PROMOTING INTEGRITY

Law, Ethics and Governance Series

Series Editor: Charles Sampford, Director, Key Centre for Ethics, Law, Justice and Governance, Griffith University, Australia

Recent history has emphasised the potentially devastating effects of governance failures in governments, government agencies, corporations and the institutions of civil society. 'Good governance' is seen as necessary, if not crucial, for economic success and human development. Although the disciplines of law, ethics, politics, economics and management theory can provide insights into the governance of organisations, governance issues can only be dealt with by interdisciplinary studies, combining several (and sometimes all) of those disciplines. This series aims to provide such interdisciplinary studies for students, researchers and relevant practitioners.

Also in this series

Governing the Heroin Trade
From Treaties to Treatment
Melissa Bull
ISBN 978-0-7546-7121-3

Islam Beyond Conflict
Indonesian Islam and Western Political Theory
Edited by Azyumardi Azra and Wayne Hudson
ISBN 978-0-7546-7092-6

Re-envisioning Sovereignty
The End of Westphalia?
Edited by Trudy Jacobsen, Charles Sampford and Ramesh Thakur
ISBN 978-0-7546-7260-9

Measuring Corruption
Edited by Charles Sampford, Arthur Shacklock, Carmel Connors and Fredrik Galtung
ISBN 978-0-7546-2405-9

Promoting Integrity
Evaluating and Improving Public Institutions

Edited by

BRIAN W. HEAD
University of Queensland, Australia

A.J. BROWN
Griffith University, Australia

CARMEL CONNORS
Griffith University, Australia

Routledge
Taylor & Francis Group
LONDON AND NEW YORK

First published 2008 by Ashgate Publishing

2 Park Square, Milton Park, Abingdon, Oxon OX14 4RN
711 Third Avenue, New York, NY 10017, USA

Routledge is an imprint of the Taylor & Francis Group, an informa business

First issued in paperback 2016

British Library Cataloguing in Publication Data
Promoting integrity : evaluation and improving public
institutions. - (Law, ethics and governance series)
1. Public interest law - Australia 2. Public interest law -
Australia - Evaluation
I. Head, Brian II. Brown, A. J. (Alexander Jonathan)
III. Connors, Carmel
342.9'4068

Library of Congress Cataloging-in-Publication Data
Promoting integrity : evaluating and improving public institutions / edited by Brian Head, A.J. Brown, and Carmel Connors.
p. cm. -- (Law, ethics and governance)
Includes bibliographical references and index.
ISBN 978-0-7546-4986-1 (hardcover) 1. Public administration--Moral and ethical aspects. 2. Public administration--Moral and ethical aspects--Australia. I. Head, Brian II. Brown, A. J. (Alexander Jonathan) III. Connors, Carmel.

JF1525.E8P77 2008
352.3'5--dc22

2008029515

ISBN 978-0-7546-4986-1 (hbk)
ISBN 978-1-138-26467-0 (pbk)

Contents

PART 3: A BEST WAY TO ASSESS INTEGRITY SYSTEMS?

List of Figures and Tables

Figures

Tables

Notes on Contributors and Editors

Stephen Bartos, Partner, Allen Consulting since 2007, has been Director of Australia's National Institute for Governance since January 2005. Prior to this he was a visiting fellow at the Australian National University, and until June 2003, Deputy Secretary of the Australian Government's Finance department. He is a Fellow of the Australian Institute of Management and Australian Institute of Company Directors, author of *Public Sector Governance – Australia* (CCH, Sydney, 2004) and *Against the Grain – the AWB Scandal and why it happened* (UNSW Press, Sydney, 2006).

A.J. Brown is a Senior Lecturer, Griffith Law School; Senior Research Fellow, Socio-Legal Research Centre; and Visiting Fellow with the ANU College of Law, Australian National University. He holds law and politics degrees from the University of New South Wales, a graduate diploma in legal practice from the ANU, and a PhD from Griffith University. He was formerly a senior investigator with the Commonwealth Ombudsman, and Associate to Justice Tony Fitzgerald AC, President of the Court of Appeal of Queensland, Australia. He now researches and teaches in a wide range of areas of public accountability, public policy and public law.

Carmel Connors is a Senior Research Assistant and Publications Manager, Key Centre for Ethics, Law, Justice and Governance, Griffith University. She was a contributing author to *Encouraging Ethics and Challenging Corruption* (with Noel Preston and Charles Sampford, Federation Press, 2002), co-editor of *Management, Organisation, and Ethics in the Public Sector* (with Patrick Bishop and Charles Sampford, Ashgate, 2003) and *Measuring Corruption* (with Charles Sampford, Arthur Shacklock and Fredrik Galtung, Ashgate, 2006).

Alan Doig is Resident Advisor, Council of Europe and was Professor of Public Services Management, Teesside Business School, University of Teesside. His areas of teaching and research are public services management, where he specializes in the impact of change and the issues of governance and fraud management, particularly in the operational and organizational issues relating to prevention, detection and investigation of fraud and corruption.

Stuart C. Gilman is the Programme Manager for the United Nations Global Programme Against Corruption and is Head of the UN Office on Drugs and Crime's Anticorruption Unit. In this role he is responsible for effective implementation of the United Nations Convention Against Corruption. His 30-year career includes positions in universities, government as well as the non-profit sectors. His work has focused on integrity and anticorruption systems in government and the private sector.

Angela Gorta PhD is Principal Analyst of the NSW Police Integrity Commission, based in Sydney. After teaching psychology and statistics at Macquarie University, she conducted criminological research for more than ten years and has spent the past 15 years focusing on better informing efforts to reduce corruption in the public sector through her work with the New South Wales Independent Commission Against Corruption (ICAC) and the New South Wales Police Integrity Commission (PIC).

Brian W. Head is a Research Professor at the University of Queensland and formerly Professor at the Key Centre for Ethics, Law Justice and Governance, Griffith University. He has held senior roles in government, academia and the non-government sector. He is currently researching integrity systems, inter-governmental relations, collaboration models and community consultation, and has published widely on public policy and management issues.

David Kimber is an Associate Professor, IESEG Business School, France and visiting faculty at the Centre for Corporate Governance and Citizenship, Indian Institute of Management – Bangalore. He was the former Associate Dean and Director of Post Graduate Studies at RMIT's Business Faculty. His teaching and research interests are in areas of business ethics, corporate governance and citizenship, international alliances, cross cultural studies, business/society relationships and values in management and leadership. He has taught at universities and colleges in China, Malaysia, Singapore, France, India and Australia.

Peter Larmour is a Reader, Public Policy and Governance, Crawford School of Economics and Government, Australian National University. His research interests include South Pacific politics and government and corruption and anti-corruption. His recent book *Foreign Flowers: Institutional Transfer and Good Governance in the Pacific Islands* (University of Hawaii Press 2005) included a chapter on the transfer of anti-corruption institutions, and he is currently working on a book on corruption in the Pacific Islands.

Colleen Lewis is an Associate Professor in the School of Humanities, Communications and Social Sciences at Monash University. Her major research interests include police accountability, complaints against police, police-government relations and models of oversight bodies such as anti-corruption commissions, crime commissions and ombudsmen functions. She has contributed widely to a number of highly regarded research publications in area of policing.

Joel Lucas is a Manager of KPMG Forensic.

Stephanie McIvor, a research assistant in Teesside Business School, has worked on various country studies with Robin Theobold and Alan Doig and contributed to a major anti-corruption project.

Jeremy Pope is a New Zealand Human Rights Commissioner and a Director of TIRI, an independent non-governmental organization that works with governments, business and civil society to find practical solutions to making integrity work. He was a founding member of Transparency International, its foundation managing director for five years, and until October 2003 the Director of the London-based Transparency International Centre for Innovation and Research, (TI-CIR), part of the Transparency International Secretariat. His 'TI Sourcebook 2000', *Confronting Corruption: The Elements of a National Integrity System,* has been translated into over 25 languages and articulates the concept of the national integrity system (which he pioneered).

Tim Prenzler is a Professor in the School of Criminology and Criminal Justice at Griffith University in Brisbane. His teaching areas include crime, crime prevention, and ethics in the criminal justice system. He conducts research on the security industry, and has a strong research interest in police corruption prevention. Tim has also published widely on the history of women police and strategies for preventing sex discrimination within policing.

Peter Roberts is a Senior Lecturer, Centre for Investigative Studies and Crime Reduction, Charles Sturt University. Previously, he was in the Australian Public Service for 30 years and was a Senior Executive for 12 years with the Commonwealth Attorney-General's Department and the National Crime Authority. Among other projects, he worked on the Commonwealth's guidelines on official conduct and managed the Commonwealth's fraud control campaign from 1988 to 1999.

Arthur Shacklock PhD is a Senior Research Fellow and Program Director Integrity and Anti-Corruption, Key Centre for Ethics, Law, Justice and Governance, Griffith University. He has extensive experience in human resource management within the Australian and Western Australian Public Services both as a manager and policy advisor. Arthur researches, teaches and consults in the areas of organizational ethics, leadership and human resource management. He was co-editor of *Measuring Corruption* (with Charles Sampford, Carmel Connors and Fredrik Galtung, Ashgate, 2006).

Rodney Smith is an Associate Professor in Government at the University of Sydney. His teaching and research centres on Australian politics. He has edited three editions of *Politics in Australia* (1989, 1993 and 1997). He is the author of *Australian Political Culture* (2001) and *Against the Machines: Minor Parties and Independents in NSW 1910–2006* (2006) and co-author of *Keywords in Australian Politics* (2006).

Jeffrey Stout is an Intern with the Ethics resource Centre, Washington and has assisted Stuart Gilman in anti-corruption research.

List of Abbreviations

ACC	Australian Crime Commission
ACC	Anti-Corruption Commission
ACLEI	Australian Commission for Law Enforcement Integrity
ADT	Administrative Decisions Tribunal
AEC	Australian Electoral Commission
AFP	Australian Federal Police
ALRC	Australian Law Reform Commission
ANAO	Australian National Audit Office
ANU	Australian National University
APS	Australian public Service
APSC	Australian Public Service Commission
AS	Australian Standard
AS/NZS	Australian and New Zealand Standards
ASSA	Australian Survey of Social Attitudes
ASX	Australian Stock Exchange
ATO	Australian Taxation Office
AUSTRAC	Australian Transaction Reporting and Analysis Centre
AWB	Australian Wheat Board
BISA	Business Integrity Systems Assessment
CAC	Commonwealth Authorities and Companies
CCC	Corruption and Crime Commission
CEO	Chief Executive Officer
CFMS	Centre for Fraud Management Studies
CFO	Chief Financial Officer
CISCR	Centre for Investigative Studies and Crime Reduction
CJC	Criminal Justice Commission (formerly Crime and Misconduct Commission)
CLERP	Corporate Law Economic Reform Program
CMC	Crime and Misconduct Commission
CPI	Corruption Perception Index
CSR	Corporate social responsibility
DAEO	Designated Agency Ethics Official
DFAT	Department of Foreign Affairs and Trade
DOFA	Department of Finance and Administration
DPP	Director of Public Prosecutions
EARC	Electoral and Administrative Review Commission
ECP	Enhanced Cooperation Program
ERC	Ethics Resource Center (Washington)
EU	European Union
FAO	Food and Agricultural Organization

FATF	Financial Action Task Force
FMA	Financial management and accountability
FOI	Freedom of information
GAO	Government Accountability Office
GDP	Gross domestic product
GOC	Government owned corporation
GRECO	The Council of Europe's Group of States against Corruption
HoCOLEA	Heads of Commonwealth Law Enforcement Agencies
IAT	Integrity Assessment Tool
ICAC	NSW Independent Commission Against Corruption
ICG	Integrity Coordinating Group
IDP	Internal Disclosure Procedures
IMF	International Monetary Fund
KCELJAG	Key Centre for Ethics, law, Justice and Governance
KICAC	Korean Independent Commission Against Corruption
MAB	Management Advisory Board
MAF	Management Accountability Framework
MBA	Master of Business Administration
MCA	Millennium Challenge Account
MIAC	Management Improvement Advisory Committee
MLA	Member of the Legislative Assembly
MNC	Multinational corporations
MP	Member of Parliament
NBES	National Business Ethics Survey
NGO	Non-government organization
NIS	National Integrity System
NISA	National Integrity System Assessment
NSW	New South Wales
OECD	Organisation for Economic Cooperation and Development
OFC	Offshore Financial Centres
OFF	Oil-for-Food Programme
OGE-PR	Office of Government Ethics of Puerto Rico
OPI	Office of Police Integrity
PIC	Police Integrity Commission
PNG	Papua New Guinea
PSHRMAC	Public Service Human Resource Management Agency of Canada
PWC	PricewaterhouseCoopers
QCC	Queensland Crime Commission
RAMSI	Regional Assistance Mission to Solomon Islands
RMIT	Royal Melbourne Institute of Technology
ROSC	Reports on the Observance of Standards and Codes
SA	South Australia
SCC	Sydney Chamber of Commerce
SME	Small to medium enterprises
SSC	State Services Commission (New Zealand)

TAFE	Technical and Further Education
TBS	Treasury Board of Canada Secretariat
TI-CIR	Transparency International Centre for Innovation and Research
UK	United Kingdom
UN	United Nations
UNGAP	Global Programme against Corruption
US	United States of America
USOGE	United States Office of Government Ethics
WA	Western Australia
WEA	Wheat Export Authority

PART 1
Understanding Integrity Systems

Chapter 1

Introduction: Integrity Systems and Democratic Accountability

A.J. Brown, Brian W. Head and Carmel Connors

A Revealing Glitch in the Integrity System

The nine Attorney-Generals of a modern, industrialized, federal democracy met to consider a specific legal reform intended to boost public integrity. The national Attorney-General proposed there should be uniform law reform across the country to protect journalists from being prosecuted for contempt of court if they refused to name a confidential source while giving evidence in a criminal trial. It was not in the public interest, the nation's senior justice minister argued, for journalists to face criminal penalties for honouring their professional ethics, in a situation where a free and independent media could not be effective unless it could promise confidentiality. Hence, journalists should be able to claim a defence in appropriate cases.

The federal Attorney-General's eight state and territory counterparts, however, representing different parts of the nation, pointed to inconsistencies with other laws (Merritt 2007). Yes, they said, journalists should be able to claim protection from having to reveal a confidential source. But especially in federal law, there was still no protection for the confidential source themselves. For example, if a public official 'blew the whistle' on failures of government, they faced criminal prosecution and up to two years in jail; indeed, the whole issue had arisen because the federal government had recently prosecuted two public servants in this way, one for leaking information about a change in policy on war veterans' entitlements, the other for blowing the whistle on systemic weaknesses in airport security (*The Australian* editorial, 28 March 2007). According to the state ministers, shielding the journalists might be legally impossible if the original disclosure was still criminal, and the public servants could not themselves raise a public interest defence. Most of the nation's state governments had a 'whistleblower protection' law, they said, offering some relief from the situation – but the federal government had none, and in fact seemed determined to prosecute as many whistleblowers as it could find. There seemed to be double standards in giving journalists a 'public interest' defence for their use of sensitive information, but not giving public interest whistleblowers any defence for supplying them with the information. Thus the proposal – which was, and is, a good reform – fell on its face.

This incident, which occurred in Australia in April 2007, reveals some of the complex problems confronting the integrity systems of the average, modern nation. As always, when different ministers from different governments and parties assemble, there was plenty of short-term politics involved. Indeed, several state ministers overlooked that while their own jurisdictions had 'whistleblowing' laws to protect public officials who made public interest disclosures, these did not protect officials who spoke to journalists any more effectively than the federal government, which had none (Brown 2006a, 42–4). On a larger scale, however, the deferral of the plan also shows the difficulty faced by political leaders and policy-makers in keeping an overall view of the systems that are, or should be, in place to protect and promote public integrity, even in developed countries. Many different aspects of politics, policy and law are involved in 'getting it right' when it comes to the institutions and strategies of integrity and accountability – and ensuring all these aspects are in place, and coordinated, is no longer easy. Linked to the Australian debate was the fact that, while some governments had different 'watchdog' bodies to investigate complaints of corruption, others including the federal government had few such bodies. The justice ministers found themselves asking a number of questions of larger importance, alongside the politics of commitment to integrity goals. What are the right institutional settings and strategies for ensuring honesty and accountability in public life? How do these settings and strategies relate to one another, and how do we know what is working and what is missing from the whole complex tapestry?

Thinking about Integrity Systems: The International Background

This book suggests some new answers to these larger questions, relevant not just in Australia but in all countries where public integrity is an issue. The book reviews a variety of existing efforts to understand, 'map' and evaluate the effectiveness of integrity policies and institutions, not just in the government sector but across all the major institutions of modern society. 'Integrity' is used in this book to mean, for the most part, the opposite of 'corruption' in public life. The English word is derived from the Latin *integritas*, meaning 'unaffected, intact, upright, reliable'; the same root has given us 'integer', the mathematical term for a 'whole' as opposed to fractional number (KCELJAG and TI 2001, 1; Uhr 2005, 194). Corruption, on the other hand, means decay, deterioration or perversion from an original or 'whole' state – physically, 'the destruction or spoiling of anything, especially by *disintegration* ...' (*Oxford English Dictionary*; Heidenheimer and Johnson 2002, 6–9). Some of its internal conflicts have been well documented (Philp 1997; 2002, 53–4).

For our purposes – in the context of governance, politics, law and public policy – corruption refers to the corrosive threats posed to society by the abuse of entrusted power (see Brown 2006b). Conversely, when powerful individuals and institutions act in a manner that is true to the values, purposes and duties for which they have been entrusted that power, or allowed to continue to hold it, then we tend to say they have integrity. Truth and honesty are not synonyms for integrity, but are elements of it; as one Canadian integrity commissioner said, 'the virtue of integrity ... includes honesty, together with worthiness, respect and an expectation that a promise made will be kept, absent some factor or circumstance beyond the control of the promiser' (Evans 1996, 7; see also Dobel 1999).

Our aim in this book is not just an academic one – of understanding systems – but also the practical goal of devising new ways for integrity reformers to reliably assess the relative strengths and weaknesses of the integrity regimes in place in their country. Every society already has some kind of 'integrity system', even if not widely understood, or recognized, or respected for its achievements. If there were no elements of an integrity system in place, then social and political order itself would collapse. The question is, what are the weaknesses and gaps in each integrity system, and how are they best addressed, in the effort to ensure that those people entrusted with political and economic power exercise it in accordance with the values and purposes for which they hold it? This is a much harder question – one which relies on a practical ability to see the 'integrity system' as a whole, and then evaluate what is working and what is not, in the search for a reliable road-map towards successful reform.

While the book has been assembled by Australian researchers, and contains considerable Australian material, the scope of the underlying project and the lessons arising are much more global. The book arose from an acknowledged lack of *practical* methods for describing and assessing modern integrity systems in all their complexity, right around the world. The research underpinning it was conducted in partnership with Transparency International, which from the mid-1990s was one of the first organizations to point out, in its international 'Sourcebooks' (Pope 1996; 2000), that the long-term success of integrity and anti-corruption depends on holistic rather than piecemeal reform. Previously, the search for higher standards – or at least appearances – of integrity saw many nations vigorously borrow and adapt institutions from one to another, in some cases establishing one single new 'anti-corruption law', or one single new 'anti-corruption agency', as a simple response to various drivers for change. In articulating the concept of a 'national integrity system' (NIS), the founding director of Transparency International, Jeremy Pope, sought to demonstrate that the task of building a robust framework of integrity into social institutions involved many more elements and a greater diversity of strategies (Pope 1996; 2000; Langseth et al. 1997; see also Stapenhurst and Kpundeh 1999).

In Chapter 2 of this volume, Pope renews and explains the rationale for this broader concept of an integrity system, including a restatement of his famous structural analogy of modern integrity systems as akin to an ancient Greek temple, emphasizing the many building blocks that go to make up its foundations, and the many different institutional pillars needed to keep it upright (see Figure 2.1). This more multi-pronged approach to integrity reform was consistent with the experience of many of Transparency International's growing number of country chapters. However, according to Pope himself, it had also been demonstrated by reforms in Australia from the late 1980s to the early 1990s – particularly the substantial overhaul of public institutions conducted in the state of Queensland in response to the Fitzgerald Commission of Inquiry (1987–1989). What began there as a limited inquiry into police corruption, resulted in wide-ranging recommendations about the reforms needed to much larger systems of political and official accountability if such corruption was to be prevented from recurring. As stated by Commissioner Tony Fitzgerald QC, there was 'no purpose in piecemeal solutions, which only serve to conceal rather than cure the defects in the existing system' (Fitzgerald 1989, 14; see Prasser et al. 1990; Finn 1994). The result was deliberate reconstruction of public institutions in the shape of, as Pope put it, an overall 'integrity system', a process whose outcomes have already been described in the background to the present project (KCELJAG and TI 2001; Preston et al. 2002).

Looking around the world, Pope and Transparency International observed the need for a similarly strategic approach in other jurisdictions, and the readiness of TI chapters to support and pursue it. Accordingly, in 1999, an international effort commenced to establish how modern integrity systems could best be described and evaluated, in order to extend this kind of strategic, multifaceted approach to the strengthening of integrity institutions. Much of this effort was focused in Australia, where Pope's observations and other international interest resulted in a five-year National Integrity System Assessment (NISA) of Australia, led by Griffith University, and supported financially by Transparency International Australia, the Corruption Prevention Network of New South Wales (NSW) and the Australian Government through its Australian Research Council. In parallel, a large number of smaller national integrity system 'country studies' were conducted in Europe, Asia and the Americas by British researchers, and in the South Pacific by a separate Australian National University team. All this focus on 'national integrity systems' took place alongside a variety of other international efforts to better evaluate systems of governance and accountability, undertaken or sponsored by a range of organizations from the World Bank to the Washington-based Center for Public Integrity. Most relevantly, the Organisation for Economic Cooperation and Development (OECD 2005) has undertaken an important project on the ways in which OECD member-countries could assess their various measures for promoting integrity and preventing corruption. As discussed below, this project drew extensively on the Australian research.

The result of this international activity was a strengthening of the ways in which the evaluation of 'integrity systems' is conceptualized and undertaken, and an enrichment of the practical experience of many bodies and organizations in doing so. However from the outset, all such efforts necessarily encounter an innocent but fundamental question – what *is* the 'integrity system' we are trying to understand and strengthen? In Chapter 3, this question is addressed by A.J. Brown, who coordinated the Australian national integrity system assessment in 2003–2005 (Brown et al. 2005). Reviewing the different institutions and strategies that form the focus of assessment methodologies around the world, Brown argues the importance of understanding the drivers and recognizing the limits of any given assessment process, and of adopting a clear conceptual framework for what is being assessed. In different nations and cultural settings, it is particularly important to understand whether the 'integrity system' is simply an alternative term for a desired form of liberal democratic political order, or a description of specific institutions and policies within a given system of governance, democratic or otherwise. For the most part, the concepts of accountability that underpin the definition of integrity outlined above, are intrinsically related to Western liberal democratic ideals, and their relevance and transferability across national and cultural boundaries need to be weighed accordingly. Nevertheless, the search for a clear understanding of an 'integrity system' helps place this book in its international context. It also has practical importance for how the task of integrity system assessment might be most safely addressed.

Assessing Integrity Systems in Practice

The second part of this book outlines many of the practicalities of institutional strengthening that can flow from effective evaluation, providing accounts of specific methods used to assess integrity systems as part of the international effort. In Chapter 4, Alan Doig and Stephanie McIvor describe the process they used to study the integrity systems of 18 countries, in 2000, using an institutional template based directly on the Transparency International 'national integrity system' concept. The results tend to confirm that public integrity is indeed reliant on a multiplicity of institutions and strategies, and confirm that an increasing array of countries use a similar web of these institutions and strategies in their integrity-building efforts. In many settings, the gaps and weaknesses suggested by this relatively simple form of comparative analysis have equipped reformers with a clearer view of where explanations for problems might lie, or where efforts to strengthen integrity institutions might yield quickest results.

Chapter 5 outlines the similar effort to study the integrity systems of 14 Pacific Island Nations, in 2006. Peter Larmour arrived at similar conclusions but also identifies some of the more fundamental issues thrown up by these country studies. On one hand, as Transparency International has noted, these studies have borne out the accuracy of the concept of the 'national integrity system' as a means of explaining many countries' approaches, typically finding that 'most countries had nearly all the pillars [of the integrity system] and few had additional or different pillars' (TI 2001, 39). On the other hand, as TI feared and Larmour's studies confirm, there is a problem that even when these 'pillars' are present, they are sometimes merely facades or 'hollow' (Larmour and Barcham 2004, 29; TI 2001, 16, 27). While a comparative analysis of the presence or absence of institutions can do much to assist policymakers and reformers, it may do little to explain *why* things are as they are, or *what is needed* to fix particular perceived gaps or weaknesses in the system. Answers to these questions rely on a deeper analysis.

The remaining chapters in this part show the evolution of some of these deeper evaluative methods in the Australian setting. By no means does Australia provide a model of integrity in public life, whatever its relatively positive ratings on measures such as Transparency International's corruption perception index. Rather, as found by the Democratic Audit of Australia (Hindess 2004) and suspected by Transparency International Australia (Costigan 2005), Australia might be regarded as a country whose apparently low level of official corruption seems to be due in part to ongoing responses to accountability scandals that have tended to maintain public vigilance on the issue.

As explained above, an early phase of the Australian research effort involved a detailed description of the public sector integrity system of the state of Queensland (KCELJAG and TI 2001). While more detailed, this description was largely consistent with the country study approaches in Chapters 4 and 5. In parallel, however, a pioneering effort was made to analyse the presence of integrity systems in the private business sector – an area of the national integrity system that had been largely ignored. Chapter 6, by Joel Lucas and David Kimber, describes the results. The recommendations of the final NISA report included the need to continue this work, and in particular, to study strengths and weaknesses in the contribution made by business regulatory agencies to integrity in public life (Brown et al. 2005, 40–43, 102). Nevertheless, this '*business* integrity system assessment' showed why a proper review of integrity systems must not simply examine large-scale laws and institutions, operating right across society, but the everyday realities of organizational culture and practice – that is, the role of integrity in the lives of individual businesses. Indeed, as Lucas and Kimber show, it is also vital to recognize personal integrity as a dimension of these systems (see Figure 6.1). Their analysis emphasizes that identifying and responding to an integrity system's 'hollow' pillars requires us to look behind the template of major or 'core' integrity institutions and to examine the 'distributed' integrity systems extending throughout the great number of organizations – public and private – that employ the nation's workforce and determine the quality of daily life. For reformers, this deeper examination also indicates the importance, for the system as a whole, of understanding the relationships between 'core' (for example, regulatory or oversight) institutions and the integrity practices of everyday businesses and agencies.

In Chapter 7, Rodney Smith deals squarely with this question of relationships – one of the most vital questions in any understanding of an integrity system. From the very outset, the realization that integrity programs depend not just on one or two institutions, but a multiplicity, demands closer study of the ways in which these work together – or fail to work together. As just noted, this is not simply a theoretical question. If integrity systems at an organizational level are not reinforced or supported by the actions of integrity agencies, they are liable to fail. And if there is a plethora of integrity bodies, how they can best work together should be a live issue in administrative practice. The Australian state of New South Wales has, in its state government, the largest number of integrity bodies of any Australian governmental jurisdiction, and perhaps any jurisdiction in the world. Smith's mission, within the framework of the Australian national integrity system assessment, was to map this complex system and gather evidence from among participants about the strengths and weaknesses of its internal interactions. The intricacy of this picture has been central to suggestions that a well-developed integrity system is perhaps better understood as a messy, organic structure such as a bird's nest, rather than Pope's stoic analogy of a Greek temple (Sampford et al. 2005). The practical challenges of maintaining the coherence of such a system also provide important worldwide lessons, as discussed in this book's concluding chapters.

Chapters 8, 9 and 10 go on to analyse, from different perspectives, the state of the integrity system at the level of Australia's federal (national) government. In Chapter 8, Peter Roberts reports on this component of the Australian national integrity system assessment project. As well as reinforcing the need for action to restore the coherence of the system at this level, his analysis emphasizes the need to take account of issues of organizational and political culture, and reviews some of the evidence of a lack of capacity in certain areas of the Australian federal government's approach. Like Smith's analysis, these findings found their place in the formal recommendations arising from the NISA assessment (Brown et al. 2005, 31–6). However, they also resonate with others' findings regarding a weakening in the culture of public accountability at Australia's federal level, whether discussing specific lapses in public honesty by political leaders (Weller 2002) or the 'puzzling' self-regulatory system (Uhr 2005, 147) on which the integrity of federal parliamentarians' conduct continues to rely, by comparison with other jurisdictions.[1]

The most notable example of integrity failure on the part of Australian institutions, in recent years, concerns the payment of around US$222 million in illegal 'kickbacks' to the government of Iraq by the Australian wheat export company AWB International Limited, in breach of the United Nations sanctions regime in 1999–2003. This saga of deceit and omission, only fully uncovered after a Royal Commission, is reviewed by Stephen Bartos in Chapter 9. The institutional failures that permitted the corruption to occur, the absence of a vigilant political culture, and a limited institutional capacity for rapid detection and rectification, provide further demonstration of the types of systemic difficulties discussed in the earlier chapters.

Chapter 10 presents a detailed examination by A.J. Brown of the institution-building choices faced by governments – in particular, Australia's national government – as political leaders struggle to respond to such pressures. Using evidence from a comparative analysis of key institutional capacities in different jurisdictions, the chapter demonstrates the ways in which integrity system assessment can help provide an objective basis for judgement as to the extent of the perceived 'hollowness' of particular integrity pillars, while also reviewing a contemporary debate over the creation of a broad and effective anti-corruption commission at Australia's federal level. This unresolved debate, directly informed

1 The recently elected Australian Prime Minister, Kevin Rudd, has announced that ministers' shareholdings and their employment after leaving office will be restricted under new transparency measures. The new ministerial code will place a 12-month ban on departing ministers having business dealings with MPs, public servants or defence personnel on any matter they dealt with in their official capacity. The code is also set to curb influence-peddling by political lobby groups. Lobbyists will be forced to disclose their details on an online public register, kept by the Department of Prime Minister and Cabinet, before seeking meetings with ministers or parliamentary secretaries. (Anderson and Morris 2007, 6)

by the recommendations of the NISA assessment project, highlights that even industrialized countries with well-entrenched democratic institutions can battle to find the right mix of integrity institutions.

A Best Way to Assess Integrity Systems?

All of the issues raised by these efforts in integrity system assessment provoke an obvious and persistent question – is there a 'best way' for such evaluations to be undertaken, if they are to have the best chance of yielding results that are both empirically accurate and politically cogent in the quest for effective reform? The third part of the book returns to the methodological choices thrown up by many earlier chapters.

Chapter 11 provides a concrete example of just some of these measures. Colleen Lewis and Tim Prenzler review the state of existing performance indicators for the independent agencies charged with ensuring the prevention and detection of corruption in which performance is being measured. No single measure, or even group of measures, provides an objective demonstration of the effectiveness of an agency in preventing corruption or effectively adjudicating allegations of misconduct, but at least it provides a starting point. Expanding on other areas where performance information is known to exist, chapter 12 presents a comparative review of organization-level integrity assessment tools compiled by Arthur Shacklock and others involved in the Australian national integrity system assessment project. This review brings much of the discussion of the Australian assessment full circle, by emphasizing that organizations – both public and private – can and do try to measure the effectiveness of their own internal integrity systems by collecting a range of evidence about the state of their own organizational culture. These tools thus provide both a rich resource for organizational managers, interested to establish whether their own integrity efforts are working, and a reinforcement of the types of evidence that, if collected on a larger scale, can also help determine whether societal programs of accountability are achieving their desired traction in the day-to-day operations of institutions and citizens' lives.

Chapters 13 and 14 begin to draw the book to a close, returning to the broad question of how best to approach the task of integrity system assessment. In Chapter 13, an analysis originally prepared for the OECD (2005, 75–122), Gilman and Stout review a number of efforts recently undertaken around the world. While they confirm that the art and science of integrity system assessment is in its relative infancy, they vigorously challenge assumptions that a more holistic evaluative approach is impossible, and reinforce the call for evaluation measures to become part of ongoing operational processes and be regarded as a natural part of program management. Gilman and Stout also oppose the idea that 'one size' can ever fit all needs in national efforts to assess integrity systems, but endorse the idea of a toolkit of evaluation instruments capable of being modified for use in a variety of settings.

Chapter 14 draws on the research and lessons described in many of the preceding chapters, to suggest just such a toolkit. In a retrospective look at integrity system assessments to date, A.J. Brown and Brian Head set out a threefold approach taking in evidence-based examinations of the 'consequences, capacities and coherence' of the various core and distributed institutions that make up a modern integrity system. This approach – which was tested in the Australian context and informed the OECD's development of a generic framework for integrity system assessment – goes beyond that framework to suggest a flexible assessment methodology with a concrete focus, adaptable to a range of settings. Moreover, the 'consequence, capacity, coherence' model provides an ability to more comprehensively track the evolution of a country's integrity system over time, providing the longitudinal information on which to build the consensus needed to support continual improvement and reform.

Whither Integrity Systems?

The analyses in this book are intended to contribute to debates about evidence-informed policymaking for the improvement of integrity systems. As Brian W. Head argues, it is unclear whether the great surge of interest in integrity strengthening and values-based governance over the last decade will be sustained by policymakers and integrity reformers around the world. The outcome may depend on whether the political will for reform is sustained and can be reinforced by international funding agencies. However, in an age of instability and heightened national security issues, the need is even greater for all societies to ensure that their integrity systems are well-coordinated and capable. Unless we demonstrate the need and benefits of change, practical measures that can lead to positive improvements in public trust and accountability, and tools for open and ongoing monitoring, we might find that the recent advances in integrity system understanding and reform will not be further institutionalized.

References

Anderson, F. and Morris, S. (2007), 'Rudd's Code Tough and Clear', *The Australian Financial Review*, 6 December.

The Australian (Sydney) (2007), 'Freedom to Speak: Whistleblowers need public interest protection', editorial, 28 March.

Brown, A.J. (2006a), *Public Interest Disclosure Legislation in Australia: Towards the Next Generation* (Canberra: Commonwealth Ombudsman, NSW Ombudsman, and Queensland Ombudsman).

Brown, A.J. (2006b), 'What are we trying to measure? Reviewing the basics of corruption definition', in C. Sampford, A. Shacklock, F. Galtung, and C. Connors (eds) *Measuring Corruption* (Aldershot: Ashgate Publishing).

Brown, A.J. et al. (2005), *Chaos or Coherence? Strengths, Challenges and Opportunities for Australia's Integrity Systems*, National Integrity Systems Assessment (NISA) Final Report (Melbourne: Transparency International Australia and Griffith University).

Brown, A.J., Uhr, J., Shacklock, A. and Connors, C. (2005), 'Developing Policy Assessment Measures for Integrity and Corruption Prevention Activities: The Australian Experience', in OECD, *Public Sector Integrity: A Framework for Assessment* (Paris: Organization for Economic Cooperation and Development).
Costigan, F.X. (2005), 'Australia's National Integrity Systems: Introducing A New Blueprint', *Australian Journal of Public Administration* 64:2, 40–41.
Dobel, J.P. (1999), *Public Integrity* (Baltimore, MD: Johns Hopkins University Press).
Evans, G.T. (1996), *'Commissioner's Remarks'*, 1995/95 *Integrity Commissioner's Annual Report* (Canada: Ontario Government Publications).
Finn, P. (1994), 'The Significance of the Fitzgerald and WA Inc Commissions', in P. Weller (ed.) *Royal Commissions and the Making of Public Policy* (Melbourne: Macmillan).
Hindess, B. (2004), *Corruption and Democracy in Australia*, Report No. 3, Democratic Audit of Australia (Canberra: Research School of Social Sciences, Australian National University).
KCELJAG and TI (2001), *Australian National Integrity Systems Assessment: Queensland Handbook* (Brisbane: Key Centre for Ethics Law Justice and Governance, Griffith University, and Transparency International Australia).
Langseth, P., Stapenhurst, R. and Pope, J. (1997), 'The Role of a National Integrity System in Fighting Corruption', *Commonwealth Law Bulletin* 508.
Langseth, P., Stapenhurst, R. and Pope, J. (1999), 'National Integrity Systems', in R. Stapenhurst and S.J. Kpundeh (eds) *Curbing Corruption: Toward a Model for Building National Integrity* (Washington DC: Economic Development Institute, World Bank), 127–48.
Larmour, P. and Barcham, M. (2004), *National Integrity Systems Pacific Islands: Overview Report* (Melbourne: Transparency International Australia).
Merritt, C. (2007), 'States Reject Journos' Sources Law', *The Australian* (Sydney), 13 April.
OECD (2005), *Public Sector Integrity: A Framework for Assessment* (Paris: Organisation for Economic Cooperation and Development).
Philp, M. (1997), 'Defining Political Corruption', *Political Studies* 45: 436–62.
Philp, M. (2002), 'Conceptualising Political Corruption', in A.J. Heidenheimer and M. Johnston (eds) *Political Corruption: Concepts and Contexts* (New Brunswick, NJ: Transaction Publishers).
Prasser, S., Wear, R. and Nethercote, J. (eds) (1990), *Corruption and Reform: The Fitzgerald Vision* (Brisbane: University of Queensland Press).
Preston, N., Sampford, C. and Connors, C. (2002), *Encouraging Ethics and Challenging Corruption: Reforming Governance in Public Institutions* (Sydney: Federation Press).
Sampford, C., Smith, R. and Brown, A.J. (2005), 'From Greek Temple to Bird's Nest: Towards a Theory of Coherence and Mutual Accountability for National Integrity Systems', *Australian Journal of Public Administration* 64:2, 96–108.
Stapenhurst, R. and Kpundeh, S.J. (eds) (1999), '*Curbing Corruption: Toward a Model for Building National Integrity* (Washington DC.: Economic Development Institute, World Bank).
TI (2001), *The National Integrity System: Concept and Practice (Country Studies Overview Report)* (Berlin: Transparency International).
Uhr, J. (2005), *Terms of Trust: Arguments over Ethics in Australian Government* (Sydney: University of New South Wales Press).
Weller, P. (2002), *Don't Tell the Prime Minister* (Melbourne: Scribe Publications).

Chapter 2

National Integrity Systems: The Key to Building Sustainable, Just and Honest Government

Jeremy Pope

What is government itself but the greatest of all reflections upon human nature? If men were angels, no government would be necessary. If angels were to govern men, neither external nor internal controls on government would be necessary.

(James Madison (1751–1836) 4th President of the USA)

Background

Creating the Foundations for Integrity in Public Life

It is often overlooked that, at the beginning of the 1900s, industrialized countries such as Canada, the United Kingdom and the United States of America were deeply corrupt. In the United Kingdom, despite a well-paid, efficient and largely honest civil service, corruption was rampant in almost every other sector. In the private sector, cartels abounded whereby the public quite literally was held to ransom. Political patronage abounded. An editorial in *The Times* had complained that headmasters were taking bribes from publishers for school text-books. Clergymen were even taking kickbacks on sales of hymn books. In response, anti-corruption groups sprang up and these proved to be the trigger for reforms which have helped lay the basis for some of the world's most successful economies.

Legislation in Canada, the United States and the United Kingdom, for example, dates back to the end of the nineteenth century, when all three suffered many of the less attractive features of today's developing economies. It was not that policymakers in these countries necessarily had a very clear concept of what they were trying to achieve, or of where their reforms would ultimately lead. The measures introduced were piecemeal, not comprehensive.[1]

---

1 In the US, for example, the law was developed progressively. First, the Sherman Act of 1890 rendered conspiracies in restraint of trade a criminal offence, but it recognized no role for the state in actively regulating what was taking place (Canada had done so a year earlier, in 1889). Then came the Clayton Act of 1914, still the primary tool for the control of anti-competitive mergers and joint ventures in the US. At the same time, the

Today, the ethical standards of the political leaders of these countries – among many others – are under sustained attack. Nevertheless, the systems of governance that have emerged – of checks and balances operating under the Rule of Law – have provided the basis for effective modern administration. What have emerged are functioning national integrity systems.

How, then, can developing countries and countries in transition – many in the grip of corruption – achieve such a change?

Although the early anti-corruption work on national integrity systems has focused on a mix of institutions, laws and practices, it is now clear that the ethical framework demands much more attention than has been appreciated. As James Madison remarked (as quoted above): 'If angels were to govern men, neither external or internal controls on government would be necessary'.

Thus, the relevance of what Charles Sampford has called an 'Ethics Regime' becomes of at least equal importance to reforms of institutions, laws and practices. By placing ethics at the forefront of the reform process, public servants come to appreciate the 'why' that lies behind a rule, and to appreciate the benefits for society of the existence of a stick with which to enforce it. Intuitively we all know that there has not been a system yet devised that cannot be outwitted by the corrupt, but the compelling need in many countries is to move from a situation where corruption is systemic to one in which it is simply episodic.

An effective ethics programme at the forefront of the reform process also helps build local ownership and commitment. Many of those working in the field of development are coming to realize that the impetus for a reform programme has to be home-grown and home-owned for it to be sustainable. There have been far too many examples of donors trying to impose anti-corruption programmes on countries as a precondition for aid, but none can be regarded as having contributed more than the most incremental of change.[2]

Federal Trade Commission Act created the Federal Trade Commission and so introduced the element of active regulation. These countries, and other developed economies, are constantly modernizing their legal framework, the United Kingdom as recently as in 1998, with its Competition Act. See the concluding discussion in the chapter on the role of the private sector in the *TI Source Book* (www.transparency.org) for a discussion on how civil society actively generated anti-corruption reform. Once anti-bribery legislation was passed in the UK in 1906, a number of its supporters formed an NGO, the Secret Commissions and Bribery Prevention League of which 'practically all the leading bankers, merchants and traders' were members. The League monitored implementation of the new law, often bringing prosecutions itself. This, coupled with the stiff sentences the judges gave to the convicted, brought about a discernible change in attitudes. A similar Anti-Bribery League was established in Germany.

2 For example, the previous insistence that the Government of Kenya establish an independent anti-corruption bureau. The institution was set up and its first victim was a senior official who many had seen as one of the most outstanding and honest in the administration. By placing him under investigation he was suspended from his post, to the relief of many. It may be the case that in time this will be developed, as a result of internal political pressures, in to an effective institution. However, its initial performance was, not surprisingly, lamentable.

The irony is that while ethics regimes are desperately needed in developing countries, it has been a number of developed countries – Australia, Britain, Canada and New Zealand among them – and the OECD itself who have recognized the prime importance of the ethics dimension, and who have been working on it studiously.

Gerald Caiden has remarked that:

> Corrupt officials, knowingly or not, display contempt for other people, no matter how minor or seemingly innocent their corrupt acts. This contempt harbours within it the seeds of megalomania that, if allowed to flourish, will eventually blossom into grosser and grosser acts … where other people are considered expendable and other people's lives are considered meaningless and useless. All corruption is a deceit, a lie, that sacrifices the common good or the public interest for something much less … [I] it gives comfort to social pathologies that divide, destabilise and desensitise. Not only does it point society in the wrong direction, but it also exhausts governmental legitimacy, supports the wrong kind of public leadership and sets the wrong kind of example for future generations. (Caiden 1988, 17)

What, then, is the 'right' direction? The First Report of the Committee on Standards in Public Life (the Nolan Committee) (1995) provides a starting point with its articulation of seven principles which it saw as applying to all aspects of public life:

- Selflessness: holders of public office should take decisions solely in terms of the public interest. They should not do so in order to gain financial or other material benefits for themselves, their family, or their friends.
- Integrity: holders of public office should not place themselves under any financial or other obligation to outside individuals or organizations that might influence them in the performance of their official duties.
- Objectivity: in carrying out public business, including making public appointments, awarding contracts, or recommending individuals for rewards and benefits, holders of public office should make choices based on merit.
- Accountability: holders of public office are accountable for their decisions and actions to the public and must submit themselves to whatever scrutiny is appropriate to their office.
- Openness: holders of public office should be as open as possible about all the decisions and actions that they take. They should give reasons for their decisions and restrict information only when the wider public interest clearly demands.
- Honesty: holders of public office have a duty to declare any private interests relating to their public duties and to take steps to resolve any conflicts arising in a way that protects the public interest.
- Leadership: holders of public office should promote and support these principles by leadership and example.

Together, these elements foster a tradition of ethics in relation to public life and an ethical environment in which politicians and officials are generally assumed to be honest. Within such an environment it is also assumed that the laws and means of detection and investigation are sufficient to make it risky and costly to break the rules, accept bribes or become involved in fraud (Doig 1994, 4). However, it is important to bear in mind several crucial points:

- the ethical environment must be owned, enforced, adapted and applied equally and consistently across the public sector;
- the ethical environment must be self-sustaining and integrated; if the ethical environment has potential weak points, new means of accountability must be introduced, or existing means upgraded and reinforced to counter these weaknesses;
- the ethical environment requires political commitment and leadership to inspire confidence and trust, but it should not always be the politicians who have the responsibility to own and enforce it; and,
- the ethical environment depends on micro-level changes (the details of reform) in order to deal with the consequences of failure.

Failure can result in: weak guidance on standards of conduct or poor compliance with procedures; management indifference or ignorance; aggregated decision-making powers; inadequate financial and management information systems; lax working practices; poor staff relations; sub-organizational autonomy; poor recruitment and training policies; and little or no attempt to control, monitor or police the increasing contact with private sector values, practices, personnel and procedures (Doig 1994, 7–8). Before discussing the advantages of the national integrity system approach, it is instructive to consider why other approaches to containing corruption have largely failed.

Why Reform Efforts Fail

Despite the flurry of activities around the globe in the last decade, the would-be reformer of corruption can still be at a loss to know where to begin. History is littered with the pretence of reform – grandiose promises and a conspicuous inability to even try to deliver.[3]

In other cases the intentions are genuine: newly elected leaders arrive determined to clean up corruption, but are quickly overwhelmed by the size of the problems facing them. Yet others simply posture, making speeches, signing laws – all in the absence of any expectation that meaningful change will follow. Some enact reforms and then privately flout them.[4]

---

3 An example is the former President of South Korea, Roh Tae Woo. He vowed at his inauguration to be the cleanest President in his country's history but wound up in prison, facing a host of major corruption charges: *The Washington Post*, 18 November 1995.

4 Former German Chancellor Helmut Kohl made great play of reforms designed to contain the problem of illicit political party funding, only for it to be revealed that his subsequent behaviour was wholly contrary to everything he claimed to believe in.

Time and again, optimistic electorates have returned governments pledged to confront corruption firmly and effectively. Governments have fallen when they have demonstrated an inability to counter the phenomenon; others have been elected in the hope that they can do better. Yet, very few can point to enduring progress. Not only must there be change, but it must be change which is sustainable.

An added difficulty in developing countries and countries in transition is the inherent weakness of government itself. Some countries are having to 'invent' government completely, rather than to 're-invent' it. The process of transition and of building democratic institutions of accountability clearly takes a long time to mature, as a generation of actors has to adapt to a new and alien political environment and to forge wholly new relationships between the executive, the legislature and the judiciary. We cannot expect this to happen quickly.

An analysis of the failure of past efforts has identified a number of causes, including the following:

- the limits of power at the top. An incoming head of state may endeavour to address the challenge, but is effectively impeded by the existing corrupt governmental machinery;[5]
- the absence of commitment at the top. Lower ranking political and administrative figures may wish to effect change but be severely restricted by an absence of commitment at the leadership level;
- reforms tend to overlook those at the top and focus only on the lower political and administrative levels, based on the assumption that those at the top either do not 'need' reform or that they would be openly hostile towards anyone who attempted it. As a result, the law is seen as being applied unevenly and unfairly, and soon ceases to be applied at all;
- overly ambitious promises leading to unrealistic and unachievable expectations. Those who promise what they cannot deliver, quickly lose the confidence of those around them;
- reforms lack a specific and achievable focus and so fail to deliver concrete change;
- reforms have taken place piecemeal and in an uncoordinated manner, leading to lack of ownership and commitment to effective implementation (Benson 1988, 149);[6]

---

5 Witness President Mkapa of Tanzania who, on his election in 1995, publicly declared his assets and those of his spouse, and called on other leaders to follow his example. The Attorney-General issued a public statement that many interpreted as implying that the President's actions were 'illegal' (in that they were not required by law) and that it would be improper for other leaders to follow suit.

6 'The rotten apple in the barrel ….' The Knapp commission, which investigated corruption in the New York Police Department, concluded that 'the interaction of stubbornness, hostility and pride has given rise to the so-called 'rotten apple' theory. According to this theory, which bordered on official Department doctrine, any policeman found to be corrupt must promptly be denounced as a rotten apple in an otherwise clean

- reforms have relied too much on the law, which is an uncertain instrument in trying to change the way people behave, or too much on enforcement, which can lead to repression, abuses of power and the emergence of another corrupt regime. If a legal system is not functioning, the problem is more likely to lie in the judicial system (with delays, corruption and uncertainties) rather than in the letter of the law itself. If existing laws are not working, it is hardly likely that a new one will have impact;
- institutional mechanisms are not implemented. Even where reform efforts are real, there still need to be institutional mechanisms to carry reforms forward after their initial champions have passed from the scene. The classic case is that of Justice Plana in the Philippines who reformed the tax administration, raising its ability to implement tax collection fairly and effectively, but as soon as he was promoted out of his post, the reforms began to unravel (Klitgaard 1988);[7] and
- a weakening of civil society on a radical change of government. When radical political change takes place, as for example, in Georgia and South Africa, frequently civil society leaders are catapulted into government and quickly learn not to listen. At the same time, civil society has to undergo a sea change; from a stance of opposing the government to a position of constructive dialogue and democratic debate. Paradoxically, civil society, which many trumpet as being part of the solution, can, in fact, be crippled just at the moment when its role is potentially at its most powerful.

Reform must also face a host of vested interests: all those who have been bending the rules, whether to supplement meagre incomes or to pad well-filled foreign bank accounts, are potentially at risk, and so are threatened by the prospect of an anti-corruption drive.

In many situations the power of vested interests is such as to be able to derail reforms; indeed, in some cases these are so powerful, or so determined, that they can resort to violence. The potential dangers to reformers in such countries are real. The changes inherent in a comprehensive overhaul of a country's integrity system may be considerable, and call for special political and managerial skills. The conduct of parliaments can also be quite outrageous, for example, refusing to remove areas of corruption in which parliamentarians personally benefit.[8]

---

barrel. It must never be admitted that his individual corruption may be symptomatic of underlying disease. Quoted in Benson, 149.

7 The case is described as an example of successful reform in Klitgaard (1988).

8 See, for example, the refusal by the Brazilian Parliament to outlaw nepotism. President Obasanjo's difficulties in 1999/2000, in having anti-corruption legislation enacted in the Nigerian National Assembly, were considered by some observers, at least in part, to be the result of some legislators feeling themselves to be at risk. There, the legislature voted itself large sums of money for its members to spend, effectively converting a 'watchdog' into a 'burglar', and destroying the healthy tensions that should exist between any legislature and an executive.

Why 'Vertical Accountability' by itself Fails

In a democracy, there are two forms of accountability at work: 'vertical accountability' by which the electors, the governed, assert control over the governors and 'horizontal accountability' where those who govern (the governors) are accountable to other agencies (the watchdogs).

In principle, the governors and the governed are alike. There is no special group with political power. Political power is vested by the people themselves in chosen representatives, for a limited period of time. If the people are dissatisfied, they can remove those in power, either through the ballot box or through demanding their resignation or punishment (Fontana 1997).

However, throughout history, mere 'vertical accountability' has proved inadequate to the task. If the governors cannot achieve re-election through support of a satisfied populace, they achieve it through a combination of secrecy (so that the electors are unaware of what is transpiring) and the building of systems of patronage. The governors may also indulge in short-term populist acts, which may be to the longer-term detriment of the public. Not only will politicians tend to stretch the limits of their power and authority so as to govern with as little opposition as possible, but in some cases they will multiply their interventions simply to prove their own importance.

Moreover, the political class, which emerges with 'professional' politicians, often shares a set of values largely at odds with the democratic ideal, and promises made whilst in opposition, as we know, are all too frequently in stark contrast to their actions on assuming power. For example, in 1997 the Labour government came to power in the United Kingdom with strong pledges to end official secrecy. Their subsequent reforms were steadily watered down, to the point where some observers argue that the resulting reforms, far from making the government more transparent, could actually increase areas of secrecy.

The ancient democracies recognized and struggled with these contradictions. In Athens, in ancient Greece, the People's Court, formed by a randomly-selected group of citizens sat in judgement on public controversies and had the power to reverse decisions of the legislative body, the People's Assembly (Hansen 1991).[9] Similarly, in ancient Rome, the right of the citizen to appeal to the tribune of the plebs against decisions of the magistrates was seen as a cornerstone of liberty (Nicolet 1976). Both systems were democratic, as they were exercised by citizens, and were characterized by horizontal accountability, as the popular courts were effectively autonomous and independent political bodies. Much the same can be said of traditional societies in sub-Saharan Africa and elsewhere.

By contrast, in ancient China, the later Roman empires and the old European monarchies there emerged a bureaucratic class. This, in its time, served as a buffer between the people and the governors. When the bureaucrats' sensitivities were

---

9 The court could vary from a few hundred citizens to over 2,000, depending on the importance of the matter in issue. Jurors were chosen by lot. The cases were argued by supporters and opponents of the measure in question. People were expected to argue their own case and the employment of professional speakers or advisors was prohibited.

infringed, they were able to indulge in passive resistance – to question, to delay and to redirect the impact of orders from above, and so exercised a limited form of vertical accountability in a non-democratic environment.

Paradoxically, in the modern nation state (whether industrialized or developing), the bureaucratic class that emerged and which often protected the citizens from the excesses of their rulers, has, in large part, itself become part of the problem. It was never designed to be answerable to the people, and to some extent its upper echelons are themselves dependant on the political class. However, in many respects the bureaucracies have wrested considerable power from the political elite, including such agencies as central banks, research boards, and those that regulate commerce. Thus, what started out as a barrier against the actions of despots can now be seen by the public as being itself despotic. On the one hand the people feel that their will is disregarded, and on the other, the people's democratically-elected representatives lament the escape from their own control of a multiplicity of bureaucratic agencies. The advent of privatization has compounded this even further. In developing countries and countries in transition, the bureaucracy often acts to block effective implementation of anti-corruption programmes, not matter how hard a political leader may press for change.

In a democratic environment, the chances of vertical accountability succeeding would seem to be most favourable. In theory, those who govern and those who are governed are one and the same, with the rulers being chosen from among the people for finite terms, and entrusted with power only temporarily. If they govern badly, the people, the governed, can vote them out. If they abuse their power, the people can demand their punishment and/or resignation.

But in spite of this, in practice the application of vertical accountability has proved to be inadequate. Politics has become a profession, and as such has acquired its own rules and standards, to which the political class subscribes – those who govern and those contesting for power alike. Transparency *vis-á-vis* the people is seldom seen as being an advantage to the rulers, who have a vested interest in controlling what the governed know and precisely how their activities are presented to them (hence the emergence of 'spin doctors').

Those who govern benefit when they can hide behind the technicalities of government and paint a less than accurate picture of their activities.

So it is that vertical accountability as a single pillar fails to sustain accountability for several reasons – the people are not adequately informed of the activities of the governed; they have no power to investigate precisely what abuses may have taken place; and the process of elections is only periodic, so that even with free elections an administration is judged by the totality of its performance over time as perceived by an electorate, rather than held to account for specific acts of abuse.[10]

---

10 Critics of the Blair government in the United Kingdom would argue that this is precisely what is happening in Britain over the controversies surrounding the run-up to the decision to invade Iraq.

Introducing 'Horizontal Accountability'

The example set by leaders and high-ranking public officials is crucial to the achievement and maintenance of just and honest government. But who will guard the guardians?

The people's courts in ancient Greece and ancient Rome could manage the task of 'horizontal accountability', but the complexity of the modern state renders the formal exercise of popular surveillance simply unmanageable. There is, of course, a growing role for civil society in assuming this responsibility (aided by an explosion of information). However, any formal surveillance must depend on other mechanisms.

In his work, *De l'Esprit des Lois* (1748), Charles-Louis Secondat, Baron Montesquieu proposed what remains the most influential theory of horizontal accountability. In his interpretation the necessary condition for a moderate (as opposed to a despotic) regime was the articulation of the activity of government in separate functions and the allocation of these functions to separate bodies.

This breaking down of the exercise of political authority offered a double advantage: (a) the different departments of government would operate in competition with each other, each limiting and controlling the other's scope of action; and (b) the necessity to gain the approval of different authorities would delay the enforcement of legislation (he was concerned about arbitrary and secret orders of arrest) and allow more opportunities to monitor and detect abuses (Fontana 1997).

What he was predicating is what we have come to describe today as a 'national integrity system' – a system characterized by both vertical and horizontal accountability, and one capable of containing specific acts of abuse as well as ensuring that an administration is judged on the totality of its performance (Pope 1995).[11]

Introducing the National Integrity System

In a country where corruption is systemic, the figure below the unhappy spectacle that greets the anti-corruption reformer when he or she examines the existing 'national integrity system'.

The concept of the national integrity system provides reformers with a 'map' against which reform efforts can be plotted and progress tracked. It is one that has been quickly adopted by the development community, including the World Bank, but it has yet to realize its full potential in terms of generating and maintaining sustainable reforms. In essence, it fosters the holistic approach that most now accept is central to the success of any sustainable anti-corruption reform.

---

11 The concept of the 'national integrity system' was first articulated in the Pope (1995). It was adopted by development agencies, among others by the World Bank: Langseth and Stapenhurst (1997).

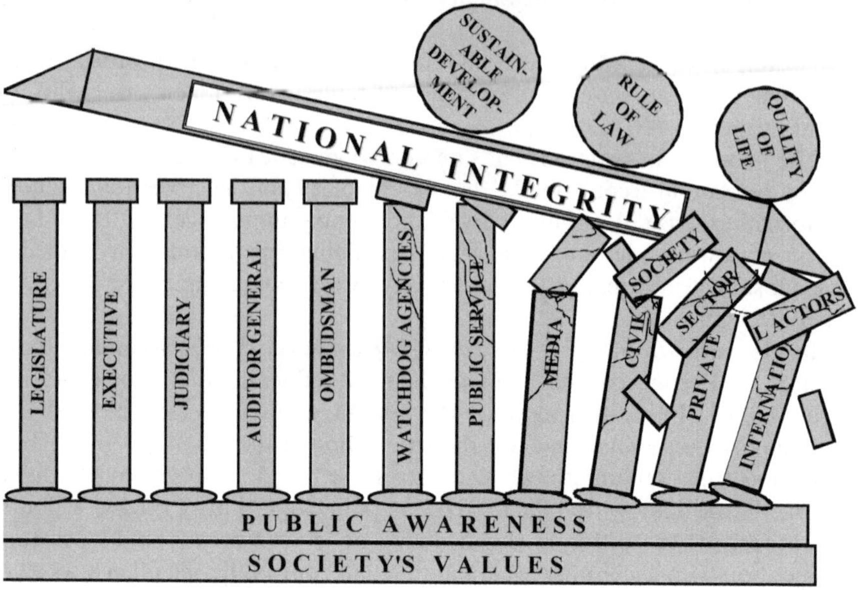

Figure 2.1 Greek temple

Not only does it assist in understanding the basic concepts and foundations of a particular country's governance system, but it also helps to ensure that the resulting remedies are grounded in practicality. Most importantly, it assists in achieving solutions that relate meaningfully to other parts of the overall system. Many anti-corruption strategies have failed to have the desired results simply because they have been too narrowly focused.

This analytical approach has been further developed into a methodology for the 'mapping' of the operations of an integrity system. This tracks the relevant inputs and outputs, and assesses why each element was created, what it expects from other institutions and agencies, and what it is supposed to deliver to them.[12]

The task in developing countries and countries in transition is to move away from a system which is essentially top down: one in which an autocratic ruling elite gives orders which are followed, to a greater or lesser degree, by those down the

12 This is being developed initially in a functioning integrity system (that of the state of Queensland, Australia) on the thesis that it makes greater sense to develop the methodology against the template of a functioning system that it would to try to achieve the same results by starting with a dysfunctional system. At a more simple level, basic analyses of some 18 countries were prepared for the Global Forum II on Countering Corruption and Building Integrity (The Hague, 2001). See http://www.transparency.org/activities/nat_integ_systems/country_studies.html. The study prepared for Ghana is of particular interest.

line. The approach is to move instead to a system of 'horizontal accountability'; one in which power is dispersed, where none has a monopoly, where none enjoys impunity and where each is separately accountable.[13]

Under a system of 'horizontal accountability'[14] a fabric of interlocking accountability and transparency requirements (sometimes described as a 'virtuous circle') is perfected: one in which each actor is both a watcher and is watched; is both a monitor and is monitored. A framework that, by effectively fracturing and disseminating 'power', both answers, and at the same time renders otiose, the age-old question of 'Who shall guard the guards'?

This is, of course, easier said than done. Age-old traditions and expectations have to be turned on their heads, and the process is obviously one that is likely to take a generation, if not generations, to perfect. Even then, ultimate perfection will always be elusive – even 'developed' countries prefer to style themselves as 'industrialized' as they, too, tread a path of continuous improvement.

Although the contemporary wave of democracy held much promise, in practice, democratic gains are being threatened and undermined by the very phenomena that were intended to be victims of the democratic process: corruption, abuse of power and nepotism. The need to refashion instrumentalities of governance runs very much deeper than simply moving away from a totalitarian system to one in which the people periodically have a voice. It means building an environment of continuous participation.

The shift is thus from a system of vertical accountability – be it the tyrant or the leadership of a one party state – to one of horizontal accountability, whereby a system of agencies of restraint and watch-dogs are designed to check abuses of power by other agencies and branches of government. These generally include the courts, independent electoral tribunals, auditors-general, ombudsman, central banks, parliaments (and their public accounts committees), professional organizations, and a free and independent media. At the core of horizontal

13 In such a system, there must, of course, be a free press. But the press, too, must respect certain limits imposed by law – for example, avoiding defamatory attacks on individuals. For even a free press is accountable, not only perhaps to a Press Council (which may or may not be a statutory body) but also, and ultimately, to the courts. For their part, the courts are no longer 'servants' of the ruling elite. Rather they are required to act with independence and to enforce the Rule of Law, and the rule under the law. Yet such independence is not absolute – judges are answerable for their individual decisions through a system of appeals, and each judge is accountable for his or her integrity and competence to another body, be it a parliament or a judicial services commission. That body, in turn, is accountable elsewhere, and ultimately to the people through the ballot box. So do the strands of accountability link the various elements, or 'pillars', and in such linking they brace and strengthen each other.

14 Anti-corruption commissions, auditors-general, human rights machinery, legislative public accounts committees, monitors of assets and liabilities of officials, criminal investigators *vis-à-vis* state agencies and civil servants, and sectoral regulatory agencies are examples of institutions of 'horizontal accountability' – state agencies that monitor other arms of the state.

accountability, too, lies the capacity for citizens to participate actively in the affairs of the day.

However, the phase of transition can be slow and painful. In some societies it has been a question of rehabilitating what was once there before; in others, notably in Eastern Europe, it can be a question of constructing the modern state literally from the ground upwards. In some there is no institutional memory of times of horizontal accountability, no living memories of how things once were, and could be again.

Such accountability mechanisms, when designed as part of a national effort to reduce corruption, comprise an integrity 'system'. This system of checks and balances is designed to achieve accountability between the various arms and agencies of government. The system effectively disperses power and limits situations in which conflicts of interest arise or have a negative impact on the common good. This involves accountability, transparency, prevention and penalty.

An integrity system embodies a comprehensive view of reform, addressing corruption in the public sector through government processes (leadership codes, organizational change, legal reforms, procedural reforms in bureaucracies etc.) and through civil reforms. The primary emphasis is on reforming and changing systems, rather than on blaming individuals. Even if corruption is endemic, it tends to be the result of systemic failures.

The whole edifice of government is thus sustained, and its integrity maintained (or undermined), by a bottom-up process. The fish may rot from the head, as is often observed, and corruption filter down through poor leadership examples and practices, but it is public awareness and, where warranted, public outrage, that is a society's ultimate defence. Where all else fails, the final sanction is revolution. However, the assumption underlying the approach advanced here is that evolution, not revolution, can be an effective and a preferable route.

Reform programmes, particularly those in developing countries and countries in transition supported by international or donor agencies, have tended to focus on a single area to the exclusion of others. These are 'single pillar' strategies. Frequently the choice has been made of a 'pillar' that is relatively 'safe', at the expense of addressing more difficult and more challenging areas. Certainly, a 'National Integrity System' reform programme can accommodate a piecemeal approach, but this must be coordinated and be within the bounds of an holistic programme which embraces each one of the relevant areas, and their inter-relationships with others.

Underpinning the integrity system concept is the conviction that all issues of contemporary concern in the area of governance – capacity development, results orientation, public participation, and the promotion of national integrity – need to be addressed in a holistic fashion. The overall goals should be to achieve:

- public services that are both efficient and effective, and which contribute to sustainable development;
- government functioning under law, with citizens protected from arbitrariness (including abuses of human rights); and

- development strategies which yield benefits to the nation as a whole, including its poorest and most vulnerable members, and not just to well-placed elites.

Building a Coherent National Integrity System

The ultimate goal of establishing a national integrity system is to eliminate to the extent possible the opportunities for people to be corrupt, and at the same time to make corruption a 'high risk' and 'low return' undertaking. As such, the system is designed to prevent corruption from occurring in the first place, rather than relying on penalties after the event – important though these are as a deterrent. The end goal is honest and efficient government.

However corrupted and however ineffective it may be, every country has the framework of a 'national integrity system' already in place. The concept helps to focus reformers on the holistic viewpoint. As we shall see, it is not enough to address a single element or 'pillar' of the system in isolation to others.[15]

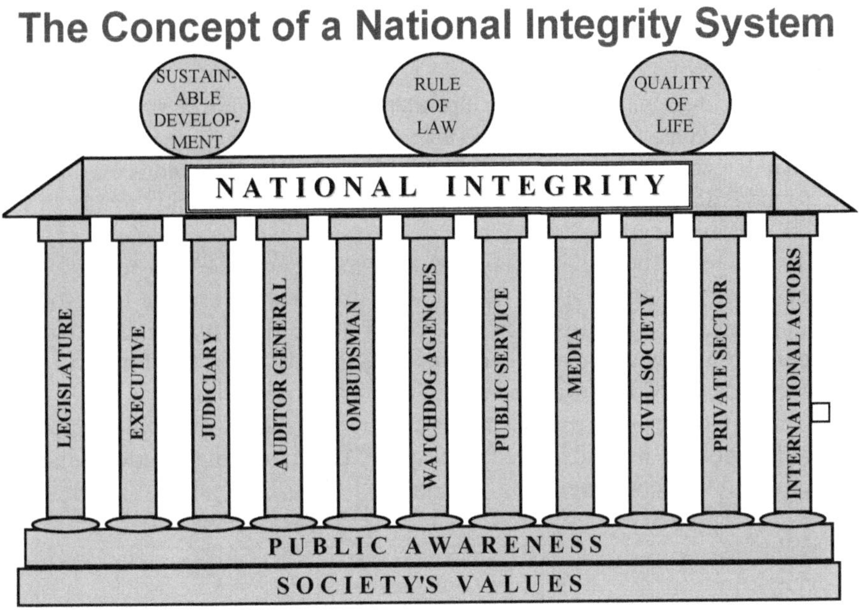

Figure 2.2 The institutional pillars of the national integrity system

15 For instance, in the closing years of the corrupt Moi administration considerable work in Kenya strengthened the operational capabilities of the Office of the Auditor-General. However, although widely featured in the media, the Auditor-General's highly professional reports were simply ignored, as the rest of the 'system' remained effectively dysfunctional.

A 'national integrity system' is rather like a Greek temple: a temple with a roof – the nation's integrity, supported at either end by a series of pillars, each being an individual element of the national integrity system. At one end of the temple are the institutional pillars – the judiciary, the parliament, the Auditor-General's Office, the Ombudsman, free media, civil society and the like. At the other end of the temple, the pillars represent the core tools, which the institutions must have at their disposal to be effective. For example, the media must have a right of freedom of speech; and civil society the legal space in which to organize itself and conduct its business.

Resting on the roof are three round balls: 'quality of life', 'Rule of Law' and 'sustainable development'. They are round to emphasize that it is crucial that the roof be kept level if these three round balls and the values they encompass are not to roll off.

The 'temple' itself is built on and continuously sustained by foundations, which comprise public awareness and society's values. If the public is apathetic and inattentive, or if values are widely lacking, then the foundations will be weak. The 'pillars' will be empty and ineffectual, and lack the underpinning necessary if they are to safeguard the nation's integrity. On the other hand, if public awareness is high and values are strong, both will support the 'pillars' which rest on them, giving them a solid foundation.

The individual 'pillars' are interdependent but may be of differing strengths. If one pillar weakens, an increased load is thrown onto one or more of the others. If several pillars weaken, the structure will tilt, and, with the whole edifice collapsing, the 'round balls' of 'sustainable development', 'Rule of Law' and 'quality of life' will fall and disintegrate,

The design of the 'pillars' may and will vary from society to society. Some will be stronger; some will be weaker. But there will always be trade-offs to accommodate this. For instance, one could argue that in Singapore, from a 'systems' point of view at least, a comparative lack of press freedom is to some extent compensated for by an intrusive anti-corruption bureau.

Although there are variations around the world, the most common 'integrity pillars'[16] that have been identified in a society that is seeking to govern itself in an accountable fashion include:

- executive;
- legislature;
- judiciary;
- Public Accounts Committee;
- Public Service;
- Auditor-General;
- Ombudsman;
- other 'watchdog' agencies (police, Anti-Corruption Agency, etc.)

---

16 The 'integrity pillars' were first presented as such by TI's Ibrahim Seushi in Tanzania. They have since found their way into a growing body of literature. The 'integrity system', as such, was developed by Transparency International.

- civil society (including the professions and the private sector);
- media;
- international agencies.

The 'Rules and Practices' Pillars

Complementing each of the national integrity system institutional 'pillars' are core 'rules and practices'. These rules and practices comprise the 'toolkit' employed by, or underpinning, the various institutions. The absence of core rules and practices are clear indicators of weakness. They are not necessarily confined to any single particular pillar, as the following illustrates:

Institutional pillar		**Corresponding core rules/practices**
Executive	=	Conflict of interest rules
Parliament	=	Fair elections
Public Accounts Committee (of legislature)	=	Power to question senior officials
Auditor General	=	Public reporting
Public service	=	Public service ethics
Judiciary	=	Independence
Media	=	Access to information
Civil society	=	Freedom of speech and assembly
Ombudsman	=	Records management
Anti-corruption[17]/watchdog agencies	=	Enforceable and enforced laws
Private sector	=	Competition policy, including public procurement rules
International community	=	Effective mutual legal/judicial assistance

The rules and practices are not, of course, exclusive to the institutional pillar to which they are assigned above. Several – such as ethics, freedom of speech and records management among them – run right across the structure. Some rules and practices that are also of paramount importance are subsumed in others in this list: for example, whistle blower and complaints mechanisms may be regarded as being covered by freedom of speech and public service ethics. In their totality, the institutional pillars in the left-hand column together with the rules and practices in the right-hand column comprise a basic national integrity system.

Establishing a sound national integrity system requires the systematic identification of deficiencies, as well as opportunities for strengthening or augmenting each of the pillars into a coherent framework.

If the system is wholly dependent on a single 'pillar' as is the case, perhaps, of a 'benign dictator', or if it depends of only a very few pillars, it will be vulnerable to

17 For example, the Independent Commission Against Corruption (ICAC), New South Wales, Australia.

collapse. The system may give the outward appearance of functioning in the short term, for instance in the case of clean-ups conducted by military governments on the overthrow of corrupt civilian regimes. However, the lack of a functioning integrity system ensures progressive decay, unless there is also a timely move toward accountable governance.

The national integrity system approach unlocks a new form of diagnosis and potential cure for corruption. Instead of looking at separate institutions (for example, the Judiciary) or separate rules and practices (for example, the criminal law) and then focusing on stand-alone reform programmes, the concept allows one to look at inter-relationships, inter-dependence and combined effectiveness in an holistic fashion.[18]

Nevertheless, the 'bracing' for the system – the 'horizontal accountability mechanisms' – is frequently the weakest point, and so renders the whole edifice liable to lurching sideways. The exclusion of civil society from these horizontal mechanisms is a cause of considerable frustration to civil society, as citizens increasingly demand participation in the workings of oversight institutions (Goetz and Jenkins 2001; Jenkins and Goetz 1999).

Checks and Balances in Building Horizontal Accountability

The objective in any integrity system is to build a system of checks and balances within the framework of agreed fundamental principles (usually enshrined in a written constitution or basic law). In effect, a self-sustaining 'virtuous circle' is achieved, in which the principles at risk are all monitored, by themselves and by others.

Although a self-sustaining circle can be constructed on integrity, it can also be based on deceit. Every post-holder is potentially at risk – be it the head of government, a judge, an auditor or a junior official – although some are obviously more vulnerable than others. The goal is to construct a transparent and accountable system, which has two primary objectives: the first is to prevent fraud from taking place, and the second to make the players believe that if there is fraud, there is a realistic chance of its being detected.

Monitoring corruption cannot be left only to public prosecutors and to the forces of law and order. Action cannot depend solely on detection and criminal prosecution. Rather, action must include a combination of interlocking arrangements, including codes of conduct and reliable complaints mechanisms. In part, this approach includes improving the transparency of relationships, and to the extent possible, preventing the development of relationships which can lead to corrupt acts. It also includes transparency in the financial affairs of key players, and the prospect of reviews being conducted by independent institutions which are likely to be beyond the reach of any particular corruption network.

---

18 For example, What is the benefit of a sound and 'clean' Judiciary ready to uphold the Rule of Law, if there is corruption in the police, investigators, prosecutors or the legal profession? The Judges would simply not receive the cases they should hear; they would then sit in splendid isolation – honest, capable, yet able to achieve little.

Although corruption can never be completely eliminated, it can be controlled through a combination of ethical codes, decisive legal prosecutions against offenders and institutional reform.

Involving Civil Society

Where genuine attempts to combat corruption have been unsuccessful, there has generally been at least one missing ingredient – the involvement of civil society. The *Times of India* has observed that: 'People's acceptance of corruption as a fact of life and their general despondency need to be tackled first' (Bayley 1966, 723).

Most people in civil society have a fundamental need for an effective integrity system: be it the private sector, religious leaders, the press, the professions or, above all, the ordinary citizen who on a daily basis bears the brunt of corruption.

Traditionally, civil society has only been involved in 'vertical accountability', voting – or not voting – in elections and in making demands for better performance. This has proved ineffectual, and now we must find increased ways of inserting civil society into oversight (or 'horizontal accountability') mechanisms. One can point to several instances of this being achieved: such as citizens serving on police complaints boards; as prison visitors; on environmental oversight bodies; and on professional misconduct bodies for lawyers and doctors. In fact, the highly successful Hong Kong Independent Commission Against Corruption has an oversight body of citizens that has to consent to any investigation being discontinued.

Mapping the Integrity System

The concept of the national integrity system has given rise to an extensive series of 'national integrity system assessments'.[19] The systems of some 100 countries have been analysed at the urging of various development agencies, most notably those of Australia, Britain and The Netherlands. Studies, typically of between 25 and 50 pages, have provided a broad outline of the tasks each country faces and helps to identify various interventions that can usefully be made by aid donors. The process has involved the gathering of informed responses to a similar set of questions about the performance of institutions and the existence and observance of rules and sound practices. This in turn facilitates inter-country comparisons.

Concurrently, experimental work has been embarked upon in Australia on an even more ambitious scale which takes the process to a more sophisticated level. The pilot state chosen was Queensland – selected because it seemed most logical to analyse a state where there had been major corruption scandals and where a comprehensive effort had been made to redress these problems. It was thought that the lessons learned would be more instructive than would the case had the first

---

19 The series has been developed and managed by Prof. Alan Doig. The studies may be seen at http://www.transparency.org/activities/nat_integ_systems/country_studies.html.

trial been conducted in a developing country where the results could be clouded by extraneous factors such as poverty, illiteracy and a weak bureaucracy.

The field test in Queensland has shown that an integrity system can be 'mapped'. The performance of institutions can be analysed by obtaining the answers to a series of standard questions: Why was a particular institutions established? What is it supposed to do? What does it in fact do? What is the institution supposed to receive from other parts of the system? What does it receive in practice? What is it supposed to provide to other parts of the system? And what does it in fact provide? For example, investigators need cooperation from prosecutors and the courts, they need adequate resources, they need to be provided with enforceable laws and their independence must be respected by the political class.

Such a 'mapping' analysis can reveal the fault lines, and remedial action can be taken. It can also be used to check the impact of reforms and to serve as a type of governance barometer.

Clearly the journey that has to be travelled is not an easy one. Companions may prove unreliable, even obstructive. The travellers, too, need to know where they are going, and be confident that they are not following false trails. They must be able to know whether they are making progress, and if so, how much. The overwhelming advantage of the 'national integrity system' concept is that it can provide a clear and unambiguous 'road map' for the journey towards just and honest governance, and a means for keeping that final destination in view.

The 'mapping' process refined in Australia is now ready to be taken into the developing world and countries in transition. It may be just in time. The developed world is growing weary of the anti-corruption struggle in the developing world, and is showing signs of concluding – without actually saying so – that the problems are too deeply embedded for their aid agencies to be able to have much impact. There have been many gallant attempts to curtail corruption, and an equal number of inglorious failures. Attempts have been made to change laws and to strengthen institutions, all to little effect. Perhaps the national integrity system and the approach of 'mapping' it in individual countries to the Queensland model is the key for which development agencies have been waiting.

References

Bayley, D. (1966), 'The Effects of Corruption in a Developing Nation', *The Western Political Quarterly*, 19:4, 719–32.

Benson, B.L. (1988), 'An Institutional Explanation for Corruption of Criminal Justice Officials', *Cato Journal* 8:1, 139–63.

Caiden, G.E. (1988),'Toward a General Theory of Official Corruption', *Asian Journal of Public Administration* 10:1, 3–20.

Doig, A. (1994), 'Honesty in Politics and Public Spending: The Ethical Environment', paper presented to the Second Seminar on the Status and Prevention of Corruption, Santiago, Chile, 4–6 July.

Fontana, B. (1997), 'The Failures of Human Agency: Accountability in Historical Perspective', unpublished paper, University of Lausanne.

Goetz, A.-M. and Jenkins, R. (2001) 'Hybrid Forms of Accountability: Citizen Engagement in Public-sector Oversight in India', *Public Management Review* 3:3, 362–83.

Hansen, M.H. (1991), *The Athenian Democracy in the Age of Demosthenes* (Oxford: Blackwell).

Jenkins, R. and Goetz, A.-M. (1999), 'Accounts and Accountability: Theoretical Implications of the Right-to-information Movement in India', *Third World Quarterly* 20:3, 603–22.

Klitgaard, R. (1988), *Controlling Corruption* (Los Angeles, CA: University of California Press).

Langseth, P. and Stapenhurst, R. (1997), 'National Integrity System: Country Studies', *EDI Working Paper* (Washington DC: World Bank).

Nicolet, C. (1976), *Le métier de citoyen dans la Rome républicaine* (Paris: Gallimard).

Pope, J. (1995), *Transparency International National Integrity System Sourcebook* (Berlin: Transparency International).

Chapter 3

What is a National Integrity System? From Temple Blueprint to Hip-Pocket Guide

A.J. Brown

In concept, a 'national integrity system' is a relatively simple notion. As suggested in chapter 1, 'integrity' describes the desirable situation when powerful individuals and institutions act in an upright and reliable manner in our society, true to the values, purposes and duties for which they have been entrusted with that power. Accordingly a national integrity 'system' means the methods used by a given society – institutions, laws, practices and attitudes – to increase the chances of this outcome by working to promote and pursue integrity in daily public life. The purpose of describing this system is also fairly simple: in order to improve it, by figuring out what developments in institutions, practices, management and education might enhance our collective assurance that the powers we entrust to elected and appointed officials are exercised in accordance with recognized public purposes and values.

Simple as this may sound, the concept of an integrity system discussed by Jeremy Pope in Chapter 2, and similar concepts used by others internationally, show that identifying and describing this system may be anything but simple in practice. The metaphor of the ancient Greek temple used by Pope (Figure 2.1) immediately emphasizes a number of key institutions as the type of 'pillars' we should look for as making up, if not the entire system, then some of its most important parts. But are these pillars the same in every country, and are there not some major differences between the types of pillars that appear in Pope's model? Most of the first 18 countries studied for the presence of such pillars were revealed to have them, taken by Transparency International as confirming 'the relevance and application of a uniform approach' (TI 2001, 39; see Doig and McIvor, this volume) – but how uniform do we believe such a system needs to be? Does tracking the presence of these institutions really tell us what kind of system is in place, let alone what makes it work, and what might be its problems? Where do the tentacles of the system begin, and where do they end?

This chapter seeks to answer these questions by reviewing some of the practical experience of agencies and researchers engaged in the description of integrity systems. How an integrity system is described is clearly important. Without a clear understanding of what this system is, it is difficult if not impossible to evaluate or assess it, and hence to mount cogent arguments for how it needs to be improved. The first part of the chapter compares the main elements that a number of recent assessment approaches have looked for, internationally, for the purposes of analysis and evaluation of integrity and related governance regimes. This throws up some immediate questions about the scope of any integrity system assessment, in terms of the true extent of the institutions and practices that are being described. Is the 'integrity system' just another term for a fully-functioning democratic model of government, or is it only part of a country's system of government, or is it just the system that ensures integrity in government itself (that is, just the public sector … or only part of a part of the society's governance as a whole)? The discussion also raises some questions about the suitability of the methods used, and the underlying policy purposes that might drive different forms of assessment – some of which may not be obvious. These 'hidden' or not-so-hidden agendas need to be flushed out and acknowledged.

The second part of the chapter puts some of these questions in a practical context, by looking at some of the challenges met when describing Australia's integrity systems. Even though Pope's idea of a national integrity system crystallized largely in response to Australian experiences, the simple fact is that even the identification of basic institutional 'pillars' in this system becomes a complex exercise. As in all countries, in Australia the institutions that matter are to be found operating in and across different sectors (public, business, civil society), at different levels of governance and regulation (federal, state, local), as well as in different institutional configurations ('core' institutions, and 'distributed' ones). Indeed even though the new assessment efforts focus on systems, all these systems are ultimately made up of individuals, and both the individual and popular culture of integrity in a society will obviously matter. Is there a practical way to map all these elements of an integrity system? Is it necessary to do so, before attempting to assess it?

The final part of the chapter concludes that while an attempt to map and assess every single element of an integrity system may well be impossible, it is fundamentally important to approach the task with a clear sense of direction. Even in predominantly Europeanized, liberal democratic countries like Australia, there are conflicting assumptions about the meaning of 'integrity', and a number of obvious and not-so-obvious assumptions about which 'systems' are most important for achieving it. These different dimensions are acknowledged throughout the English-speaking and industrialized worlds, making it important for reformers in any country to stop and think about these fundamentals before they adopt an assessment framework based on any particular template. The clear need is for flexibility in the type of template that is adopted, so that above all else, when the integrity system is described and assessed, those who need to recognize its features and accept the results of the evaluation, have no choice but to accept its logic. Some final suggestions are made for a flexible approach to identifying what makes up the system – but however it is done, it is clear from the experience that clarity matters, and little should be taken for granted.

Integrity System Assessment: An International Growth Industry?

The study of integrity systems, of the kind identified by Pope and Transparency International, is not confined to the single model of Greek temple pillars set out in chapter 2. The 'national integrity system' is but one of a number of major ideas occupying the field of governance assessment and reform – a global industry that few would have contemplated 15 years ago. Another major effort to describe and evaluate 'good' governance in recent times is comparative analysis of the 'ethics infrastructure' of many member-countries by the Organisation for Economic Cooperation and Development (OECD 1996; 1999; 2000). Another is the construction of a Global Integrity Index comparing and ranking the anti-corruption 'architecture' of 25 countries, published by the Washington-based Center for Public Integrity (Lewis 2004; Camerer 2004). On an ongoing basis, the World Bank has compiled quantitative data on a series of 'Governance Indicators' to help measure the progress of aid-receiving countries against the Bank's development goals (Kaufmann et al. 2003), a major response to the lifting of the veil on the corruption problems of aid-receiving societies in the early-mid 1990s (Glynn et al. 1997; McCoy 2001).

As Table 3.1 shows, the elements or dimensions of the systems assessed by each of these different efforts are often very similar. Like Pope, many international actors look immediately to a range of institutions as the key defining parts of an integrity system, including corruption-specific bodies such as anti-corruption commissions and ombudsmen, but also setting these in the context of major democratic institutions and accountability mechanisms including an active civil society and the rule of law. Indeed the similarity of the lists suggests some deceptively answers to the question, 'what is an integrity system?', because it would be easy to assume that any country that can demonstrate the presence of all these major institutions does have such a system, while conversely, a society missing any or all of these elements does not.

Of course, this is not actually the case. If indeed these lists were identical, this would throw up a problem of its own. Contrary to some of the early suggestions by Transparency International, a uniform approach to the building and maintenance of integrity is not necessarily desirable, if only because long experience suggests it is never likely to work. As Michael Johnson has observed, there are known problems with governance reform proposals that 'emphasise the same factors everywhere, and thus do not really fit anywhere' (as quoted by Quah 2003, 244; see also Lindsey and Dick 2002). To the extent that the different assessment models are all looking for the same thing, this is potentially the sign of a problem.

In fact, on closer inspection these 'laundry lists' of the elements of good governance have at least three significant differences, throwing up even more basic questions about exactly what it is that is being assessed. A first difference lays in the fact that only the list of 'integrity pillars' suggested by Transparency International mentions the private business sector. The remainder are more clearly focused on good 'government' rather than governance as a whole. In some cases this is quite deliberate. The OECD's projects have been focused on public sector management within the industrialized economies of its member-countries, and

Table 3.1 Elements of Western governance assessments

Assessment model/approach				
National integrity system	**OECD anti-corruption mechanisms**	**OECD ethics infrastructure**	**Public Integrity Index**	**Governance matters**
Transparency International – NIS Country Studies and NISA	OECD, Paris	OECD, Paris	Centre for Public Integrity, Washington DC	World Bank
Pope 1996, 2000	OECD 1996	OECD 1999, 2000	Camerer 2004	Kaufman 2003
Key elements to be assessed				
Legislature Executive	Oversight by legislature	Political will	Electoral and political processes	Political stability
Judiciary	Specialised bodies to prosecute corruption	Effective legal framework	Branches of government	Rule of law
Auditor-General	Supreme financial audit authority	Efficient accountability mechanisms	Oversight and regulatory mechanisms	Control of corruption
Ombudsman	Ombudsman			
	Anti-corruption regulation			
Watchdog agencies	Corruption investigation bodies	Ethics coordinating body		
	Human resource mgt procedures	Supportive public service conditions		
	Financial management controls			
Public service	Organisational management controls		Administration and civil service	
	Guidance and training for public officials	Workable codes of conduct Professional socialization mechanisms		Regulatory quality
Media Civil society Private sector International actors	Transparency mechanisms	Active civil society	Civil society, public information and media	Voice and accountability

have not attempted to suggest this 'ethics infrastructure' was devoted to integrity in all institutions of society, nor indeed to prescribe any global model. However in the case of the Global Integrity Report (Camerer 2004), the lack of attention to private sector accountability was an acknowledged deficiency, identified as one of four major limitations of the study.

In fact, even in the case of Transparency International's list, there has been confusion over exactly what part the private business sector plays as part of the integrity system. Initially it appears that the private sector was listed as an integrity 'pillar' because of the positive role being played by some (presumably not all) international business in fighting international bribery (Stapenhurst and Sedigh 1999, 2). When it came to systems for ensuring integrity on the part of business itself, the mechanisms examined were primarily voluntary and self-regulatory, and did not extend to the types of stronger regulatory 'pillars' being used to ensure integrity in government (see Langseth et al. 1999, 145; Pope 2000, 137–51). So when it comes to the integrity and regulatory regimes needed to govern business, are these in or out of the national integrity system? The conclusion reached in the Australian assessment was that they are definitely in, even if assessing them is a large and complex undertaking in its own right (see Lucas and Kimber, this volume; Brown et al. 2005). Indeed the interrelationships between causes of corruption and integrity failure that can be found on both sides of the 'public-private divide' necessitate this wider approach, as demonstrated clearly in Australia by the AWB scandal (Bartos, this volume).

A second, related difference can be found between the Transparency International, OECD and Global Integrity lists of system elements on one hand, and the World Bank's approach on the other. Even where the major dimensions of the system appear very similar, what is *actually* being measured, and the reasons for doing so, can be very different things. Like the other agencies, the World Bank was concerned with government, and not overly concerned with the integrity systems needed to effectively regulate the business sector. Of the several hundred variables from 25 surveys used as Governance Indicators, just four measured corruption within business (not including organized crime), with two surveys each asking about levels of insider trading and tax evasion in the particular countries (Kaufmann et al. 2003, 78, 85). Even more telling was the Bank's inclusion of 'telephone wait times' and 'phone faults' among the 'Objective Indicators of Good Governance' (Kaufmann et al. 2003, 50) – when clearly, these only provide objective evidence of the state of the phone system, or at most of ease of communication, rather than necessarily pointing to high or low quality governance. Similarly the evidence collected to describe the state of a country's 'rule of law' focuses on enforceability of contracts and private property rights (Stapenhurst and Kpundeh 1999, 238; Kaufmann et al. 2003, 4, 19, 85, 96 etc; Knack et al. 2003, 360) – rather than, say, access to justice or freedom from arbitrary torture.

While the World Bank's six dimensions of governance indicators (voice and accountability, political stability, government effectiveness, regulatory quality, rule of law, and control of corruption) appear to set out a comparable method of describing an integrity system, in fact they do not measure 'good governance' or even 'good government' as much as whether government appears to be conducting itself in a manner conducive to efficient and effective economic development. This should be no surprise. Since at least 1992, the Bank has explicitly defined 'governance' to mean 'the manner in which power is exercised in the management of a country's economic and social resources *for development*' (see Marquette 2001, 399), even though most political scientists and public policy-makers take a wider definition. It is important to recognize, however, that with this particular approach to anti-corruption reform comes a number of assumptions. At least as important, and probably more important than institutional ethics and effective regulatory oversight of officials and companies, is 'state of the art' macroeconomic reform based on reduced public sectors, minimized official discretion, deregulation, privatization, enhanced competition and market liberalization; according to Kaufmann (1999, 95), 'virtually all economic, deregulation, and government reform measures' will help curb corruption as well as sustaining national growth. Ultimately, as Williams (1999, 122) commented, a 'very specific, Western-based understanding of market discipline' underlies this idea of how corruption should be addressed, and where integrity systems fit into society.

For obvious reasons, assumptions that free-market economic liberalization should be a mainstay of the integrity system – and that the integrity system should do nothing to compromise the market – have come under attack (for example, Kotkin and Sajo 2002). The important lesson here is that even the World Bank's assessment model, far more detailed and drawing together far richer sources of empirical evidence than any other, cannot necessarily be relied upon as supplying an 'instant' list of the elements or items that need to be checked in order to establish how a country's governance system is composed, let alone whether it works as an 'integrity' system or not.

Inevitably, attempts to describe integrity systems are shaped by the underlying goals or 'drivers' of the assessment. Defining the integrity system can have at least four different starting-points – economic, democratic, administrative and/or personal – depending on where perceived problem and preferred solutions happen to lie (Brown and Uhr 2004). Integrity system assessment can be undertaken in order to (a) pursue greater, liberalized economic development, as seen above; it can also be pursued in order to (b) promote and enhance democratic reform, (c) establish simply whether agreed ethics programmes are performing cost-effectively within existing economic and political circumstances, and/or (d) promote honesty and integrity as desirable personal qualities. In the Australian setting, the purposes of assessment were a clear mix of (b) and (c), with a strong awareness of (d), but very little to do with (a) despite its dominance of much international governance reform. Any similar assessment needs to proceed on the basis of frank acknowledgement as to what is being assessed, and why.

Even if we accept that a major strategy of an integrity system is to enhance democratic accountability, as a means of ensuring appropriate use of power in society, we still face important decisions as to what exactly the integrity system *is*. Clearly we are less concerned with systems for maximising economic efficiency and growth, or systems for ensuring that individual citizens are always honest with one another. But we need to determine whether our integrity system is *one and the same* as the regime of parliamentary democracy we use to govern our society, or whether it is simply a constituent part of that regime. If the former, then the institutional elements that make up the integrity system may include every part of our system of governance, perhaps calling for a methodology akin to a Democratic Audit (such as developed by the Stockholm International Institute for Democracy and Electoral Assistance). If the integrity system is a discrete part of the system of governance, however, it would be described differently; indeed, parts of it might have nothing to do with democracy at all.

These questions raise their own problems of the potential limit of any definition of an integrity system that relies on identifying particular institutions, such as democratic ones. Clearly many of the system elements listed earlier in Table 3.1 are closely interrelated with the theory and practice of Western-style, liberal, representative, parliamentary democracy, even removing any neoliberal economic elements. The Global Integrity Index explicitly targeted 25 countries 'that hold elections', making it fairly unremarkable why it would equate integrity with effective democracy. The World Bank's indicators of political participation, under the dimension of 'voice and accountability', are overwhelmingly democratically-focused. The Transparency International concept is even more closely based on liberal democratic principles as an integrity-building strategy, not just in the nature of institutions – for example in the inclusion of parliaments and the judiciary as obvious pillars in the system – but in how those institutions interrelate.

The implications of this for societies that do not share, or do not particularly wish to share the same political traditions as Western democracies are further discussed towards the end of the chapter. The practical problem is how to start describing the disparate elements that make up the system. Elsewhere in this volume, while still seeing a particular association between integrity systems and democracy, Gilman and Stout (this volume) tend to view an 'integrity system' as a discrete and deliberate part of this democratic order, 'one of the most innovative anti-corruption programmes developed by governments in the last one hundred years'. If so, it should be reasonably easy to describe and map. However as already seen, describing the system is not so simple, especially when its operations are so intertwined with such a wide array of fundamental institutions. The practical question of what makes up such a programme, or system, can really only be usefully pursued in context.

Describing the System in Practice: Lessons from Australia

In Australia, the choice between seeing the integrity system as a discrete and finite part of the overall system of governance, and as something more diffuse running throughout it, can be found reflected in two quite different perspectives. On one hand, the first and easiest point of focus clearly remains on those major institutions – anti-corruption commissions, ombudsmen, audit offices, company regulators – whose primary reason for existence is to ensure accountability, promote integrity and fight corruption. In Australia, there is a wide array of such bodies. Often these have been constituted as independent statutory authorities, still notionally part of the 'executive' arm of government but legally protected from undue interference by the government of the day, and hence ultimately only accountable to parliament. One way of conceiving the integrity system is to focus primarily on these bodies, and view these institutions as constituting a 'fourth branch' of government alongside the legislature, executive and judiciary, as suggested by Chief Justice of New South Wales:

> … there have been a number of candidates for a 'fourth branch' designation over the years. The number does not matter. The idea does. The primary basis for the recognition of an integrity branch as a distinct functional specialisation, required in all governmental structures, is the fundamental necessity to ensure that corruption, in a broad sense of that term, is eliminated from government. However, once recognised as a distinct function, for which distinct institutions are appropriate, at a level of significance which acknowledges its role as a fourth branch of government, then the idea has implications for our understanding of constitutional and legal issues of broader significance. (Spigelman 2004)

A similar 'functional specialisation' might be found in a number of key bodies with influence over integrity in the private sector, which also necessarily form part of the system as outlined earlier. Taking this approach, a number of institutions are relatively easy to map. Figure 3.1 sets out how this might be done, taking both private and public sectors together. The 'fourth branch' described by Spigelman CJ is reflected in the hatched bodies in the top-right quadrant.

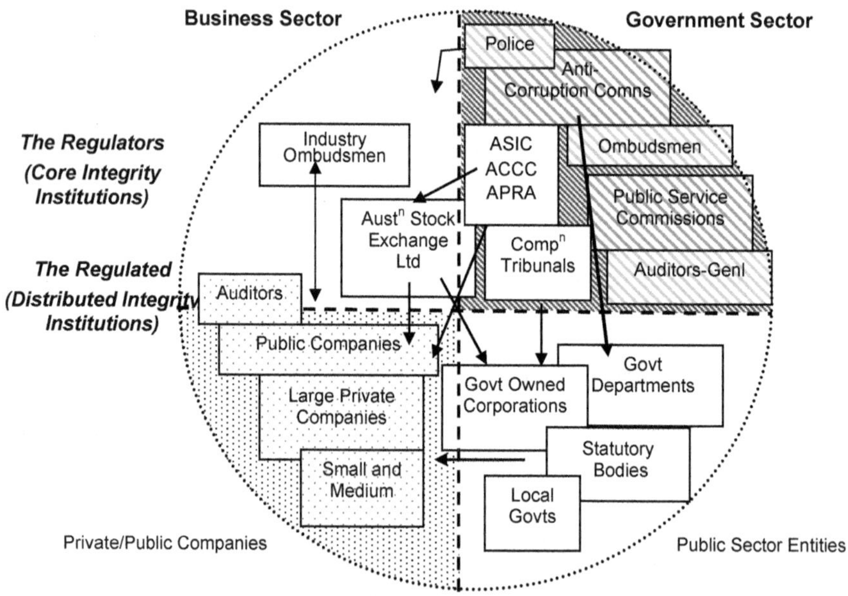

Figure 3.1 Key integrity institutions by sector and level

However while these organizations are important, they clearly do not represent the entirety of the integrity system. On a different view, it immediately becomes obvious that integrity – in either sector – is also dependent on the commitment and management strategies of the institutions regulated by the 'fourth branch', not simply as a direct result of regulation but also of their own free will, in the service of recognized duties and values. Speaking again primarily of government, Uhr points out that in practice, integrity is a complex exercise in which all participate, and in which critical differences are made by individuals in positions of influence throughout organizations, in their own right and in relationship with one another, as well as within the democratic-political context that determines the 'terms of trust' defining integrity at any given time. On Uhr's view, the integrity system can be understood as a more diffuse 'lattice of leadership':

> The 'lattice ...' implies that public trust in government is more reliably placed when the various institutions of government share the task of self-regulation, with each relevant institution acting in ways that bring out the greatest public responsibility in those institutions with which they share public power. (Uhr 2005, 155)

Both these accounts reinforce the call for a clearer picture of the integrity system, because they each show that the ways in which the parts of the system interrelate, and the methods for keeping them coordinated, are vital to understanding how the system works. However they focus on different elements. In particular, without losing sight of the significance of major 'core' institutions in the integrity system, it is important to recognize that to rely on these alone is only to recognize one dimension. In addition to listing the types of institutions and formal programmes that make up 'integrity systems' or 'ethics infrastructure', a number of bodies and analysts point to a number of approaches. Transparency International suggests that in addition to its 'institutional pillars', the Greek temple relies on a number of 'rules and practices pillars' albeit not reflected graphically in the model. Sampford and others point to ethical standard-setting and institutional reform as equal partners to legal regulation in the pursuit of public integrity (Figure 3.2a). The OECD has pointed out that while some elements of the 'ethics infrastructure' are directed towards control, others are directed to guidance or management (Figure 3.2b). The American political scientist Pat Dobel (1999) fleshes out why three different models of integrity have to be considered, and how these models – 'institutional-legal', 'effectiveness/implementation' and 'personal-responsibility' – may also work against one another (Figure 3.2 c).

Clearly, taking into account these different dimensions, there are more elements to the integrity system than listed at the outset in Table 3.1. Even in terms of institutions, it is necessary to include both 'core' institutions, whose sole or primary purpose is the pursuit of integrity in other organizations, but the 'distributed' integrity institutions that extend into the work of the vast bulk of organizations. These 'distributed' ethics programmes include everything from codes of conduct to values-building programmes to internal audit programmes to whistleblower protection systems, and they may have everything or nothing to do with external legislative requirements or the activities of 'core' oversight

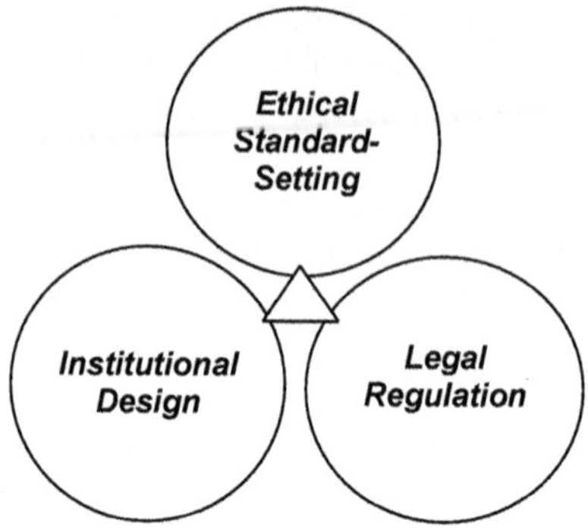

Figure 3.2a Sampford's trinity of reform

Figure 3.2b Elements of OECD ethics infrastructure

Figure 3.2c Dobel's models of integrity

bodies. While they can be usefully described as distributed integrity institutions, they are embedded in the management structures and systems of organizations, and are as much to do with institutional practice and the leadership culture of management in those organizations as they are to so with legal requirements. They exist across the public and private sector alike, and are found in the bottom two quadrants of Figure 3.2 above.

A third practical issue in identifying what makes up an integrity system, even in these basic institutional terms, is the reality that formal systems of governance and regulation are configured at different levels in all societies. All these institutions, in any or all of these sectors, may exist in multiple jurisdictions within the same country – and moreover, the extent of replication may be different in different sectors. In Australia, the systems of business regulation are increasingly unitary (that is, one system operating under uniform national laws), but in addition to the federal (national) government there are eight state and territory governments, and around 800 local governments. In other words, while the left-hand half of Figure 3.2 accurately summarizes some key institutions relating to integrity in the business sector, the right-hand half of the figure would need to be repeated nine times to describe the main public sector integrity frameworks. Not surprisingly for a federal country, each of those nine pictures would also be slightly different, because no two governmental jurisdictions in Australia take exactly the same institutional approach. Table 3.2 below, repeated from Chapter 10 (Brown, this volume), demonstrates this in respect of select 'core' public integrity bodies.

Table 3.2 Some core public integrity institutions in Australia

	Auditor-General	**Ombudsman**	**Police Complaints Authority**	**Police Integrity Commission**	**Anti-Corruption Commission**	**Crime Commission**
NSW	1	2	3		4 (ICAC)	5
Commonwealth	1	2		3 (ACLEI)		4
Queensland	1	2	3 (CMC)			
WA	1	2	3 (CCC)			
South Australia	1	2	3			
Victoria	1	2 (inc. Office of Police Integrity)				
Tasmania	1	2				

Note: This table does not include Health Care Complaints Commissions and a range of other specialist independent integrity bodies, other than those dedicated to police.

Even when describing a relatively small number of key institutions, therefore, giving an effective account of the nation's integrity systems begins to become quite complex. In most cases, descriptions and assessments of integrity systems are restricted to the situation at just one level of government (typically the national government), even though some of the most important influences on integrity and opportunities for corruption may lie at other levels. Another acknowledged limitation of the Global Integrity Report (Camerer 2004) was this problem of geographic superficiality. In the Australian assessment, analysis began with two state governments (see also Smith this volume), and extended to the federal level (Roberts this volume), but the state of the system as it pertained to other jurisdictions was judged simply through desktop research and extrapolation.

In a democratic country, the integrity system is clearly more than simply a neat subset of the system of governance – rather it permeates that system, including its parliamentary and political elements. Some particular bodies or programmes may be new and distinct, but their operation as part of the system will inevitably depend on a wide variety of often older, more diffuse elements, some probably so old that their role is little understood or simply taken for granted. Indeed, it may be these parts of the integrity system that are most difficult to locate and describe, even though they may be atrophying and particularly conducive to integrity failure. An example might be the independence and integrity of the news media, which in many developed societies is assumed to be still playing its conventional and crucial role in ensuring public accountability, but which in reality is subject to commercial pressures that often leave it superficial and compromised.

Despite the simplicity of the concept, an integrity system is not easily described and assessed in the same relatively straightforward way as other types of public policies and programmes. Even within a single democracy, let alone between them, let alone between a larger diversity of systems, the institutional elements can vary markedly. Nevertheless, taking the above lessons, it is conceptually possible to figure out how a taxonomy of all the elements of an integrity system might be drawn. In Australia, an attempt to thoroughly describe the system across eleven sectors and jurisdictions (nine government, one business and one civil society) would do so looking at all the ways in which three different approaches to integrity (ethical standard-setting, institutional design and legal regulation) were being pursued, at two institutional levels (core and distributed). There is little doubt that studying each of these 66 categories would yield a comprehensive description. This conceptual approach could be expanded to any number of sectors, jurisdictions or organizational levels, as shown by Figure 3.3.

Whether such an exhaustive, reductionist approach to describing the integrity system is necessary, is not really the issue. What is important is the recognition that even to understand the integrity system as it exists in a relatively average industrialized democracy – moreover one from which Transparency International's concept of the national integrity system was partly drawn – it is necessary to abandon specific institutional templates and adopt a deliberate strategy for describing the system from 'the bottom up'. The key lesson is that the system is multidimensional, with tentacles that reach into politics and public attitudes in addition to law enforcement and public sector management. Decisions about how to focus the assessment need not be made arbitrarily, or limited by default assumptions that have never been critically analysed, but can and must be approached consciously, with extensive public discussion. While an attempt to map and assess every single element of an integrity system may well be impossible, it is fundamentally important to approach the task with a clear sense of direction. By adhering to an imported template, in-country researchers or reformers may satisfy the needs of external funding agencies, but are unlikely to present a truly recognisable analysis of the integrity system, of the kind needed to persuade the local community and decision-makers of the case for any particular proposed reform.

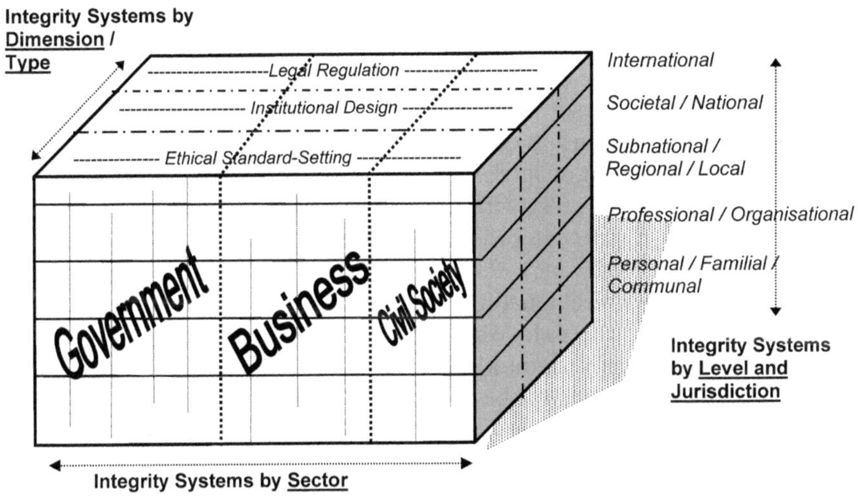

Figure 3.3 A conceptual approach to integrity system design

Integrity and Democratic Accountability: Are They Inseparable?

While the understanding of an integrity system suggested so far emphasizes that the nature of that system will be impossible to untangle from its larger political system, does this mean that integrity systems and liberal democratic institutions are inextricably related? The short answer is yes, but only in a democracy or a country (or for reformers) already committed to building liberal democratic institutions of that kind. In other settings, including societies where 'pre-democratic' values and social institutions continue to play a stronger role in the governance of society than in some Western liberal democratic societies, then key parts of the existing integrity system may have nothing to do with democracy at all, and may be impossible to locate on the imported templates. In Table 3.1, for example, the role of religious organizations is reduced to, at best, a hidden place as one of the many interest groups that might make up an active 'civil society'. In many countries, religion would be a much more pivotal element of the integrity system, not simply in terms of organized institutions but in terms of the values permeating much more obviously through the daily ordering of society.

The need to 'de-link' the definition of an integrity system from a specific model of political system is again demonstrated by the fact that, even in Australia, there is sometimes an uncomfortable fit between concepts of integrity and assumptions that all will be well if only democracy can be made to work more effectively.

On one hand, liberal representative democracy and the type of public integrity being discussed here do closely align, because both concepts often turn on questions of 'accountability' and 'public trust'. By definition, our concern with corruption is about the abuse of power by those entrusted with that power by others, whether through election or appointment or legislation or other recognized relationships. This is an inherently democratic concept, reflective of the social and economic conditions under which complex modern societies now find themselves. In these conditions, human beings need 'as far as they can, to economize on trust in persons and confide instead in well-designed political, social, and economic institutions' to ensure that trust is not abused (Dunn 1988/2000, 85–6). The development of intricate integrity systems, working through such a diversity of institutions, reflects the way in which modern societies now set about 'institutionalising distrust' in order to 'enculturate trust' in the life of business and government (Braithwaite 1998). Hopefully this is not as negative as it sounds; rather it appears to reflect a natural human reaction to the growing inability to rely on interpersonal trust to hold society together, and so, in relation to people we don't know, we are happy to consider the worst and set up institutions accordingly, as a means of encouraging the best to happen. The development of the concept of 'accountability', when it emerged in the late nineteenth century, was originally described as 'awful' (Hoskin 1996). However it is an approach that has grown with, and out of, a political culture based on democratic relationships, in which power is indeed consciously entrusted to others, and if it is abused, we have a general expectation of being able to call the abuser 'to account'.

For many integrity reformers, the connection between integrity and this concept of 'accountability' made possible by democracy is more than close enough to justify a conflation. Alongside economic reform, international agencies consistently promote democratization as the key to reducing corruption 'in the long run' (Elliott 1997, 176), usually because strengthening of democracy is presumed to 'afford less fertile ground in which corruption can flourish' (Stapenhurst and Sedigh 1999, 2). Even where corruption is known to occur in well-developed democracies, as indeed it does in countries like Britain, the United States and Australia, the situation is generally presumed to be less bad than in less developed, undemocratic ones (Lipset and Lenz 2000, 122; Pope 2000, 1). As Gilman and Stout argue in this volume, 'in truth, democracy provides the vehicle to make corruption public, whereas in most authoritarian regimes it remains hidden through intimidation and secrecy'. As explained by Braithwaite, this also means that democratic countries are in need of more machinery to deal with corruption, and to prevent its recurrence; but many integrity reformers are alert to this fact. Thus, Oscar Arias Sánchez, former President of Costa Rica, opened the Transparency International sourcebook (Pope 2000, xiii) with an open call for a new 'age of Enlightenment … of great philosophical debates about the merits of democracy, the constitution of liberty, and the obligations of citizenry'. Malaysia's Syed Hussein Alatas has professed a similar need for an Asian popular-political transformation comparable with European democratization since the eighteenth century (Alatas 1999, 127–32).

All this helps explain why, when it comes to describing the integrity system, the 'the most usual "integrity pillars" observed by integrity reformers in any 'society which is seeking to govern itself in an accountable fashion' are those associated with representative democracy (Pope 2000, 36). But in fact, even though it is closely aligned, 'accountability' of the kind made possible by vaguely functional democratic systems is not actually synonymous with integrity in public life. These terms are often used interchangeably when describing many of the institutions involved, but an 'integrity' system is about more than simply ensuring accountability, or even responsibility. Some of the key differences between these terms, depending on the way in which they are being used, are set out in Table 3.3. Drawing on the different models of integrity discussed earlier, this analysis shows that while persons of integrity are generally also persons who successfully hold themselves open to account, the reverse does not necessarily apply. Even in democratic societies such as Australia, officeholders can be perfectly accountable in many legal and technical senses while still breaching standards of 'integrity'. Similarly, their actions can sometimes be defended as highly responsive or responsible, in policy or political terms, even when quite corrupt in others (see Brown and Uhr 2004; Uhr 2005a, 189). Perhaps the most prominent Australian example of fast-footwork between concepts of integrity and accountability occurred in electoral debate in 2004, when the Prime Minister carefully – and successfully – recast the concept of 'trust' from one based on honesty and honour (not then his strong point) to one of responsiveness ('who can you trust with the economy?'), using the democratic process to expunge criticism of the former in a manner that was itself entirely open and therefore 'accountable'.

Table 3.3 Defining accountability, responsibility and integrity

Meaning	**Technical** (***Process-rational***)	**Substantive** (***Value-rational***)	**Personal** (***Pre/post-rational***)
(Dobel's model)	(Institutional-legal)	(Implementation/ effectiveness)	(Personal-responsibility)
'Accountability'	Individual actions are, or can be held to account	Individual actions invite, are open to accountability	Accountability *makes* person trustworthy
'Responsibility'	Individual actions are, or can be held responsible	Individual actions are responsive, responsible	Person *is* responsible, trustworthy
'Integrity'	Actions accord with stated purposes/values; trust is honoured	Actions are honest, honourable	Person *is trusted*, has honour

Source: A.J. Brown applying Weber (1954) and Hoskin (1996) to Thynne and Goldring (1987: 4–7), Davis et al. (1993: 79), Uhr (1993, 1999), Schedler (1999), Dobel (1999) and Mulgan (2003: 7–22, 240).

It is important to recognize that in a democratic political system, concepts of accountability work in particular ways to influence the concept of 'integrity', and accountability processes automatically tend to dominate our view of what makes up an integrity system. In particular, the dominant role played by accountability further reflects and entrenches some dimensions of integrity at the potential expense of others, because this focus immediately requires a weight of analysis to be placed on studying the *processes and machinery* by which officeholders are held to account, and in particular the institutions – creating, once again, a tendency to prioritize what Dobel calls the 'institutional-legal' model of integrity over its other dimensions.

This fact may help explain why many efforts to describe and assess integrity systems have difficulty moving past the relatively superficial search for like institutions, and reach behind institutions to understand the other elements of the integrity system – including sociological conditions, attitudes, values, education and the like – that may provide more fundamental explanations. A further limitation of its own methodology acknowledged in the Global Integrity Report (Camerer 2004) was this over-emphasis on institutions, but the question is how to compensate for it. The answer lies first in recognising that concepts of public integrity do have these different dimensions, including a 'personal-responsibility' dimension where judgements as to integrity are shaped less by formal processes and institutions, and more closely linked to personal and social values. Even though the new assessment efforts focus on systems, all these systems are ultimately made up of individuals, and both the individual and popular culture of integrity in a society will obviously matter. It is important to recall that even in the analogy of the national integrity system as a Greek temple, in Chapter 2, the institutional 'pillars' all stand on a foundation called 'society's values'.

In Conclusion: Some Starting Points

The discussions above reinforce, once again, that if the meanings of such basis terms as 'integrity' and 'accountability' can have different meanings even within a stable democracy such as Australia, it becomes all the more important to identify the constituent parts of the integrity system using a description that works from first principles, not an imported template. Even the definition of 'integrity' cannot be taken for granted. Rather, multiple meanings of integrity need to be considered, if necessary through additional linguistic and cultural analysis, if the scoping phase of an integrity system assessment is to adequately identify all the key institutions and processes that should logically be assessed. Rather than assuming a consensus, differences in the meanings given to key terms like 'integrity' should themselves be used as analytic tools to explore what is by its nature likely to be a contested landscape.

Finally, therefore, what are the very first starting points for the process of defining the integrity system? Taking all these lessons, in a democratic context, it is actually possible to start with three fairly simple questions. While still firmly located in an accountability-dominated concept of integrity, they are not limited to it, nor do they assume any particular cultural, organizational or institutional answers:

- *How do we identify the values, purposes and duties for which power is entrusted to, or held by, individuals and institutions?* In a given context, the answers provide the benchmarks against which integrity itself will be assessed. Often these vital benchmarks are publicly stated and defined in advance, in law or explicit agreements, undertakings or codes; but they can also be implicit, understood, or change in meaning or implication over time. They may be rooted in wider social or religious values, or economic practice, rather than legal codes. Often, they only become subject to discussion after things appear to go wrong, making it important to try to flush them out at the beginning of any assessment.
- *When and how do we expect officeholders to justify their actions with reference to these benchmarks?* Often this occurs publicly, as a matter of routine or in response to controversy. However most of the time we also expect integrity to be achieved through ongoing self-discipline and good management, relying on leadership, professionalism, self-reflection by individuals and organizations, and the simple intuitive adherence to relevant fundamental values by officials. In the former case, 'core' integrity institutions will play a role; but in the more frequent, latter scenarios, it is our more diffuse network of 'distributed' institutions and strategies that play the vital role; and again, the personal dimensions of integrity, based directly on social values and education, remain important.
- *How do we determine whether or not actions are true to these values, purposes or duties – i.e., how do we decide when the justifications are satisfactory?* Only after an examination of the first two questions, does this final question call for closer analysis of the processes used to hold persons in power to account. It demands as close a focus on how those processes work, including the different definitions of integrity and accountability that may be in play, as who or what undertakes the judgement. For example, just because someone 'wins' a publicity campaign or a democratic election, we do not necessarily accept that their actions displayed integrity. A wide range of institutions and processes play a role in deciding whether official actions are 'true' to key values and purposes, and these may vary widely according to the circumstances.

The institutions and processes we identify in response to all these questions make up a society's 'integrity systems'. While still simple, and still dominated by the concepts of integrity interwoven through any system of representative democracy, this rough guide can help reformers and policy-makers escape the prison of the institutional templates on which many assessment processes are based. As the chapters that follow show, there is no such thing as an 'ideal' integrity system to which all societies should aspire, simply by copying the same institutions in a similar configuration. Such an 'ideal' is no more achievable than the idea that any particular country, or group of countries, currently possesses an ideal form of democracy. However using these questions, it is possible to take a holistic approach to identifying the key elements of existing integrity systems in order to then use a range of flexible assessment techniques to determine where their strengths and weaknesses might lie. What type of assessment techniques appear to work best is a question to which this book returns in its final chapters. The important lesson from the outset, is that these approaches cannot succeed if they are concerned with importing or mimicking supposed 'best practice' templates when what is needed is a greater capacity for communities to take stock of their own systems, so as to more easily find their own particular path to their own version of public integrity.

References

Alatas, S.H. (1999), *Corruption and The Destiny of Asia* (Malaysia: Prentice Hall and Simon and Schuster).

Brown, A.J. (2003), *The Australian National Integrity System Assessment (NISA): Towards a Framework Methodology*, paper presented to the 'Integrating Integrity' Workshop, Griffith University, Brisbane, November.

Brown, A.J. and Uhr, J. (2004), 'Integrity Systems: Conceiving, Describing, Assessing', refereed paper to the Annual Conference of the Australasian Political Studies Association, Adelaide, September.

Camerer, M. (ed.) (2004), *Global Integrity Report* (Washington DC: Centre for Public Integrity, www.publicintegrity.org).

Carter, S.L. (1996), *Integrity* (New York: HarperCollins).

Davis, G., Wanna, J., Warhurst, J. and Weller, P. (1993), *Public Policy in Australia*, 2nd edn (Sydney: Allen and Unwin).

Dobel, J.P. (1999), *Public Integrity* (Baltimore, MD: Johns Hopkins University Press).

Doig, A. and McIvor, S. (2003a), 'The National Integrity System: Assessing Corruption and Reform', *Public Administration and Development* 23, 317–32.

Dunn, J. (1988/2000), 'Trust and Political Agency', in D. Gambetta (ed.) *Trust: Making and Breaking Cooperative Relations* (Oxford: Basil Blackwell 1988; electronic edition 2000 Department of Sociology, University of Oxford, <http://www.sociology.ox.ac.uk/papers>).

Elliott, K.A. (1997), 'Corruption as an International Policy Problem: Overview and Recommendations', in K.A. Elliott (ed.) *Corruption and the Global Economy* (Washington DC: Institute for International Economics).

Glynn, P., Kobrin, S.J. and Naim, M. (1997), 'The Globalization of Corruption', in K.A. Elliott (ed.) *Corruption and the Global Economy* (Washington DC: Institute for International Economics).

Hoskin, K. (1996), 'The "Awful Idea of Accountability": Inscribing People into the Measurement of Objects', in R. Munro and J. Mouritsen (eds) *Accountability: Power, Ethos and the Technologies of Managing* (London: Thomson Business Press).

Johnston, M. and Doig, A. (1999), 'Different Views on Good Government and Sustainable Anti-Corruption Strategies', in R. Stapenhurst and S.J. Kpundeh (eds) *Curbing Corruption: Toward a Model for Building National Integrity* (Washington DC: Economic Development Institute, World Bank).

Kaufmann, D. (1999), 'Economic Reforms: Necessary But Not Sufficient to Curb Corruption?', in R.Stapenhurst and S.J. Kpundeh (eds) *Curbing Corruption: Toward a Model for Building National Integrity* (Washington DC: Economic Development Institute, World Bank).

Kaufmann, D., Kraay, A., Mastruzzi, M. (2003), *Governance Matters III: Governance Indicators for 1996–2002* (Washington: World Bank).

KCELJAG and TI (2001), *Australian National Integrity Systems Assessment: Queensland Handbook* (Brisbane: Key Centre for Ethics Law Justice and Governance, Griffith University, and Transparency International (Australia)).

Knack, S., Kugler, M. and Manning, M. (2003), 'Second-generation Governance Indicators', *International Review of Administrative Sciences* 69:3, 345–64.

Kotkin, S. and Sajo, A. (eds) (2002), *Political Corruption in Transition: A Skeptic's Handbook* (Budapest: Central European University Press).

Langseth, P., Stapenhurst, R. and Pope, J. (1999), 'National Integrity Systems', in R. Stapenhurst and S.J. Kpundeh (eds) *Curbing Corruption: Toward a Model for Building National Integrity* (Washington DC: Economic Development Institute, World Bank).

Larmour, P. and Barcham, M. (2004), *National Integrity Systems Pacific Islands: Overview Report* (Melbourne: Transparency International Australia).

Lewis, C. (2004), 'Speech at Launch of Global Integrity Report', in M. Camerer (ed.) *Global Integrity Report* (Washington DC: Centre for Public Integrity, www.publicintegrity.org).

Lindsey, T. and Dick, H. (eds) (2002), *Corruption in Asia: Rethinking the Governance Paradigm* (Sydney: Federation Press).

Lipset, S.M. and Lenz, G.S. (2000), 'Corruption, Culture and Markets', in L.E. Harrison and S. . Huntington (eds) *Culture Matters: How Values Shape Human Progress* (New York: Perseus/Basic Books).

Marquette, H. (2001), 'Corruption, Democracy and the World Bank', *Crime, Law and Social Change* 36:4, 395–407.

McCoy, J.L. and Heckel, H. (2001), 'The Emergence of a Global Anti-Corruption Norm', *International Politics* 38, 65–90.

Mulgan, R. (2003), *Holding Power to Account: Accountability in Modern Democracies* (Basingstoke and NY: Palgrave Macmillan).

OECD (1999), *Public Sector Corruption: An International Survey of Prevention Measures* (Paris: Organisation for Economic Cooperation and Development).

OECD (2000), T*rust in Government: Ethics Measures in OECD Countries* (Paris: Organisation for Economic Cooperation and Development).

Pope, J. (1999), 'Elements of a Successful Anticorruption Strategy', in R. Stapenhurst and S.J. Kpundeh (eds) *Curbing Corruption: Toward a Model for Building National Integrity* (Washington DC: Economic Development Institute, World Bank).

Pope, J. (2000), *Confronting Corruption: The Elements of a National Integrity System (The TI Source Book)* (Berlin and London: Transparency International).

Preston, N., Sampford, C. and Connors, C. (2002), *Encouraging Ethics and Challenging Corruption: Reforming Governance in Public Institutions* (Sydney: Federation Press).

Quah, J.S.T. (2003), *Curbing Corruption in Asia: A Comparative Study of Six Countries* (Singapore: Eastern Universities Press).

Sajo, A. (2003), 'From Corruption to Extortion: Conceptualization of Post-commmunist Corruption', *Crime, Law and Social Change* 40, 171–94.

Sampford, C. (1991), 'Law, Institutions and the Public/Private Divide', *Federal Law Review* 20, 185–222.

Sampford, C. (1994), 'Law, Ethics and Institutional Reform: Finding Philosophy, Displacing Ideology', *Griffith Law Review* 3:1, 1–38.

Sampford, C. and Wood, D. (1992), 'The Future of Business Ethics? Legal Regulation, Ethical Standard Setting and Institutional Design', *Griffith Law Review* 1:1, 56–72.

Sedigh, S. and Muganda, A. (1999), 'The Fight Against Corruption in Tanzania', in R. Stapenhurst and S.J. Kpundeh (eds) *Curbing Corruption: Toward a Model for Building National Integrity* (Washington DC: Economic Development Institute, World Bank).

Stapenhurst, R. and Kpundeh, S.J. (1999), 'Conclusion', in R. Stapenhurst and S.J. Kpundeh (eds) *Curbing Corruption: Toward a Model for Building National Integrity* (Washington DC: Economic Development Institute, World Bank).

Stapenhurst, R. and Sedigh, S. (1999), 'Introduction: An Overview of the Costs of Corruption and Strategies to Deal With It', in R. Stapenhurst and S.J. Kpundeh (eds) *Curbing Corruption: Toward a Model for Building National Integrity* (Washington DC: Economic Development Institute, World Bank).

Thynne, I. and Goldring, J. (1987), *Accountability and Control: Government Officials and the Exercise of Power* (Sydney: Law Book Company).

TI (2001), *The National Integrity System: Concept and Practice (Country Studies Overview Report)* (Berlin: Transparency International).

Uhr, J. (1993), 'Redesigning Accountability: From Muddles to Maps', *Australian Quarterly* 65:2, 1–16.

Uhr, J. (1999), 'Institutions of Integrity: Balancing Values and Verification in Democratic Governance', *Public Integrity* 1:1, 94–106.

Uhr, J. (2002), 'Competing Models of Integrity', *Res Publica* 11:2, 13–16.

Uhr, J. (2003), *Creating A Culture of Integrity* (London: Commonwealth Secretariat).

Weber, M. (1954), *Law in Economy and Society* (Cambridge, MA: Rheinstein Ed.).

Williams, J.W. and Beare, M.E. (1999), 'The Business of Bribery: Globalization, Economic Liberalization and the "Problem" of Corruption', *Crime, Law and Social Change* 32, 115–46.

PART 2
Integrity System Assessment in Action

Chapter 4

Using National Integrity Systems to Assess Corruption: An International Perspective

Alan Doig and Stephanie McIvor

Much attention is given internationally to the assessment, measurement and monitoring of corruption, both between countries and across time. In part it is considered necessary to determine which countries face what types and levels of corruption, and thus propose relevant reforms. In part monitoring the success or otherwise of those reforms is central to what works and what does not.

What approach is most suited to the identification of the extent of, or seriousness of, country corruption – or of improvement – is very much a subject of continuing debate, not in the least because of the source, context and relevance of some of the indicators and their datasets currently in use. This chapter looks at the use of the National Integrity System (NIS), a holistic assessment framework, to consider what it says about corruption and then to consider its value as a tool against other types of measures or assessment.

Introduction: What is the NIS?

The NIS is a set of objectives which, supported by key strategies or approaches (elements), are delivered by or through key institutions, sectors or specific activities (the pillars). The approach was developed by Jeremy Pope when with Transparency International (TI). Collectively, the NIS is proposed as a system which, when in existence and working both interactively and effectively, is concerned with two goals: first, in combating corruption as part of the larger struggle against misconduct and misappropriation; and, second, in creating a efficient and effective government working in the public interest:

> The issue of corruption has come to center stage. The economic consequences of pervasive corruption, and recent trends toward democratization, have increased the pressure for accountability and transparency from those in public office. This paper does not suggest that there are easy solutions or models that can be applied in the fight against corruption; nor does it suggest that any country has yet designed an ideal model, or indeed that such an ideal model exists. What this paper does argue is that while each country or region is unique in its own history and culture, its political

systems, and its stage of economic and social development, similarities do exist and that experience and lessons are often transferable. A 'national integrity system' is proposed as a comprehensive method of fighting corruption. It comprises eight pillars (public awareness, public anti-corruption strategies, public participation, 'watchdog' agencies, the judiciary, the media, the private sector, and international cooperation) which are interdependent. Establishing and strengthening such an integrity system requires identifying opportunities for reinforcing and utilizing each of these pillars in the fight against corruption. (Langseth et al. 1997)

The ultimate driver of the NIS is about promoting good governance:

the conviction that all of the issues of contemporary concern in the area of governance – capacity development, results orientation, public participation, and the promotion of national integrity – need to be addressed in a holistic fashion. The overall goals should include:

- Public services that are both efficient and effective, and which contribute to sustainable development;
- Government functioning under law, with citizens protected from arbitrariness (including abuses of human rights); and
- Development strategies which yield benefits to the nation as a whole, including its poorest and most vulnerable members, and not just to well-placed elites. (Pope 2000, 34)

Overall … the aim is not complete rectitude or a one-time cure or remedy, but an increase in the honesty or integrity of government as a whole …. (Pope 1997, 5–6)

The NIS was not intended as a passive tool, and nor was it necessarily dependant on existing pillars or on a specific permutation of pillars, with the development of an NIS pursued by introducing new pillars, strengthening core pillars in an incremental approach to the development of an NIS or working through one pillar to develop an agenda or national plan involving other pillars, all within the context of the NIS objectives. The NIS also promotes the requirement that individual pillars are as resistant to corruption as possible in pursuit of their functions (corruption-proofing) and to thus ensuring that the individual pillars would not only be effective within the overall NIS but also reflect internally the objectives of the NIS.

Such an approach also promotes a comprehensive and holistic framework because of perceived failures of past reform initiatives from a number of causes: the inability of any single individual or agency to address the extent of corruption; the absence of top-level commitment; overly-ambitious programmes; piecemeal and uncoordinated reform; over-reliance on the laws as the vehicle for reform; lack of focus or uneven application of reforms; lack of sustainable institutional mechanisms:

Monitoring corruption cannot be left only to public prosecutors and to the forces of law and order. Action cannot depend solely on detection and criminal prosecution. Rather, action must also include a combination of interlocking arrangements. In part, this approach includes improving the transparency of relationships, and to the extent possible, preventing the development of relationships which can lead to corruption. It includes transparency in the financial affairs of key players and the prospect of reviews being conducted by independent institutions which are likely to be outside any particular network. Although corruption can never be completely monitored, it can be controlled through a combination of ethical codes, decisive legal prosecutions against offenders, organisational change, and institutional reform. (Pope 1997, 19)

The NIS as a concept thus offers a framework within which and through which to assess a country's corruption profile and those institutions tasked to deal with it, directly or indirectly, their effectiveness and their interaction with each other. This in turn allows assessment to be made on the weaknesses and strengths of, and reforms relating to: specific pillars in terms of their centrality to the working of an NIS; the added-value of pillar interaction both in terms of addressing corruption and the wider NIS goals; promoting coordinated donor support to pillars; national plans for dealing with corruption and wider public service reform; measuring individual pillar and NIS performance, and reconfiguring the NIS pillars as a consequence.

Why Assess, Measure or Monitor Corruption?

The NIS is not a measurement tool since it describes rather than assigns a value to or rank-orders countries according to levels or types of corruption. On the other hand, description by itself does provide a (subjective) sense of what country may appear more corrupt than another, and why. There are currently a number of qualitative and quantitative approaches that claim that they can assess, measure and monitor corruption, including: indicators that seek to 'measure' corruption (such as the TI Corruption Perception Index – CPI), or assess institutional propensity to be corrupt (such as the World Bank 'state capture' indices), or to place a numeric ranking on described levels and patterns of corruption (the Centre for Public Integrity). There are surveys relating to the provision of basic services (such as service delivery surveys) and there are also 'context' indicators relating to pillars (such as levels of military expenditure in relation to overall expenditure or the size of the informal economy).

The existence of the various approaches is in part based on assumptions that link dealing with corruption to promoting a more efficient and effective state. There are arguments that such a state is a precursor not just to dealing with corruption but wider social, economic and political progress. Carol Lancaster, former deputy administrator at USAID and a deputy assistant Secretary of State for Africa, makes an important point about precondition and context that has general resonance: 'despite the relatively large flows of foreign aid to African countries since independence, econometric studies correlating aid with growth have found no significant relationship (either positive or negative) between the two … (A) study, undertaken by World Bank staff and covering fifty-six countries worldwide (twenty-one of which were in Africa), found that aid had a positive effect on growth in countries with good fiscal, trade and monetary policies. There was no such effect in countries with poor policies' (Lancaster 1999, 59, 17). This has been validated elsewhere (see Burnside and Dollar 2000) while Danny Kaufmann at the World Bank has argued that 'good governance is strongly correlated with better development. But we can go further than this obvious correlation, which might simply reflect the fact that richer countries are able to "afford the luxury of good governance" – as is argued by some of the practitioners of the worst governance in the world. In our research, we found a large causal effect running from improved governance to better development outcomes' (Kaufmann et al. 2000, 4).

It is hardly surprising that donors now want to link funding to those indicators that suggest development progress. The most overt example of this is the Millennium Challenge Account (MCA), a multi-billion dollar fund provided by the United States for those countries adjudged to be: governing justly; investing in people; and promoting economic freedom. The MCA has made it plain that the first of these three categories has a number of components – civil liberties, political rights, accountability, rule of law, government effectiveness and the control of corruption – which are expected to be present (or emerging) to provide the political and institutional framework for economic liberalization, basic health provision and educational expenditure. For the countries concerned, MCA aid will be dependent on an assessment of the components through quantitative means. This will be undertaken by a limited number of agencies, some of whom are closely allied to the Washington Consensus that currently dominates the donor agenda on economic liberalization and political conditionality (Doig 2006). As one of those agencies – Freedom House – noted on its own evaluation work for the MCA: 'the corruption section was an especially important feature of the report, since this is the only MCA criterion that can eliminate an otherwise eligible country' (Repucci 2005, 255).

Who Measures and Monitors?

There are now an extensive range of measures and indicators. Recent TI Global Corruption Reports discuss a range of one-off and repeated perception and measurement activities; those undertaken more than once include:

- the Bribe Payers Index to assess which countries are likely to pay bribes in or to developing countries, as a measurement of the effectiveness of the OECD Convention through interviews with private sector leaders in a range of countries;
- the CIVICUS Civil Society Index assessing the state of civil society on a country-by-country basis and using national workshops (and which notes a relatively strong correlation with the TI CPI);
- the Index of Budget Transparency, a five-country study in Latin America on the accessibility and usefulness of the information provided by governments on their finances, revenue and expenditures;

- the New Europe Barometer – mass public opinion surveys assessing change in the former Soviet countries (smaller surveys have also been undertaken by other initiatives in Southeast Europe);
- the Latinobarometro – annual public opinion surveys on corruption in Latin America.

The World Bank has developed a wider governance framework which seeks to assess countries in terms of key themes of political stability, government effectiveness, regulatory framework, rule of law and control of corruption The extension of this approach through expanding the components of each core theme into developing a governance matrix (see Kaufmann et al. 2002). This considers improvements or deteriorations to the components. The US-based Centre for Public Integrity uses general governance categories within which in-country researchers review country reports, corruption notebooks, questionnaires (all of which draw heavily on the NIS model) and then develop rankings to report, as the NIS approach also does, on 'the *de jure* as well as *de facto* reality of corruption and anti-corruption mechanisms'. This is followed by a ranking-review process intended, it claims, to produce a balanced and comparative integrity index. The index claims that does not measure corruption itself, 'but rather the opposite of corruption: the extent of citizens' ability to ensure their government is open and accountable' by considering 'the existence of mechanisms, including laws and institutions, that promote public accountability and limit corruption; the effectiveness of these mechanisms; (and) the access that citizens have to public information to hold their government accountable'.

Many of the quantitative measurement come with methodology caveats. The most well-known, the TI CPI accepts its role as an composite perception indicator, although with relevance to any assessment of real levels of corruption (see Lambsdorff 2000 and 2002). Others take themselves much more seriously although they also have issues on the source, comprehensiveness and interpretation of the data sets used. The study that presents data to indicate a correlation between corruption and military spending – not in the least on the grounds that military equipment is expensive whose purchase is often shrouded in secrecy and driven by predatory arms salesmen (and their governments) from developed countries – warns, for example, that its evidence is 'suggestive' and 'by no means conclusive' (Gupta et al. 2000).

Overall, such data, while offering the means to rank countries and to draw attention to specific issues – such as media freedom or 'capture' of parts of the state by sectional or business interests – are often indicators rather than an analytical tool to unpick causes and consequences. Indeed, there is not necessarily a uniformity across the various quantitative measurements. The basic state capture/governance components (stability, government effectiveness, regulation, rule of law, and control of corruption) both coincide with, and diverges from, the TI CPI. Neither military expenditure as a percent of overall government expenditure nor levels of press freedom mirror either measurement (although there is a convergence between, say, the TI CPI and the size of the informal economy).

While quantitative measurements have a role, that role lacks country-specific knowledge and focus on patterns of corruption and on the role of and reform to those institutions that must be the focus of reform initiatives. As one of the proponents of the quantitative approach notes, 'even the best cross-country governance indicators remain imprecise and say little about the specific institutional failures that bring about weak governance in a particular setting' (Kaufmann et al. 2000) and that 'we recognise that there are limitations to what can be achieved with this kind of cross-country, highly aggregated data. This type of data cannot substitute for in-depth, country specific governance diagnostics as a basis for policy advice' (Kaufmann and Kraay 2004, 302).

Testing the NIS in Practice

In 2000 the Dutch government funded TI to assess the NIS in practice.[1] The first phase sought to identify the pillars of the NIS in each country and assess issues concerned with their effectiveness and credibility in combating corruption, internally, externally and interactively. The second phase concerned completion of an overview report, incorporating a review of the NIS as a framework and findings from the country reports. The focus and contents of the country reports were assessed against a range of practitioner, media and academic material. The country reports, supporting material, and the overview report were used to inform the work of the 2000 Global Forum II conference. Following the completion of

1 TI worked with the Centre for Fraud Management Studies, Liverpool Business School, [CFMS; later the Fraud Management Studies Unit, Teesside Business School] to deliver the project. Jeremy Pope was the TI Project Director; Gillian Dell was the TI Project Coordinator and Alan Doig and Stephanie McIvor of CFMS supervised the research and edited the country studies. TI devised the questionnaire on the basis of previous surveys and, for this particular project, secured formal government acknowledgement of the project. CFMS developed the terms of reference and project framework.

The project involved two phases. The first involved the preparation of reports from 18 countries, chosen to give an approximate mix of regions and developmental paths, and based on the framework and questionnaire – both devised to assess the NIS in practice. The countries chosen were: Argentina; Botswana, Brazil; Bulgaria; Canada; Colombia; Fiji; Ghana; Jordan; Kazakhstan; Lithuania; Mexico; Mongolia; Nepal; Netherlands; Senegal; Republic of Korea; Trinidad and Tobago. Authors were selected on the basis of a functioning TI chapter with research capability, or an external researcher, or – where there was not an established TI national Chapter – a university or research institute with identified research experience. All researcher curricula vitae were submitted for approval and an appropriate timetable for delivery agreed. In all but one country the researchers were from the country concerned. All had applied academic and professional backgrounds in corruption research and reform programmes. The individual country projects included interviews and focus groups, as well as analysis of published material, within the terms of reference and framework.

the conference, country authors revised their reports which were then standardized in format, indexed and published.[2]

Overall Project Findings

What the studies revealed about what types and patterns of corruption, within country specific contexts, was, of course, fundamental to an understanding of what reforms would be fit for purpose and what should be monitored or measured to ensure improvement. Corruption is pervasive – present, practised and not particularly concealed in most of the countries. The reports described patronage appointments throughout public sectors, widespread abuse of procurement procedures, misappropriation of decentralized funds, widespread petty administrative bribery, prevalent and unregulated receipt of gifts and hospitality by parliamentarians, vote buying, and government expenditure bypassing scrutiny by the audit institutions and the legislature. The nature, levels and impact of corruption, however, were very much reflective of a country's development and current political and institutional configuration although there were also degrees of comparability between countries with similar development trajectories or similar country types.

A repeated assessment in the reports was the need for the pillars to take the necessary steps to implement their own regulations and procedures. The pillars' impartiality, credibility and effectiveness was, in a number of countries, compromised by a range of countervailing influences that fell into a range of categories, including: lack of commitment, self-interest, skewed formal or constitutional arrangements, failings in other pillars, and, above all, the primacy of political influence. Overall, many of the pillars were weakened in terms of an inability to implement, or to adhere to, the rules and practices that would enhance their effectiveness and develop their capacity and capability to work within an NIS.

As was expected, the country reports confirmed the general absence of effective vertical and horizontal accountability. In many countries, the Executive dominated the political landscape and accountability through the ballot box was limited. Similarly, electoral accountability exercised upward through legislature representatives was equally constrained, especially when faced with the downward control being pursued by the Executive. Elections based on ideology and manifesto remain underdeveloped and unlikely to be organized from the bottom-up. Further, the overt links between the Executive and parties, especially the use of state resources for party-political purposes, diluted both the development of an effective opposition, the Legislature as an independent check on governmental power, and the correlation between the vote and policy-making that could convince the public that participation would help deliver the democratic dividend.

A significant issue arising from the reports was not only about agencies' individual effectiveness but the impact on that effectiveness, and on their inter-

2 They are available on the TI website at: http://www.transparency.org.

dependence, of their relationship with the Executive. A number of the country reports noted that many of the control agencies (audit, anti-corruption) were at best operational, but only within their particular spheres of responsibility. A number were weak or limited in their impact as a consequence of limited terms of reference, or inadequate resources, or location within the Executive suite of institutions.

Many of the reports underlined the inheritance, and continuing predominance, of the Executive or Presidency in many countries. Whether the consequence of the legacies of colonial independence, communism or military rule, the Executive, invariably dominated by a single party or elite grouping, used state resources for coercion and patronage in order to protect tenure of office and to disadvantage opponents. It has also has continued to reflect the traditional 'high politics' configuration with a focus on elite gain or regime survival rather than the broader public interest. In such circumstances there wee structural implications for – and thus for potential reform initiatives relating to – the development of an NIS.

In terms of future development, the democratization route, noted by various reports, had inherent threats as well as providing the opportunities and incentives for both new, and modifications of existing, types, levels and patterns of corruption. The first issue was that democracy as a process may not be necessarily intrinsically more honest than other processes concerned with the exercise of power, and the winning and retention of office. The 'new' areas of corruption included party funding, electoral misconduct and the development of new patronage networks to sustain electoral support. The second point relating to the democratization route is that, for some states, the veneer of democracy was being cemented over the old political systems and power plays which continued to operate beneath the surface.

Decentralization was often seen by donors keen on democratization as complementary to democratization, in pushing down the potential for political engagement to district or local levels. Again the reports noted that, as with democratization, existing elite groupings sought to colonize reform or selectively misuse their constitutional powers: both, of course, ensured the continuity of centralized networks of control persist. At the same time, the means of horizontal accountability had not been developed at the same rate, or with the same level of support, to offer a counterbalance to the opportunities opened up to local elites.

The reports raised a number of concerns about the choice and implementation of reforms intended to address the public sector and public services delivery. The first concerns the often negative consequences of donor economic enthusiasms from the 1980s and 1990s. Thus the neoliberal revolution of the 1980s and the enforced adoption by many countries of Structural Adjustment Programmes with subsequent cuts in public spending along with privatization programmes, resulted in a significant reduction in many states' development capabilities. Transitional countries had to cope with an over-concentration on economic liberalization, without concomitant reforms to the previously-discredited state, which left a policing and legitimacy vacuum. Key reforms such as privatization often transferred the economic power into elite hands with little evidence of improved efficiency or lower prices while the majority of the public services remained underfunded, unreformed and unresponsive to the public. Such reforms also impacted on the state's capacity to raise revenue, deliver basic services such as health, housing, sanitation and education, to nurture indigenous industry, to control urbanization and provide utilities and transport infrastructure.

Why? The Added-value of an NIS Approach

The overall finding was that the presence, permutation and impact of varieties of political corruption, individually and collectively, were complex, unpredictable and often resistant to reform. Underlying cultural and power trends ensured that corruption – or at least the opportunities and activities that facilitate corruption – can be reconfigured, transposed, metamorphosized because, as Simon Werner noted (1983), corruption has a self-perpetuating and adaptable dynamic that is as integral to public life as the tensions between public service and private gain which leads to its occurrence. It is this, often subjective, assessment about the trends and dynamics relating to the causes and consequences of corruption that provides the edge to the NIS approach. As Crawford (2002) effectively argues in his critique of recent evaluation of EU-funded projects, any country evaluation studies would be informed by the need 'to understand and analyze the various economic, social and political forces, including their relative strength, that influence and shape the prospects for democratic reform' (922). These forces are, however, not necessarily susceptible to quantitative measurement but an understanding of them is fundamental to any assessment process. In other words, the NIS approach provides the body for any quantitative skeleton – describing the 'why' to the quantitative 'where' in the rankings.

As a concept and approach, the NIS is also being promoted up, implicitly and explicitly, by a range of academics, institutions and agencies undertaking country assessments – on some occasions, seeking to re-invent an approach that already exists. Thus Michael Collier in 2002 proposes 'a middle-range, interdisciplinary theory of the causes of corruption built through employment of an institutional choice analytic frame … (which) concludes that ongoing international and national anti-corruption programs will likely fail unless they include reforms to state internal power structures and political culture' (Collier 2002, 1) while Hung-en Sung argued in 2002 that:

> A strategy to dismantle opportunities for corruption cannot and need not change each of the structural, political and institutional factors described. Rather, a strategy should fit the particular circumstances of a country, taking into account the nature of the corruption problem as well as the opportunities and constraints for addressing it. Therefore, designing a strategy requires an assessment of the extent forms and causes of corruption for the country as a whole and for specific government institutions. At the same time, strategy formulation demands not only closely examining the political will of the government to reform vulnerable monopolistic and regulatory practices but also carefully assessing the historical circumstances and institutional weaknesses of the broader society. Such an assessment entails a political economy analysis as well as

a sociocultural study of the reform process to identify both supporting and opposing forces of anti-corruption reform. (Sung 2002, 156)

Certainly the use of an NIS-type approach and an acknowledgement of the value of the descriptive approach is already reflected elsewhere in practitioner work. The Council of Europe's GRECO project was established in 1999 'to improve its members' capacity to fight corruption by monitoring the compliance of States with their undertakings in this field. In this way, it will contribute to identifying deficiencies and insufficiencies of national mechanisms against corruption, and to prompting the necessary legislative, institutional and practical reforms in order to better prevent and combat corruption'. (See 'What's the GRECO? www.greco.coe.int.) The project clearly sees a value in the roles of, and interaction of, what are to all intents and purposes, NIS pillars, as was implied in the evaluation of the Slovak Republic:

Moreover, in order to ensure an effective implementation of the measures indicated above, the evaluators recommend that the following complementary action be taken:

- develop awareness among the population at large of the dangers of corruption with respect to the stability of democratic institutions as well as economic and social progress;
- inform the population of the measures taken to counter corruption, the sanctions that can be imposed in cases of corruption, the effective regret mechanism and the institutions involved in combating corruption to which the public can turn to;
- involve the media as well as non-governmental organisations in a coordinated awareness raising campaign. (GRECO 2000a, para. 36)

In the GRECO review of Slovenia, the evaluators:

could only confirm the absence of an official, comprehensive anti-corruption policy in Slovenia. Indeed, contrary to other countries in the region, no special anti-corruption legislation or programmes have been adopted in Slovenia, no independent anti-corruption authority has been established, no awareness campaign has been organized among public officials or among professions exposed to the danger of corruption. Even if some actions have been undertaken by different Government departments, which are relevant for preventing and combating corruption, there is no comprehensive document, based on the thorough reflection on the present shape of the phenomenon and reflecting the strategy of the Government to prevent and combat corruption. Such a strategy seems to be necessary in order to ensure co-ordinated action of different authorities and organizations. (GRECO 2000b, para. 55)

In 1999, a formal institutional analysis was undertaken of Palestine by a US Council of Foreign Relations-sponsored independent task force (Council of Foreign Relations 1999). Their report was highly critical of the Palestine state, noting serious institutional shortcomings. It argued that, 'the risk is that if present structures and practices go unreformed, they will shape and even predetermine future ones in negative ways' (Council of Foreign Relations 1999, 13). The team noted the range of functions accruing to the Presidency and proposed 'the institutionalization of citizens' rights, establishment of the rule of law, creation of a viable and independent system of justice, empowerment of civil society, invigoration of the private sector, and delegation of authority and assertion of institutional autonomy throughout the public administration' (Council of Foreign Relations 1999, 14). Further, an NIS-type study of the emergent Palestinian state a year later underlined:

> The Palestinian state is not democratic, transparent or accountable, and its legitimacy is unsettled and contested. Moreover, the rule system and the state institutions are developing certain institutional and decisionmaking characteristics, which have been labeled neopatrimonial. Primarily, the ruling elite emanates from the 'extra-territorial' PLO with its proper interests, political agenda and internal cohesion, but without the proper political will to share political power and economic opportunities. Secondly, an informal, clientalist, monopolist and coercive mode of rule is being developed at the detriment of popular participation, transparency and accountability. Both factors point to an enduring mal-development of the political institutions and to increasing levels of corruption. (Amundsen 2000, 2)

This appreciation illustrated by the two reports on Palestine – what are the components of a democratizing state and what are the underlying influences that may affect them – have highlighted issues that would not have been identifiable from any quantitative measure but clearly predictable from the descriptive approach. It is this type of assessment that quantitative measurements cannot address or which could even give the wrong basis for interpretation. To assert 'that corruption is simply a consequence of underdevelopment runs the risk of embracing a crude evolutionism which envisages a proportionate decline in the volume of abuse with each percentage improvement in GDP' (Theobald 1990, 164), when the governance reforms to deal with corruption 'require a fuller political consideration of each case; its state culture, the intertwining of public office and private accumulation, and the prevailing ideological reference points that bind elites together' (Harrison 2005, 256).

Conclusion: Quality and Quantity – Contradiction or Complementarity?

What the NIS approach offers is an effective qualitative approach to provide the context for a robust, uniform and regular measurement of the pillars, of the NIS and, especially, the delivery of the NIS goals:

> it must be noted that one of the most important tasks in any anti-corruption effort is to ensure that progress is actually being made. Statistics by themselves are no reliable indicators of progress. (Pope 1997, 23–4)

The fact that quantitative data exponents, and others, are moving toward the qualitative perspective suggests that the reverse may be more effective and relevant – leading with the qualitative approach, supplemented by quantitative measurement.

There is a strong and continuing argument to measure and monitor how countries address and deal with corruption. The NIS, through its constituent parts offers a systematic, cohesive and coherent approach not only to what is being measured, and how, but using that measurement to encourage countries and donors to use it as the basis for a national plan and as the basis for wider reform.

Measurement is crucial to assess performance and delivery; it is also crucial to an evaluation of the levels and intensity of corruption facing the pillars and a shaping of future donor initiatives. Here Carothers' comments (1997, 122, 123) on the centrality of an informed qualitative assessment pertain:

> A second problem with the basic strategy of US democratic assistance is that it tends to ignore the power relations that underlie and in many ways determine a country's political life ...
>
> The deeper causes of the failings of the institutions in question are not factored into the diagnosis and therefore not reflected in the assistance response ...
>
> By giving short shrift to the realities of political life in the countries in which they operate, US democracy assistance programmes take on an artificial technical quality ...

Thus the NIS approach provides the depth to any assessment of the causes and consequences of corruption that goes beyond quantitative rankings and crude modeling (such as the agent-principal approach). What type of corruption, and its genesis, in what types of state (from transitional to small-island), the exercise of political power, the continuing legacies of specific development trajectories, and the descriptions of how macro-reform, such as democratization or decentralization, are assimilated or manipulated make a significant case for structured, tailored, sequenced and sustained reform approaches. It also emphasizes how much of these must be home-grown – which in turn posits a particular and specific role for external donors and other agencies.

In so doing the NIS provides two advantages over quantitative approaches to measurement. First, its use across a range of countries underlines the somewhat obvious conclusion that there is no end-game of the eradication of corruption but also raises some interesting perspectives on how developed countries contain and manage continuing areas of concern. The awareness that not all reform in developed countries (such as public management) is unequivocally successful and nor are they necessarily suitable for unadapted transfer, may inform the crucial shift from reactive firefighting or off-the-shelf corruption reforms to a more proactive, country-specific approach.

Second, as noted above, the NIS gives donors both a road map to reform and a probability profile of the effectiveness of targeted reform that will resolve many of the weaknesses of past and current reform initiatives and donor support. Quantitative data might suggest where a country is in terms of comparison with other countries but causes, consequences and future directions cannot be effectively addressed. One major failing by donors and others has been the lack of awareness of (and planning for) some of the negative consequences of the unequivocal and unstructured promotion of democratization, decentralization and the public management reform. A number of countries comment on the adverse implications of party funding; others note the time lag in the decentralization of the compliance and regulatory agencies (and the over-stretching of limited of resources). Inter-country comparisons also reveal not just the importance of continuous attention to the maintenance of standards but also what types of controls and procedures must be introduced to mitigate some of the consequence of wider reforms.

In summary, the NIS provides an assessment of the weaknesses and strengths of, and reforms relating to, specific pillars in terms of their centrality to the working of an NIS, or the added-value of pillar interaction both in terms of addressing corruption and the wider NIS goals, or promoting coordinated donor support to pillars, or measuring individual pillar contribution to the NIS performance. The NIS provides the context for designing country-relevant reform programmes. The impact of such programmes, again using the NIS, may be measured over time and assessed against lessons from other countries. Too often donors approach reform through single agencies in recipient countries which, in itself, may be worthwhile but whose impact and effectiveness is diluted by the environment in which they work. What is needed is an assessment of why that environment inhibits the effectiveness of that agency and an approach that looks at the timing, sequence and purpose of reform initiatives. At the same time, the NIS approach provides context and country-specificity to the questions of where, why and how corruption occurs – and thus the appropriateness of proposed reforms.

References

Amundsen, I. (2000), *State Formation and Rent Seeking in Palestine* (Norway: Chr. Michelsen Institute).

Burnside, C. and Dollar, D. (2000), *Aid, Policies and Growth* (Washington, DC: World Bank).

Carothers, T. (1997), 'Democratic Assistance: The Question of Strategy', *Democratization* 4:3.

Collier, M. (2002), 'Explaining Corruption: An Institutional Approach', *Crime, Law and Social Change* 38:1.

Council of Foreign Relations (1999), 'Strengthening Palestinian Public Institutions', chaired by Michel Rocard and directed by Henry Siegman; Principal Authors: Yezid Sayigh and Khalil Shikaki.

Crawford, G. (2002), 'Evaluating European Union Promotion of Human Rights, Democracy and Good Governance: Towards a Participatory Approach', *Journal of International Development* 14.

Doig, A., McIvor, S. and Theobald, R. (2006), 'Numbers, Nuances And Moving Targets: Converging the Use of Corruption Indicators or Descriptors in Assessing State Development', *International Journal of Administrative Sciences* 72:2, 239–52.

GRECO. (2000a), *Evaluation Report on Slovak Republic*, GRECO Secretariat, Council of Europe.

GRECO (2000b), *Evaluation report on Slovenia*, GRECO Secretariat, Council of Europe.

Gupta, S., de Mello, L. and Sharan, R. (2000), *Corruption and Military Spending*, Fiscal Affairs Department: International Monetary Fund.

Harrison, G. (2005), 'The World Bank, Governance and Theories of Political Action in Africa', *British Journal of Politics and International Relations* 7.

Kaufmann, D. and Kraay, A. (2004), 'Governance Matters III; New Indicators for 1996–2002 and Methodological Challenges', *Global Corruption Report* (Berlin: Transparency International).

Kaufmann, D., Kraay, A. and Zoido-Lobatón, P. (2000), 'Governance Matters: From Measurement to Action', *Finance and Development* 37: 2.

Kaufmann, D., Kraay, A. and Zoido-Lobaton, P. (2002), *Governance Matters II*, Policy Research Working Paper 2772 (Washington, DC: World Bank Development Research Group and World Bank Institute).

Lambsdorff, J.G. (2000), *The Precision and Regional Comparison of Perceived Levels of Corruption – Interpreting the Results*, Transparency International and Gottingen University.

Lambsdorff, J.G. (2002), *Framework Document*, Transparency International and Gottingen University

Lancaster, C. (1999), *Aid to Africa* (Chicago: University of Chicago Press).

Langseth, P., Stapenhhurst, R. and Pope, J. (1997), *The Role of A National Integrity System in Fighting Corruption* (Washington, DC: World Bank).

Pope, J. (1997). *The TI Source Book* (Berlin: Transparency International).

Pope, J. (2000), *The TI Source Book (Second Edition)* (Berlin: Transparency International).

Repucci, S. (2005), 'A Survey of Governance in 30 Underperforming States', *Global Corruption Report* (Berlin: Transparency International).

Sung, H.-E. (2002), 'A Convergence Approach to the Analysis of Political Corruption: A Cross-National Study', *Crime, Law and Social Change* 38:2.

Theobald, R. (1990), *Corruption, Development and Underdevelopment* (Basingstoke: Macmillan).

Werner, S. (1983) 'The Development of Political Corruption: A Case Study of Israel', *Political Studies* 31:4.

Chapter 5

Evaluating International Action against Corruption in the Pacific Islands

Peter Larmour

Introduction

Action against corruption is now often required of governments seeking loans from development banks, or applying to join international organizations like the European Union. The chapter compares and evaluates several attempts to induce governments to act against corruption in the Pacific Islands where small states are particularly dependent on the international community. It considers the coerciveness and effectiveness of the use of loan conditions by development banks; peer review by a regional organization; franchising NGOs; blacklisting of banks; and the more recent 'cooperative intervention' in Solomon Islands, where Australian officials enforce local laws against corrupt police and politicians.

Since the 1990s, the problem of corruption has come on to the agenda of intergovernmental organizations such as the World Bank and the OECD. The banks are concerned that domestic corruption will inhibit economic growth so they promote anti corruption reforms in developing countries. The European Union makes similar demands on countries in Eastern Europe seeking to join it. The new international interest in corruption has been stimulated by the influential non-governmental organization, Transparency International. It was founded in 1993 by disaffected international civil servants, frustrated at the World Bank's tolerance of corruption in aid projects, and angry at the way Western governments tolerated their own companies' bribery of foreign officials (Larmour 2006).

Policy Transfer

This international effort to reach into domestic politics can be seen as an infringement of national sovereignty, or as a new form of colonialism. Or it can be analysed less judgementally as a form of 'policy transfer', defined as 'the process by which knowledge about policies, administrative arrangements, institutions and ideas in one political system (past or present) is used in the development of policies, administrative arrangements, institutions and ideas in another political system' (Dolowitz and Marsh 2000, 5). The anti corruption model most admired internationally is the Independent Commission Against Corruption (ICAC), devised in Hong Kong in the 1970s, with its characteristic three pronged approach to corruption: investigation; prevention and education. In the Pacific Islands, PNG's model of a 'leadership code', requiring senior officials to avoid conflicts of interest, was borrowed from East Africa, and has in turn influenced Solomon Islands and Vanuatu. Dolowitz and Marsh (2000) note there is a continuum in policy transfer, from voluntary adoption at one end through to coercive imposition on the other. At the voluntary end are study tours and consultancy reports on 'best practice'. At the coercive end are colonial rule or military defeat. In the middle are processes of conditionality or accession criteria that say, in effect, 'If you want a loan, or to join our club, you must accept our conditions'.

A more sociological approach to transfer argues that coercion and voluntarism are not polar alternatives. Di Maggio and Powell (1991) start from the surprising similarity of organizational forms throughout the world. This 'isomorphism' may be the result of the exercise of force, such as by colonial rule. But it may also be the result of emulation of prestigious overseas models, or of the gradual professionalization of work, involving shared standards and curricula in training and credentialing institutions. For example, the ICAC model could be imposed, perhaps as a condition for a loan from a multilateral bank, or as a requirement for joining an international organization. Equally, without external pressure, local leaders may desire to emulate the prestigious overseas model. The lawyers and investigators who would staff the organization are likely to have received professional training in international best practice, and so are predisposed to adopting it.

Policy Evaluation

It is now over a decade since these new international interventions against corruption began. Nobody commends corruption, but a small critical literature on the anti- corruption movement is emerging, particularly from Eastern Europe where scholars have found externally sponsored anti corruption campaigns encouraging a populist style of politics that could undermine the legitimacy of newly established democracies (Kotkin and Sajo 2002; Tisne and Smilov 2004). Bryane Michael has assessed anti corruption campaigns in Africa, finding a standard model that paid little attention to variable local conditions (2004a; 2004b; 2004c).

As these examples suggest, anti-corruption campaigns can be evaluated against different, potentially conflicting, criteria. The standard criteria in the study of public administration have been the several 'e's: economy; efficiency; effectiveness and equity. The first looks at costs, and asks if the policy was implemented cheaply or without waste. The second – typically the concern of economists – looks at the relationship between inputs and outputs. It asks if the maximum was got from the resources committed to a project (so-called technical efficiency) or if the resources might have been better used elsewhere (so called allocative efficiency). For example, the police may conduct a technically efficient campaign against corruption, but could their time have been more usefully spent dealing with other kinds of crime? The third looks at the impact or effects of a policy, and asks if it achieved what it set out to do. Did it, for example, actually reduce corruption? The fourth looks at justice or fairness of policy, either in its processes or outcomes. For example, did the anti-corruption campaign trample on human rights to achieve its goals? Did it only target the 'little fish'? Campaigns for 'good governance' introduce additional criteria for policy evaluation, such as transparency and accountability.

Any anti-corruption campaign is, of course, hard to assess. There are disagreements on what exactly counts as corruption, and popular perceptions may underestimate or overestimate the amount that takes place. The phenomenon itself often takes place in secret, between more or less willing partners, who have no interest in revealing that it has taken place. Increased levels of prosecution may reflect a more effective judicial system, rather than changes in the underlying rate of corruption (Sampford et al. 2006). It is hard to disentangle the effects of the anti-corruption campaign from other changes taking place anyway. It all takes time. Similar difficulties bedevil evaluation of campaigns against other kinds of crime, shameful activity, and public policy more generally.

These international campaigns are typically one step back from the problem they address. They are campaigns to persuade other governments to campaign against corruption. However, as we shall see, in one case the donor (Australia) has become more directly involved in action against corruption within another country (Solomon Islands) whose Prime Minister has accuses it of running a 'parallel government' (Sogavare 2006).

Here, we focus on two criteria: coerciveness and effectiveness. The first is theoretically interesting for the theories of policy transfer we sketched above. Dolowitz and Marsh proposed a continuum of coerciveness, whereas Di Maggio and Powell saw coerciveness as only one of several sources of isomorphism. Coerciveness is also related to the issue of national sovereignty. Governments of sovereign states do not like being pushed around by foreign governments or international organizations. The second criterion, effectiveness, is of practical interest to the banks and donors sponsor anti-corruption campaigns. They want to know if they are working, and donors are paying increasing attention to aid effectiveness.[1]

The chapter introduces the region, and the particular Australian interest in it. Then, it considers how corruption is defined in the region, and by donors. It then identifies international dimensions of corruption, and international initiatives against it. Finally, it considers the coerciveness and effectiveness of these initiatives, and asks whether they were related.

---

1 This chapter is an output of a larger Australia Research Council 'linkage' project with AusAID on aid effectiveness in the Pacific being carried out with Satish Chand and Ben Reilly at the ANU. I am grateful for comments from Clive Moore, Barry Hindess, Anthony Regan and several anonymous reviewers, while I remain responsible for the content. An earlier version was published in the *Asian Journal of Political Science*.

The Pacific Islands

The small island states of the Pacific are particularly dependent upon the international system. Many are what Jackson (1990) characterized harshly as 'quasi states', sustained by international recognition of their governments, and foreign aid, rather than domestic capacity and taxation. So – like it or not – they are more open to international pressure than larger or more self-sufficient countries. Island governments club together in regional organizations like the Pacific Islands Forum (henceforth 'The Forum'). They also form sub regional groupings in larger organizations like the Asian Development Bank, the Commonwealth, or the Africa Caribbean and Pacific grouping in relation to the EU. During the 1990s, these international organizations became conduits for policies of 'good governance', including public sector reform, accountability and anti-corruption (Larmour 2005).

The Pacific Islands also constitute regions of influence for relatively powerful neighbours. Australia – also a member of the Forum – has decided to become actively and directly involved in the government of what it sees as potentially 'failing' states Solomon Islands, Nauru and Papua New Guinea (PNG) (Dinnen 2004). Nauru and PNG had been colonies of Australia until they became independent in the 1970s (whereas Britain ruled Solomon Islands until 1978 and has shown little interest in it since). The Australian Prime Minister explained:

> The South Pacific has the enduring problems of poverty, bad governance and corruption, and what we're trying to do is do something about both. It's in our interests strategically, historically and sentimentally. If we just throw up our arms and go away, you'll end up with these places being taken over by interests that are very hostile to Australia. It's also walking away from our moral responsibility. We are far and away the most powerful and influential country in the whole area, and nobody else will do the job if we don't. (*The Daily Telegraph*, 31 December 2006)

It is possible to compare the 14 states listed in Table 5.1 as each of these have been subject to detailed independent surveys of what Transparency International calls their 'national integrity systems': the institutions in place to control corruption, and their performance in practice. I will examine the international dimensions of corruption uncovered in these surveys, and the international action being taken against it. The latter includes public sector reform promoted by the Asian Development Bank and the World Bank; improved accountability promoted by the Pacific Islands Forum; support for local chapters of Transparency International; and a crackdown on offshore financial centres by the Financial Action Task Force (FATF), an offshoot of the OECD. Recently, Australia has provided soldiers, policemen and other government officials to 'strengthen' institutions in Solomon Islands, PNG and Nauru. The chapter then draws some conclusions about the coerciveness and effectiveness of these international campaigns.

Corruption is famously difficult to define, and these difficulties are likely to be great in international campaigns that juxtapose different legal systems and

Table 5.1 Pacific Islands population GNP growth and aid

	Population (2004, estimated)	GNP per capita $ US purchasing power parity (2000)	Average annual growth of GNP per capita 1970–2000	Average annual aid per capita since 1970 ($US)	Aid as % GDP
Papua New Guinea	7,236,000	2180	0.3	104	7
Solomon Islands	589,700	1710	–0.4	110	20
Vanuatu	289,400	2960	–0.3	217	14
Fiji	891,100	4480	2.7	65	2
Samoa	182,700	5050	0.8	213	14
Tonga	98,300	1660	2.6	233	15
Cook Islands	14,000	5000	na	646	na
Tuvalu	9,600	1100	–1.4	647	na
Niue	1,600	3800	na	3558	na
Federated States of Micronesia	112,700	2000	na	178	50
Kiribati	166,100	950	–1.2	217	33
Marshall Islands	55,400	1600	na	232	61
Palau	20,700	9000	na	933	27
Nauru	10,100	5000	na	51	na

Sources: Secretariat of the Pacific Community 2005; Chand 2003.

different popular understandings. For example, a recent survey in Solomon Islands found 62 per cent of the rural population, and 46 per cent of the urban population believed the government was corrupt, though focus groups found 'no universal agreement on what constituted corruption (and some tendency to challenge the conventional Western view of it)' (RAMSI 2006, 2). So, first, I look briefly at how 'corruption' is understood within the region, and by international organizations.

Domestic Understandings of Corruption

Most Pacific Island countries' penal codes prohibit bribery of officials, and most public service regulations prohibit conflicts of interest. Papua New Guinea (PNG), Solomon Islands and Vanuatu have constitutionally mandated codes of practice applying to all politicians and senior officials, so called 'Leadership Codes'. Accusations and counter-accusations of 'corruption' are also part of the normal language of politics in the region, as loose coalitions of ideologically indistinct politicians rotate office, and its spoils, with one another.

Each country's legal system is inherited from colonial rule or – in the case of Tonga, which was never formally colonized – copied from models circulating internationally. Laws are often criticized as being out of step with indigenous traditions and popular opinion. Politicians sometimes defend as 'traditional' or 'customary' behaviour that outsiders might regard as corrupt. Ethical commitments to family and kin may contradict official duties. Traditional gifts and payments to chiefs and pastors may be hard to distinguish from bribes made to secure advantage. Thus, a PNG Prime Minister, criticized for paying money to an MP to cross the floor in parliament, replied 'corruption is part of our culture' (Larmour 1997). Elections often involve substantial public payments by candidates to local leaders, and directly to voters.

Popular opinion often seems to cast the net of corruption widely to include the personal misbehaviour of elites, and signs of wealth such as four wheel drives, and overseas travel. Perceptions of corruption are often biased against trading minorities such as the Indians or Chinese who provide the backbone of a local private sector in most of the region. As Krastev (2002) found in post-communist Balkans, new, visible and unwelcome inequalities of income are often more easily explained as the result of corruption, rather than luck, effort, or the working of the market or the merit principle. Foreign aid and bribery are conceptually similar (Morgenthau 1962) and the relatively high salaries of foreign aid workers and consultants are often regarded as corrupt.

International Understandings of Corruption

International governmental organizations tend to take a more economic view of corruption. The World Bank adopted TI's definition, 'the use of public office for private gain' (while TI has since moved on to a more expansive definition 'the use of entrusted power for private gain'). While this definition focuses on the acts of individuals, rather than the character of a whole system of government, international organizations have generally shied away from campaigns against particular corrupt individuals. They are not like Interpol, coordinating international action against particular villains. Nor do they want to act like an international court of appeal against local acts of corruption. TI decided to avoid chasing individuals out of prudence. Its local members would be subject to litigation or violent retaliation. Intergovernmental organizations prefer prevention to investigation, and approach the harsh word 'corruption' through the softer language of 'governance' and 'accountability'.

International Surveys of Corruption

Of the 14 countries we are comparing, only PNG and Fiji have featured in the Transparency International's Corruption Perceptions Index (CPI). The CPI is a poll of polls, based on existing surveys, when available, of each country by local and foreign businessmen, academics and journalists. It treats corruption as an attribute of countries rather than individuals. In 2006, PNG scored 4 on a scale of 1–10 (where 10 is 'highly clean' and 0 is 'highly corrupt'). TI thus ranked PNG at 130 of the 163 countries surveyed in that year, tied with Burundi, Cambodia, the Congo, Kyrgyzstan and Venezuela (Transparency International 2006). Fiji wasn't ranked in 2006, but a year earlier received the same score as PNG (4/10). So both PNG and Fiji have below average reputations for corruption, but no worse than many developing countries, which tend to cluster at the low end of the rankings.

TI has also subjected the same 14 countries to more detailed qualitative assessments of their 'national integrity systems' (NIS). A local consulting firm surveyed Fiji (Olaks Consulting Services 2001). PNG was surveyed by two PNG academics (Mellam and Aloi 2003), and the remaining twelve small island states were surveyed in a project Manu Barcham and I coordinated from the Australian National University. We commissioned foreign and local academics or retired officials to carry out the surveys, and compared the results (Larmour and Barcham 2006). These NIS surveys provide the basis for the accounts of international corruption below.

International Dimensions of Corruption

The median population for the 14 island states is a little over 50,000 (Table 5.1). In very small countries, without natural resources, there is often little to sell overseas but the symbols and tokens of sovereignty, such as stamps, work permits, passports, international telephone access codes and internet domain names. Back in the 1970s, the Philatelic Bureau – selling exotic stamps – was looted by the government to fund campaign expenses in Cook Islands. There have been scandals over the sale of passports to foreigners in Tonga, Kiribati and Samoa.

Tonga leases out its right to put a communications satellite in orbit, while Tuvalu has tried to lease out the right to use its catchy internet domain name suffix '.tv' (Ta'afaki 2004). Several countries use their sovereignty to run offshore banking regimes congenial to companies and individuals wanting to avoid tax in their home countries.

Local opportunities for profitable investment are small in most of Polynesia and Micronesia. Phosphate revenues in Kiribati are placed in a portfolio of shares offshore, whereas in Nauru ministers have invested directly in offshore hotels and an airline. They have often been the victims of scams, or at least poor advice. In each of these three cases – passports, tax avoidance, and overseas investment – it was often not clear if ministers involved were benefiting personally, or acting recklessly on behalf of the national treasury.

Often the most valuable thing a small country has to sell is its vote in international forums, such as the International Whaling Commission or the United Nations. Japan has cultivated island governments and their officials to support its positions on whaling. Governments switch sides between support for China and Taiwan. Currently, six Pacific Island states recognize Taiwan rather than China, and they amount to one quarter of the dwindling number of states to do so (Dobell 2007, 9). The Chinese Premier toured the region in 2006, promising preferential loans, trade access, training opportunities and debt forgiveness to the seven states with which it currently has diplomatic relations (*Peoples Daily Online* 6 April 2006). The Premier offered trade as well as aid, and did not nag island leaders about 'good governance'. Fiji's 2006 coup leader, regretting the sanctions applied by Australia and New Zealand, promised to turn to China for support.

Taiwanese government funding has contributed to corruption in Solomon Islands. In 2001, the Taiwanese government loaned the Solomon Islands government $US25 million to pay compensation to victims of the recent ethnic conflict. Its rapid and chaotic distribution led to claims of unfairness and extortion, and accusations that particular ministers had improperly benefited. Taiwan is accused of financially supporting candidates in the 2006 general election (Dobell 2007, 11). Later in the year, the Taiwanese ambassador in Solomon Islands was announcing that his government would be paying $400,000 Solomon Islands dollars ($US49, 000) in 'Rural Community Development Funds' annually to every MP to spend as they wished in their constituencies (Maesulia 2006).

The three largest countries, Papua New Guinea, Solomon Islands and Fiji face the opposite risk, a variety of what economists call a 'resource curse'. Log exports have been a major source of corruption in PNG, Solomon Islands and Fiji. Politicians often act as intermediaries between local landowners and the foreign, mainly Malaysian and Indonesian, loggers. A timber project seems to offer traditional landowners in isolated areas access to cash, jobs and services that are otherwise only available in the capital cities, or abroad. The larger-scale mining industry in PNG is more centralized, and any corruption that might take place more hidden, or of the 'policy' kind, where interested politicians and officials get the law changed in their favour.

The region – except Fiji and Nauru – depends heavily on foreign aid (Table 5.1). The multilateral banks rely on the recipient governments' accountability structures.

Smaller amounts at the discretion of ambassadors or mobilized for emergency relief, are often used or seen as forms of political patronage. In Solomon Islands, for example, the first Prime Minister resigned over claims that French hurricane relief funds were disproportionately channelled to his own village. The funding under the first Compact of Free Association that the US signed with its former colonies became so plagued with problems of accountability and suspicions of corruption that the revised Compact contains provision for a special audit office based in Hawai'i.

International Initiatives to Prevent Corruption

Public Sector Reform by the ADB, the World Bank and the IMF

Fiscal crises in the mid 1990s led six Pacific Island countries to seek loans from the Asian Development Bank. The Bank used the opportunity to nudge them towards 'public sector reform'. Loan conditions typically included asset sales, downsizing, the introduction of Value Added Tax, and output budgeting. Existing heads of department were removed, their jobs put on contract, and advertised outside the civil service. Corruption was not targeted as such, but new consultation and accountability mechanisms were to be introduced, such as national summits with the private sector and NGOs. In Cook Islands, for example, private sector accountants were brought on to a new committee to oversee government public expenditure.

Corruption in the forest industry was targeted more directly and explicitly in the World Bank's loan negotiations with PNG. In the late 1990s the Bank began to work closely with international environmental NGOs (and at the same time became friendlier towards TI). It pushed to make reform of the logging industry a condition of loans proposed for PNG. Negotiations broke down, amid accusations from PNG that the World Bank was interfering with domestic policy. A change of government bought both sides back to the table in 2000. The PNG government seemed to agree to new loan conditions including a moratorium on new forestry agreements and a case-by-case review of the legality of existing ones (Filer 2004).

Peer Review by the Forum

During the early 2000s, Australia began using the Forum to press island states to improve their systems of governance, attempting first to persuade its members to adopt a leadership code (something Australian parliaments have found difficulty applying to themselves). The Forum has also been promoting a process of 'peer review' of countries' success in implementing 'eight principles of accountability' for which they have jointly affirmed support. These processes do not deal directly with corruption, though their adoption might make it less likely, or easier to detect. Several of the principles rely on power of a democratically elected legislature to oversee the executive and the bureaucracy, through approving expenditure in an annual budget, approving loans entered into by ministers, and considering reports of Auditors-General and Ombudsmen. They do not address corruption in parliaments themselves, an issue identified as problematic in most of the NIS studies. The Forum's financial and economic ministers have signed up to these principles, and are meant to report to each other on progress in adopting them.

Franchising NGOs

The founders of TI were mainly international civil servants, but they soon realized that its campaign against international corruption would not attract popular support unless they also dealt with corruption within countries. So they began to franchize their name to local anti-corruption campaigns. TI's structure leaves local groups to fund and fend for themselves, simply franchising its name to any local group that adopts its standards and policies, and sometimes helping with seed money. A PNG group was set up after a political crisis that followed the government's botched attempt to hire foreign mercenaries to subdue a provincial rebellion (Larmour 2003). Smaller groups have coalesced in Fiji, Solomon Islands and Vanuatu, and TI's Australian chapter has taken a particular interest in their tutelage – including funding the 14-country survey of National Integrity Systems referred to above.

Cleaning Up Offshore Financial Centres

In 1989, the Group of Seven rich countries set up a Financial Action Task Force (FATF) attempting to persuade the governments which sponsor Offshore Financial Centres (OFCs) to regulate such centres more closely. The OECD was originally concerned with loss of tax revenues, but since September 11 has shifted its emphasis to money laundering defined as 'the process of converting cash, or other property, which is derived from criminal activity, so as to give it the appearance of having been obtained from a legitimate source' (Asia Pacific Group on Money Laundering Secretariat 2003).

The FATF tried to get governments to adopt what it called its 'Forty Recommendations', which included obligations to criminalize laundering the proceeds of serious crimes, to require financial institutions to be able to identify their clients, and to report suspicious transactions. Governments were to introduce systems to control financial institutions, and to enter into agreements allowing international cooperation. The Task Force published annual lists of 'non-cooperative' countries, starting in 2000. The US also sharply increased its own pressure on the OFCs, as part of its counter-terrorist activity after 11 September 2001. Section 312 of Patriot Act required US banks to exercise 'due diligence' towards risks of money laundering in 'correspondent accounts' that foreign banks might hold with them (US Department of Treasury 2005). A further eight, then nine, recommendations were added to FATF's original forty, to deal with the implications of the Patriot Act.

Among South Pacific countries, Cook Islands, Marshall Islands, Niue and Nauru appeared on the first FATF list. Listing invoked countermeasures included warning non-financial businesses dealing with listed countries that the transaction might run the risk of money laundering. In December 2001, FATF members agreed to apply additional countermeasures to Nauru for its failure to abolish four hundred shell banks, which had no physical presence in the country.

Australian-led Action Against 'State Failure'

Solomon Islands suffered a period of what was called inter-island 'ethnic tension' before elements of the police led a *coup d'état* in 2000 and forced the Prime Minister to resign. Though a civilian government stayed in place, and a general election was later held, government officials, particularly those in the finance department, continued to be intimidated by thugs and gangs often believed to be linked to political leaders. Solomon Islands leaders made several requests for Australian intervention which were rejected by the Australian Foreign Minister on the grounds that 'foreigners do not have answers for the deep-seated problems afflicting Solomon Islands' (quoted in Fullilove 2006, 6).

Australian policy then shifted for several reasons. The success of Australia's intervention in Timor in 1999 and its alliance with the US in its 'war on terror' emboldened the Prime Minister, John Howard. These international events happened against a steady loss of Australian official faith in more traditional approaches to aid and development in the region. Economic growth since the countries became independent had been slow to negative, particularly if measured in *per capita* terms (Table 5.1). The International Financial Institutions, and bilateral donors like Australia, increasingly believed that bad governance was the reason for low levels of growth, and that good governance should be addressed in aid programs. Pacific Island governments (demonized as 'elites') came to be seen as part of the problem as much as part of the solution.

In July 2003, Australia sent over 2,000 troops, police and other officials in a 'regional assistance mission' to Solomon Islands (RAMSI) to restore law and order – particularly by disarming combatants – and stabilising government finances. The mission was framed as a Forum initiative, and included small contingents of police and soldiers from other countries in the region. The intervention was invited by the Solomon Islands government, and regulated by a special act of the Solomon Islands Parliament.

PNG is much the largest country in the region, with an estimated population of over 7 million (Table 5.1). It is the largest recipient of Australian aid, and Australia is the largest donor to PNG. The latter's low rate of economic growth and its law and order problems continue to cause despair and impatience in Canberra, and PNG's leaders are regularly offended when their country appears in Australian lists of potentially 'failing' states. In 2003, Australia devised an 'Enhanced Cooperation Programme' which would put several hundred Australian police on patrol in PNG, and Australian officials in line positions in departments concerned with finance and criminal justice, including the prosecution of corrupt officials and politicians.

Nauru – at the opposite extreme of scale, with a population of only 10,000 – used to have one of the highest *per capita* incomes of the island states, as a consequence of phosphate mining. Corruption and mismanagement of its offshore investment portfolio and regional airline have led to Nauru's near bankruptcy. A new source of sovereignty-based revenue became available in 2002 when Australia persuaded the Nauru government to act as host to an offshore detention centre for illegal immigrants to Australia. Detainees could be held without the protections of Australian law while Australian officials assessed their applications for asylum.

Coerciveness of International Interventions

The international, regional and Australian approaches differed in the degree of coercion they involved. In the case of public sector reform, governments needed loans to get them through fiscal crises, and reform became conditional on the loans. Governments were not forced to borrow though the alternatives might be dire. In PNG's negotiations with the World Bank, the Bank tried to ratchet up tougher conditions, as well as to hold the PNG government to its own stated policies and legislation.

In the second case, the Forum lacked the tool of conditionality, but relied, like the World Bank, on a steady stream of consultancy reports and reviews to chivvy reluctant leaders to stick to commitments they, or their predecessors, had made in other times and circumstances.

In the third case, NGOs lacked coercive powers, though they might hope to mobilize community support to put pressure on individual MPs, or governments to adopt anti corruption measures. TI's doctrine, however, did not dispose the organization to an adversarial approach. It sought to build coalitions and engage rather than confront governments. Its members were part of the elite that they were criticizing – sometimes their sons and daughters.

In the fourth case, 'non-cooperative' governments were threatened with increasing scrutiny and eventual boycotts by the foreign banks, particularly those in the US, that they had regular dealings with.

Coercion was intrinsic to the fifth case, RAMSI. The initial landing in July 2003 was heavily armed. Australian forces did not know what to expect, and were relieved at the signs of popular welcome. People were encouraged to surrender their guns through shows of military strength, and the promise of future security. A new police force was introduced side by side with the discredited Solomon Islands force, and it used its powers to arrest under Solomon Islands law. A new jail was built to house those convicted, or refused bail. The coercion was not directed at the Solomon Islands government as such (though some individual officials MPs and ministers were its targets).

The international and regional approaches range along Dolowitz and Marsh's continuum between voluntary and forced adoption of foreign models. The World Bank's use of conditionality, as the authors suggested, falls somewhere in the middle. The Forum's attempt to use peer pressure falls more towards the voluntary. The FATF's blacklisting moved sharply towards the coercive after the passing of the US Patriot Act imposed heavier requirements on US banks. RAMSI is more complicated. In many ways, it lies on coercive end of the continuum.

RAMSI physically invaded the Solomon Islands. It occupies the coercive end of a domestic government's powers in police law and justice. But it was invited and legitimated by an act of Solomon Islands parliament and RAMSI's officials work alongside Solomon Islands officials within Solomon Islands legislation. It has not defeated, colonized or taken over the Solomon Islands government, but inserted some of its officials within it, and partly displaced some of its functions for an indefinite period.

Effectiveness of International Interventions

The Public Sector Reforms in the 1990s aimed, among other things, to improve financial accountability, and budget control, which would thereby reduce opportunities for corruption. Yet, aspects of the reforms created new opportunities for corruption, and popular perceptions of it. Putting heads of departments on contract reduced their independence from ministers. The process of privatization was vulnerable to favouritism and insider dealing. There was controversy over the way a government owned hotel was sold in the Cook Islands and over the privatization of the Bank of PNG.

'To-ing' and 'fro-ing' continued between the PNG government and the World Bank over the terms of the moratorium on new logging agreements, and the review of hundreds of existing agreements. Extensions to some permits were issued, others threatened with rescission (Filer 2004). The World Bank suspended its loan. In 2004, a new permit was issued to the largest foreign company involved, Rimbunan Hijau. The company had become increasingly vocal on behalf of logging, through the local newspaper it conveniently owned, and by commissioning its own consultancy report to counter the welter of documentation produced by the World Bank and the conservation movement (ITS Global 2006). In 2005, the government and the World Bank jointly announced the cancellation of the project to finance forestry reform (ITS Global 2006).

A 'stocktake' of the Forum's accountability process found agreements made at the Forum were not being well communicated and implemented back home (Pacific Islands Forum Secretariat 2002). Another stocktake two years later found some changes, mainly to legislation, but only among the seven countries which replied to the questionnaire. The main constraints were lack of political will, technical capacity and human resources (Filer 2004). Island ministers rejected the lengthy draft leadership code proposed by Australian consultants, though Tuvalu went on to pass its own legislation based on the Forum model (Taaafaki 2004, 10). The Forum reported that Nauru, Kiribati and Marshall islands were preparing similar legislation (Somare 2005).

Five years after its inception, TI (PNG) conducted a review of its own effectiveness, finding some success in the development of school curricula and awareness raising. But it reported less success with attempts to promote Integrity Pledges among election candidates, and Integrity Pacts amongst companies bidding for tenders. Its campaign to establish an ICAC had fallen on deaf ears in parliament (Siaguru 2001).

The threat of commercial isolation has brought about legal changes in OFCs. Nauru held out longest but by 2006 it had legislated sufficiently for the FATF to remove it from its blacklist.

RAMSI quickly restored law and order and has turned its attention to supporting institutions involved with finance, accountability, and criminal justice. According to RAMSI's website three thousand six hundred guns were given up. Six thousand three hundred people have been arrested – roughly one in fifty.[2] One hundred and sixty Solomon Islands policemen now face corruption and other serious charges brought under local legislation. Six former ministers have been charged with corruption. Government finances have been stabilized, with economic growth running at 5 per cent per annum (after a fall of 25 per cent through the conflict). Audit reports are once again being presented to parliament (Wasuka 2006).[3]

However, relations between the Australian and Solomon Islands governments turned sour after a riot that followed the parliamentary election of a new prime Minister in 2006. Rioters burned Chinatown, the capital's business district. Australia resisted Solomon Islands government attempts to set up a commission of enquiry into the cause of the riots, arguing it could prejudice legal action against two MPs already facing charges for inciting it. It might also embarrass the RAMSI police who failed to anticipate or control it (Moore 2006, 9–10). In September 2006, the Solomon Islands government declared the Australian High Commissioner *persona non grata*, claiming he was interfering in domestic politics (Sogavare 2006). Then, the two governments got into a public row over Solomon Islands' plan to appoint Julian Moti, a Fiji born Australian citizen, as its Attorney General (and therefore responsible for the proposed commission of inquiry).[4] In October, the Forum reaffirmed its support for RAMSI, and moved to set up better mechanisms for consultation about its direction. However, tempers flared again when RAMSI criticized a Solomon Islands government proposal to rearm the police. The Solomons Prime Minister accused Australia of infringing the country's sovereignty. The Australian Foreign Minister went over his head in publishing an 'open letter' in a Solomons newspaper defending RAMSI's achievements and warning of a 'deliberate push to undermine' it. The Prime Minister responded

---

2 The population between 15–64 years amounts to 53 per cent of the total (http://www.spc.int/popadvocacy/COUNTRY%20PROFILE-5.SVP.htm).

3 One of these reporting that an Australian government corporation, Air Services Australia, had been involved in the corruption that RAMSI was sent to clean up. The corporation had held the contract to manage Solomon Islands airspace, and had collected revenue from international airlines on Solomon Islands behalf. Apparently, $2.2 million of this revenue had been diverted 'to third parties, at the direction of senior Solomon Islands officials' (Air Services Australia 2006).

4 Australia claimed that Moti was wanted under Australian anti-paedophile legislation, which covers Australians overseas. Australian police have prosecuted an average of two such cases a year since the legislation was introduced in 1994 (Australian Federal Police 2004). However, Moti's alleged offence took place in Vanuatu, several years ago, and had already been dealt with by the Vanuatu courts – perhaps improperly, but raising questions about why this old matter was being raised now.

angrily, saying Australia was trying to run a 'parallel government' in Solomon Islands (AAP 7 February 2007).

Meanwhile, the ECP was implemented in PNG in late 2004, after a year of negotiations over the immunities from local legislation that its Australian officials might enjoy. One hundred Australian police were briefly on patrol in the capital, and 45 Australian officials in position in PNG government departments. The ECP programme was halted in May 2005 after PNG's Supreme Court found that immunities against prosecution promised to Australian officials were unconstitutional, but the non-police officials have remained in 'advisory' rather than 'line' positions.

The Australian Police Commissioners in Fiji and Solomon Islands were both expelled in late 2006. Fiji's commissioner was dismissed after the December coup, and Solomon Islands Commissioner declared an undesirable immigrant, preventing his return from Christmas holidays in Australia.

Conclusions

The degree of coerciveness and the degree of effectiveness varied across these five cases of policy transfer. Were the two linked? Do the cases suggest that coercion was effective – at least for this policy (anti-corruption) in this region (the Pacific Islands)? And do they suggest that other, non-coercive, sources of isomorphism, such as emulation and training, were more or less effective?

The coerciveness and effectiveness of the FATF were clearly linked. It is unlikely that tax havens would have reformed themselves without the threat of boycotts. Nor were they particularly susceptible to non-coercive processes of emulation and training. They were, after all, set up as alternatives to metropolitan banks, and were technically competent. RAMSI's coerciveness was also linked to its effectiveness, at least in the first three years, though a backlash set in when the new Prime minister accused it of 'bullying'. RAMSI also incorporated more traditional, non-coercive forms of aid, such as training public servants.

By comparison, the World Bank's attempt to set conditions on its loans to PNG became a sullen bureaucratic struggle against political and official backlash. The Bank's threats were unconvincing and ultimately ineffective. Filer (2004) concludes that the PNG government must have decided that the forest industry, even if unsustainable, was worth more to it than a loan from the World Bank. The Asian Development Bank, however, was somewhat more successful in using conditionality to achieve public sector reform among its island members, perhaps because it did try to engage popular opinion, and did not create resistance among politicians by targeting corruption as such. Indeed, in the new powers they gain to hire and fire department heads, politicians gained from public sector reform.

The other interventions – by the Forum, and through local chapters of TI – were less coercive, but not completely ineffective. Tuvalu eventually adopted the Leadership Code proposed by the Forum, and TI (PNG) chalked up some successes in developing an anti corruption curriculum. Both are good examples of the non-coercive processes of institutional isomorphism proposed by Di

Maggio and Powell – emulation and training. However, the prestigious foreign model of anti corruption activity – the ICAC – was often talked about, and actually proposed by TI in PNG, but nowhere implemented. Tuvalu adopted the different model proposed by consultants to the Forum. In each of the cases, training was short term and technical rather than the longer term credentialing and professionalization of work envisaged by Powell and DiMaggio. So these cases do suggest coercion works, up to the point at which it generates a backlash, which requires further intervention to prevent or overcome. Less coercive approaches were not necessarily effective either.

This chapter has focused on effectiveness, but as we saw at the start, it is only one of many criteria against which policy can be evaluated. RAMSI, the most complicated and innovative intervention, has been highly effective in the short term. Effectiveness relates to achievement of purposes, but RAMSI's have shifted over its short life, so evaluation is in danger of becoming a circular process of adjusting goals to current activities. It cries out for evaluation on other criteria as well. Michael Fullilove's comparisons of RAMSI with other recent international interventions suggest some of these (2006; 2007): efficiency, popularity, and sustainability. For example, he finds Australia's dominant role in the intervention makes it more efficient than other multinational interventions, with their problems of coordination. Its manifest popularity with ordinary Solomon Islanders – attested to by an independent review by an Eminent Persons Group appointed by the Forum – has helped it in rows with reluctant politicians and officials. Fullilove worries about its sustainability, and RAMSI's own research finds that 65 per cent of the population thought that violence would return if RAMSI left (RAMSI 2006, 2). Meanwhile, the protagonists propose other more complex and contradictory criteria for evaluation. Prime Minister Sogavare evaluated RAMSI's processes according to their impact on 'sovereignty' while Prime Minister Howard evaluated its outcomes according to their impact on 'good governance'.

References

Air Services Australia (2006), 'Solomon Islands: Payments to Officials', *Media Release* 23 June.

Asia Pacific Group on Money Laundering Secretariat (2003), 'History and Background', available at <http://www.apgml.org/content/history_and_background.jsp>, accessed 30 October 2004.

Australian Federal Police (2004), *Media Release*, 24 August.

Barnett, T. (1989), *Report of the Commission of Enquiry into Aspects of the Forest Industry: Final Report* (2 vols), unpublished report to the Government of PNG.

Chand, S. (2003), 'Economic Trends in the Pacific Island Countries', *Pacific Economic Bulletin* 18:1, 1–15.

Common, R. (2001), *Public Management and Policy Transfer in South East Asia* (Aldershot: Ashgate).

Dinnen, S. (2004), 'Aid Effectiveness and Australia's New Interventionism in the Southwest Pacific', *Development Bulletin* 65, 76–80.

Dobell, G. (2007), 'China and Taiwan in the South Pacific: Diplomatic Chess versus Pacific Political Rugby', *Policy Brief* (Sydney: Lowy Institute for International Policy).

Dolowitz, D. and Marsh, D. (2000), 'Learning from Abroad: The Role of Policy Transfer in Contemporary Policy-making', *Governance* 13:1, 5–23.

Filer, C. (2004), 'A Serious Case of Conditionality: The World Banks Gets Stuck in the Forests in PNG', *Development Bulletin* 65, 95–99.

Fullilove, M. (2006), *The Testament of Solomons: RAMSI and International State Building* (Sydney: Lowy Institute for International Policy).

Fullivove, M. (2007), 'AIIA President's Forum – Remarks by Michael Fullilove', available at <http://www.aiia.asn.au/national/T5_Michael_Fullilove.html>, accessed 28 February 2006.

Financial Action Task Force (2003), available at <http://www1.oecd.org/fatf/>, accessed 22 February 2006.

ITS Global (2006), 'The World Bank and Forestry in PNG', *Report for Rimbunan Hijau (PNG) Group* (Melbourne: ITS Global).

Jackson, R. (1990), *Quasi States: Sovereignty, International Relations and the Third World* (Cambridge: Cambridge University Press).

Kotkin, S. and Sajo, A. (eds) (2002), *Political Corruption in Transition: A Skeptic's Handbook* (Budapest: Central European University Press).

Krastev, I. (2002), 'The Balkans: Democracy without Choices', *Journal of Democracy*, 13:3, 39–53.

Krastev, I. (2004), *Shifting Obsessions: Three Essays on the Politics of Anticorruption* (Budapest/NY: Central European University Press).

Larmour, P. (1997), 'Corruption and Governance in the South Pacific', *Pacific Studies* 20:3, 1–17.

Larmour, P. (2000), 'Issues and Mechanisms of Accountability: Examples from Solomon Islands', *State Society and Governance in Melanesia Discussion Paper No. 1* (Canberra: Research School of Pacific and Asian Studies, Australian National University).

Larmour, P. (2003), 'Transparency International and Policy Transfer in PNG', *Pacific Economic Bulletin* 18, 115–20.

Larmour, P. (2005), *Foreign Flowers: Institutional Transfer and Good Governance in the Pacific Islands* (Honolulu: University of Hawaii Press).

Larmour, P. (2006), 'Civilizing Techniques: Transparency International and the Spread of Anti-corruption', in B. Bowden and L. Seabrooke (eds) *Global Standards of Market Civilization* (Abingdon: Routledge).

Larmour, P. and Barcham, M. (2006), 'National Integrity Systems in Small Pacific Island States', *Public Administration and Development* 26, 173–84.

Maesulia, A. (2006), 'Fund for Millenium Development Fund Released', available at <www.pmc.gov.sb>, accessed 7 January 2007.

Mellam, A. and Aloi, D. (2003), *National Integrity Systems Country Study Report Papua New Guinea* (Berlin: Transparency International).

Michael, B. (2004a), 'The Globalization of Anticorruption Policies: the Diffusion of Best Practices and the role of Knowledge Management', in D. Levi-Faur and E Vigoda-Gadot (eds) *International Public Policy and Management: Policy Learning Beyond Cultural and Political Boundaries* (New York: Marcel Dekker).

Michael, B. (2004b), 'Explaining Organizational Change in International Development: the Role of Complexity in Anti Corruption Work', *Journal of International Development* 16, 1067–88.

Michael, B. (2004c), 'What do African Donor-sponsored Anti-corruption Programmes Teach us about International Development in Africa?', *Social Policy and Administration* 38:4, 320–45.

Moore, C. (2006), 'Helpem Fren: The Solomon Islands and RAMSI 2003–2006', *National President's Forum 14 July 2006* (Sydney, Parliament House: Australian Institute of International Affairs).

Morgenthau, H. (1962), 'A Political Theory of Foreign Aid', *The American Political Science Review* 56:2, 301–9.

Olaks Consulting Services (2001), *National Integrity Systems Country Study Report Fiji* (Berlin: Transparency International).

Pacific Islands Forum Secretariat (2002), *Stocktake of the Implementation of Forum Economic Ministers Meeting Decisions* (Suva: Pacific Islands Forum Secretariat).

Pacific Islands Forum Secretariat (2004), *Forum Finance and Economic Ministers Biennial Stocktake Session 3 Paper PIFS (04) FFEMR.06* (Ministers Meeting Rotorua, New Zealand: Forum Economic).

Regional Assistance Mission to the Solomon Islands (RAMSI) (2006), *Annual Performance Report 2005/2006* (RAMSI performance assessment advisory team, Camris International).

Roughan, P. (2004), *National Integrity Systems Country Study Report: Solomon Islands* (Berlin: Transparency International).

Sampford, C., Shacklock, A., Connors, C. and Galtung, F. (eds) (2006), *Measuring Corruption* (Aldershot: Ashgate).

Secretariat of the Pacific Community (2005), 'Pacific Islands Populations Poster', available at <http://www.spc.int/demog/English01-02/RecentStats/2004/Pacific%20Island%20Populations%202004.xls>, accessed 31 September 2006.

Siaguru, A. (2001), 'The Chairman's address to the 5th General Meeting of Transparency International (PNG) Inc.' (Port Moresby: Transparency International).

Sogavare, M. (2006), 'Address to the Nation by the Prime Minister', available at <http://www.pmc.gov.sb/?q=node/636 >, accessed 18 February 2007.

Somare, Sir M. (2005), 'Opening Address of the 36th Pacific Islands Forum', 25 October, Sir John Guise Stadium PNG.

Taafaki, T. (2004), *Tuvalu' National integrity Systems Country Study Report* (Berlin: Transparency International).

Tisne, M. and Smilov, D. (2004), *From the Ground Up; Assessing the Record of Anticorruption Assistance in Southeastern Europe* (Budapest: Center for European Policy Studies, Central European University).

Transparency International (2006), *Corruptions Perceptions Index*, available at <http://www.transparency.org/policy_research/surveys_indices/global/cpi>, accessed 31 December 2006.

United Nations (2006), available at <http://www.unescap.org/stat/data/apif/solomon_islands_apif2004.pdf>, accessed 9 January 2006.

United States Department of the Treasury (2005), 'Fact Sheet: Section 312 of the USA Patriot Act Final Regulation and Notice of Proposed Rulemaking', available at <http://fincen.gov/312factsheet.html>, accessed 18 February 2007.

Wasuka, E. (2006), 'Corruption Reports: Casualty of Fallout', *Islands Business*, 25 December.

Chapter 6

Corporate Business Systems for Integrity: A Case Study

Joel Lucas and David Kimber

Introduction

The Business Integrity Systems Assessment (BISA) was undertaken by RMIT School of Management as part of the Australian National Integrity Systems Assessment (NISA). The primary aim of this project was to identify, analyse and record the institutions, laws, procedures, practices and attitudes in Australia that raise business standards (including increasing transparency and accountability) and inhibit corruption (the 'integrity system') with a view to:

- assessing the strengths and weaknesses of the present Australian integrity system and recommending improvements;
- identifying areas of potential risk from which corruption might develop;
- surveying attitudes to the extent and nature of corruption in Australia and to the effectiveness of its integrity system;
- identifying the ways in which elements of the integrity system interrelate and any gaps or overlaps between them;
- providing a benchmark for comparison between jurisdictions and against which changes in the effectiveness of the integrity system can be measured;
- providing a basis for action by relevant Australian governmental and non-governmental agencies and organizations including Transparency International Australia; and
- providing examples and case studies for other countries both developed and developing.

An assessment of business integrity systems is relevant to the national assessment of integrity systems because Australia's reputation as a payer of international bribes rests principally on the conduct of the Australian business community. Further, companies may seek to obtained or retained business from, or influence with, the federal, state or local governments by corrupt means. This risk is particularly evident when the increasing rate of fraud in the community is considered.

The scope of this project has been, in effect, to 'map' Business Integrity Systems (BIS) within Australia. It was recognized that the enormous complexity and depth of business integrity issues requires a far more comprehensive analysis beyond the means of this project. The objective therefore became a map of integrity within business; an identification of those elements within organizational culture, policy, procedures and practices, that contribute to or hinder the maintenance and development of business integrity.

In achieving the main project objective, it was also important to define the range of issues that those within business perceive as being related to corruption and corruption prevention. This approach was adopted through the pilot project and continued throughout the main project as key findings were discovered.

Methodology

Aspects of Data Collection

The aspects of the primary data collection consisted of the following research areas:

Qualitative research The qualitative research had two themes – individual interviews and departmental focus groups. The individual interviews were for senior and departmental managers, as well as industry or organizational function specialists. The focus group interviews were conducted mainly for operational or entry level employees and normally consisted of about three to six employees at a time. Focus groups were conducted rather than individual interviews because of time and resource restrictions. However they also provided opportunities for the analysis of interaction between employees and insight into the way employees discussed integrity issues amongst themselves. In two of the large organizations, focus group interviews were conducted with the senior management team, which provided further insights to the focus groups with employees. In small to medium enterprises (SMEs), interviews would often only be conducted with the manager of the business. However because of simpler structures and operations, the depth of analysis achieved was similar if not better than that achieved in large organizations. Those individuals that participated in the quantitative component were not excluded from participating in the interviews.

While the issues discussed in the interviews for the research were very similar, the structure did alter somewhat between the various organizations. This was mainly due to the number of staff in organizations and the departmental structure, which was influenced by size and the industry. Within some organizations, we were also able to interview groups of managers as focus groups. Twenty-three organizations agreed to contribute to the research as case studies. Interviews and focus group discussions were held with 72 people from these organizations.

Company documentation Company documentation was collected from those organizations that participated in the research. The types of documents collected were mission statements, codes of ethics/conduct, values statements and specific departmental policy that related to integrity, if in existence. An example of departmental policy that specifically relates to integrity might be a HR recruitment procedure to assess the character of candidates eligible for employment. Company documentation was provided by 16 of the organizations that contributed to the research project as case studies.

The integrity documentation was analysed in an attempt to identify ways of espousing company values throughout organizations, and to compare differing types of words used in the promotion of proper conduct.

Quantitative Research

A quantitative research tool call IntraSight^{SM} Assessment was made available to us for exclusive use in this project by Andersen. This was used to assist in understanding the awareness and perception levels of Australian business as a whole. Normally a minimum of ten responses from various levels was asked for of the case-study organizations. IntraSight is a perception and awareness based ethical climate survey tool. It was also completed anonymously as a web-based questionnaire. Questionnaires were completed by 160 participants.

The results from the IntraSight quantitative component were used to two ways. Where a significant number of responses were gained from a particular organization, the results were analysed in conjunction with the integrity documentation from the company. This was to review the awareness of the existence of the documentation amongst employees, and to measure the effectiveness of it in terms of attitude and perception. For the most part, the quantitative results for the various organizations were aggregated to provide data on the perception and awareness of integrity in Australia as a whole. This data was analysed in conjunction with the qualitative interview data to provide validation of arguments developed or identify discrepancies. In view of timing problems relating to the analysis of the data the statistical data has not been separately reviewed. Rather it provided corroborating evidence for the findings emerging from interviews, documentation and focus groups.

Secondary Research

Secondary research was also used as a means of validating themes drawn from the primary research and to compare and contrast this research with similar work performed in varying contexts. Much of the validation and discussion of integrity within the Australian context, as well as the identification of integrity risks, all of which were drawn from secondary research has been omitted from this extract to preserve the focus on the primary research findings.

When accessing the data on business integrity systems in organizations we were required to ensure that we as researchers were discussing the same issues and themes of the respondents. One of the initial questions that we asked in all of the interviews was 'What does integrity mean to you?' This question was asked to ensure that we were discussing 'apples and apples' and not 'apples and oranges'. There is little value in writing a report for business which uses a philosophical meaning of integrity, if that is not what integrity means within organizations.

After that initial insight had been achieved, the questions were largely based on the role and function of the individuals within their area of the organization.

The main areas of the concentration with data collection within organizations were strategy, human resources and operations. The strategy aspect involved the senior echelon of organizations, which comprised of compliance, risk management, public relations, corporate governance and ethics management. This area was expected to give insight into the top-down messages that are espoused through the organization. Human resource management was considered important because of the relationship between individual's personal integrity and the integrity expectations inherent in their organizational role. Lastly, operations, including areas of international operations, information technology, accountancy, and sales and marketing, was of particular interest as it was expected to clarify the day-to-day aspects of integrity management. It also displayed the effectiveness of management communicating values and expectations throughout the organization.

The diagram below (Figure 6.1) outlines the theoretical research framework used when approaching each of the cases researched:

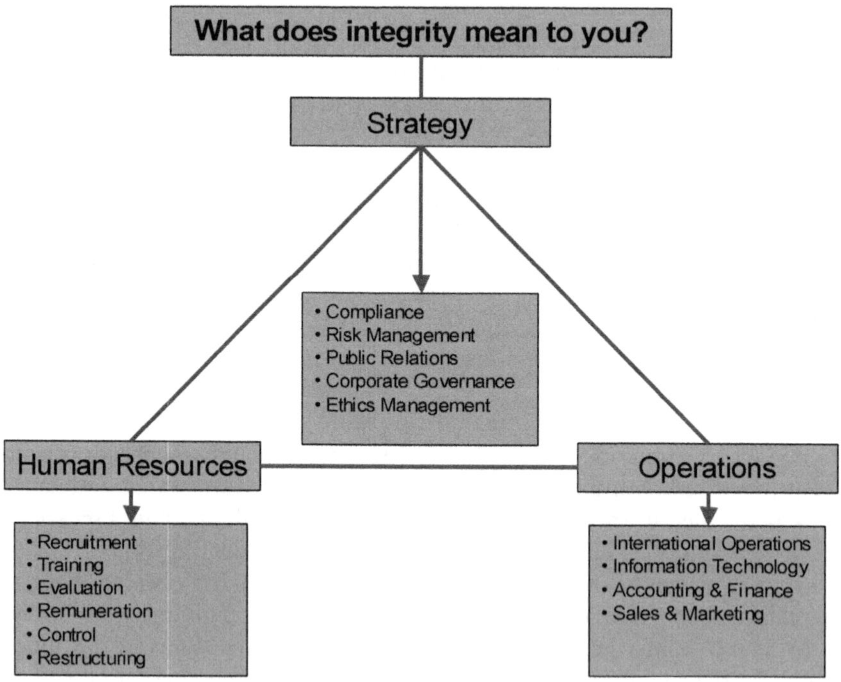

Figure 6.1 What does integrity mean to you?

The Pilot

A pilot for the Business Integrity Systems Assessment project was conducted from September to December 2000. This pilot involved two large organizations and two small organizations, and assisted us to get some initial understanding of the major concerns and benefits of business integrity systems. There were few major changes to the initial methodology construct following the pilot project, however some areas were refined and it assisted in the clarity and phrasing of questions.

One major change from the pilot project was the inclusion of the influence of regulatory bodies in driving the maintenance of integrity systems.

Validation of Findings

After the pilot stage was completed, the direction, scope and depth of the project was monitored by the advisory group. This was achieved though the use of workshops that met at set intervals during the post-pilot phase. The workshop participants consisted of representatives from Transparency International Australia, RMIT and the sponsoring organizations. The key project contributions of the workshops were assistance with the planning, ensuring that the content of the final report was directed to business, topic identification and structuring for the report and validation of the findings. The workshops were conducted at the outset of the major project, midway through the project and at the beginning of the report production stage.

Limitations

Identifiable limitations that we recognized and were conscious of while conducting the research were:

Perceptions of the researcher Any research of this nature is likely to be influenced by perceptions of the researchers. To combat this concern, a number of workshops and meetings with people outside the scope of the research activity were conducted. These meetings assisted the researchers to 'stay on target' with the research and ensure that we continued to report on the reality of the situation as it was observed.

Desirable responses Particularly with research being conducted within various businesses, we were conscious that some portion of the responses may well have been answers that respondents 'thought we wanted to hear', rather than their perception of what was actually occurring.

Inability to conduct one-on-one operational interviews Time pressures within the project resulted in an inability for the research to involve one-on-one interviews with operational staff. While we were able to interview management staff on an individual basis, research of employees in the lower echelons of integrity management could only be conducted as focus group interviews. This may have been a potential hindrance in situations were lower-level employees may have held back from discussing sensitive issue amongst their colleagues.

Definitions Some clarification about the term 'integrity' is necessary to understand the term 'business integrity'. It also assists in identifying what are the business systems aimed at maintaining integrity.

Dr Noel Preston discussed the meaning of integrity at length in the first report arising from this project (KCELJAG/TI 2001). The word 'integrity' is derived from the Latin *integritas*, meaning 'unaffected, intact, upright, reliable'. The same root word has given us 'integer', the mathematical term for any whole number, one that is not fractionalized. When something is 'integrated' its many parts have been brought together, unified.

Integrity and systems go together. We hear of 'maintaining the integrity of the eco-system' which implies protection of species diversity and our reliance on natural landscapes and vegetation. We do not find that usage of the term strange when it refers to ecological interconnectedness because the word, integrity, names a unifying, connecting, relating process in a system.

'Integrity' signifies also that a person, a profession, an institution knows what it stands for, values that knowledge and acts on it.

This definition is close to Sampford's view of institutional ethics (including business ethics) of 'asking hard questions about your values, giving honest and public answers, and trying to live by them' (Sampford 2002).

This concept of integrity is, to an extent, procedural rather than substantive – related to consistency of values and actions/words and deeds. They involve being honourable, honest, loyal, faithful, and trustworthy.

However, integrity is often used in a more substantive sense – as adherence to particular substantive values of being decent, good, conscientious, and scrupulous.

Researching Integrity

Figure 6.2 describes our initial thinking behind the function and purpose of integrity systems in business. It allowed us to identify those areas of the organizations that significantly impacted the purpose and development of systems.

This diagram identifies, in effect, a theoretical and practical element to integrity, both within and outside the organizations. Within the organization the theoretical element comprises of the formal systems, being those structures, codes, guides, policies and manuals that contribute to the development of integrity. On the practical side is the organization culture, which includes the behaviours, processes, actions and day-to-day functions that those within the organization perform. Organizational integrity systems are also impacted by the 'practical' social culture outside the organization. This social culture includes the values, principles and beliefs of the society in which the business operates. A further external element that impacts on business integrity is the regulatory environment. This includes public policy and legislation, the Australia Standards

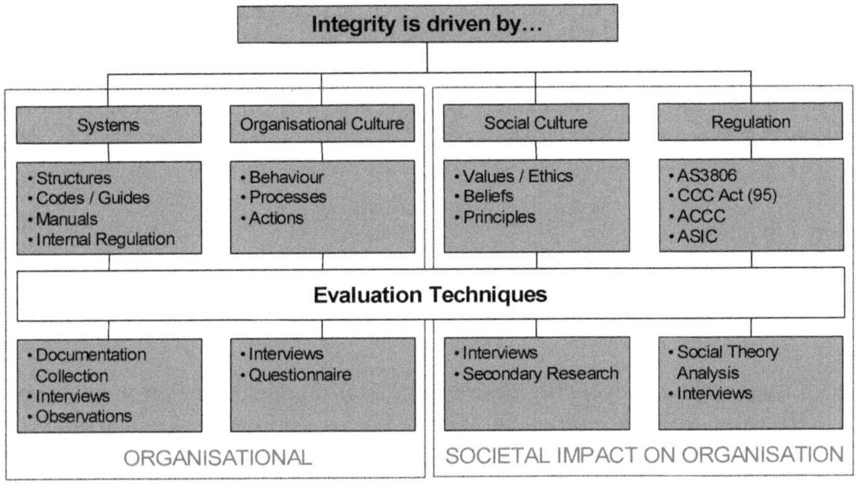

Figure 6.2 Integrity driven by ...

Board, the Australian Stock Exchange for listed companies, and formal regulatory bodies such as Australian Securities and Investments Commission, Australian Prudential Regulation Authority and the Australian Competition and Consumer Commission. It also includes the impact of professional accounting and legal associations' standards and systems of compliance.

Findings: Sources of Business Integrity

In the context of this research, BISs are developed in organizations to help establish personal, organizational and societal congruence, integration and stability. Hence integrity maintenance in business is seen to respond to a range of legal and ethical norms, internal and external systems and processes and areas, including:

- the personal values held by individuals - owners, employees, customers, suppliers, and other stakeholders;
- norms developed within the various groups of which they are members (including the business itself);
- the systems, practices, processes, policies and ways of acting, etc. developed by the business and organizations involved with business;
- legal norms and regulation; and
- the political and social environment.

Clearly the arena is a wide and complicated one. As Preston (2000) has noted it is a 'slippery notion' – one which many would prefer to avoid because of its inherent complexity. However this would only lead to inappropriately simplistic understandings about how business integrity systems have been established. It is necessary to grapple with the multiple meanings and try to reconcile them. One way of doing this is to review the socio-cultural roots of integrity in Australia and how it has affected both past and current business practices. This analysis was performed as part of this research and can be found in the full report on the BISA project.

Key Findings

A number of significant issues emerged from the research project. They are as follows:

- Integrity is a universally desired and well-understood factor in business. However understandings and management approaches vary significantly. Some organizations did not consider it in a conscious and formal fashion. Others sought to promote it in clear, systematic, well-articulated ways.
- Leadership, clear policy, stability, consistency, a concern for reputation, 'good' staff and communication were regularly identified as key factors which sustained business integrity.
- BIS were most evident in two types of business enterprise. First, large, stable, often multinational corporations (MNCs) who had developed well articulated values principles, clear objectives and policy guidelines, and well documented operational procedures, which took account of integrity management issues. Secondly, in SMEs whose strong leaders had a well-articulated perspective on integrity, which was communicated and accepted by employees. In such circumstances it was part of the organizational culture and driven by a known, informal, peer supported 'way things are done around here'.
- In a number of cases, especially large national entities undergoing considerable change, a well integrated BIS could not be easily identified. A number of organizations declined to be involved in the project because they felt it would be difficult to review their operations from this perspective, because of restructuring and/or major industry changes.
- Whilst integrity was commonly identified as an important personal attribute, directly related to the character traits of individuals, few organizations directly or consciously incorporated integrity assessment as part of employee selection processes. At best it was indirectly identified via the experience and intuition of those involved in recruitment and selection, reference checking, multiple interviewing, or trial employment. Whilst some recruiting firms recognized its importance, most selection processes concentrated on the assessment of personal competence and proof of work skills, rather than formulating judgements about personal integrity.
- In some cases, whilst integrity perspectives were being emphasized in strategy and policy documentation by senior management, line managers and operational staff were openly cynical about BIS influencing work practices.
- Accounting and audit procedures, legal compliance, asset protection, quality control, health, safety and security were often identified as key integrity system

issues. Technology is increasingly being used to manage such systems. Proper resourcing and maintenance of such systems was noted as a concern, especially if cost minimization is a strong policy driver.

- Competition, cost pressure, and the desire for 'lean organizations' were cited as factors which inhibit the development of fully integrated BIS.
- The ways integrity systems are developed and managed varies considerably. They depend on the nature of the business operations, the industry, the size of the business, the philosophy of its governors and leaders, and the regulatory, political and social environment. The control over business integrity was seen as influenced by:
  - leadership – strategy, policy development, planning and governance,
  - ethics management, business conduct, regulation and legal compliance
  - public relations and marketing in relation to reputation
- Senior and operational management in relation to product quality, performance, reliability, standard setting etc.
- Human resource management in relation to staff selection, training and education, etc.
- Accounting, audit and asset security in relation to legal compliance, fraud and corruption protection etc.
- Most organizations surveyed did not appear to have a co-ordinated approach that ensured integrity management in all these arenas took place or was aligned.
- In many SMEs, integrity was noted as a key factor preserving reputation and sustaining the business. It was evident that a strong organizational culture, built on the personal integrity of employees, managers and owners, appeared to successfully create an environment which maintained high business integrity. It was primarily related to good leadership and management practices. Open and regular communication reinforced appropriate behaviour. Formal documentation did not appear to be an important element in such organizations. Informal systems were recognized as the most effective. In fact 'red-taping the systems' was seen as a potentially negative influence. Integrity systems were not seen as separate or add-on elements, rather simply as part of the daily operational management
- In the micro-business environment, integrity maintenance related to networking, good relationships, trust, and loyalty. Cost and time pressures limit the capacity of small businesses to develop formal or systematic approaches even though risk of failure may be high. Consequently reputation and 'word of mouth' is most likely to be relied upon in terms of dealing with customers and suppliers.
- Documentation provided by organizations identified two opposing orientations towards integrity maintenance. At one extreme, formal, rule based, regulation focused systems emphasized that the recognition of law and compliance with it underpin the integrity of organizations. At the other end of the spectrum, aspirational, values focused, statements suggest that integrity relates to the innate goodness of human beings, which will emerge when suitably recognized encouraged and rewarded.

Reflections on Findings

When organization did not have well established BIS, they apparently relied on external influences – the personal integrity of their employees and the influence of strong regulatory environment, to maintain their business integrity. As employee selection processes do not appear to focus on character assessment, integrity risk factors may be inherent in such entities.

Rapid technological and social changes pose a major threat to organizations that do not consciously address integrity maintenance. Individuals faced with job insecurity experience conflict between personal needs and loyalty for the organization. Their disillusion and anger could lead to personal justification for a 'work to rules' mentality which in turn feeds a more compliance driven focus on BIS management. The development of such environments, especially in large organizations, is likely to reduce personal commitment to organizational integrity.

Those organizations that appeared to have embedded integrity into the organizational culture were seen by staff as 'good places to work'. They were often the smaller entities. Relationships and personal connectedness in the work place was part of, and supported, BIS.

The pressure to reduce costs in business entities may mean that the growth of outsourcing and contracting is having a negative impact on integrity and reputation, especially in a global environment. This awareness is likely to cause MNC's strengthen integrity maintenance as part of their supply chain management processes.

Business integrity management is becoming an increasing societal concern. There is increasing pressure for businesses to take account of their social and environmental responsibilities as well as their financial performance. The relationship between business integrity and sustainability is being slowly recognized. However the pressure for short-term financial performance by investors is creating significant tension for business. The paradox and contradictions inherent in this arena, especially as the impact of global business increases, are creating increasing stress for Australian businesses and may impact on their ability to maintain BIS.

Different philosophies relating to human and organizational behaviour and moral development influence the perspective which different organizations appear to adopt. At one end of a philosophical spectrum, people are viewed as motivated by self-interest, greed, envy, deviousness, etc. – the factors likely to threaten business integrity. Power, control and fear are seen as the prime forces needed to motivate their behaviour. At the other end of the spectrum people are seen as fundamentally caring, honest, and capable of being relied upon to personally seek high levels of integrity. Factors that encourage their achievements are aspiration, self-reliance, independence, mentoring, education/training and personal support. Corporate philosophies seemed to move in between these two extreme positions. The nature of the industry, legal risk and size seemed to be significant factors influencing which of these approaches dominates. Further research would help determine their appropriateness, efficiency and/or effectiveness.

The two different philosophies outlined above are related to the two different approaches found in business integrity systems (compliance and aspirational). Like many dichotomies, it is a false one. What is needed is a combination of the two approaches. Aspirational codes should not be expected to rely merely on the innate goodness of human beings and the ability to persuade people of the benefits of virtue. They need the support of remuneration systems that reward those who are furthering the values that the business publicly stands for, and compliance systems which identify and punish those who fall well below those standards.

The NISA project argued that integrity systems/ethics regimes involve ethical standard setting, legal regulation and institutional design (Sampford 1990) or guidance, control and management. Most of these elements have been considered separately. This project sought to consider how they interact with each other in regimes where there has been an attempt to co-ordinate them.

Conclusions and Recommendations from the Business Integrity System Assessment (BISA)

The analysis and synthesis of the data collected and the findings reached from that data enabled us to draw some significant implications and specific recommendations relating to the development and maintenance of BIS in Australian businesses. They are listed below:

- There is growing evidence that organizations who rely heavily on individual integrity, and who do not systematically address its maintenance, risk decline or failure. Increased workloads and stress, senior executive mobility, reduced organizational loyalty, an aging and increasingly cynical workforce, an emphasis on individualism, the increasing differential between upper and lower remuneration levels, the emphasis on work and wealth as success indicators, are all factors which point to greater risk of integrity failure. The increased emphasis on compliance in a number of organizations could be attributed to these concerns.
- Destabilizing influences such as significant business growth or decline, continual movement of senior staff, and major technological change affecting communication, are likely to adversely affect BIS. Consequently the current economic climate, both globally and in Australia, creates considerable pressure for BIS maintenance.
- A number of the issues noted above which may contribute to business decline can be related to tensions between business practice trends and the cultural values developed in Australia. Principles relating to egalitarianism, equity and fairness, care for others, team support, etc. have been challenged by business philosophies of the past three decades. An erosion of Australia's 'social capital' is likely if corporations' strategic planning and government policy do not foster a culture in which integrity is valued and practised.

- The BISA project has identified a number of complex and interwoven personal, business and social integrity issues. There is clearly a need for further and deeper research. Whilst Australia seems to have developed a well-regarded framework for business integrity, it is based on compromise between multitudes of pressures that are often contradictory. Ensuring the balance is sustained requires a conscious effort from individuals, organizations and government. A co-ordinated perspective is essential for effective BIS development. Public policy and subsequent legislation needs to be carefully reviewed from a BIS perspective to ensure the framework is not eroded.
- The review of BIS in Australia provides important and valuable data to be considered in a global context. This project highlights that social history and context are a important factors influencing the development of BIS. Simple or single focused perspectives that do not take account of a multiplicity of influences are unlikely to be effective in the long term.

Recommendations

The following recommendations were drawn from the findings of the BISA project:

- Many organizations in Australia need to take a more holistic approach to BIS development and maintenance. Strategy, planning, policy development and implementation processes need to take account of all factors outlined above which influence business integrity, in particular those that directly influence the organizational culture of the enterprise. Figure 6.3 demonstrates the conceptual model or 'map' of the different paradigms and processes that influence integrity in a business context, as revealed by our project:
- Greater attention needs to be given to the impact of decision-making on personal integrity within organizations. This relates to issues ranging from recruitment and selection to daily operational practices. There was clear evidence that many in business feel troubled by apparent contradictions and tensions created by organizational decision making which ignores the impact on peoples personal values and principles.
- Public policy and subsequent legislation must take account of business integrity maintenance as a key social concern. It is important to recognize the inter-relationships between personal, organizational and social integrity and ensure public policy supports and sustains all themes. It is highly desirable that these are mutually reinforcing rather than in conflict and that dialogues between those responsible be furthered.
- Integrity awareness must become a more recognized theme in leadership training and development. Greater emphasis in university postgraduate management programmes such as MBAs, professional training programmes, in-house training etc. Unless this develops, the recent financial collapses of major corporations both in Australia and overseas can be expected to continue.

Figure 6.3 Integrity systems

- Systems integrity and specific industries: further investigation of specific industries where integrity systems are not well developed is necessary. Industry practices in certain fields, such as the building industry, indicate there is a need to increase awareness of the value of well-developed integrity systems.
- There is a clearly identified need in many organizations to effectively integrate integrity management systems into all aspect of their business practices. Greater awareness of the dangers of 'window dressing' and 'lip service' is required. Like health and safety or appropriate risk assessment, it seems that a serious threat to BIS development is the pressures for immediate business results.
- Increased emphasis on how BIS activities influence international trade is required. It is evident that Australian businesses vary significantly in their understandings about business practices in other countries and how they need to respond to integrity issues relating to international trade.
- A major potential barrier to BIS development is the scepticism evident towards senior management in many Australian organizations. This has been exacerbated by media coverage emphasizing the differentials of rewards between executives and employees. This theme needs to be tackled in a number of ways. Greater transparency relating to role expectations and remuneration, as well as genuine moves to limit inequitable reward systems, are necessary to underpin general acceptance of broad based BIS in organizations.
- Greater emphasis on the themes outlined above is necessary in general undergraduate and TAFE business programmes. The past two decades have

seen a strong focus on vocational skills and knowledge in such courses at the cost of educational activities strengthening personal integrity awareness and development. Universities should be openly encouraged to ensure studies in areas of ethics, philosophy, sociology, civics, etc. are maintained in business programmes. Increased consciousness of the value of integrity to business, and ultimately to society, is an essential aspect of business education.

Ultimately a well structured BIS works for a business because it is appropriate, relates to the context and conditions, and has been consciously developed and maintained. It seems evident from the research undertaken for this project how this occurs in business, both globally and in Australia will have significant impact on the sustainability of the economic framework currently in existence.

References

Albrecht, W.S., Wenz, G.W. and Williams, T.L. (1995), *Fraud: Bringing Light to the Dark Side of Business* (Burr Ridge, IL: Irwin Professional Publishing).

Barton, L. (1995), *Ethics: The Enemy in the Workplace* (Cincinnati, OH: South-Western College Publishing).

Birch, D. (ed.) (1999), *The First National Conference on Corporate Citizenship: A New Research Impact. Proceedings* (Melbourne: Corporate Citizenship Research Unit, Deakin University).

Birch, D. (2001), 'Corporate Citizenship: Rethinking Business beyond Corporate Social Responsibility', in J. Andriof and M. McIntosh (eds) *Perspectives on Corporate Citizenship* (Sheffield: Greenleaf Publishing).

Birch, D. and Batten, J. (2001), *Corporate Citizenship in Australia* (Melbourne: Corporate Citizenship Research Unit, Deakin University).

Collins, J.C. and Porras, J.I. (1996), *Built to Last – Successful Habits of Visionary Companies* (London: Random House).

Covey, S.R., Merrill, A.R. and Merrill, R.R. (1994), *First Things First: To Live, to Love, to Learn, to Leave a Legacy* (New York: Simon and Schuster).

Cox, E. (1995), *A Truly Civil Society* (Sydney: ABC).

Delaney, J.T. and Sockell, D. (1992), 'Do Company Ethics Training Programs Make a Difference? An Empirical Analysis', *Journal of Business Ethics* 11:9, 719–28.

Estes, R. (1998), *Tyranny of the Bottom Line: Why Corporations make Good People do Bad Things* (Washington DC: Berret-Koehler).

French, P. (1995), *Corporate Ethics* (Orlando, FL: Harcourt Brace).

French, W.A. and Granose, J. (1995), *Practical Business Ethics* (Englewood Cliffs, NJ: Prentice Hall).

Fukuyama, F. (1995), *Trust: The Social Virtues and the Creation of Prosperity* (London: Penguin Books).

Gowler, D. and Legge, K. (1996). 'The Meaning of Management and the Management of Meaning', in S. Linstead, R. Grafton Small and P. Jeffcutt (eds) *Understanding Management* (London: Sage Publications).

Grace, D. and Cohen, S. (1998), *Business Ethics: Australian Problems and Cases*, 2nd edn (Melbourne: Oxford University Press).

Greenleaf, R.K. (1998), *The Power of Servant Leadership* (San Francisco, CA: Berret Koehler).

Hilmer, F. and Donaldson, L. (1996), *Management Redeemed* (New York and Sydney: Harper and Row).

Hoffman, W. and Frederick, R. (1995), *Business Ethics: Reading and Cases in Corporate Morality* (New York: McGraw-Hill).

KCELJAG/TI (2001), *Australian National Integrity Systems Assessment: Queensland Handbook* (Melbourne: KCELJAG/TI).

Kohlberg, L. (1981), *The Philosophy of Moral Development, Vol. 1* (San Francisco, CA: Harper and Row.

Mackay, H. (1993), *Reinventing Australia: The Mind and Mood of Australia in the 90s* (Sydney: Angus and Robertson).

Mackay, H. (1999), *Turning Point* (Sydney: Pan Macmillan).

Mcdonald, G. and Nijhof, A. (2000), 'Beyond Codes of Ethics: An Integrated Framework for Stimulating Morally Responsible Behaviour in Organisations', *Leadership and Organisation Development Journal* 20:3, 133–46.

McKenna, R (1999), *New Management* (Sydney: Irwin McGraw-Hill).

Murphy, R. (1996), 'Defining and Practising Business Ethics', in K. Woldring (ed.) *Business Ethics in Australia and New Zealand* (Melbourne: Thomas Nelson).

Petrick, J. and Quinn, M. (1997), *Management Ethics: Integrity at Work* (New York: Sage Publications).

Ping, A. (1999), *Sensitive Chaos* (Sydney: Hale and Iremonger).

Preston N. (2000), 'What is Integrity', National Integrity Systems Workshop, Key Centre for Ethics Law Justice and Governance, Griffith University, September.

Priest, J. (2000), 'Managing Investments in Information Systems – Exploring Effective Practice', unpublished DBA thesis (Melbourne: RMIT School of Management).

Putnam, R.. Leonard, R. and Nanetti, R.Y. (1993), *Making Democracy Work: Civic Traditions in Modern Italy* (Princeton, NJ: Princeton University Press).

Reaghan, G. (2000), 'Counting the Cost: Effectively Managing Risk of Worker Fraud', *Birmingham City Journal*, 3 November, available at <http://birmingham.bcentral.com/birmingham/stories/2000/11/06/focus6.html>.

Sampford, C. (1991), 'Law, Institutions and the Public/Private Divide', *Federal Law Review* 20, 185–222.

Sampford, C. (1994), 'Law, Ethics and Institutional Reform: Finding Philosophy, Displacing Ideology', *Griffith Law Review* 3:1, 1–38.

Sampford, C. (1998), 'Cautionary Reflections on Corporatisation and Privatisation', in J. Malbon (ed.) *Corporatisation and Privatisation: Who Benefits?* (London: Routledge).

Sampford, C. and Wood, D. (1992), 'The Future of Business Ethics: Legal Regulation, Ethical Standard Setting and Institutional Design', *Griffith Law Review* 1, 56.

Sampford, C. (2002), 'Institutionalising Public Sector Ethics', in R. Elliott (ed.) 'Institutional Issues Involving Ethics and Justice Theme', *Encyclopaedia of Life Support Systems* (Oxford: EOLSS Publishers Co.).

Shaw, A.G.L. (1955), *The Story of Australia* (London: Faber and Faber).

Shaw, W. (1999), *Business Ethics* (London: Wadsworth).

Sinclair, A. (1998), *Doing Management Differently: Gender Power and Sexuality in a Changing Business Culture* (Melbourne: Melbourne University Press).

Solomon, R. (1992), 'Ethics and Excellence: Co-operation and Integrity in Business', quoted in K. Woldring (ed.) (1996), *Business Ethics In Australia and New Zealand* (Melbourne: Thomas Nelson).

Solomon, R.C. (1994), *Above the Bottom Line*, 2nd edn (Sydney: Harcourt Brace).

Taylor, G. (1981), 'Integrity', *Proceedings of the Aristotelian Society* 55 (Supplementary).

Vogel, S. (2001), 'Corporate Integrity and Globalisation: The Dawning of a New Era of Accountability and Transparency', *Shoemaker Lecture*, Pennsylvania State University, 23 March, available at <http://www.ethics.org/articles.html>.

Woldring, K. (ed.) (1996), *Business Ethics in Australia and New Zealand: Essays and Cases* (Melbourne: Thomas Nelson).

Chapter 7

Is There a New South Wales Public Integrity System? A Preliminary Assessment

Rodney Smith

This chapter outlines the methodology and work-in-progress conclusions of the New South Wales public sector component of the National Integrity System Assessment. It describes the approach taken to assessing the NSW system, highlighting the difficulties of developing an assessment methodology from first principles, the possibly unique jurisdictional factors that arise to colour such an assessment, inherent limitations in the approach, and questions for how such assessments might be done in the future. The chapter focuses most heavily on issues of coherence in the NSW public sector integrity system, which is relatively complex. Although NSW integrity agencies can be divided into core, peripheral and specialist agencies, the relationships of different NSW agencies to the suite of integrity agencies vary considerably. Moreover, while NSW public sector agencies seem to be divided on whether the integrity agencies are well coordinated enough, the existence of multiple integrity agencies appears to have disadvantages for complainants, integrity agencies and agencies under their scrutiny. The coherence of the NSW integrity system must therefore be questioned. Major steps to improve the integrity system's coherence are likely to prove politically difficult, leaving open the possibility for smaller steps toward greater coherence worked out by agencies themselves.

Introduction

In May 2004, the joint parliamentary committee overseeing the NSW Independent Commission Against Corruption recommended that the government establish a judicial review into the agency. The committee criticized ICAC for investigating petty matters, low conviction rates and a lower burden of proof than criminal courts. ICAC's governing legislation was due for review after 15 years. ICAC should be refocused onto serious, systemic and costly corruption. Petty matters could be dealt with internally by public sector agencies or by the police, while the integrity of elected officials could be overseen by a new agency modelled on the Canadian Ethics Counsellor (Totaro 2004).

Two elements of this story repeat familiar patterns in the recent history of NSW integrity politics. The first is the ongoing search to find the best match between agencies and integrity issues. In this search, parliamentarians and others critical of the apparent failures of an integrity agency call for it to be disbanded or overhauled. The agency's functions are redistributed to other integrity agencies, including agencies themselves under continued scrutiny for ethical and investigative failures. The second is the gradual expansion of the number of integrity agencies, as new specialist agencies are proposed and established in an attempt to meet the deficiencies of the agencies whose functions they inherit. Although counter-swells of reform sometimes subsume smaller integrity agencies into larger bodies, the general tendency is for creeping increases in the number of integrity agencies that make up the NSW integrity system.

The purpose of this chapter is to conduct a preliminary mapping of the NSW public sector integrity system within the wider framework of the National Integrity System Assessment (see Pope 2000; Brown and Uhr 2004). The main data reported in this chapter are drawn from judgements and perceptions of senior NSW public sector officials concerning public sector integrity in NSW. In this context, integrity is understood broadly to encompass all efforts to ensure that NSW public sector activities fall within acceptable legal and ethical boundaries. This includes matters such as codes of conduct, fulfilling agencies' stated corporate missions, honesty and transparency in the culture of agencies, fraud and corruption control, staff training in ethics, investigation of maladministration, corruption or ethical lapses, disciplinary and other compliance or monitoring activities. The chapter adopts the coherence, capacity and consequences framework for analysing integrity systems proposed by A.J. Brown and John Uhr (2004).

The evidence of this chapter suggests that the NSW public sector integrity system is relatively complex. Although NSW integrity agencies can be divided into core, peripheral and specialist agencies, the relationships of different NSW agencies to the suite of integrity agencies vary considerably. Moreover, while NSW public sector agencies seem to be divided on whether the integrity agencies are well coordinated enough, the existence of multiple integrity agencies appears to have disadvantages for complainants, integrity agencies and agencies under their scrutiny. The coherence of the NSW integrity system must therefore be questioned. Major steps to improve the integrity system's coherence are likely to prove politically difficult, leaving open the possibility for smaller steps toward greater coherence worked out by agencies themselves.

The capacity of integrity agencies is hard to determine. Comparative data on staffing levels and budgetary expenditure suggest that NSW integrity agencies are relatively well resourced; however, the data hide fluctuations in the jurisdictional responsibilities of agencies that must be taken into account when estimating capacity. Money and staffing levels do not in themselves resolve the debate over where capacity ought to be directed. The evidence in this chapter suggests that the long-running debate between those who want capacity directed to coercive investigations and those who want it aimed at systemic and cultural change is a false one. The best integrity activities couple the two types of activity.

The consequences of integrity activity are also notoriously difficult to pin down. In NSW, judgements differ on the state of public sector integrity. Greater agreement exists that public sector integrity has improved over the last decade or so. While external integrity oversight appears to be responsible for some of that improvement, activities within public sector agencies appear to have been equally important.

Methodology

On the face of it, New South Wales has many of the 'pillars' and 'rules and practices' of an 'integrity system' suggested by Transparency International (Pope 2000).[1] These pillars and practices include an elected parliament, independent judiciary, free and fair elections, an independent media, a range of watchdog bodies and vibrant public debate within its civil society (see, for example, Smith 2003). Simply identifying and ticking off each of these institutions and practices may, however, give a misleading picture of the integrity system. The ways in which these institutions and practices inter-relate and combine, or fail to do so, provides a more important test of an integrity *system* than their mere presence (see Pope 2000, 37).

To get at these inter-relations and combinations requires moving beyond a checklist approach. This chapter proposes an alternative approach in which integrity institutions are understood as being part of a network. Jean Cartier-Bresson (1997) has argued that much public sector corruption can be conceptualized in terms of networks that develop between officials in bureaucratic agencies. To mobilize resources and get things done in compartmentalized bureaucracies, officials need to establish networks across institutions. These networks are characterized by 'concrete hidden practices' – legal and illegal – that do not register on the official charters and practices of institutions (Cartier-Bresson 1997, 53). As Cartier-Bresson (1997, 55) puts it:

> ... the network creates a web of pertinent interlocutors who are concerned with the definition of problems needing to be resolved and by their solutions. The network takes shape by assuming from the start that the legal boundaries of organizations are already scrambled ....

These ideas can be adapted to conceptualize networks of integrity efforts across institutions. The presence of a number of integrity agencies means that each is unlikely to be effective without a workable day-to-day relationship with others. No matter how carefully compartmentalized their formal powers, the

---

1 Perhaps this is not surprising, since the Transparency International pillars and practices grew partly out of an examination of Australia. The legal, political and societal elements in TI's suggestions for developing integrity are not particularly novel. See, for example, the similar prescriptions at the conclusion of P.N. Grabosky's (1989) analysis of public sector illegality in Australia.

nature of the integrity problems that they are trying to resolve will scramble the legal boundaries between them. The Ombudsman, for example, may be formally established to deal with maladministration and the ICAC to deal with corruption; however, some events brought to the attention of these agencies will involve both types of integrity failure. Similarly, specific integrity failures will scramble formal lines of division of agencies between those concerned with minor corruption and those that deal with significant corruption. If the goal of officials within these agencies is to resolve integrity problems, they will have to develop the sorts of networks based on concrete anti-corruption practices that mirror Cartier-Bresson's depiction of corruption networks. The nature and strength of these integrity networks, rather than the mere formal presence of integrity agencies, will define the integrity system and help determine its success or failure.

The development of these integrity networks could best be researched at the micro level through detailed observation of agency practices. The practical disadvantage of this methodology is that it would be very difficult to build up enough observations to draw system-wide conclusions. For this reason, the current study uses an alternative research tool, a series of structured interviews with senior NSW public sector agency officials covering the relationships between different NSW integrity agencies. While this approach yields fewer details of the precise practices that comprise NSW integrity networks, it allows those networks to be mapped in a reasonably consistent way across the NSW public sector.

The interview schedule on which this NSW mapping was based was initially adapted from the questionnaire used in the Queensland section of the NISA research (KCELJAC and TI 2001). The instrument was refined by subsequent discussions among the NISA researchers. A group of NSW public sector members of the Corruption Prevention Network offered critical comments on the interview schedule at a focus group meeting in November 2003, which led to further minor refinements.[2] The final interview schedule covered perceptions of integrity across the NSW public sector and in respondents' own agencies, assessments of the importance, quality and promptness of a range of specific NSW integrity agencies, the most important types of integrity-related activity, the level of coordination across integrity agencies, areas for integrity improvement and impediments to improvement in the NSW public sector. A self-completion questionnaire mirroring the questions and structure of the interview schedule was also developed.

Major NSW public sector agencies, including agencies whose primary responsibility was integrity protection, were identified from a larger list of 130 'Key NSW Government Agencies' posted on the New South Wales Government web pages (New South Wales Government 2004). Letters were sent to the heads of 37 agencies from February 2004, setting out the goals of the study and requesting

2 The NSW-based Corruption Prevention Network began in 1994 as a 'networking and self-help group' within the public sector sharing 'information and experiences in dealing with the challenges of fraud control'. It later expanded its focus to wider forms of corruption and now 'welcomes the participation of anybody in Australia and internationally, from both the private and public sector, who is interested in preventing fraud and corruption' (Corruption Prevention Network 2004).

a face to face interview. A self-completion questionnaire was offered as an alternative. Participants were assured of their anonymity unless they agreed to be identified in the study. The first of the eleven interviews reported in this chapter took place on 10 February 2004 and the last on 24 June 2004. Interviews were conducted by the author, Michelle Savage and Richard Mills. Four other agencies responded by questionnaire. About one-half of all interview and questionnaire respondents were heads or assistant heads of agencies; the remainder were senior agency officers with specific probity roles.[3]

The 15 NSW public sector agencies whose responses form the basis for much of this chapter included six integrity agencies, two central coordinating agencies and seven line agencies. The seven line agencies range considerably in function and size. Most of the respondents from agencies requested anonymity, including almost all of the respondents from line agencies. Because of this, agency responses are generally identified by number throughout this chapter (Agency 1 etc.) and quotations from interviews have had identifying comments removed. Although these measures to preserve anonymity mean that some details of the relationships within the integrity network cannot be adequately conveyed in this chapter, the overall patterns of those relationships can be reported.

Coherence

The possible ideal type models of integrity agency coherence are relatively limited. At one end of the spectrum we could imagine a single super integrity agency with comprehensive powers and responsibilities. This agency would almost certainly be divided internally into specialist sections. The problem of coherence in such a model would lie within the organization, in the relationships between its sections.

The other end of the spectrum would be occupied by many small, more or less specialist agencies, each formally independent of the others. In this model, the problem of coherence becomes externalized in the relationships between the agencies. Problems of coherence manifest themselves in duplication of integrity effort and gaps in integrity coverage. The extent to which these become problems is likely to differ according to the attitudes of the agencies to each other. Agencies that cooperate with each other seem more likely to reduce duplication but allow gaps to develop, as hard cases are left for other agencies to pick up. Agencies that compete with each other are likely to reduce the gaps in integrity coverage as they fight over jurisdictional territory but they are likely also to increase duplication of effort. Agencies that operate in indifference to each other – neither cooperating nor competing – will most likely engender both gaps and overlap.

3 Interviews and questionnaire for the study are continuing. The results will be incorporated into later publications. The final list of participants will include key NSW integrity focused non-government organizations, as well as key NSW news media organizations.

Actually existing integrity systems like that in NSW lie between these two poles, with a combination of larger generalist agencies and smaller specialists agencies. Thus the problems of coherence are both inter- and intra-agency. While intra-agency coherence is an important issue, this chapter focuses on inter-agency coherence.

In NSW, integrity efforts are spread across a wide range of agencies. The senior public servants interviewed for this study were asked to nominate the relative importance to their own agency of integrity agencies and organizations. Ten public sector agencies or types of organizations were listed in the interview schedule and questionnaire. Respondents were invited to supplement the list with any agencies or organizations they thought important.[4]

The results are presented in Table 7.1 The table shows the mean rating of each agency's importance as judged by the 15 respondents (the lower the figure, the more important the agency or organization) and the number of respondents judging each agency or organization to be at least 'fairly' important.

Twenty-three agencies and organizations are included in the table, with 21 judged fairly important to at least one agency. This in itself suggests that issues of inter-agency coherence are likely to be significant in New South Wales. A closer examination of the table suggests, however, that the NSW integrity system can be roughly divided into four groups of agencies or organizations. The core of the system consists of the generalist investigative agencies – the ICAC, the Ombudsman and the Audit Office. These core agencies are seen as important by almost all other agencies. Less central, but still relatively important, are the central legislative, judicial and executive agencies – parliamentary committees, courts and police, and the Premier's Department. The third and fourth groups consist of progressively less important organizations with general oversight (the Administrative Decisions Tribunal, the Privacy Commissioner and so on) and specialist integrity agencies that are important only for the particular agencies over which they have specific oversight (the Police Integrity Commission and the Health Care Complaints Commission).

Moreover, if we examine the relationships between the integrity agencies identified as most important within the overall system, they appear to be relatively coherent, at least on the measure of their own judgements. We would expect coherence between the ICAC, Ombudsman and Audit Office to be reflected in reinforcing judgements by each that the other two agencies are important, provide good quality advice and service, and provide it promptly. Figure 7.1 suggests that this is the case, although it is worth at least noting in passing that the ICAC judged its fellow integrity agencies more critically than did the Ombudsman or

4 The item also asked respondents to rate the importance of the news media and non-government organizations in dealing with integrity issues. Both rated reasonably highly. The mean score for news media was 1.8 and they were seen as at least fairly important by 11 of 14 agency respondents. Non-government organizations were scored 2.2 and seen as at least fairly important by eight of 14 respondents. The role of these integrity actors from within New South Wales civil society will not be covered here but will be discussed in other publications resulting from the research.

Table 7.1 NSW public sector agency perceptions of the importance of integrity agencies and organizations

Agencies and organisations[a]	Mean rating of importance[b]	Numbers thinking agency at least fairly important[c]
Independent Commission Against Corruption*	1.4	13 of 14
Ombudsman*	1.6	12 of 14
Audit Office*	1.7	13 of 14
Premier's Department*	2.0	9 of 14
Courts*	2.4	9 of 15
Parliamentary Committees*	2.4	7 of 15
Police force*	2.6	8 of 15
Administrative Decisions Tribunal*	2.8	5 of 15
Health Care Complaints Tribunal*	2.9	2 of 14
Police Integrity Commission*[d]	3.1	3 of 15
Office of the Children's Guardian	3.3	3 of 15
Privacy Commissioner	3.3	2 of 15
Commission for Children and Young People	3.6	2 of 15
Coroner	3.8	1 of 15
Police Integrity Commission Inspector	3.8	1 of 15
Official Visitors	3.8	1 of 15
Royal Commissions	3.8	1 of 15
Joint Investigative Response Teams	3.8	1 of 15
Judicial Commission	3.8	1 of 15
Director of Public Prosecutions	3.9	1 of 15
NSW Crime Commission	3.9	1 of 15
Anti-Discrimination Board	3.9	0 of 15
Legal Services Commission	3.9	0 of 15

Notes:

a Agency respondents were shown a list of agencies and organizations and asked to rate the importance of each in dealing with integrity issues for their own agency. The listed agencies are indicated with an * in this table. Respondents were invited to add further agencies to the list and rate them.

b The response categories were: 'very important', scored 1; 'fairly important, scored 2; 'not very important', scored 3; and 'not at all important' and 'can't say', both scored 4. Mean scores can thus range from 1.0 to 4.0, with a mid-point of 2.5. The lower the score, the more important the agency or organization in the eyes of the respondents.

c Since respondents were not asked to rate their own agencies in this question, some agencies have been rated by only thirteen respondents, rather than fourteen.

d At the time of writing, the authors had not interviewed a respondent from the NSW Police Force, the agency most likely to rate highly the importance of the Police Integrity Commission.

Audit Office. Interviews with these agencies suggest that these close links were maintained in a range of ways, including formal referrals of matters, cooperation on investigations, staff movements from one agency to another, and sharing of each others' perspectives through agency publications.

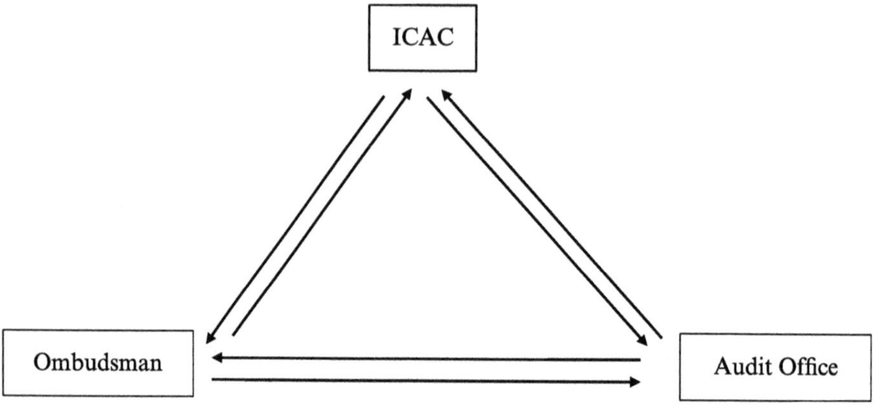

Figure 7.1 Relationships between the Independent Commission Against Corruption, the NSW Ombudsman and the NSW Audit Office

Note: The direction of the arrows indicates the direction of judgements made by the agencies. Each score is the mean of three items covering judgements about the importance of an agency on integrity matters, the quality of the agency's advice and actions, and the promptness of the agency's advice and actions. Potential scores range from 1.0 (very important, very good quality and very prompt) to 4.0 (not at all important or can't say, poor quality and poor on promptness), with a midpoint of 2.5.

Taking a bird's eye view, then, the NSW integrity system appears relatively coherent and manageable, with just a handful of closely aligned agencies centrally concerned with integrity work and a larger number involved only in a relatively peripheral or specialized way. From the perspective of individual agencies on the ground looking out into the system, however, the picture is often quite different. Table 7.2 shows this perspective.

A greater potential problem of system coherence can be seen in this table. The median number of important integrity agencies and organizations with which NSW public sector agencies have to deal is six, with some dealing with up to nine or ten. There is no clear relationship between the broad type of public sector agency and the number of integrity bodies which it views as important, although line agencies with clients who pose clear integrity or vulnerability risks tend to fall above the median figure. The anomalous agency in this table is Agency 15, whose respondent claimed that none of the integrity agencies were important. This did not mean that Agency 15 had no contact with integrity agencies. Instead, it reflects the respondent's judgement that those integrity agencies had uniformly

Table 7.2 Relationships between NSW public sector agencies and integrity agencies and organizations

	ICAC	Omb	Aud-Gen	Prem	Courts	Parl	Police	ADT	HCCC	PIC	OCG	Other 1	Other 2	Other 3	Total
Agency 3	+	++	+		++	++		+			+	++	++	++	10
Agency 7	++	++	++	++	++	+	++	+				++			9
Agency 9		+	+	++	+	+	+			+		+	+		9
Agency 13	++	++	+		++		++	+	++	++		++			9
Agency 4	++	++	++	+	+		++	++			+	++			8
Agency 8	++	++	++	++			+		++		+	++			8
Agency 10	++	+	++	++	++	++									6
Agency 11	++		++			+	++			++		+			6
Agency 5	++		+	++	++		+								5
Agency 6	++	+	++	++	+										5
Agency 12	+	+	+			+						++			5
Agency 14	+	++	+	+				++							5
Agency 1	++	++		+		+									4
Agency 2	++	++	+		+										4
Agency 15															0

failed and therefore were not important. From Agency 15's point of view, the source of integrity system failure seemed to lie with capacity rather than coherence. For the majority of NSW agencies, who see working with a number of integrity agencies, coherence is a potentially pressing problem.

How much coherence do NSW agencies see in the integrity system? As one indicator, respondents were asked to rate the level of coordination they perceived between NSW integrity agencies. The responses were widely dispersed. Of the 13 agencies that answered this question, two thought the level of coordination between integrity agencies was very good and five that it was fairly good. Agency 13 represented this view:

> [Y]ou have this matrix of watchdogs in New South Wales, and you won't find them stepping over each other's bodies to get to an issue. There's a very professional, well-honed process and interrelationship. For instance, if anyone makes a complaint about a judicial officer, the Ombudsman or the ICAC would defer to the Judicial Commission to undertake that investigation, because it's best placed.

On the other hand, four agencies thought the level of coordination was not very good and two that it was poor. Agency 6 commented:

> [It's n]on-existent. There's a level of comparison between Ombudsman and ICAC. Both refer to each other in dealing with matters such as conflicts of interest. Apart from that, it's poor.

An agency's judgement about the level of coordination was not related to the number of integrity agencies with which that agency had important relationships. Instead, a fairly clear division emerged between the integrity and central agencies on the one hand and the line agencies on the other. All but one of the integrity and central agencies judged the level of coordination to be at least fairly good, while the strongest critics of the lack of coordination were found among the line agencies. The line agencies seemed to feel the consequences of a lack of coordination more sharply than the integrity and central agencies. According to Agency 8, these consequences included resource diversion and staff fatigue in agencies responding to overlapping investigations of the same incident, the encouragement of 'gaming' among complainants who know they can lodge complaints with a range of agencies, poaching of staff by integrity agencies competing for the small pool of personnel with forensic skills and, as a result, a loss of corporate memory within integrity agencies.

Regardless of their judgements about the level of coordination between the agencies, all the agencies interviewed implicitly or explicitly acknowledged that cooperative relationships between agencies were important. Only one respondent raised the idea in passing that competition between integrity agencies could be in itself be desirable. None seemed satisfied with a situation in which integrity agencies operated without regard for the operations of each other.

Eliminating competition and indifference between agencies as acceptable models leaves greater cooperation between integrity agencies and partial or full merging of agencies as the two available alternatives to the issue of coherence. Agency merger has proved politically difficult, as the interviewee from Agency 13 notes:

> I think it's worked out pretty well, in recent times. We've had a bit of a rationalisation with the Ombudsman taking on the responsibility of the Children's Services Commissioner, and the ADT [Administrative Decisions Tribunal] being set up .... And people have thought, over the years, of the idea of merging ICAC and the Ombudsman and the Police Integrity Commission into one. But I think it's the way the system has grown up. ... [T]here's no ideal structure. It's part of the history, and I think it's working okay, and they seem to have worked out relationships between them.

The last attempt to partially merge the Ombudsman and ICAC was proposed in 1999, when the outgoing Ombudsman Irene Moss became ICAC Commissioner. She proposed merging the two jobs to allow better coordination and division of responsibilities between the two agencies. Premier Bob Carr immediately embraced the idea but just as quickly dropped it due to opposition from the Coalition parties and some minor parties in the Legislative Council (see Humphries 1999).

The most important NSW integrity agencies have evolved in a piecemeal way, largely as a direct or indirect result of partisan imperatives. The oldest NSW watchdog body, the Audit Office, can trace its history back to 1870 with the establishment of the Auditor-General as an independent official; however, it is only since the 1980s that the agency has played an expanded role in integrity investigation and monitoring through expansion of its auditing powers (see the *NSW Public Finance and Audit Act 1983*; Parker 1978, 283–4, 361; Funnell and Cooper 1998, 282–6). The parliamentary Public Accounts Committee that has in recent years worked closely with the Audit Office in this expanded role was until the late 1970s seen as having an 'ignominious history' (Parker 1978, 236) until it became a stepping stone for ambitious MLAs such as Nick Greiner, Peter Collins and Bob Carr (Funnell and Cooper 1998, 286; Collins 2000, 139–40; West and Morris 2003, 134–5).

The establishment of the NSW Ombudsman came ten years after the Liberal Party included the idea in its 1965 election manifesto. The *NSW Ombudsman Act 1974* allowed the Ombudsman to investigate complaints against public agencies on its own initiative but exempted a range of offices from scrutiny, including ministers, courts and tribunals, police, local councils. The Wran Government extended the Ombudsman's scrutiny to local government and later to police (Parker 1978, 441–4). As noted earlier, in the 1990s, the Community Services Commission (a watchdog body primarily interested in the Department of Community Services) was incorporated into the Ombudsman, while its role in child protection increased following the Wood Royal Commission.

The Coalition Government of Nick Greiner set up the Independent Commission Against Corruption in 1988, partly because of its apparent potential to investigate actions of its Labor opponents while they had been in power over the previous decade. Then Opposition Leader Bob Carr supported the establishment of ICAC, against the wishes of strong elements in his party (Chaples and Page 1995; Dodkin 2003, 13–15, 46; West and Morris 2003, 168–74, 206). By the mid-1990s, Coalition critics were calling for the disbanding of ICAC. This hostility was largely driven by ICAC's 1992 corruption findings against Greiner and Tim Moore, later overturned in the Supreme Court. It was also directed at ICAC's failure to uncover police corruption and organized criminal activity. The Independents and Labor passed a motion supporting a royal commission into police corruption (Chaples and Page 1995, 69; West and Morris 2003, 258–9). The consequent Police Royal Commission under James Wood in turn proposed the creation of the Police Integrity Commission (PIC) to deal with police corruption. While the Ombudsman retained its role in investigating minor complaints against police, the PIC took over the ICAC's former role of investigating police corruption (Lagan 1996).

This brief historical excursion indicates that the prospect of mergers between NSW integrity agencies based on considerations of the desirable overall pattern of integrity coverage is no strong. That leaves the possibility of the agencies themselves forging closer cooperative networks as the most likely avenue for increased coherence. As was indicated above, willingness to cooperate often seems present. Two further barriers stand in the way of greater cooperation. The first is legal barriers, and particularly the operation of the *NSW Privacy Act*, which inhibits agencies sharing information:

> Most of the agencies are more than happy to cooperate but coordination's the problem, given all of our various secrecy provisions and the Privacy Act has made that more difficult. With the Privacy Act, it wasn't drafted to clearly keep in mind that public officials shouldn't be able to use it to avoid scrutiny. We managed near the end to delay the act for a while we built in various exemption clauses, but that was an afterthought. ... So you've got all these different watchdog bodies, they all have varying jurisdictions and a number of them overlap to one extent or the other. You need to coordinate the activities of those bodies, as I say it's difficult because to a large extent all of us can't talk to each other. (Agency 11)

The second is the refusal of budgetary bodies to allow funds to be spent on cooperative projects between agencies. The interviewee from Agency 11 gives two examples of this barrier:

> We managed to convince the heads of most of the complaint handling bodies in NSW that we should co-locate. ... [W]e could have a common reception, meeting rooms, hearing rooms, libraries, etc, etc. A one stop shop and the Premier's Department was quite keen and they started to do all the costings but this was rolled at the last minute by the Government Accommodation Management Committee who said ah no no, it would cost too much money.
>
> So then we came up with another approach which was the complaint counter and this would be an electronic portal. So, faxes, phones, emails, web pages, all the rest of it, one place. You just went in there and all that material would be assessed and work out which place it should go to. So you didn't need to know about all the different agencies and whatever, you just needed to know about the complaint counter, send it in. And we had our webpage booked, all the agencies had agreed, we'd gone through the privacy issues, worked it all out. We had a grant from the information technology people to improve electronic access to the public. ... It was all on the go. And then the Treasury said that's fine about the capital money but you're not allowed to spend it ... Basically the [project] was put on hold.

Treasury later withdrew the funding and the project closed down.

These examples help to make the point that failures of coherence among the NSW integrity agencies cannot be laid entirely at the feet of the agencies themselves. The political, legal and budgetary frameworks within which integrity agencies operate are just as important in promoting or frustrating coherence.

Capacity

The capacity of integrity agencies is often understood in terms of resources. As R.S. Parker observed some years ago, '... the Public Service Board and Treasury between them, or perhaps the Treasury alone, could make the Auditor-General himself ineffectual, because they control his staff and its salaries' (Parker 1978, 285). By this simple measure, the capacity of the NSW integrity system is relatively high. Figure 7.2 indicates that compared with Victoria, NSW spends a higher proportion of its state budget on central integrity agencies. Indeed, NSW seems to spend a higher proportion than Victoria on its Ombudsman, despite also having other agencies such as ICAC and the PIC who share the integrity work done by the Ombudsman alone in Victoria. The comparative NSW and Victorian figures for staffing are similar.

While these figures undoubtedly point to real differences between the two states, they must be treated with some caution. Viewed from the inside, the New South Wales Treasury has not always seemed a generous provider of capacity to its integrity agencies. In 1998, then Ombudsman Irene Moss complained that her annual budget of $5.8 million would not meet public service pay increases, while her staff faced an increased workload of 25 per cent (Murphy 1998). Soon

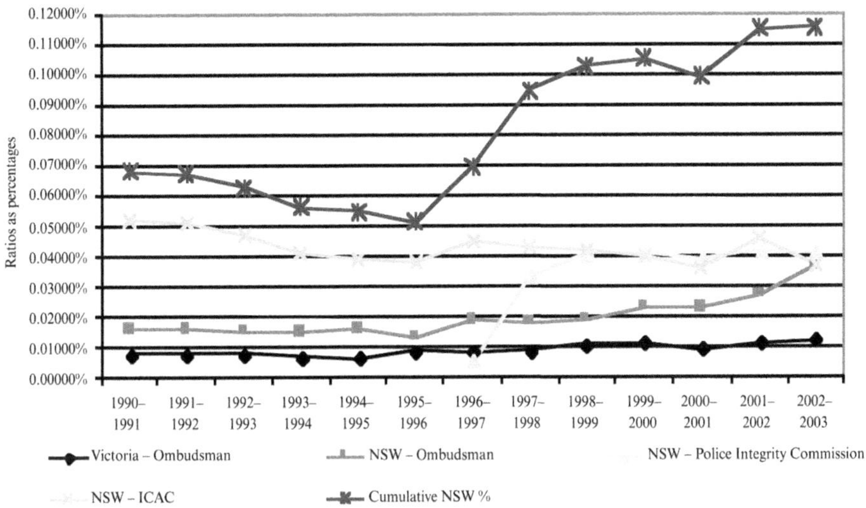

Figure 7.2 NSW v Victoria public sector watchdogs – individual and cumulative comparison of ratios

after Moss made her complaint, her agency came to an 'informal agreement' with NSW Treasury to increase the Ombudsman's funding in line with the range of new statutory responsibilities it was acquiring. The incorporation of the former Community Services Commission into the Ombudsman, for example, brought with it 48 staff and increased funding (interview). Thus although the NSW Ombudsman has the largest staff in Australia – its 168 in 2002–2003 compares with 82 for the Commonwealth and 50 for Queensland – a good deal of this growth in capacity is due to growth in the Ombudsman's statutory responsibilities.

Similarly, although the Police Integrity Commission has received solid funding since 1996–1997 and has built a staff of around 100, some of this capacity has come at the expense of the ICAC. The ICAC has, since 1998–1999, lost around one quarter of its staff and has also seen its budget drop. Once responsibility for police corruption shifted from the ICAC to the PIC, resources soon followed. In these circumstances, judging whether the overall capacity of the NSW integrity system has been enhanced is difficult.

Resourcing levels affect the investigative capacity of individual integrity agencies. Irene Moss has spoken of an '80 per cent rule' – integrity agencies get 80 percent of what they need, so they have to refer most issues back to agencies for internal examination (Rayner 2003, 27). An interviewee from Agency 9 put the same point in a more positive way:

> Of course more resources would help but we also accept that we're part of a state budget. The state has its objectives and the budget is divvied out accordingly. That's sort of like saying to the Department of Community Services – would it help you if you have more resources? Yes it would – of course it would. But, you have to manage

with what you've got and it's a bit like how long is a piece of string. We could be the super agency with super resources and still not get it all done.

... But, from our perspective, we encourage the public sector to take responsibility for their integrity issues. ... [A]t the end of the day, its for them to build their integrity systems and we'll help them with that but we can't be the enforcer of integrity in their organisations because that's got to come from within – it won't work if it comes from outside. And that's why you get such a good outcome following an investigation because then you've go the CEO's attention. It relates back to the leadership issue.

These comments address the crucial issue of where existing capacity ought to be directed. Increases in funding and staffing may not represent real integrity gains if they are directed ineffectively. A long-running debate exists in the ethics and integrity literature between those who want capacity directed to coercive investigations and those who want it aimed at improving systems and changing cultures. The implicit model in the comments above is that both are important and that external investigations are valuable to the extent that they drive organizational reform and cultural change.

This model seems to be shared by most of the agencies interviewed for this study. Asked to identify the most significant types of contact between their agency and integrity agencies, the most common responses were information from integrity agencies, followed by investigations, ad hoc assistance and meetings. Asked to identify the most important types of activity for achieving a high level of integrity across the New South Wales public sector, the most common responses were education and training, followed by organizational leadership and then external and internal investigations. Several respondents explicitly linked investigations with organizational leadership and cultural change in the same way as the interviewee from Agency 9.

These findings suggest that external investigative resources should not be the sole measure of integrity agency capacity. External investigations are important – failed investigations underlie the negative judgements of the integrity system made by two agencies in this study. Integrity agencies must retain the resources to carry out external investigations. Nonetheless, the crucial element of capacity is the capacity to use these investigations to bring about wider change.

Consequences

The consequences of integrity activity are notoriously difficult to measure. As is widely recognized, increases in reported corruption may indicate the success rather than failure of integrity agencies. The measure used in this chapter is the judgements of senior NSW public servants. Their judgements differ widely on the state of NSW public sector integrity. Asked how well they thought integrity issues were currently handled generally in the New South Wales public sector, some respondents found it difficult to make blanket judgements:

[I]t's handled better in some agencies than in others. There are some, like the Police and like this one, that are dealing with these issues all the time, and they have an established

> machinery to handle them. There are others that come across examples infrequently, and need advice and support when it happens. So, it's a variable picture, but certainly in the bigger agencies, one that's dealt with at a high level. (Agency 4)

Two-thirds of those who did give a clear answer judged integrity issues to be handled 'very' or 'fairly' well across NSW, with the remainder answering 'not very well' or 'not at all well'. The pattern was almost identical when they were asked to judge their own agencies.

The most striking similarity in their answers was their assurance that the NSW public sector and their agencies had both improved their handling of integrity issues over the past ten years. This was true of all but one of the respondents who judged integrity issues to be relatively badly handled in the NSW public sector. The respondent from Agency 6, for example, thought that integrity issues were not handled very well across NSW, but still saw improvement over time: 'There's more effort now when issues come to notice. Ten years ago, it was "Who cares?" Now there's the expectation of third party scrutiny by the ICAC.'

Can this perceived improvement be attributed to the activities of NSW integrity agencies? The answer given by the senior NSW public servants seems to be 'at least in part'. Asked to explain what they saw as the most important factors behind the trends in their own agencies' handling of integrity issues, over half of the respondents raised the activities of integrity agencies in their answers. The other factors mentioned were, on the face of it, internal to agencies, including the development of codes and procedures and risk assessment activities. Whether these internal changes were prompted indirectly by the activities of NSW integrity agencies is difficult to determine.

Conclusion

This chapter has, in a preliminary way, indicated the value of an approach to mapping and assessing integrity systems that goes beyond checking off the presence or absence of particular institutions. The relationships between those institutions have been shown to be more important in the NSW context than the mere presence of institutions. In this sense, a network analysis seems to have much to offer analysts of integrity systems.

This chapter has gone some way to developing the concepts of coherence, capacity and consequences suggested by Brown and Uhr (2004). None of these concepts is as straightforward as they initially seem. This chapter has also suggested some measures for each concept that could be applied to compare different integrity systems.

Finally, the chapter has mapped in a rather crude way, the coherence, capacity and consequences of the NSW integrity system. New South Wales has an integrity system that is relatively complex. The main hope for greater coherence in the system lies in removing barriers to cooperation between its multiple integrity agencies. The NSW integrity system appears comparatively resource rich. The challenge is to continually direct these resources into investigations that promote organizational reform and cultural change. The final section of this chapter suggests that, with one or two notable exceptions, this consequence is being increasingly achieved.

References

Brown, A.J. and Uhr, J. (2004), 'Integrity Systems: Conceiving, Describing, Assessing', paper prepared for the 2004 Australasian Political Studies Association Conference, 29 September–1 October (Adelaide: University of Adelaide).

Cartier-Bresson, J. (1997), 'Corruption Networks, Transaction Security and Illegal Social Exchange', in P. Heywood (ed.) *Political Corruption* (Oxford: Blackwell).

Chaples, E. and Page, B. (1995), 'The New South Wales Independent Commission Against Corruption', in M. Laffin and M. Painter (eds) *Reform and Reversal: Lessons from the Coalition Government in New South Wales 1988–1995* (Melbourne: Macmillan).

Collins, P. (2000), *The Bear Pit: A Life in Politics* (Sydney: Allen and Unwin).

Corruption Prevention Network (2004), *Corruption Prevention Network* (updated 9 June 2004) <http://www.corruptionprevention.net//>.

Dodkin, M. (2003), *Bob Carr: The Reluctant Leader* (Sydney: University of New South Wales Press).

Funnell, W. and Cooper, K. (1998), *Public Sector Accounting and Accountability in Australia* (Sydney: University of New South Wales Press).

Grabosky, P.N. (1989), *Wayward Governance: Illegality and Its Control in the Public Sector* (Canberra: Australian Institute of Criminology).

Humphries, D. (1999), 'Super Watchdog Concept Dies in Upper House', *Sydney Morning Herald* 19 September, 3.

KCELJAG and TI (2001), *Australian National Integrity Systems Assessment: Queensland Handbook* (Brisbane: Key Centre for Ethics, Law, Justice and Governance, Griffith University, and Transparency International).

Lagan, B. (1996), 'Inquiry Sparks Police Shake-Up', *Sydney Morning Herald* 5 February, 1.

Murphy, D. (1998), 'Ombudsman Reveals Staff and Pay Crisis', *Sydney Morning Herald* 9 July, 3.

New South Wales Government (2004), *Key NSW Government Agencies*, <http://www.nsw.gov.au/search_results.asp?SEARCH_KEYS=Home+Pages+NSW+key&SEARCH_FLAG=sub_link_type_search>.

Parker, R.S. (1978), *The Government of New South Wales* (St Lucia: University of Queensland Press).

Pope, J. (2000), *Confronting Corruption: The Elements of a National Integrity System* (Berlin: Transparency International).

Rayner, M. (2003), 'Watchdogs Put Down', *Eureka Street*, 26–27 April.

Smith, R. (2003), 'New South Wales', in J. Moon and C. Sharman (eds) *Australian Politics and Government: The Commonwealth, The States and the Territories* (Cambridge: Cambridge University Press).

Smith, R. (2006), 'NSW Parliamentary Committees and Integrity Oversight: Comparing Public Sector Agency, News Media and NGO Perspectives', *Australasian Parliamentary Review* 21:1, 47–62.

Totaro, P. (2004). 'Corruption Watchdog to Face Judicial Review', *Sydney Morning Herald* 24 May, 3.

West, A. and Morris, R. (2003), *Bob Carr: A Self-Made Man* (Sydney: HarperCollins).

Chapter 8

A Federal Integrity System at the Crossroads: Australia

Peter Roberts

Introduction

In assessing the strengths of Commonwealth's integrity arrangements, the overwhelming issue is the lack of evidence that there is a significant corruption problem in Commonwealth administration. The statistical information from the Australian Federal Police and the Director of Public Prosecutions indicates low levels of corruption being detected and prosecuted. Nor are there any press reports of endemic problems in Commonwealth administration. With the exception of the issues relating to accountability, it is notable that the overwhelming majority of reports in the media about corruption are reports of cases that were detected internally. Also, all officials interviewed or surveyed in the course of this study expressed the view that corruption in Commonwealth administration is not a serious problem.

In terms of the systemic elements, the following arrangements are assisting in preventing corruption:

- there are highly sophisticated financial management arrangements with a statutory basis;
- independent and highly regarded investigation, prosecution and judiciary processes;
- there is active and independent monitoring by the Ombudsman and the Auditor-General; and
- the statutory accountability arrangements are backed up by review by the upper house of Parliament, using its powers, and were the government does not have a majority.

The major weaknesses identifies in this study ones are:

- subsuming corruption within the fraud arrangements means that some corruption activity may go unnoticed and that the prevention emphasis may be skewed towards fixing systems rather than on the cultural dimension;
- reporting mechanisms make it difficult to ascertain the exact level of corruption. This has policy implications for the government in that were

systemic corruption problems arise, they may not be recognized early enough;

- whistleblowing arrangements are inadequate;
- the emphasis upon encouraging agencies to manage their own governance arrangements means that the whole-of-government integrity system does not have any clear leader or champion. The Australian Public Service Commissioner has *de facto* filled this role, in part. The announcement by the government that a national anti-corruption body is to be established will not address this issue because that proposal, even if implemented, would be limited to investigation of police corruption; and
- there are issues about the independence of senior officials from the political process.

Methodological Issues

Because the Commonwealth component was the second looking at a public sector administration, it follows upon the methodology developed for the Queensland component. Some modifications to the approach were made for the Commonwealth study. Because the author of the Commonwealth study had considerable experience of the Commonwealth's integrity arrangements, the interviews could dispense with much of the fact-finding function and were able to explore more deeply the attitudinal approaches to integrity among the participants. The interviews were semi-structured based around a series of questions.[1] Interviews were conducted with representatives of eight agencies with central responsibility for integrity matters:

- Attorney-General's Department;
- Australian Electoral Commission;
- Australian Federal Police;
- Australian National Audit Office;
- Australian Public Service Commission;
- Department of Finance and Administration;
- Office of the Director of Public Prosecutions;
- Office of the Commonwealth Ombudsman.

Interviews were conducted with representatives of five 'line' agencies, i.e. responsible for the implementation of the integrity policies set by the central agencies:

- Australian Taxation Office;
- CSIRO;
- Department of Defence;
- Department of Education Science and Technology;
- Department of Employment and Workplace Relations.

---

1 See Annex A.

Also, the questionnaire developed for the Queensland study was modified and circulated to a number of agencies, with ten agencies responding:

- Attorney-General's Department;
- Australian Electoral Commission;
- Australian Public Service Commission;
- Department of Environment and Heritage;
- Department of Health and Aging;
- Department of Industry Tourism and Recreation;
- Health Insurance Commission;
- National Library of Australia;
- National Museum of Australia;
- Office of the Commonwealth Ombudsman.[2]

Before leaving the description of the methodology, there are some observations about the methodology that need to be made. First, the notion of an integrity system is not one that has universal understanding among all participants. Representatives of some agencies, particularly large line agencies like the Australian Taxation Office and the Department of Defence, made the linkages between the various elements that go to make up an effective integrity system. Many participants saw integrity in terms of a quality of the programmes that their agency was running, rather than a quality that defined the totality of the way in which the federal level of government operated. Another aspect of this narrower perspective was the way in which many participants saw the issues of integrity among public sector employees as an issue not closely related to the issue of integrity of Ministers or Members of Parliament.

Second, agencies were contacted and asked to nominate a representative to participate in the study. Consequently, the researcher was in the hands of the participants as to the knowledge and experience that they brought to the study. In some instances participants were very senior officers and able to synthesise the large amount of information necessary to provide answers to the questions that were put to them. In many cases, agencies had not internally brought together the systemic issues of integrity and were reluctant to expend the resources necessary to come to a point that could be seen as a collective view.

Finally, there is the extent to which asking senior officials to evaluate the effectiveness of integrity mechanisms for which they have responsibility leads to defensive responses. As will be outlined below, the Commonwealth has some very strong accountability and transparency mechanisms that mitigate the effect of this natural defensiveness – the administrative law package, annual report requirements, Senate Estimates Committees and the public reporting of the Ombudsman and the Auditor-General. To a significant extent, the keen researcher has access to a large range of public material that can enable responses to be verified. Also, some of the key integrity agencies like the AFP, Ombudsman and the Auditor-General have such a degree of autonomy that they are able to make

2 See Annex B.

robust evaluative comments that can be used to assess the degree to which other agencies are being overly defensive.

Quantitative Data on Corruption

One of the key aims of the NISA project was to look at a country that had a low level of corruption and to analyse why and how this was so. A preliminary step in the study was to reach some conclusions about the level of corruption in the Commonwealth.

Australia is not generally regarded as a country with a major corruption problem. It ranks eighth, in corruption free nations, in Transparency International's Corruption Perception Index for 2003. Noting the propensity of the Commonwealth to concentrate on fraud rather than corruption, the Director of Australian Institute of Criminology, Adam Graycar (2000) estimated that the total amount of fraud in Australia is somewhere between A$3 billion and A$3.5 billion, that estimate including fraud at all levels of government and in the private sector. In the 2000/01 financial year, Australia's GDP was A$670 billion.

To try to get some more precise measurement, it is necessary to go to a variety of sources. The Annual Reports of the Australian Federal Police (various dates) show the following for the number of cases of fraud and corruption investigated.

Table 8.1 Cases investigated by the Australian Federal Police

Year	Number of corruption cases investigated	Number of fraud cases investigated	Estimated value of fraud cases investigated
2002–2003	24	208	(not provided)
2001–2002	39	192	$252 million
2000–2001	40	272	$98 million
2000–2001	43	312	$207 million
1998–1999	143	308	$93 million
1997–1998	134	360	(not provided)

Of course, not all cases that are investigated are prosecuted. The Annual Reports of the Director of Public Prosecutions (various dates) show the following for the number of prosecutions of cases related to fraud and corruption.

Looking at these statistics, a number of issues are of interest.

- the ambiguity of subsuming corruption within fraud is evident. (This issue is discussed in detail later in this report). What the AFP refers to as 'corruption' is clearly being dealt with predominantly by the fraud provisions in the Criminal Code;

Table 8.2 Cases prosecuted by the Director of Public Prosecutions

Year	2002–2003		2001–2002		2000–2001		1999–2000		1998–1999	
Legislative provision**	S*	I*	S	I	S	I	S	I	S	I
Imposition (s29B Crimes Act)	118	23	93	31	116	55	128	61	150	87
Fraud (s29D Crimes Act)	95	143	107	133	104	59	67	159	73	111
Bribery (ss73&A Crimes Act)	–	1	1	1	0	1	1	4	1	2
Financial benefit by deception (Criminal Code s134.2)	15	32	10	3						
Obtaining financial advantage (Criminal Code s135.2)	730	1	19	0						
False information (Criminal Code s137.1)	4	0	1	0						
False Documents (Criminal Code s137.2)	7	0	0	0						
Corrupting benefits to C'wealth official (Criminal Code s142.1)	1	0	0	0						
Social Security Act	4681	3	5218	–	3953	–	3525	–	3638	–

Notes

* S = Summary, I = Indictable.
** Relevant provisions in the Criminal Code enacted recently.

- the quite extraordinarily low numbers for the incidence of bribing a Commonwealth official or paying corrupting benefits;
- the role of the AFP as investigator is limited to a relatively small proportion of the cases that are going through the prosecution process; and
- the preponderance in the prosecution of large numbers of cases of welfare fraud which are generally of quite small amounts and are handled by investigators in the payment agency, Centrelink, rather than by the police.

The information provided above does not really give any indication of the amount of what is reported, as fraud is corruption. Surveys by the Australian National Audit Office (ANAO) (2000a; b; c) found that a very significant extent of fraud was defined as 'internal' which would fall within the TI definition of corruption. The following table is reproduced from the report:

From this data, some observations can be made. Over the four-year period, 'internal fraud' was:

- 22.2 per cent of the total allegations;
- 22.5 per cent of the total number of cases;
- 2.9 per cent of the total value of the cases.

However, these observations have to be treated with caution. From the ANAO report itself:

Table 8.3 Extent of fraud reported by surveyed APS agencies in response to ANAO's 1999–2000 and 2002–2003 surveys

Financial years	Number of fraud allegations	Number of fraud cases	Value of fraud cases ($'000)
Internal fraud			
1997–1998	1,310	352	1,039
1998–1999	1,220	348	9,289
2000–2001	2,271	1,605	1,690
2001–2002	2,782	1,540	2,629
External fraud			
1997–1998	5,775	3,510	152,137
1998–1999	5,257	3,702	136,573
2000–2001	7,328	4,002	115,127
2001–2002	8,380	4,971	90,700

- not all agencies provided responses;
- not all agencies that responded were able to provide information on the value of cases;
- there were inconsistencies in what was regarded as fraud with some 32 per cent of agencies using an outdated definition of fraud; and
- in the later of the two surveys, 99 per cent of the reported fraud against Commonwealth agencies was committed against 10 per cent of agencies.

This issue about access to data about levels of corruption is not assisted by the Commonwealth's approach of not making public the data collected by virtue of the Fraud Control Policy (Guideline 8) (Minister for Justice and Customs 2002).

Before leaving the discussion of the level of corruption against the Commonwealth, it is worth mentioning three recent cases that received considerable publicity.

The first is the case of David Muir, a contract accountant with the Department of Finance and Administration. In 1998 he used his access rights to the Department's computer system to transfer some A$8.25 million into a series of private accounts. Very little of the funds were recovered. In 2000, David Muir was found guilty of defrauding the Commonwealth and given a sentence of seven years.

The case of Nick Petroulias[3] was even more startling. He had been recruited into the Australian Taxation Office (ATO) in 1997 from the private sector and quickly rose to be First Assistant Commissioner (a very senior position, with only

3 Nick Petroulias (a former senior executive with the ATO) who was charged with a series of offences related to abuse of office.

one layer of management between him and the CEO) (Lampe 2001). Part of his duties was to crack down on tax evasion schemes. He also had authority to issue private binding rulings where the operators of complex financial schemes could get advice from the ATO whether the ATO considered the proposed schemes were within the scope of the taxation legislation. Petroulias left the ATO in early 1999, and in 2000 the Australian Federal Police arrested him. It is alleged that rather than controlling tax avoidance schemes, he used his authority to issue private binding rulings to assist in their marketing, and profiting from the arrangement. He was charged with defrauding the Commonwealth and corrupt conduct. The case was vigorously defended but Petroulias was found guilty of two offences in June 2008 and sentenced to two years imprisonment.

In May 2002, Andrew Theophanous, the former Labor member for Calwell in the federal House of Representatives, was convicted of four charges of bribery and defrauding the Commonwealth. He was sentenced to six years jail, but served only 20 months. One of the charges was quashed on appeal. Theophanous was accused of seeking or obtaining thousands of dollars to help Chinese nationals with visa applications and other immigration matters. The charges also alleged that in one case Theophanous sought sexual favours from a woman.

The Office of the Commonwealth Ombudsman stated that it sees nothing to suggest that endemic corruption in Commonwealth administration exists; observing that corruption within agencies appears more individual than systematic.

Study Observation

It needs to be acknowledged that, as a jurisdiction, the Commonwealth makes a vast amount of information public about its operations. The particular pursuit of data about corruption is confounded primarily by the definitional issues surrounding the subsuming of corruption within the fraud control framework.

The comment can be made that the Commonwealth is not helping itself by this lack of definitive data. While there is no reason to doubt the assumption that the levels of corruption in Commonwealth administration are generally low, the lack of data would make it difficult for the Commonwealth to be sensitive to any sudden rise in the incidence of corruption and to take the steps to deal with it.

Leadership in Integrity

When considering the notion of an integrity system, an important consideration is the uniformity of the systemic elements across the administration.

Working in a Decentralized Environment

Like many other public sectors in the developed world, the Commonwealth has been deeply affected by the changes in public sector management. Over the last two decades, it has undergone substantial change, both in its internal management processes and in its methods of service delivery. These changes commenced in the Commonwealth public sector with the election of a centre-left Labor government in 1983. The first raft of changes was internal with the substantial weakening of the central coordinating agencies, flattening of complex administrative hierarchies and the devolution of management authority to agency heads.

The changes continued, with gathering momentum, through the 1980s and early 1990s. Performance pay was introduced for senior executives, and the more commercial of the government agencies were privatized. The pace of change picked up considerably with the election of the Howard government in 1996. The major changes that have occurred since then are:

- *Employment* – the terms and conditions of employment, particularly remuneration, became subject to agency-specific agreements, rather than being set centrally. Heads of agencies appointments moved to direct decision of the Executive;
- *Management* – the introduction of accrual budgeting in the 1999–2000 Budget, an emphasis on reaching performance targets, the costing of government 'outputs' and the imposition of capital use charges, the devolution of responsibility to departments;
- *Service delivery* – a policy was introduced requiring the justification of why each public sector activity could not be provided by the private sector. Consequently all information technology infrastructure was outsourced, virtually all government property sold and leased back, and the Commonwealth Employment Service abolished with virtually all employment programmes provided by the private sector and non-government agencies. Many agencies have moved to have human resources functions and internal audit provided by the private sector. In this process the Australian Public Service was reduced in size by some 12,000; and
- *Technology* – there has been a trend towards providing information and other services on the Internet.

There are a number of implications of these changes for dealing with integrity that have some negative aspects:

- fragmentation of the bodies to deal with corruption and promote integrity;
- complexity of accountability arrangements; and
- potential for the dilution of public sector ethics.

Looking at fragmentation, at a policy level, the Australian Public Service Commission and the Department of the Prime Minister and Cabinet jointly share responsibility for ethics and values, Attorney-General's Department and Department of Finance and Administration jointly sharing responsibility for fraud control and no single agency taking responsibility for corruption.

At an investigation level, what was once the sole responsibility of the police is now shared with a large number of internal investigation units. Further fragmentation is occurring as small agencies contract private sector providers to undertake or assist in investigations.

The fragmentation is also evidenced by the varying degrees of priority being given to anti-corruption and fraud control programmes within agencies. A survey by the Australian National Audit Office (2003) points to wide variations in how seriously the programmes are being taken. Clearly, anti-corruption and fraud control programmes have to jostle for attention when managers are being held accountable for producing results in delivery.

It should not be assumed that the arrangements that the Commonwealth has for dealing with ethics, fraud and corruption apply universally across the whole of the federal public sector:

- There is a wide variety of employment arrangements at the federal level. While the *Public Service Act 1999* covers the single largest group of employees, there are many statutory authorities that have the power to set their own terms and conditions. Consequently the public sector values that are an essential part of the *Public Service Act 1999* and the associated disciplinary procedures do not apply universally in the Australian government public sector. Also, employment categories like those persons employed to serve Ministers and Members of Parliament have their own employment schemes;
- The financial management provisions in the *Financial Management and Accountability Act 1997* that provide the authority for the fraud control policies (and therefore the anti-corruption policies) similarly do not extend beyond the group of 'core' budget funded public sector agencies;
- The provisions of the Criminal Code dealing with fraud and corruption have a very wide application and cover most persons working for, or on behalf of the Commonwealth; and
- The extensive arrangements for the provision of services by the private sector are governed by an array of contractual arrangements, with, according to the Australian National Audit Office, relatively little uniformity.

Leadership in Integrity

In the Commonwealth administration, it is not easy to identify which agency (or agencies) is actually providing leadership in the area of integrity. The central coordinating agencies appear to have adopted the practice of setting the policy framework, through statute, guidelines, best practice, etc. Having done that, the central coordinating agencies then rely upon the broader governance arrangements to make sure that the procedures are followed. Individual agencies do have the opportunity to comment upon the procedures while they are being developed, which is why they take so long to come into effect. And of course the larger agencies have a lot more influence than smaller agencies while this is being done.

Once the procedures are in place, it appears that monitoring agencies such as the Ombudsman have a lot more influence upon the day-to-day practice of agencies. The Australian Taxation Office indicated quite clearly that the Auditor

General and the Ombudsman were engaged continually in identifying integrity issues and then negotiating with the ATO on how best to improve procedures.

The common theme running through the external review processes is that there is preparedness by the external scrutiny bodies (ANAO, Privacy Commissioner, Ombudsman, and Parliamentary Committees) to take up issues that bear upon integrity and to undertake detailed examinations of the relevant administrative systems. The Commonwealth agencies which are the subject of this scrutiny are then left with little option other than to implement the recommendations made.

One senior participant in the study gave a personal opinion that the central agencies took the view that the integrity of the overall system was very high – and, by and large, this is a quite reasonable position to take. As a result of this view, central agencies have not seen the necessity for pulling integrity issues together and making it a high priority. This gives the impression that those agencies are complacent about integrity issues. The participant put the view that both the Auditor General and the Ombudsman have taken an interest in integrity issues whereas the Secretaries of the central coordination agencies have other things on their minds.

The interviews indicated significant differences of approach between the Commonwealth agencies which come under the *Public Service Act 1999* and those which come under other legislative schemes. Agencies away from the centre tended to give less emphasis to many of the compliance requirements that are placed upon the agencies. (Again, this is a view put by other NISA participants and is a constant theme in ANAO reports.) In observing the difference between agencies at the centre and at the periphery, there is also another dimension related to the profile of the portfolio Secretary as regards to integrity issues. Some portfolios Secretaries make a specific effort to bring together the heads of all the statutory authorities in the portfolio to discuss governance issues. In this environment it is far more likely that integrity issues will be taken seriously.

The Office of the Commonwealth Ombudsman expressed the view that the current formal integrity processes are not completely adequate in that they vary from agency to agency, particularly in their implementation. The devolution of authority for governance issues is seen as contributing to this situation with the recent requirement for agencies to approve their own Fraud Control Plans cited as an example of this trend. The Office expressed the view that this devolution is only good if agencies pick up on what is required, which, the Office says, some have not. There is also recognition that while many areas of an organization have an interest in fraud, they are not always consulted in matters of policy and practice. There is also acknowledgment that integrity and professionalism are often difficult to amalgamate into a risk management function.

By a quite overwhelming majority, most of the agencies interviewed and/or surveyed indicated that they believed that the integrity issues were being handled well.

In the questionnaire, respondents were asked to list the three most important (other) agencies for dealing with integrity issues. The ranking of the responses was:

1 Australian National Audit Office;
2 Australian Public Service Commission;
3 Parliamentary Committees;
4 Office of the Commonwealth Ombudsman.

Respondents were also asked to rank agencies as to their contribution to dealing with service-wide integrity. The 'very important' ratings were given to:

- Australian Public Service Commission (5);
- Australian National Audit Office (4);
- Office of the Commonwealth Ombudsman (3);
- Parliamentary Committees (3);
- News Media (3);
- Australian Federal Police (2).

Respondents were also asked to rank agencies as to the quality of their advice on integrity issues. The 'very good' ratings were not as freely given, and the results were:

- Australian Public Service Commission (3);
- Australian National Audit Office (2);
- Office of the Commonwealth Ombudsman (2);
- Parliamentary Committees (3).

Study Observation

These results indicate that the 'big three' in Commonwealth integrity are the Australian Public Service Commission, Australian National Audit Office and the Office of the Commonwealth Ombudsman, with the Commission receiving the most recognition. Given that, out of the agencies mentioned, the Commission has the least legal authority, this ranking is indicative that the Australian Public Service Commission has demonstrated a high degree of leadership and credibility in the field of integrity.

A noticeable absence in the leadership stakes is law enforcement agencies.

The Coherence Mechanisms

Having looked at the major elements of the Commonwealth's integrity system, it is now possible to look at the important issue of coherence. In particular, how these elements are matched to form some unifying process.

Fraud Control Policy

The first of these unifying mechanisms is the Commonwealth's fraud control policy issued in May 2002 (Minister for Justice and Customs 2002). The policy was issued in the form of guidelines issued by the authority of regulations made under the *Financial Management and Accountability Act 1997* (FMA Act). A much more detailed description of this policy is provided in paragraph 7 of the *Source Material* document.

One of the curiosities of the Commonwealth's approach is the way in which corruption is subsumed within its fraud control framework. The *Commonwealth Fraud Control Guidelines* 2002 (Minister for Justice and Customs 2002) define fraud as 'dishonestly obtaining a benefit by deception or other means'. The definition of fraud used in the Guidelines includes (*inter alia*), 'bribery, corruption or abuse of office'.

The relevant legislation treats fraud and corruption quite separately (Minister for Justice and Customs 2002) and it is reasonable to draw the conclusion that the Commonwealth legislature did not see corruption as a subset of fraud, nor fraud as a subset of corruption.

Notwithstanding that the *Commonwealth Fraud Control Guidelines* include corruption, there is a fundamental issue as to why the Commonwealth has chosen to emphasize fraud, to the almost total exclusion of corruption. Indeed, in conflating these two concepts in the one term 'fraud', that term then takes on a meaning well beyond that meant in normal discourse.

There would appear to be a number of possible reasons for this redefining of terms:

- The impetus for the Commonwealth's campaign against fraud was the community concern of widespread tax evasion and welfare fraud in the early 1980s. While there have been some high profile cases of corruption being perpetrated by Commonwealth public servants, clearly the past and continuing emphasis is upon fraud being perpetrated upon the Commonwealth from outside sources; and
- The emphasis upon fraud, rather than corruption, has a closer fit with the administrative reform agenda pursued by successive Commonwealth governments. In particular, the policies on the contracting out of public sector services lend themselves more to a commercial rationale for dealing with potentially improper behaviour than those that are based upon a commitment to shared moral values.

The above consideration is helpful in appreciating why the Commonwealth reports such low rates of corruption.

The authority of the policy stems from its legislative basis. However, the *Financial Management and Accountability Act 1997* only covers budget funded agencies. Other Commonwealth agencies are covered by the *Commonwealth Authorities and Companies Act 1997* (CAC Act). The policy does not purport to cover all of these agencies, many of which have a quasi-commercial status. There are certain implications of these coverage arrangements:

- there is a clear presumption that the fraud control mechanisms prescribed will be equally effective whether the agency is a large entity or a small advisory board;
- effectively CAC Act agencies have an 'opt-in' facility, with those agencies which receive at least 50 per cent of funding for their operating costs from the Commonwealth under the added pressure of the Minister to comply; and
- there is no easy way of determining which of the CAC Act agencies[4] have more than 50 per cent of funding for their operating costs from the Commonwealth and which have less. Nor is there any mechanism established to report on compliance with the policy for any of CAC Act agencies.

The policy also covers the small Parliamentary Departments and the *Guidelines* write in the Presiding Officers with the same role as Ministers vis-à-vis those Parliamentary Departments. Before leaving the issue of coverage, it is useful to note that the definition of the Commonwealth and of a Commonwealth employee in the Commonwealth Criminal Code is very broad and would comprehend all of the agencies discussed above.

The framework for dealing with fraud and corruption is quite comprehensive and the major components of the framework need to be examined. The first major element is prevention. The policy requires the application of risk management techniques linked to the Australian/New Zealand Standard, *Risk Management* (AS/NZS 4360:1999). All agencies are required to regularly assess their risks of fraud and corruption and prepare and implement plans for mitigating those risks. The requirement to produce this plan has a statutory base in Section 45 of the FMA Act and the policy requires CEOs to certify in agency annual reports that this process has been undertaken.

A survey of fraud control arrangements undertaken by the ANAO (2000a) found that:

- 36 per cent of responding agencies had not undertaken a fraud risk assessment within the last two years as required by the policy;
- 15 per cent of agencies covered by the FMA Act (where it is a specific requirement of s45) had not prepared a fraud control plan; and
- of the agencies that had prepared a fraud control plan, 13 per cent had not undertaken a fraud risk assessment.

---

4 The Department of Finance and Administration website contains lists of those 76 agencies covered by the FMA Act, available at <http://www.finance.gov.au/finframework/docs/FMA.Agencies.List.26.4.02.rtf>; 112 covered by the CAC Act, available at <http://www.finance.gov.au/finframework/docs/CAC_body_list_22_4_2002.rtf>. However, there is no list of CAC Act agencies delineated by proportion of funding for operating expenses.

The ANAO reviewed a sample of fraud control plans as part of the survey and found that few met all the criteria set out in the policy, some did not address fraud risks identified and a significant proportion did not include an adequate timetable for implementation nor responsible areas designated and mechanisms to monitor implementation were absent.

The fraud prevention component of the policy is almost entirely devoted to risk management and the application of risk management techniques to fraud control. Not only does the language of the policy omit any mention of corruption, the nature of the processes outlined are even more sensitive to the criticism that, to be effective, they need a significant law enforcement input. While it can be reasonably argued that examining and rectifying financial and management systems can significantly inhibit fraud, that argument is less persuasive when it comes to corruption. This is because the corrupt officer is much more likely to be actively seeking out the flaws in the system and using inside knowledge to subvert them. Thus the motivations and techniques are more closely aligned to the domain of criminal deviance than financial management and the input of skilled investigators is even more crucial.

The second major element in the fraud control policy is how cases are investigated and dealt with as they arise. The policy encourages agencies to investigate and prosecute fraud and states that individual agencies are responsible for investigation of routine and minor cases of fraud. More serious cases of fraud are referred to the Australian Federal Police (AFP) for investigation. The Commonwealth has developed a comprehensive set of investigation standards to be applied to fraud investigations. (As an indication of their usefulness, HoCOLEA (the Heads of Commonwealth Law Enforcement Agencies) has adopted the standards generally for all Commonwealth investigations). These Standards are not publicly available.

The third major element of the policy is the requirement for training and awareness raising. Agencies are required to alert staff to the dangers of fraud and corruption. More importantly, the policy links to an elaborate set of employment competencies that are a part of the national training framework. The policy (Guideline 6) requires agencies that employ investigators to have them trained to a minimum competency standard and to obtain accreditation from a formally recognized training authority.

The final major element of the policy is the requirements for reporting. The policy (Guideline 8) sets down highly detailed and elaborate requirements for collecting data about cases. However, this information is submitted to the Commonwealth Attorney-General's Department, which analyses the information and prepares a report for the Minister for Justice and Customs. This information is not made public. Agencies are required to provide information on fraud in their annual reports but this information does not differentiate fraud from corruption and is of limited assistance to the external researcher.

The Commonwealth's fraud control policy performs the role of a bridge between the Commonwealth's law enforcement responsibilities and its financial accountability structures. The fact that it is issued under the authority of the primary financial accountability statute is of considerable significance. The link between the ethical structure and the fraud control policy is not as obvious.

Study Observation

Notwithstanding the awkwardness of subsuming corruption within fraud control and the inherent problems of consistent implementation in a decentralized environment, the fraud control policy is by far the closest systemic element existing in the Commonwealth which can be described as a whole-of-government approach with strong support from the Ministerial level of government. Its strengths lie in the bridging between the very comprehensive financial accountability arrangements in the Commonwealth to the criminal justice regime and setting it in the organizational context of the increasingly pervasive corporate governance mechanisms being adopted across the Commonwealth.

All participants in the study were very familiar with the fraud control policy and were keen to portray their agencies as fully meeting its requirements.

Promotion of an Ethical Climate

In 1999, the Commonwealth Parliament enacted a totally revised legislative package for the employment of the Australian Public Service. In terms of anti-corruption activities the most important elements of this legislative package are the statement of values (Section 10), the code of conduct (Section 13) and the procedures for handling breaches (Section 15).

The distinction in the Act between the values[5] and the code of conduct is both deliberate and important. It is an attempt to be aspirational and to set down ethical requirements in terms of positive aims rather than a selection of behaviours that are proscribed. As the Commonwealth has moved rapidly away from uniform employment arrangements and a centralized human resources approach, this statement of values performs a crucial role in setting down what it means to be a public servant.

However, the framework has a sharper edge with the code of conduct. It includes[6] a number of provisions that could relate to corrupt behaviour, for example, the employee must:

- behave honestly and with integrity;
- comply with all applicable Australian laws;
- comply with any lawful and reasonable direction;
- disclose, and take reasonable steps to avoid, any conflict of interest (real or apparent);

5 See Australian Public Service Commission (no date).

6 The full version of the code of conduct – Australian Public Service Commission (no date) *APS Code of Conduct*, available at <http://www.apsc.gov.au/conduct/index.html>, accessed 8 June2004.

- use Commonwealth resources in a proper manner;
- not make improper use of:
  - inside information, or
  - the employee's duties, status, power or authority, in order to gain, or seek to gain, a benefit or advantage for the employee or for any other person;
- at all times behave in a way that upholds the APS Values (Section 10 of the *Public Service Act 1999*) and the integrity and good reputation of the APS.

An agency head (or delegate) can impose the following sanctions for breaches of the APS Code of Conduct (APS 2000):

- termination of employment;
- reduction in classification;
- re-assignment of duties;
- reduction in salary;
- deductions from salary, by way of fine;
- a reprimand.

The Commonwealth's fraud control policy does not provide any specific guidance to agencies as to when they should be contemplating a prosecution using that policy and when they should resort to administrative remedies, such as using the disciplinary procedures of the *Public Service Act 1999*. Guideline 4 states 'agencies should consider prosecution in appropriate circumstances in accordance with the Prosecution Policy of the Commonwealth'. While the policy does not provide assistance on this issue, an attempt has been made by the Commonwealth to define what a 'serious' crime is and what a 'serious' civil contravention is – setting down criteria for each.[7]

Australian Public Service Commissioner

The role of the Australian Public Service Commissioner is not only limited in its reach, it is limited by the highly decentralized structure of the Australian Public Service. The changes brought about by the 1999 revision of the legislation formalized that much of the authority of the statute flows to agency heads, rather than to the Commissioner. The Commissioner has very limited employment powers because Section 20 of the *Public Service Act 1999* gives agency heads, not the Commissioner, the powers of employer.

While it is easy to see the Commissioner as being the centre point of the APS integrity system, a close examination of the statute reveals that, arguably, it would be more accurate to attribute that role to agency heads. Section 12 of the Act states 'An Agency Head *must* uphold and promote the APS Values' (emphasis added).

Section 41 describes the Commissioner's functions:

(1) The Commissioner's functions include the following functions:

---

7 See Attorney-General's Department (no date).

(a) to *evaluate* the extent to which Agencies incorporate and uphold the APS Values;
(b) to *evaluate* the adequacy of systems and procedures in Agencies for ensuring compliance with the Code of Conduct;
(c) to *promote* the APS Values and the Code of Conduct; and
(d) to *inquire* into alleged breaches of the Code of Conduct by Agency Heads and to report to the appropriate authority on the results of such enquiries (including, where relevant, recommendations for sanctions). (Emphasis added)

In describing the ethics framework of the APS in his State of the Service report, the Commissioner said:

> Part of that effort, to provide assurance that the Values are being upheld, is to ensure that a rigorous and systematic approach to conducting investigations and dealing with breaches of the Code of Conduct. This is particularly important if agencies are to gain and maintain the commitment of employees to values-based behaviour. The agency survey results indicate that there is a large variation amongst large agencies in the number of investigations of suspected breaches as well as in the imposition of the high impact sanctions.
>
> While I recognise that this may reflect, at least in part, the different importance of particular APS Values and elements of the Code of Conduct to the work of different agencies, I believe that the considerable differences suggests agencies are not using a sufficiently rigorous and systematic approach (APS Commission 2003).

This is a realistic (and frank) acknowledgment that ultimately; responsibility for ethical leadership in the APS is much more diffuse than it would appear at first glance.

The reason for going through this analysis is to highlight that the leadership role clearly attributed to the Commissioner is more a result of activism of the occupant rather than through the exercise of legal authority. This is both a compliment to the individual and a potential shortcoming in the system. The occupant of the position has a wide range of functions and another occupant could give these other functions a far higher priority that could be to the detriment of the integrity of the APS, and ultimately to the whole public sector.

Allegations of Politicization of Senior Officials

There is a vigorous and continuing public debate[8] about what is termed the politicization of senior levels in Commonwealth administration and failures in accountability processes. Not all of the issues raised in this debate refer to officers of the Australian Public Service (APS); it involves military officers, statutory office holders and the role of advisers to ministers.

---

8 Indicative of the material published on this subject are these two excellent analyses: Mulgan (1998) and Parliament of Australia (1998).

At the core of this debate are concerns that senior officials are placing more emphasis upon their obligations to be responsive to their ministers than on requirements to be politically non-partisan, provide frank and fearless advice as well as acting in the broader public interest.

While not all the persons involved in this dilemma are public servants, the relevant provisions of the *Australian Public Service Act 1999* provide a useful illustration of the ambiguity facing senior officials. Subsection 10 (1) sets out the values of the Australian Public Service. There are 15 in total, but the ones relevant to this discussion are:

- (a) the APS is apolitical, performing its functions in an impartial and professional manner;
- (d) the APS has the highest ethical standards;
- (e) the APS is openly accountable for its actions, within the framework of Ministerial responsibility to the government, the Parliament and the Australian public;
- (f) the APS is responsive to the government in providing frank, honest, comprehensive, accurate and timely advice and in implementing the government's policies and programmes.

A cursory analysis of these values indicates that there is the potential for conflict between (f) and the other three.

Also, this statement of intent needs to be read in conjunction with other provisions in the Act and other legislation. The heads of APS agencies are appointed by the Prime Minister (section 58) on fixed terms and can be dismissed at will (section 59). Below the level of the heads of APS agencies is a Senior Executive Service of 2,253 officers (APS 2006). While the majority of these officers have permanent appointments made by the Australian Public Service Commissioner, within that framework they are required to have individual workplace agreements (Division 3, Part VID, *Workplace Relations Act 1996*) where specific performance requirements are set out.

In summary, while senior public servants have a values framework in which to operate, they work within an employment framework with a heavy emphasis upon meeting government aims. The government does not see these ambiguities being of major significance.[9]

A good way of exploring this issue further is to look at a number of recent incidents that have attracted public debate. The first is known as 'children overboard'.[10]

On 7 October 2001, the Minister for Immigration, Mr Philip Ruddock, announced to the media that 'a number of children had been thrown overboard' from a vessel suspected of being an 'illegal entry vessel' just intercepted by

---

9 A article by the Australian Public Service Commissioner (Podger 2002) is indicative of the arguments in support of these arrangements.

10 This material is derived from the Executive Summary of Parliament of Australia (2002).

the Australian Defence Force. The 'children overboard' story was repeated in subsequent days and weeks by senior government ministers, including the Minister for Defence, Peter Reith, and the Prime Minister, John Howard. The story was in fact untrue.

The sensitivity associated with the claim that children had been thrown overboard was that it was made at the beginning of and sustained throughout a Federal election campaign, during which 'border protection' and national security were key issues. That asylum seekers trying to enter Australia by boat were the kinds of people who would throw their children overboard was used by the government to demonize them as part of the argument for the need for a 'tough' stand against external threats and in favour of 'putting Australia's interests first'.

The issue was examined at length by a Senate Committee. At the broadest level, the Committee has found that a number of factors contributed to the making and sustaining of the report that children had been thrown overboard. They included genuine miscommunication or misunderstanding, inattention, avoidance of responsibility, a public service culture of responsiveness and perhaps over-responsiveness to the political needs of ministers, and deliberate deception motivated by political expedience.

The Committee was highly critical of the responsible Minister (who resigned after the election and immediately took up a position with a defence contractor), ministerial staff who intervened in administrative processes but who were not accountable to Parliament and senior public servants and military officers who knew that the story was false but failed to clearly indicate this to the responsible ministers.

The second issue has been the debate around the advice the government received on weapons of mass destruction prior to the invasion of Iraq in 2003. This debate took place in the context of similar debates in the United States and the United Kingdom. The issue came to a head when Andrew Wilkie, an intelligence analyst with the Office of National Assessments, resigned and made public statements alleging political interference in the intelligence process. Specifically, he alleged that the Government ignored the qualifications in the intelligence reports that it had received to back up the case for war. A Parliamentary Committee examined the issue and came up with an equivocal report – essentially the allegation had not been proved (Parliament of Australia 2004). In the light of the fact that no WMDs have been found and the doubts about the role intelligence agencies in the United States and the United Kingdom, many commentators are portraying the issue as one of politicization of the intelligence services.

Another incident that has been interpreted as politicization was the Government's reaction to some comments made by the Commissioner of the Australian Federal Police. In March 2004 the Commissioner appeared on a national current affairs programme and said that Australia's involvement in the Iraq war had increased the likelihood of a terrorist attack on Australia. As the Australian Federal Police plays a key role in counter terrorism and is the focal point for national criminal intelligence, the Commissioner's views received wide publicity. However, his views were contradicted immediately by the Prime Minister who argued that the threat of international terrorism had existed before the invasion of Iraq. The Minister for Foreign Affairs went further and said that the Commissioner was 'expressing a view which reflects a lot of the propaganda we're getting from al-Qaeda'. Press reports indicated that the Commissioner considered resigning (*The Age* 19 March 2004). Very soon after, the Commissioner issued a 'clarifying' press release which has been widely interpreted as being released because of political pressure (AFP 2004).

These three case studies are not meant to be exhaustive, but to indicate that there is an active public debate about issues that are central to the issue of the ethical climate of Commonwealth administration.

Study Observation

Despite the pervasiveness of this debate that occurred throughout the duration of the study, it was noticeable that none of the participants raised the issue either in the interviews or in the responses to the questionnaire. The most probable explanation for this is that the study only approached officials and did not attempt to engage with ministers or members of their staff.

Whistleblowing

Most Australian jurisdictions have legislation that protects officials (and sometimes members of the public) from reprisals caused by reporting wrongdoing. These schemes[11] are fairly similar across jurisdictions, except for the Commonwealth scheme under s16 of the *Commonwealth Public Service Act 1999* that is very minimal indeed.

In very general terms what these other schemes offer is:

- the capacity for officials (and in some cases member of the public) to bring forward concerns about improper conduct, waste, abuse, environmental damage, conflict of interest;
- a requirement that these matters be investigated;
- protection of the complainant against unlawful reprisal, usually it is made a criminal offence;
- requirements that disclosures be handled confidentially; and
- capacity for complainant to seek damages if a reprisal occurs.

11 The use of the term 'whistleblowing' to describe public disclosure processes is misleading. What is being described is not, to be precise; a whistle blower system because it does not permit officials to make there concerns public. An Australian exception is s19 of the *New South Wales Protected Disclosure Act 1994* that permits disclosure to a journalist under very limited conditions. With that exception, officials in any Australian jurisdiction who make public disclosures, as against disclosures to an approved public agency, would be liable to legal sanctions for breaching confidentiality provisions.

The Commonwealth whistleblowing provision has been widely criticized as being weak. A Parliamentary committee (Finance and Public Administration Legislation Committee) observed that the scheme had the following deficiencies:

- The scheme only applied to half of the Federal public sector;
- Only public servants can raise issues, not members of the public;
- The nature of the matters that are covered by the scheme is vague;
- Reports can only be received by the CEO and Public Service Commissioner – the latter having no power to take remedial action; and
- The protection from reprisal is limited to those from within the agency relevant to the complaint. (Parliament of Australia 2002)

The Committee found the whistleblower scheme to be inadequate but noted that all the parties to the scheme were quite satisfied with it. The Australian Public Service Commissioner has publicly reported that the scheme was working well.

The Commissioner in his State of the Service report said:

> The agency and employee surveys indicate that more than 30 per cent of agencies do not use measures to make employees aware of whistle blowing provisions, and only 65 per cent of employees indicated that they had been made aware by their current agency that they could report a serious breach of the Code to an authorised person in the agency. (APSC 2003, Ch. 7)

He also reported that in the course of the year, the Merit Protection Commissioner had received two reports and he concluded that in both cases the allegations were not supported. The Public Service Commissioner himself received 13 reports, only one of which proceeded to investigation. These figures are remarkably low in an organization the size of the APS and are a fraction of the number of cases investigated by the Independent Commission Against Corruption in New South Wales and the Crime and Misconduct Commission in Queensland.

Study Observation

The lack of a credible public disclosure regime in the Commonwealth is immediately obvious when the comprehensiveness of the legislative regimes in every other Australian jurisdiction is considered. In the course of the study, the Office of the Ombudsman was critical of the existing Commonwealth arrangements and lack of specific whistleblower legislation.

Law Enforcement

The Commonwealth has an array of offences dealing with defrauding the Commonwealth and bribing officials. The major ones are in Divisions 7.3 and 7.6 of the *Commonwealth Criminal Code Act 1995.* Many other statutes like the

Commonwealth Social Security Act 1991 and the *Income Tax Assessment Acts 1936 and 1997* contain offence provisions that relate to the broader area of integrity.

Until recent times, the Commonwealth law enforcement institutions that dealt with integrity issues were the Australian Federal Police (AFP) the Office of the Director of Public Prosecutions (DPP) the Australian Crime Commission (ACC) and the judiciary.

The obvious omission in the Commonwealth's law enforcement arrangements was the lack of an anti-corruption body. They existed in other Australian jurisdictions – the Independent Commission Against Corruption in New South Wales, the Crime and Misconduct Commission in Queensland and the Anti-Corruption Commission in Western Australia. Following allegations in the media that some police officers in the ACC who had been seconded from state police services were corrupt; the government announced the set up a 'national anticorruption body' (Minister for Justice and Customs 2004). This body only examines corruption in the police working in the AFP and ACC and does not deal with corruption by officials as all the anti-corruption bodies listed above are empowered to do. The institution of this body is a belated acceptance of a proposal made by the Australian Law Reform Commission in 1996 that had not been actioned (ALRC 1996).

Study Observation

The considerations as to whether a national anti-corruption body is needed are usually argued on the basis of a cost/benefit analysis taking into account the perceived level of corruption that is present. However, there are other considerations that are relevant.

As demonstrated by the evolution of the Independent Commission Against Corruption in New South Wales and the Crime and Misconduct Commission in Queensland, these 'peak' anti-corruption bodies take on a variety of roles that supplement the primary role of being an independent standing commission on corruptions. These roles are:

- a high-profile agency for the of promulgation of prevention strategies;
- a publicly recognized 'lightening rod' for any suspicions or allegations of corruption by member of the community. Any member of the community who had suspicions about corruption in Commonwealth programmes would find it difficult to identify the appropriate agency to approach and, more importantly, to see the handling of the allegation as a matter of high priority; and
- providing a final point of review for a public interest disclosure regime.

Financial Accountability

The Commonwealth has a highly sophisticated financial accountability framework that operates across Commonwealth administration, of which public procurement is one important part. The core of the financial accountability system is statutory. Section 83 of the Constitution requires that all expenditure by the Commonwealth be appropriated by Parliament. Then there are the foundation statutes – the *Commonwealth Financial Management and Accountability (FMA) Act and Regulations 1997*, the *Commonwealth Companies and Authorities (CAC) Act*, the *Auditor-General Act 1997* and the *Public Accounts and Audit Committee Act 1951*.

Australian National Audit Office

The key institutional players in the financial accountability system are the policy-setting agency, the Department of Finance and Administration, the Auditor-General and the Australian National Audit Office (ANAO) as well as the Joint Committee of Public Accounts and Audit.

The ANAO does a range of types of auditing[12] – performance audits, financial control and administration audits, financial statement audits and assurance and control assessment audits. It tables around 60 audit reports every year. As well the ANAO plays an active role in defining and promulgating best practice in a wide range of financial management areas and the current Auditor-General plays an active role in the debate about financial management.

The ANAO sees the acceptance of fraud control and anti-corruption procedures into the broader corporate governance framework as a crucial element in integrity. It observed that there is some variation between Commonwealth agencies, depending on the culture of the organization concerned, in the extent to which this process occurs. Business decisions made by individual agencies can simply ignore suggestions made by the ANAO, raising the possibility that some organizations may not have the ideal attitude towards ethical issues. However, the ANAO refrains from commenting directly upon policy matters, but relies on the independence of agencies.

The ANAO noted that the perception of the seriousness of an agency's fraud and corruption problem can be skewed by a lack of adequate reporting mechanisms. In the ANAO's view, a significant proportion of frauds come to notice when incidents are reported by concerned employees, thus highlighting the importance of an ethical culture within Commonwealth organizations.

With regard to the overall effectiveness of the Commonwealth's integrity system, the ANAO noted that the task of auditing such a large and diverse administration involves a series of decisions where best to expend the finite resources available to the ANAO. While the ANAO is confident that it has the mix about right, clearly it would like to be able to do more. This is particularly the case with the outsourcing of auditing.

The ANAO is highly regarded by the participants in the study as an organization of competence, integrity and independence. It has not hesitated to criticize the government for policy decisions that have, in the view of the Auditor-

---

12 The description of the audit functions is drawn from the 2003 ANAO Annual Report.

General, been in the best interests of the Commonwealth. Two examples of this independence are reports on the outsourcing of information technology (ANAO 2000a; b; c)[13] and the sale and leaseback of virtually all property. Both these reports attracted an extremely critical response from the government.

Financial Accountability Procedures

The other elements in the financial accountability process are the myriad of procedures and guidelines. As well as those that explain the workings of the system, these include the procurement guidelines promulgated by the Department of Finance and Administration (DOFA 2002), and the Best Practice Guides promulgated by the ANAO.[14]

Complementing the comprehensive procurement guidelines, the Commonwealth's financial accountability system has a number of other features that make it very robust:

- the provision requiring the 'ethical use of resources' by Commonwealth managers (Section 44, *FMA Act 1997*);
- the requirement for every Commonwealth agency to have a fraud control plan (Section 45, *FMA Act 1997*). This has attached to it a regulation making power as well as the power to issue Ministerial directions which have the authority of statute. Stemming form this head of power is the Commonwealth's fraud control policy and processes; and
- the requirement for every agency to have an Audit Committee (Section 46, *FMA Act 1997*).

Financial Accountability Review

While all those mechanisms are good, by far the most powerful is the overview of the Commonwealth's financial activities by Senate Estimates Committees. Noting that the government does not have a majority in the Senate, these Committees play a role in the integrity process that is difficult to overestimate. These Committees use the full powers of Parliament to regularly bring before them public officials and question them on public spending. Transcripts of the hearings are published

---

13 In 1996, the Commonwealth embarked upon a radical plan of outsourcing all information technology services. They were bundled into very large 'clusters' and tendered. The results were less than expected; with high costs in arranging the outsourcing, less than predicted savings and service difficulties for the public sector agencies. The programme has been curtailed and no new clusters are being outsourced. At around the same time, the Commonwealth commenced a programme of selling Commonwealth property and leasing it back from the purchasers. The ANAO found that the Commonwealth will suffer significant losses over the long term with this policy as a result of miscalculations in the costings.

14 There is a wide variety of Guides: one dealing with procurement is Australian National Audit Office (1998).

online[15] and hearings are televised. These officials are under oath to answer questions and (theoretically) their Departments and agencies can have documents subpoenaed.

The Estimates Committees have developed a reputation for doggedly following through into the details of public sector administration. Ministers are present at the hearings and frequently complain that members use the process to grill officials on matters beyond the immediate issue of the expenditure of public funds. However, any neutral observer can only welcome the direct intervention of Parliamentary authority into the complexities of the Executive's administration.

Transparency

The Commonwealth has a complex and impressive array of transparency mechanisms. At a basic level there are highly specified requirements for what is included in agency annual reports,[16] which are tabled in Parliament.

The Commonwealth has enacted a package of administrative law protections that enable citizens to seek reasons for decision, review of decisions and access to documents.

Many statutory provisions that affect the lives and well being of citizens contain such provisions, for example, the *Social Security Act 1991*, the *Income Tax Assessment Act 1997*, and the *Migration Act 1958*. More importantly, there are specific statutes like the *Administrative Decisions (Judicial Review) Act 1977* that gives a legal right to citizens for a review of a decision under an enactment, with some exceptions (Section 13), and enables the citizen to apply to a court for a review of the decision. Also the *Administrative Appeals Tribunal Act 1975* allows for the review of decisions in other enactments – like those mentioned above. Citizens have a right to access to documents by virtue of the *Freedom of Information Act 1982*. Under that statute, there is a presumption of access to documents unless specific exemptions apply (for example, section 36 allows an exemption for internal working documents. There are appeal rights to the Administrative Appeals Tribunal, with the capacity for Ministers to ultimately refuse to release particular documents.

It is noticeable that most of the enactments were made ten to 15 years ago, at a time when there was pressure from legal and academic commentators to make the Commonwealth more directly accountable to the community. This impetus has largely dissipated. The administrative law package has come under pressure recently with the Howard government removing the rights of asylum seekers to review migration decisions. Also, there have been criticisms of the wide discretions in the *Freedom of Information Act 1982* being used to unreasonably withhold sensitive information (O'Brien 2004).

---

15 See Parliament of Australia (various dates).

16 See Department of the Prime Minister and Cabinet (2004).

Ombudsman

A key element of the Commonwealth's integrity system is the Ombudsman's office. It has a statutory basis: created under the *Commonwealth Ombudsman Act 1976*. The Office describes its responsibilities as:

- identifying problems from the approximately 33,000 complaints and inquiries it receives each year (around 60 per cent of them being welfare based); and
- identifying systemic, underlying issues such as poor practices, lack of supervision and guidance, and lack of training which also may relate to integrity issues.

The office has always had a reputation for being occupied by persons with reputations of the highest integrity. The current occupant, Professor John McMillan, is recognized as a leading academic and practitioner in the field of administrative law. His predecessors have also been persons with excellent credentials and have imbued the organization with the reputation of total independence.

The functions of the Office are to investigate the administrative actions of Commonwealth Agencies within certain limitations. For example, the Ombudsman may not investigate some actions related to Commonwealth employment, or the actions of judges and ministers.

Since the formation of the Office, it has taken on a number of specific roles:

- Taxation Ombudsman (section 4 of the *Ombudsman Act 1976);*
- Defence Force Ombudsman;
- Australian Capital Territory Ombudsman *(Ombudsman Act 1989 (ACT)*
- inspecting the records of telephone interceptions by Commonwealth law enforcement agencies, the Australian Federal Police and the Australian Crime Commission (*Telecommunications (Interception) Act 1979*)
- handling complaints about Australian Federal Police (*Complaints Australian Federal Police Act 1981*)

The authority of the Office stems, in a large part, from its capacity to report its findings. The *Commonwealth Ombudsman Act 1976* provides a comprehensive and layered approach to the reporting of the results of investigations. The first level provides for a report to the agency with the Ombudsman authorized to require a response, within a specified time frame, to deal with any actions the Ombudsman may propose to remedy administrative problems identified (Section 15). Where the agency does not respond, the Ombudsman can refer the matter to the Prime Minister (Section 16). The Ombudsman can also refer matters to Parliament (Section 17) and even after reference to Parliament, the Ombudsman can also discuss with agency a resolution of the matter (Section 18).

For an organization with such a central role in the integrity system, with such an array of functions and handling a large number of complaints, the Office is quite modestly resourced. It has approximately 85 staff a budget of around A$9 million. By way of comparison, the Australian Federal Police has 2,800 sworn officers and a budget of A$334 million.

Like the Auditor-General, the Commonwealth Ombudsman has a well-justified reputation for independence. An example is the controversial report written about the administration of Australia's detention centres that criticized conditions in the facilities (Ombudsman 2001).

Democratic Processes

The fundamentals of the Australian federal government are set down in the Constitution and the detailed operation of the electoral system is set down in the *Commonwealth Electoral Act 1918*. The institution responsible for the well being of the democratic process is the Australian Electoral Commission (AEC). The organization operates as an independent statutory authority under the *Commonwealth Electoral Act 1918* and is responsible for the federal electoral system in Australia.

Besides the important minutiae of the electoral arrangements which all bears upon the integrity system, there are two issues that are worthy of close examination, if only because they have been long recognized as likely areas of unethical practice.

The first is political donations. Australian political parties are highly active in seeking external sources of funding. This funding is predominantly from the business sector. The trade union movement has traditionally been a large donor to the Australian Labor Party, although it as well now obtains significant funding from the business sector. Under section 17(2) of the *Commonwealth Electoral Act 1918,* the Australian Electoral Commission is required, as soon as practicable after a federal election, to provide to the Minister for tabling in the Parliament a report on the operation of the Funding and Disclosure scheme in Part XX of the Electoral Act. The scheme does not place any limit upon the amounts that can be donated to political parties.

The purpose of the scheme is to prevent political corruption by making the financing of political parties and candidates as transparent as possible. Notwithstanding the rules on political donations, there are frequently scandals about improper influence. The 'Manildra' case was one in which an Australian company producing ethanol received very favourable treatment from the government by virtue of protective tariffs placed upon the importation of industrial ethanol. The company was a prominent donor to the Liberal party (Riley et al. 2003).

An closely associated with political donations is public funding of political parties. The purpose of public funding was to avoid the problems of political parties having to raise large amounts of money to run campaigns – in particular the potential for political corruption. Registered political parties, independent candidates and Senate groupings which receive more than 4 per cent of the total, formal, first preference vote are entitled to funding. Currently, the rate of funding is $1.84 per vote. Some A$33 million of public funding was paid to the political parties for the 1998 federal election.

There has been some criticism of the scheme in that it tends to favour the larger, existing political entities at the expense of the smaller parties that are struggling to gain recognition. A right wing, populist political movement (One Nation) went against this trend by obtaining enough support at its first entry into the federal political arena in the 1998 election and qualifying for public election funding. That short-lived political movement was the focus of investigation for providing misleading information about its status as a political party and the diversion of funds by its leader, Pauline Hanson, for her personal use. She was imprisoned but her conviction overturned upon appeal.

References

The Age (2004), 'Honest Copper Emerges Victor', 19 March, available at <http://www.theage.com.au/articles/2004/03/18/1079199363688.html>, accessed 31 May 2004>.

Attorney-General's Department (no date), *Overarching Principles for Selecting Cases for Investigation and Administrative, Civil and Criminal Sanctions*, available at <http://www.ag.gov.au/aghome/commprot/crjd/LECD/overarching.html>, accessed 5 August 2002.

Australian Federal Police (AFP) (2004), *Press Release*, 16 March, available at <http://www.afp.gov.au/page.asp?ref=/Media/2004/1604MediaStatement.xml>, accessed 31 March 2004.

Australian Federal Police (AFP) (various dates), *Annual Reports*, available at <http://www.afp.gov.au/page.asp?ref=/Publications/AnnualReports/Home.xml>, accessed 31 May 2004.

Australian Law Reform Commission (ALRC) (1996), *Integrity but not by Trust Alone*, available at <http://www.austlii.edu.au/au/other/alrc/publications/reports/82/ALRC82.html>, accessed 8 July 2004.

Australian National Audit Office (ANAO) (1998), *Selecting Suppliers: Managing the Risk*, available at <http://www.anao.gov.au/WebSite.nsf/Publications/4A256AE90015F69B4A25691B007DD47D>, accessed 3 June 2004.

Australian National Audit Office (ANAO) (2000a), *Report No. 53, 2000–2001: Commonwealth Management of Leased Office Property*, available at <http://www.anao.gov.au/WebSite.nsf/Publications/4A256AE90015F69BCA256A7800196C61>, accessed 3 June 2004.

Australian National Audit Office (ANAO) (2000b), *Report No. 9, 2000–2001: Implementation of Whole-of-Government Information Technology Infrastructure Consolidation and Outsourcing Initiative*, available at <http://www.anao.gov.au/WebSite.nsf/Publications/4A256AE90015F69BCA25695E00194EC2>, accessed 3 June 2004.

Australian National Audit Office (ANAO) (2000c), *Survey of Fraud Control Arrangements in APS Agencies: Report No. 47 1999–2000*, available at <http://www.anao.gov.au/WebSite.nsf/Publications/4A256AE90015F69B4A25691400161DFB>, accessed 1 August 2002.

Australian National Audit Office (ANAO) (2003a), *Annual Report*, available at <http://www.anao.gov.au/annual_reports/02_03/index.html>, accessed 3 June 2004.

Australian National Audit Office (ANAO) (2003b), *Survey of Fraud Control Arrangements in APS Agencies: Report No. 14 2003–2004*, available at <http://www.anao.gov.au/

WebSite.nsf/Publications/A99ABD97799669E2CA256DE900754906>, accessed 31 May 2004.

Australian Public Service Commission (APSC) (no date), *Values in the APS* , available at <http://www.apsc.gov.au/values/index.html>, accessed 8 June 2004.

Australian Public Service Commission (APSC) (2000), *Managing Breaches of the APS Code of Conduct*, available at <http://www.apsc.gov.au/publications00/breaches.htm>, accessed 5 August 2002.

Australian Public Service Commission (APSC) (2006), *State of the Service Report*, available at <http://www.apsc.gov.au/stateoftheservice/0203/chapter1.htm>, accessed 11 April 2006.

Department of Finance and Administration (DOFA) (2002), *Commonwealth Procurement Guidelines and Best Practice Guidance*, available at <http://www.dofa.gov.au/ctc/publications/purchasing/cpg/commonwealth_procurement_guide.html>, accessed 3 June 2004.

Department of the Prime Minister and Cabinet (PM&C) (2004), *Requirements for Annual Reports for Departments, Executive Agencies and FMA Act Bodies*, available at <http://www.pmc.gov.au/pdfs/annual_report_requirements.rtf>, accessed 8 July 2004.

Director of Public Prosecutions (DPP) (various dates), *Annual Reports*, available at <http://www.cdpp.gov.au/AboutUs/AnnualReports/>, accessed 31 May 2004.

Graycar, A. (2000), 'Fraud Prevention and Control in Australia', paper presented at the Australian Institute of Criminology Fraud Prevention Conference, Gold Coast, August 2000, available at <http://www.aic.gov.au/conferences/fraud/graycar.html>, accessed 1 August 2002.

Lampe, A. (2001), 'Comfort Letter Misused after Tax Complaint', *The Sydney Morning Herald,* 22 March 2002,13.

Minister for Justice and Customs (2002), Commonwealth Fraud Control Guidelines: Issued by the Minister for Justice and Customs as Fraud Control Guidelines under Regulation 19 of the Financial Management and Accountability Regulations 1997, available at <htttp://www.ag.gov.au/www/criminaljusticeHome.nsf/AllDocs/RWP69DEF50BCECE0F58CA256BD0007EF5EF?OpenDocument>, accessed 8 June 2004.

Minister for Justice and Customs (2004), media release: 'Commonwealth to Set Up Independent National Anti-corruption Body', 16 June, available at <http://www.ag.gov.au/www/justiceministerHome.nsf/Web+Pages/85FFECE1F7A2D27FCA256EB40081E90A?OpenDocument>, accessed 8 July 2004.

Mulgan, R. (1998), 'Politicisation of Senior Appointments in the Australian Public Service', *Australian Journal of Public Administration* 57:1, 3–14.

O'Brien, Senator Kerry (2004), media statement: 'Government uses Bureaucracy to Hide Truth', 28 June, available at <http://www.alp.org.au/media/0604/20007821.html>, accessed 8 July 2004.

Ombudsman (2001), *Report of an Own Motion Investigation into the Department of Immigration and Multicultural Affairs' Immigration Detention Centres*, available at <http://www.comb.gov.au/publications_information/Special_Reports/IDCMarch1.pdf>, accessed 3 June 2004.

Parliament of Australia (1998), Research Paper Number 3 1998-99: Politicising the Australian Public Service? (Canberra: Parliamentary Library).

Parliament of Australia (2002), *Public Interest Disclosure Bill 2001* (Canberra: Finance and Public Administration Legislation Committee).

Parliament of Australia (2002), *Report of the Select (Parliamentary) Committee for an inquiry into a certain maritime incident*, available at <http://www.aph.gov.au/Senate/committee/maritime_incident_ctte/>, accessed 31 May 2004.

Parliament of Australia (2004), *Inquiry into Intelligence on Iraq's Weapons of Mass Destruction (WMD)* (Canberra: Joint Standing Committee on ASIO, ASIS and DSD).

Parliament of Australia (various dates), *Hansard Senate*: *Finance and Administration*, available at <http://www.aph.gov.au/hansard/senate/commttee/s-fpa.htm>, accessed 3 June 2004.

Podger, A.S. (2002), 'Defining an Australian Approach to the Roles and Values of the Public Service in the Twenty-firstCcentury', *Canberra Bulletin of Public Administration* 104, 1–5.

Riley, M., Seccombe, M. and Garnaut, J. (2003), 'Government Protection of Manildra was "Treacherous"', *Sydney Morning Herald*, 15 August, available at <http://www.smh.com.au/articles/2003/08/14/1060588528321.html?from=storyrhs>, accessed 3 June 2004.

Annex A

Interview Format

Need to identify which parts of the integrity system the agency is handling, identify key documents.

1 In your view, are the formal integrity processes adequate? Have they been updated to keep in harmony with other changes in administrative culture?
2 What are the impediments standing in the way of your agency performing its role in supporting integrity?
3 Are the systems in place formalized to the extent that they do not rely upon individuals for their continuation?
4 What is your agency's contribution to the 'integrity' of the system, and how do you see your agency's place in the overall Public Sector 'system' in the Commonwealth?
5 In the area of integrity, what would you identify your source of leadership? (Ministers, Secretary). How is it evidenced – by speeches, issue raised at key meetings, staff bulletins. If so how regular/recent?
6 In your view, is the response to integrity properly coordinated across the Commonwealth?
7 In your view, are all the elements of a properly coordinated response in place?
   i (Strategies, regulatory framework, promulgation, training, mechanism for handling breaches, reporting, evaluation, linkage to ethics structure).
8 In your view, is there an appropriate balance between an awareness culture and an enforcement culture (in the integrity area that the agency is responsible for)?
9 Is there an impartial application of standards between the top and the bottom? Are there any records available that can be analysed to measure this?
10 In order to play your part in the integrity system, what inputs/ supports do you require from other agencies? (eg. information, investigation, prosecution, funding, etc.)
11 Do you consider that you provide a quality service in the integrity area that you are responsible for? Follow up on capacity, perception of unmet demands.
12 In order to play your part in the integrity system, would you like to receive greater support? Is there more that you could offer to other agencies?
13 Where do you go for advice on issues related to ethics and integrity?

The following questions refer to the agency *in terms of its internal integrity processes.*

14 What procedures does your agency have in place to ensure integrity where a service is provided by a non public sector provider?

Values

15 Do you support formal processes outside those laid down in the *Commonwealth Australian Public Service Act 1999* that support ethical behaviour - such as ethics clauses in contracts, etc?

Corruption

16 Does your agency have any specific anti- corruption procedures in place?
17 Does your agency have any specific procedures for handling whistleblowers?

Fraud control

18 In fulfilling the requirements of the fraud control policy, does your agency have any specific procedures for involving individuals with law enforcement experience in the risk assessment process?
19 Is your fraud risk assessment and fraud control plan prepared by agency staff or by a non public sector provider?

Annex B

Questionnaire

Preliminary Note: For the purposes of this questionnaire, 'integrity issues' should be understood broadly to encompass all efforts to ensure that Commonwealth public sector activities fall within acceptable legal and ethical boundaries. This includes matters such as codes of conduct, fulfilling agencies' stated corporate missions, honesty and closest to your view.

Q1. Thinking generally, how well do you think integrity issues are handled in the Commonwealth public sector today? Please circle the answer closest to your view.

Very well   Fairly well   Not very well   Not at all well   Can't say

Q2. How would you compare the handling of integrity issues in the Commonwealth public sector now with the situation 10 years ago?

Improved now   About the same   Better in the past   Can't say

Q3. Thinking about the agency in which you work, how well do you think integrity issues are handled there today? Please circle the answer closest to your view.

Very well   Fairly well   Not very well   Not at all well   Can't say

Q4. How would you compare the handling of integrity issues in your agency now with the situation 10 years ago?

Improved now   About the same   Better in the past   Can't say

Q4a. Please list some of the key factors that you think have contributed to the situation you have outlined for your agency in Questions 3 and 4. Please be as specific as you can.

Q5. Please rate the importance of each of the following agencies or organizations to your own agency when it comes to dealing with integrity issues. (If there are any relevant Commonwealth agencies or organizations missing from the list, please add and rate them at the bottom of the list.)

Ombudsman				
Very Important	Fairly Important	Not very Important	Not at all Important	Can't say
Australian Federal Police				
Very Important	Fairly Important	Not very Important	Not at all Important	Can't say

Parliamentary Committees				
Very Important	Fairly Important	Not very Important	Not at all Important	Can't say
Australian Public Service Commission				
Very Important	Fairly Important	Not very Important	Not at all Important	Can't say
Australian National Audit Office				
Very Important	Fairly Important	Not very Important	Not at all Important	Can't say
Administrative Appeals Tribunal				
Very Important	Fairly Important	Not very Important	Not at all Important	Can't say
Courts				
Very Important	Fairly Important	Not very Important	Not at all Important	Can't say
Non-Gov't bodies (eg unions advocacy groups)				
Very Important	Fairly Important	Not very Important	Not at all Important	Can't say
News Media				
Very Important	Fairly Important	Not very Important	Not at all Important	Can't say
Other (please specify)				
Very Important	Fairly Important	Not very Important	Not at all Important	Can't say
Very Important	Fairly Important	Not very Important	Not at all Important	Can't say
Very Important	Fairly Important	Not very Important	Not at all Important	Can't say

Q6. Identify the *three* agencies or organizations that you see as most important to your own agency when it comes to dealing with integrity issues. Circle any significant types of contact regarding integrity issues that your agency has had with each of the three agencies/organizations you nominated.

Name of Agency/Organization 1	Name of Agency/Organization 2	Name of Agency/Organization 3
....	....	....
Informal contact	Informal contact	Informal contact
Ad hoc Assistance	Ad hoc Assistance	Ad hoc Assistance
Correspondence	Correspondence	Correspondence
Meetings	Meetings	Meetings
Inter-Agency Committees	Inter-Agency Committees	Inter-Agency Committees
Training	Training	Training
Investigations	Investigations	Investigations
Policy Disputes	Policy Disputes	Policy Disputes
Conferences	Conferences	Conferences
Problem-Solving	Problem-Solving	Problem-Solving

Other (please specify)	Other (please specify)	Other (please specify)
....	....	....
....	....	....
....	....	....
....	....	....

Q7. How would you rate the *quality* of advice, information or other action on integrity issues that you receive from the following agencies and organizations?

Ombudsman				
Very good	Fairly good	Not very good	Not at all good	Can't say
Australian Federal Police				
Very good	Fairly good	Not very good	Not at all good	Can't say
Parliamentary Committees				
Very good	Fairly good	Not very good	Not at all good	Can't say
Australian Public Service Commission				
Very good	Fairly good	Not very good	Not at all good	Can't say
Australian National Audit Office				
Very good	Fairly good	Not very good	Not at all good	Can't say
Administrative Appeals Tribunal				
Very good	Fairly good	Not very good	Not at all good	Can't say
Courts				
Very good	Fairly good	Not very good	Not at all good	Can't say
Non-Gov't bodies (eg unions advocacy groups)				
Very good	Fairly good	Not very good	Not at all good	Can't say
News Media				
Very good	Fairly good	Not very good	Not at all good	Can't say
Other (please specify)				
....				
Very good	Fairly good	Not very good	Not at all good	Can't say
....				
Very good	Fairly good	Not very good	Not at all good	Can't say
....				
Very good	Fairly good	Not very good	Not at all good	Can't say

Q8. How would you rate the *promptness* of advice, information or other action about integrity issues that you receive from the following agencies and organizations?

Ombudsman				
Very good	Fairly good	Not very good	Not at all good	Can't say
Australian Federal Police				
Very good	Fairly good	Not very good	Not at all good	Can't say
Parliamentary Committees				
Very good	Fairly good	Not very good	Not at all good	Can't say
Australian Public Service Commission				
Very good	Fairly good	Not very good	Not at all good	Can't say
Australian National Audit Office				
Very good	Fairly good	Not very good	Not at all good	Can't say
Administrative Appeals Tribunal				
Very good	Fairly good	Not very good	Not at all good	Can't say
Courts				
Very good	Fairly good	Not very good	Not at all good	Can't say
Non-Gov't bodies (eg unions advocacy groups)				
Very good	Fairly good	Not very good	Not at all good	Can't say
News Media				
Very good	Fairly good	Not very good	Not at all good	Can't say
Other (please specify)				
....				
Very good	Fairly good	Not very good	Not at all good	Can't say
....				
Very good	Fairly good	Not very good	Not at all good	Can't say
....				
Very good	Fairly good	Not very good	Not at all good	Can't say

Q9. How would you rate the general *level of coordination* between the different agencies with which you deal on integrity issues?

Very good	Fairly good	Not very good	Not at all good	Can't say

Q10. Which of the following types of integrity-related activity do you think are *most important* for achieving a high level of integrity within the Commonwealth public sector? Please circle the numbers beside the item listed below for up to three activities.

1 Workplace education and training in ethics/integrity matters.
2 External Investigations (for example, by Ombudsman, ICAC, or Police).
3 Internal investigations (for example, by internal audit teams or deputized managers.
4 Agency codes of conduct.
5 nvestigations by the news media.
6 High standards of education for appointments and promotions.
7 Parliamentary oversight.
8 Internal disclosures ('whistleblowing').
9 Leadership from senior managers.
10 Leadership from middle and junior managers.
11 1More detailed laws and regulations to follow.
12 Pressure from non-government organizations (e.g advocacy groups or trade unions).

Q11 Which of the following agencies or organizations could potentially do more to assist your agency on integrity issues? Circle the agencies.

Ombudsman

Australian Federal Police

Parliamentary Committees

Australian Public Service Commission

Australian National Audit Office

Administrative Appeals Tribunal

Courts

Non-Gov't bodies (eg unions advocacy groups)

News Media

Other

____

Q12 What do you think are the main barriers that prevent these agencies and organizations from achieving this potentially larger role? Circle the numbers beside the main reasons you think apply.

1 1 Unwillingness by the agency or organization itself.
2 2 External pressure on the agency or organization.
3 3 Lack of reward for greater activity.
4 4 Resource constraints.
5 5 Legislative or regulatory restrictions.
6 6 Other (please specify)

____

____

Finally, just a few details about yourself. If you have requested that your identity not be revealed in publications arising from this study, these details will be kept confidential and will not be used in ways that can identify you. They are nonetheless useful for describing characteristics of the whole sample of people who participated in the study.

Agency: ____

Position: ____

Number of years you have worked in the Commonwealth public sector: _____________ years.

Thank you once again for participating in the study. Please post your completed questionnaire to Peter Roberts, Centre for Applied Philosophy and Public Ethics, LPO Box A260, ANU, Canberra ACT 2601 in the stamped envelope provided.

Chapter 9

When Integrity Breaks Down: The Australian Wheat Board Example

Stephen Bartos

Introduction

From 1999 to 2003 AWB (International), the international wheat trading arm of Australian agribusiness company AWB, made clandestine payments of some $US222m in illicit kickbacks to the Saddam Hussein regime in Iraq. These payments were associated with sales of wheat under the United Nations' Oil-for-Food Programme (OFF). Sale of wheat was a legitimate objective of that programme, but through sham 'transport' payments the AWB and the Iraqi government were able to subvert the intent of the programme that no funds would be transferred to the Iraqi government for spending on non-humanitarian purposes. Although the scandal was labelled 'wheat for weapons' by the Labor Opposition party in Australia, the actual disposition of the funds by the Iraqi government is impossible to determine – dollars are fungible, and the proceeds of the kickbacks simply found their way into the national treasury. It is, however, clear that this was directly contrary to the intent of the OFF programme, and represented a breach of both international and national standards.

Exactly which individuals were responsible, and what the legal consequences might be for them, was at time of writing still being resolved through protracted investigative and court proceedings. The concept of corruption, as discussed elsewhere in this book can, at times, be ambiguous and capable of diverse and multiple definitions. Not in this case. Even though charges are yet to be laid, there is a sufficient body of evidence about the facts of the case, gathered in consecutive United Nations and Australian investigations, to make it unnecessary to debate whether or not this was a case of illicit, unethical or corrupt behaviour: the evidence suggests it was all three. The important questions, examined in this chapter, are what caused such an egregious breach of standards to occur in the first place – and why oversight and regulatory arrangements failed to monitor and control the conduct of the company involved? It is a story involving privatization of a previously government-owned statutory marketing body without adequate due diligence; the privatized body maintaining a monopoly over export of Australian wheat without strong regulatory safeguards over abuse of monopoly powers or corporate misbehaviour by the monopolist; failings in corporate governance in the company; and a government that took no action on warnings it was given that kickbacks were occurring. It has lasting lessons both for regulatory design and for the governance arrangements for corporations involved in international trade.

The Anatomy of the Scandal

The kickbacks owe their existence to a regime of sanctions that was put in place after the first Gulf War in 1990–1991. Following the Iraqi invasion of Kuwait in August 1990, the United Nations condemned the invasion (Security Council resolution 660) and instituted a regime of economic sanctions (Security Council resolution 661). Fierce diplomatic pressure on Iraq ensued involving numerous deadlines and ultimatums; eventually the United States led a coalition of forces that ended the Iraqi occupation of Kuwait in January–February 1991 (Freedman and Karsh 2003). However, economic sanctions continued while the US and its coalition partners – with support from UN resolutions – conducted their ultimately fruitless search for the weapons of mass destruction allegedly possessed by Iraq.

Within a few years, the sanctions regime was inflicting enormous suffering on the ordinary people of Iraq. This suffering began to be covered in news reporting, and leapt to prominence in 1995 when according to Cortright (2001) researchers with a Food and Agricultural Organization (FAO) study in Iraq wrote to *The Lancet*, the journal of the British Medical Society, asserting that sanctions were responsible for the deaths of 567,000 Iraqi children. *The New York Times* picked up the story and declared 'Iraq Sanctions Kill Children'. CBS followed up with a report on *60 Minutes*. The weight of public opinion began to turn against sanctions, and it became clear to a sufficient number of the world's opinion leaders that the sanctions regime had either to be abandoned (a course of action the US government was reluctant to support) or to be modified in some way.

The solution found by the United Nations was a programme called 'Oil-for-Food' instituted under UN Security Council resolution 986 of 14 April 2005. The OFF programme allowed the Iraqi government to raise money through sales of the country's key export, oil, in order to buy food, medical supplies and other humanitarian needs. Revenues from the sale of oil were paid into an escrow account and the Iraqi government was (in theory) permitted to use these funds only to buy humanitarian goods that had been approved by the United Nations.

Sanctions, and the Oil-for-Food programme, ended in 2003 for obvious reasons. Among the documents discovered following the second Gulf War were records of the various transactions under OFF that suggested *prima facie* that kickbacks of funds directly to the Saddam Hussein government had accompanied the Programme. The United States' Government Accountability Office (GAO 2005) conducted an investigation, into the matter, reported as testimony before a US Senate committee hearing, which found clear evidence of kickbacks.

The United Nations itself in 2004 appointed former US Federal Reserve chairman Paul Volcker to conduct an inquiry. The Volcker report (IIC 2005), released in October 2005, found numerous and widespread irregularities in the

Programme: total 'illicit income' of \$1.8b, of which \$1.5b was paid as kickbacks. Importantly for Australia, the inquiry found that by far the biggest single contributor to kickbacks had been AWB, which had paid \$221.7m of kickbacks to the Saddam Hussein regime. The next biggest, Chiyaporn Rice Co. Ltd. of Thailand came in at less than on fifth of that sum, \$US42.8m. Volcker clearly had no doubt as to the identity of a major culprit; even the graphics used to illustrate the mechanisms whereby kickbacks were paid include a wheatsheaf symbol – the same symbol, although not the same design, that AWB uses as its corporate logo (IIC 2005, Chart F, 291)

Although OFF nominally started in 2005, it took some time to get underway; AWB(I) only began winning wheat contracts under OFF from 1999. Payments for transport costs associated with these wheat shipments were made through a front company, Alia, nominally a Jordanian trucking company that, in fact, was controlled by Iraqi interests, and which did no actual trucking of the wheat. Alia's role was to funnel the payments to the Iraqi government, while taking a small percentage of the transaction. It was a subterfuge to allow Iraq to circumvent the rules of OFF. In retrospect, either or both of the UN and the Australian government should have been able to identify, as did Volcker and the subsequent Australian inquiry (Cole 2006) that these were what the IIC (2005) calls 'illicit payments' – that is, payments designed to circumvent the sanctions regime. However, the parties did at the time take pains to disguise the payments, and AWB when queried by Australian government officials denied that any kickbacks were being paid. Given they were illicit, it is hardly surprising they were hidden; what concerns us here is why AWB allowed itself to be drawn into the scheme, and why its wrongdoing was not uncovered at the time.

Due Diligence and Oversight

The kickbacks regime started at much the same time as the former Australian Wheat Board was privatized. Privatization was a protracted process, with government agreement to the move in 1997, transfer of assets to subsidiaries of the statutory authority in 1998, issue of shares to wheat growers in July 1999, and a public float in August 2001 (AWB 2007). From 1999, the privatized organization became known only by the acronym AWB, and in its new corporate form diversified considerably, including not only the subsidiary, AWB (International) Limited, which maintains Australia's monopoly in relation to wheat exports, but also various domestic corporations, some of which (such as rural finance and operations company Landmark) have no direct connection with wheat exports. The subsequent growth and diversification of AWB means it is now a somewhat different body from its parent. That does not however imply retrospective exculpation for government; the Minister for Agriculture up until the end of 1998–1999 had responsibility, under the government's arrangements for statutory marketing authorities, for approving the strategic plan of the Australian Wheat Board. Although negotiations with the Iraqis were underway by mid 1999, we can presume that the Board did not advise the Minister that the Board had kickback plans: more likely any kickback plans were still at a lower operational level within the organization, and in any case the Board had weightier matters such as its own privatization to deal with. Ministerial responsibility in a traditional sense applied, but it would take a very strict reading of the Westminster conventions of responsibility to suggest that even before any actual payments were made the Minister ought to have become aware of the events through the strategic planning process.

There was, however, a fundamental failing in the processes adopted for privatization for which ministers do have to take responsibility – because it was made possible by legislation. The AWB privatization was not a privatization of the sort we are familiar with from the history of Australian government business privatizations – ranging over the present Howard government and previous administrations, including companies such as Qantas, the Commonwealth Bank, various airports, just under half of Telstra, and literally dozens of other bodies. In such privatizations, there is always what is called a due diligence process. Documents relating to the assets, liabilities, financial prospects, strategies, risks – anything that might affect the value of the body to be privatized – are collected, and these documentary materials made available under strict confidentiality rules to prospective purchasers (Bartos 2004). Due diligence is a detailed discovery process that aims to find out what if any skeletons are hidden in the closet of the organization about to be privatized. The privatization of the AWB was a different matter. It was not a sale aimed at raising funds for the government – it represented rather a transfer of responsibility, from the government to wheat growers. There was an extensive publicity campaign designed to convince wheat growers of the desirability of the transfer – but as far as can be gleaned from evidence on the public record, there was no due diligence of the sort conducted for the privatization of other government business enterprises. The Australian Wheat Board's Chief Financial Officer, Mr Ingleby, continued in the CFO position in the newly privatized AWB; Cole (2006) found that 'in the period from about June 1999 to March 2003' (Cole 2006, IV, 247) – that is, over the entire period of the kickbacks regime – he was one of the persons whose acts and conduct might have breached sections of the *Corporations Act 2001.* In other government privatizations, the CFO would be involved in depth in a due diligence and scrutiny of the dealings of the company – but that does not seem to have happened in this case.

Post privatization, the government remained the primary backer of the AWB's operations. Since 1939, the Australian government had given the Australian Wheat Board a monopoly over Australia's bulk wheat exports (known as the 'single desk'). After 1999, AWB was notionally grower controlled but dependent on government support in order to exercise an export monopoly in much the same way as had its predecessor. The body that took over the enforcement and policing role was a new statutory authority, the Wheat Export Authority (WEA); it had some limited supervisory powers, but was established primarily to enforce the monopoly. It was given the power to impose severe fines on any person or company exporting bulk wheat without a permit, and AWB (I) was given a veto over WEA issuing permits to any other company. The WEA did not, however, have any significant power to supervise and regulate AWB (I) itself.

The structure of the WEA is not in any case conducive to it exercising strong monitoring role. It has five members. The chair is independent and well respected, and there is one other independent member; of the remaining three, one is an official of the Minister's department, and two are appointed by the Minister on the recommendation of the Grains Council of Australia. Nor does its legislation give it investigative powers; the WEA did indeed ask AWB if it had been involved in kickbacks, but as indicated by the WEA to a Senate hearing 'they showed our person who went down there. There was no reference to agency payments for Iraq on it. They denied it' (Senate Rural and Regional Affairs and Transport Committee, 14 February 2006). In this and other subsequent Senate hearings the chair of WEA has repeatedly made the point that the body's role is limited by its legislation – it is not equipped by law to be a tough regulator.

Both economic theory and Australia's history of agricultural marketing monopolies suggests that without independent supervision and tough regulation, a monopoly is likely to exploit its position and engage in untoward behaviours of various sorts. There is a strong historical parallel. In the late 1970s Asia Dairy, a subsidiary of the Australian Diary Corporation, had paid kickbacks and engaged in tax evasion, while keeping the government of the day in the dark (AIC 1989). A Senate Inquiry ensued (SSCFGO 1981) and for a time scrutiny of marketing authorities and monopolies was tougher. By the late 1990s it seemed these lessons had been forgotten. But not by all: the need for a tougher regulator was something recognized widely, and well before the Cole Inquiry, including on the government side (for example, 'the WEA is a toothless tiger because it had its own hands tied within months of the legislation going through … do you think the WEA is fundamentally flawed in relation to its ability to be a monitoring agency in the future?' (Sen. Ferris, Hansard, Thursday, 29 May 2003, Rural and Regional Affairs and Transport Legislation Committee, Reference: Wheat Marketing Amendment Bill 2002).

Corporate Governance within AWB

The terms of reference for the Cole Inquiry confined it to examining 'whether decisions, actions, conduct or payments by Australian companies … breached any Federal, State or Territory law'. Corporate governance and ethical standards were excluded; even so, Cole made the observation in the introduction to his report that 'the conduct of AWB and its officers was due to a failure of corporate culture. The question posed within AWB was: what must be done to maintain sales to Iraq? The answer given was: 'Do whatever is necessary.' He identifies the problem as 'a closed culture of superiority and impregnability, of dominance and self-importance. Legislation cannot destroy such a culture or create a satisfactory one. That is the task of boards and the management of companies'. The evidence before the inquiry clearly points to a failure of corporate governance. While AWB staff, with the involvement of senior managers of the company, was making illicit payments in order to secure wheat sales to Iraq, where was the Board? There is no evidence that the Board did anything other than encourage a culture of 'whatever it takes'. Rewards and incentives within the company were geared around wheat sales, and there was nothing advanced in argument or evidence before Cole to suggest that the Board applied itself to considerations of how to ensure ethical conduct. The Board was also criticized as the scandal unfolded – an Australian Financial Review columnist summed up the mood in an article of 26 March 2006 suggesting that the affair 'highlights once again the fact that a good board performs well when disaster hits. AWB directors have so far failed this test miserably'.

The decision to pay kickbacks was not taken in isolation – Cole established that knowledge of the arrangements became widely known within the company over the course of the period 1999 to 2003; he names 11 of the senior staff and refers their cases to a Task Force to consider possible prosecutions. If the Board did not know that the kickbacks were going on, the question is whether they exercised effective governance in relation to the conduct of management. If they did know, that knowledge was never documented (Cole found no evidence to this effect). Allan Hawke, Chancellor of the Australian National University, in a speech in August 2006 argues that:

> The AWB Board's role has received little attention. Indeed their 'performance' was rewarded by all six standing for re-election being reappointed for another term at the recent AGM. The majority of the shareholders seem more interested in displacement activity – blaming anyone and everyone – rather than extracting accountability from the AWB itself.

A generalizable corporate governance lesson can be drawn from the short-term nature of the transactions involved. The payoff was immediate – for four years, AWB secured sales of Australian wheat into Iraq which it might not otherwise have achieved. It is not possible to say definitively whether or not the kickbacks secured the deal – had AWB declined to pay the kickbacks, it might still have obtained wheat contracts based on the desirability of Australian wheat for Iraqi bread, its established network of contacts in Iraq, and the unwillingness of other competitors in the market to engage in kickbacks. Nevertheless, it is clear by their actions that AWB executives saw a need to pay the kickbacks to obtain sales in this market. It was short term thinking. Selling some additional wheat at a small premium then has led to a collapse of the AWB corporate reputation (and share price) and widespread questioning of whether it should retain its export monopoly. Short term thinking is a failure in governance, but as demonstrated in this case, also part of the mindset that accepts corrupt behaviour as necessary or allowable.

The other important governance lesson relates to the virtual absence on the AWB Board of independent directors with no personal interest in wheat sales. The 'grower control' shibboleth at the time of privatization meant that under the company constitution an overwhelming majority of directors were themselves wheat growers, with an interest in selling as much wheat as quickly as possible for as high a price as possible. Not only the Board but crucial committees such as the audit committee were dominated by wheat growers. It should make no difference in theory, given directors' fiduciary duties, but in reality it is easy to see how it might have been harder for this particular Board to ask searching questions of management about the means used to sell the wheat. In any corporation, it is important that some directors have a deep understanding of the business; but a leavening of directors from outside not just the company but the industry concerned can be useful in avoiding scandals such as that which engulfed AWB.

Government Responsibility

There is no evidence that the government had a deliberate policy of turning a 'blind eye' to the kickbacks while they occurred. The evidence gathered by Cole suggests that ministers genuinely had no knowledge of what was going on; and that it was not fabricated ignorance (the doctrine of 'plausible denial' identified in the 1975 Church Committee sense) but genuine. This level of ignorance about a crucial area of foreign policy does, however, raise important questions about the policy stance and attitudes of the government agencies involved – particularly the Department of Foreign Affairs and Trade (DFAT). There is also a strong case that there was not a deliberate but rather a tacit policy in place that AWB and its officials were to be trusted and believed.

Actions (or inaction) by government were outside the terms of reference of the Cole Inquiry, which as noted earlier was only allowed to examine the actions of the companies specifically mentioned in the 2004 United Nations report on OFF, and only the extent to which such actions might have breached the law. Cole was not given a mandate to examine the extent to which government policy encouraged or discouraged kickbacks, whether Ministers ought to have inquired further once they received warnings that something was amiss, or how the government has managed its relationship with AWB.

It is, however, not easy for the Australian government to entirely distance itself from the scandal. It is responsible for various international covenants against the sort of kickbacks in which AWB engaged. Australia is a signatory to both the UN *Convention Against Corruption* 2005 and the Organisation for Economic Cooperation and Development (OECD) *Convention on Combating Bribery of Foreign Public Officials in International Business Transactions* 1999. The *Criminal Code Amendment (Bribery of Foreign Public Officials) Act 1999* (*Bribery Act*) is the Commonwealth Parliament's legislative implementation of that latter convention. These various conventions mean that the government is responsible for monitoring the activities of Australian firms that might be engaged in illicit activities in other countries (Kurtz 2006).

Under the relevant Security Council resolutions, there was a clear obligation on national governments (as well as the United Nations) to monitor compliance with the sanctions regime. Resolution 661 (which first imposed the sanctions regime, and was subsequently reaffirmed several times, with some modifications that took account of the Iraqi withdrawal from Kuwait after the first Gulf War) provides that:

> ... all States shall not make available to the Government of Iraq or to any commercial, industrial or public utility undertaking in Iraq or Kuwait, any funds or any other financial or economic resources *and shall prevent their nationals and any persons within their territories* from removing from their territories or otherwise making available to that Government or to any such undertaking any such funds or resources and from remitting any other funds to persons or bodies within Iraq or Kuwait, except payments exclusively for strictly medical or humanitarian purposes and, in humanitarian circumstances, foodstuffs. (UN Security Council resolution 661; my emphasis)

There is room for debate about whether this imposes an active obligation on states to investigate companies' *potential* dealings; but almost certainly it does indicate an obligation on any state to take action if it has clear evidence of actions by its citizens or companies to circumvent the sanctions. During the course of the Cole Inquiry, there was some polite disagreement between DFAT and UN officials as to where responsibility lay; DFAT claiming it was 'just a post-box' in relation to passing the AWB grains contracts (with their damning transport clauses) to the UN so it could monitor them, and the UN in turn claiming it was the responsibility of member states to do the monitoring. It is a matter of judgement as to where the buck stops: the Volcker report (IIC 2005) does not spare the UN from criticism, and officials from that organization have since resigned or left office as a result of the evidence of mismanagement uncovered by the report; but at the same time, the wording of the relevant UN Security Council resolution does make it clear that member government have obligations that go beyond merely a postbox role.

Probably the most damning implication for government from the findings of the Cole Inquiry was its failure to take action even when alerted to the existence of a potential problem. The government was alerted to the potential existence of kickbacks via cables received in the Department of Foreign Affairs and Trade in Canberra from its post at the United Nations; referring to 2001 cables, Cole concluded in relation to their author Bronte Moules, 'it is apparent, however, that Ms Moules appreciated the risk that AWB might be the subject of Iraq's attempts to circumvent the sanctions' (Cole 2006, 30.110). Nevertheless, Cole found that DFAT did not have 'actual knowledge' of the kickbacks. Actual knowledge seems from the context of Cole to require probative evidence to the effect, not simply second-hand reports. Given the government accepted assurances from AWB that there were no kickbacks, no further inquiry into the activities of AWB (and therefore no actual knowledge) was forthcoming.

Why did government fail to undertake proper inquiries? As noted above, it is apparent that there was a fundamental lack of realization by the government at the time of privatization that monopoly behaviour in relation to reporting to ministers would be different in private than in public hands, and led to a failure to put in place regulatory oversight. That does not however explain the failure to initiate investigations once the alarms began to be sounded. Those warnings, according to evidence provided to the Cole Inquiry by Trade Minister Mark Vaile and Foreign Minister Alexander Downer, were either not read or discounted following denials by AWB. Ministers clearly believed the AWB, as shown by the testimony to the Cole Inquiry from each of the Prime Minister, Foreign Minister and Trade Minister. As the Prime Minister indicated in response to questions from John Agius SC, senior counsel for the Cole Inquiry:

> Q. Well, in that connection, did you ever have any suspicion that any Australian company, including AWB, one of the largest exporters to Iraq, might have been involved in that rorting?
> A. No, I didn't.
> Q. Are you able to say why it was that you never had any such suspicion?
> A Well, because I'd never been presented with any hard evidence. I was, I guess, conscious only of AWB because of the predominant role of AWB in the wheat trade, and I had always believed the best of that company, as had most people in the government. It had been associated with the Australian wheat industry since the 1930s, and it hadn't crossed my mind that it would have behaved corruptly. (Transcript, Cole Inquiry, 13 April 2006)

AWB was a rural icon, its leadership very closely connected to the government, and in the 'Yes Minister' tradition, as 'decent chaps' they were to be left alone. Nowhere in the evidence presented to the Cole Inquiry is there a formal government instruction to this effect – but the actions of the DFAT officers, those of the then Department of Primary Industries and Energy (DPIE) and subsequently Agriculture, Forestry and Fisheries, those in *Austrade* and in the Prime Minister's department demonstrate a shared understanding of the expectations of government.

Bartos (2006) identifies these shared expectations as fundamental to understanding the AWB scandal. Tacit public policy can be defined as a type of policy that is understood among the key policy players, has an effect on government action, but is never defined, articulated, or recorded. AWB had an undue influence in the tacit understandings between Ministers and government officials because it was a fully paid up member of a small and influential agri-political club. The Ministers concerned (especially Mark Vaile as Trade Minister and a senior National Party Minister) knew the AWB senior people and interacted with them frequently. Grains Council, National Party, senior Trade officials, senior Agriculture Department officials, were closely connected; for example, Warren Truss (deputy leader of the National party and subsequently Minister for Trade) and Brendan Stewart (Chair of the Board of AWB) are both former office holders in the Queensland Graingrowers Association, as is the Liberal Party Minister for Industry, Tourism and Resources Ian Macfarlane. The Chairman of the AWB Board at the time the kickbacks began, Trevor Flugge, was former President of the Australian Wheat Growers Federation (now Grains Council) and former Director of the Grains Research and Development Corporation (a ministerial appointment); the present chairman, Brendan Stewart, is not only former president of the Queensland Graingrowers' Association but also former president of the Grains Council of Australia and vice president of the National Farmers' Federation; a majority of other AWB directors have held political positions in farmers' representative or marketing organizations of one sort or another. Bartos (2006) provides details of the agri-political backgrounds of the

AWB Directors, showing how closely they engage with this closed policy network, and how closely their backgrounds parallel those of the ministers and senior advisers in government who deal with agriculture.

In the literature on policy communities (Grant and MacNamara 1995; Marsh and Smith 2000; Botterill 2005), agri-political networks are recognized as the paradigmatic case of a closed, isolated group that excludes outsiders and resents any scrutiny or criticism. While the AWB case clearly fits that mould, and is further distinguishable from other corporations by the privilege extended to it of a government monopoly over exports, there are nevertheless more broadly applicable lessons in governance and ethics that stem from the degree of respect in which it was held by government and wheat growers: that this respect of itself can mask corrupt conduct and waylay proper investigation.

There is a useful comparison to be drawn here with the United States' experience with Enron. In their analysis of the Enron affair, *The Smartest Guys in the Room,* McLean and Elkind asked why analysts has not been more questioning – even when alarm bells were rung.

> ... from time to time analysts would quiz Enron's investor relations department [about one of the devices for creating illusory profits] ... but they refrained from pointing them out in the reports they issued to investors. Analysts who worked for Wall Street banks later claimed that they had been deceived by Enron. But if they were indeed victims, they were willing ones. (McLean and Elkind 2004, 231)

Not only the analysts, who feared for their jobs (the one major analyst who went against the herd was targeted by Enron who established a relationship with his bank and then had him sacked) but also the ratings agencies were willing participants in deception. It seems, in a striking parallel with the failure by Ministers and departments to join the dots on the AWB affair, that 'while the credit analysts saw many of the pieces that made up Enron's convoluted financing structure, they never connected them all up' (McLean and Elkind 2004, 238–9). They were caught up in the herd mentality, decided to go along with the illusion just because all the others were too.

But one of the key lessons from Enron was that hard questions do need to be asked, especially if doubts about a corporation are raised. This did not happen with AWB because ministers considered the company was just too well respected. Enron too was highly respected – in each of the five years before it filed for bankruptcy in December 2001 it had made it into the top ranks of the Fortune magazine Fortune 500 listings of America's most admired companies, and in 2001 was rated America's most innovative company in that same list. Being respected is not necessarily a guarantee of honesty.

References

Australian Institute of Criminology (AIC) (1989), 'Wayward Governance: Illegality and its Control in the Public Sector', in P.N. Grabosky (ed.) *Australian Studies in Law, Crime and Justice* (Canberra: Australian Institute of Criminology).

Australian National Audit Office (1998), 'Accountability and Oversight Arrangements for Statutory Bodies in the Former Primary Industries and Energy Portfolio', *Report* (Canberra: ANAO).

AWB (1999–2004), *Annual Reports*.

AWB (2007), *Corporate History*, available at <http://www.awb.com.au>, accessed 2 March 2007.

Bartos, S. (2006), *Against the Grain – the AWB Scandal and Why it Happened* (Sydney: UNSW Press).

Bartos, S. (2004), *Public Sector Governance Australia* (Sydney: CCH).

Botterill, L. (2005), 'Policy Change and Network Termination: The Role of Farm Groups in Agricultural Policy Making in Australia', *Australian Journal of Political Science* 40:2, 33–50.

Church Committee (1975), *United States Senate Select Committee to Study Governmental Operations with Respect to Intelligence Activities* (Washington, DC: United States Senate).

Cole, T. (2006), *Report of the Inquiry into Certain Australian Companies in Relation to the UN Oil-for-Food Programme* (The Cole Inquiry) (Canberra: Australian Government).

Cortright, D. (2001), 'A Hard Look at Iraq Sanctions', *The Nation*, 3 December.

Freedman, L. and Karsh, E. (2003), *The Gulf Conflict, 1990–1991: Diplomacy and War in the New World Order* (Princeton, NJ: Princeton University Press).

GAO (2005), 'GAO–05–346T Testimony Before the Permanent Subcommittee on Investigations, Committee on Homeland Security and Governmental Affairs', US Senate, 15 February (Washington, DC: United States Government Accountability Office).

Grant, W. and MacNamara, A. (1995), 'When Policy Communities Intersect: The Case of Agriculture and Banking', *Political Studies* 43, 509–15.

IIC (2005), *Independent Inquiry Committee into the United Nations Oil-for-food Programme* (The Volcker Report) (New York: United Nations).

Kurtz, J. (2006), 'A Look Beyond the Cole Inquiry: AWB Ltd, Bribery and Australia's Obligations under International Law', *Discussion Paper 18/06 Democratic Audit of Australia* (Canberra: Australian National University).

Marsh, D. and Smith, M. (2000), 'Understanding Policy Networks: Towards a Dialectical Approach', *Political Studies* 48, 4–21.

McLean, B. and Elkind, P. (2004), *The Smartest Guys in the Room: The Amazing Rise and Scandalous Fall of Enron* (New York: Penguin).

Parliamentary Library (1997–1998), 'Wheat Marketing Legislation Amendment Bill 1998', *Bills Digest No. 220* (Canberra: Parliament of Australia).

Productivity Commission (2000), 'Single-Desk Marketing: Assessing the Economic Arguments', *Staff Research Paper* (Canberra: Productivity Commission).

SSCFGO (1981), *Report The Australian Dairy Corporation and its Asian Subsidiaries* (Canberra: Senate Standing Committee on Finance and Government Operations).

Weller, P. (2002), *Don't Tell the Prime Minister* (Carlton North: Scribe Publications).

Weller, P. (1994), *Royal Commissions and the Making of Public Policy* (Melbourne: Macmillan Education Australia).

Chapter 10

Towards a Federal Integrity Commission: The Challenge of Institutional Capacity-Building in Australia

A.J. Brown

Introduction

How can society be satisfied that any government has established the right institutions to safeguard public integrity? Even if those institutions exist on paper, when can citizens be confident these bodies have been given the capacity to do their job properly? As shown by preceding chapters, these questions are basic to the methods used to assess the state of any government's 'integrity system', and the political judgements about the adequacy of that system reached as a result. They are also basic to the decisions that have to be made by any government as to whether their integrity institutions are adequate for the task, and if not, how developments in those institutions should be designed.

This chapter analyses the institution-building questions that have confronted, and continue to confront, Australia's federal government in its search to establish a complete and coherent integrity system. In mapping the institutional choices that lie before the national government, Australia's national integrity system assessment was able to use the comparative analysis made possible by a federal system, to compare the differing institutional approaches of different jurisdictions within the same political system.

The first part of the chapter examines some of the fundamental issues that need to be addressed in any such comparison. How does the institutional framework for integrity currently vary between these jurisdictions? Given underlying differences between the jurisdictions, what is the most intelligent way to compare the 'net value' of the resources being dedicated to the anti-corruption effort? Are there differences in the integrity risks faced by different jurisdictions, that would justify major differences in frameworks or resourcing?

These questions also set the scene for the remaining analysis, by introducing the parallel – but different – institutional choices made by two Australian jurisdictions: the federal (Commonwealth) government, and the government of the state of Victoria. Since 2003, these jurisdictions have confronted, but responded differently to, relatively similar challenges regarding institutional capacity in the integrity field. Despite pressure from the federal government to do so, the Victorian government elected not to create a new anti-corruption commission in response to allegations of police corruption, instead initially grafting new anti-corruption functions onto an existing body. In parallel, the federal government also decided *not* to follow its own advice about the right 'model', establishing a new specialist body – the Australian Commission for Law Enforcement Integrity (ACLEI) – but not a generalist anti-corruption commission for the public sector.

Together, these developments point to some major unresolved issues of institutional design – not least the continuing need for Australia's federal government to further invest in generalist anti-corruption capacity. The growing evidence for this includes the unanimous assessment of the Senate Legal and Constitutional Legislation Committee, and the federal government's own track record in instituting at least three additional *ad hoc* inquiries into alleged abuses of federal power, outside the standing institutional framework, even while professing that the creation of ACLEI was enough to address any overall 'gap' in the federal integrity system.

The second part of the chapter sets out a new schema for addressing these unresolved issues. Applying principles of institutional design developed through the national integrity system assessment (Brown and Head 2004, 2005; Brown et al. 2005a, 62–78), five important issues of institutional design are highlighted:

1 how to bring all federal officeholders within a realistic scheme of integrity scrutiny (either by expanding the jurisdiction of the Australian Commission for Law Enforcement Integrity, or rolling that agency into an existing or new body with appropriate investigative capacity);
2 how to include senior officials such as ministers within the scheme;
3 how to ensure that information about integrity breaches is rapidly transmitted to the place where most effective action can be taken, including effective management of 'whistleblowing';
4 how proactive integrity-building and corruption resistance strategies, rather than reactive investigations into alleged integrity breaches, are best pursued and monitored across the public sector; and
5 how the different integrity institutions are best to be coordinated.

With relatively clear answers available to each of these questions, addressing them has become a clear test for current and future federal governments. As discussed in conclusion, this next phase of institutional development relies on an approach that complements and integrates the roles of existing institutions rather than proposing new bodies as a 'silver bullet' solution to perceived problems. Only through a more comprehensive process of institutional design can public integrity systems be properly strengthened.

Comparing Institutional Capacities and Needs

How do Integrity Institutions Differ?

In an integrity system, questions of institutional design frequently go to the heart of a system's capacity. As one of the three key themes in the assessment of Australia's integrity systems, 'capacity' can be seen as taking at least seven different forms, including (Brown et al. 2005a, 62):

- Legal capacity – are integrity institutions properly constituted, and do they have the formal powers or jurisdiction they need to fulfil their tasks?
- Financial capacity – are the budgets of integrity bodies right for their tasks?
- Human resource capacity – are sufficient numbers of employees dedicated to integrity functions in both core and distributed integrity institutions?
- Skills, education and training – do managers and integrity practitioners have the right professional training and background to discharge their roles?
- Political will – do senior officeholders possess, or are they sufficiently empowered by the community to find, the will to provide genuine leadership?
- Community capacity – is there sufficient broader social or community understanding and support for integrity processes?
- Balance in distribution of capacity – are resources adequately shared between positive and negative strategies?

The institutional frameworks that make up the integrity system are not necessarily neatly concentrated. Often they are 'distributed' throughout the larger networks of governmental and other institutions that permeate society. However, 'core' integrity agencies, such as independent anti-corruption commissions and Ombudsman's Offices, clearly play a key role in the development of integrity systems, and in questions over whether those systems are working.

Where the number or configuration of these core integrity agencies differs significantly, there is frequently debate about the relative adequacy of different systems. Figure 10.1 sets out some of the basic differences in Australia, and charts the history of recent debates showing the institutional configurations as at the end of calendar years 2003 and 2007. At the top of the spectrum, the state of New South Wales has developed the largest number of independent integrity agencies (see also Smith, this volume). Having been the first Australian jurisdiction to institute an Independent Commission Against Corruption (ICAC) in 1988, perceived failures in the handling of police corruption matters led to a further commission of inquiry and establishment of a separate Police Integrity Commission in 1997.

At the bottom of the spectrum, as at 2003 several jurisdictions retained a model in which the only independent agency apart from an auditor-general was the office of the Ombudsman, instituted in most jurisdictions in the 1970s (Brown et al. 2005b; ACLEI 2007, 7–9).

Figure 10.1 Some core public integrity institutions in Australia, 2003–2007

2003

	Auditor-General	Ombudsman	Police Complaint Authority	Police Integrity Commission	Anti-Corruption Commission	Crime Commission
NSW	1	2		3	4 (ICAC)	5
Qld	1	2	3 (Crime and Misconduct Commission)			
West Aust.	1	2	3 (Corruption and Crime Commission)			
Sth Aust.	1	2	3			
Cth	1	2				3
Victoria	1	2				
Tas.	1	2				

2007

	Auditor-General	Ombudsman	Police Complaint Authority	Police Integrity Commission	Anti-Corruption Commission	Crime Commission
NSW	1	2		3	4 (ICAC)	5
Cth	1	2		3 (ACLEI)		4
Qld	1	2	3 (Crime and Misconduct Commission)			
West Aust.	1	2	3 (Corruption and Crime Commission)			
Sth Aust.	1	2	3			
Victoria	1	2		3 (OPI)		
Tas.	1	2				

Notes

1 These tables do not include Public Service Commissions or equivalents, or Health Care Complaints Commissions and a range of other specialist independent integrity bodies, other than those dedicated to police.
2 See also Brown and Head 2004, 2005; Brown et al. 2005: 13.

The key institutional shifts in 2003–2007 relate to the federal (Commonwealth) and Victorian governments, both of which moved from that original model by creating a further independent agency to deal with police corruption. First, in 2004, the Victorian government expanded the roles and resources of its public sector Ombudsman to include a new Office of Police Integrity (OPI). This body was akin to the NSW Police Integrity Commission but still housed within, and headed by, the Victorian Ombudsman – until separated in late 2007. The creation of OPI followed a major police corruption scandal (see Gilchrist and Bachelard 2004; Rennie 2007). However the Victorian government resisted public and media pressure to follow the same path as taken by the three other jurisdictions notable for their prior similar problems: Queensland, NSW and Western Australia. As shown in Figure 10.1, in each of those states, an independent royal commission into police corruption had led to establishment of a separate permanent anti-corruption commission, with the added functions of a crime commission in Queensland and Western Australia.

In contrast to the Victorian government's decision to build the capacity of *existing* institutions to fight corruption, the federal government reacted to similar issues by committing to the creation of a wholly new anti-corruption agency. In June 2004, the relevant federal ministers announced the creation of an 'independent national anti-corruption body' in terms that also explicitly criticized the Victorian government for failing to do so (Ruddock and Ellison 2004). This announcement led eventually to the passage in June 2006 of the *Law Enforcement Integrity Commissioner Act* (Cth), and establishment of the Australian Commission for Law Enforcement Integrity (ACLEI) in January 2007. For the first six months of the Commission's operation, the establishment commissioner was the Commonwealth Ombudsman (ACLEI 2007, 1–5).

Ultimately, in fact, the paths chosen by the Victorian and federal governments were not dissimilar. Both jurisdictions ended up with an independent new police integrity agency, in both cases via a transitional arrangement in which the existing Ombudsman oversaw the agency's establishment.

Nevertheless, the contentious nature of the public debate over the initial differences (see Brown and Head 2005, 86–7) helps bring into sharp relief many of the intersecting questions of institutional design at the heart of this chapter. Furthermore both jurisdictions have contributed to the diversity of Australian arrangements, rather than helping focus the debate over the 'right' integrity framework, because together they have added to rather than reduced the number of available models. This is because, despite having moved away from the original Ombudsman-based model, neither government has actually moved to the more general anti-corruption models adopted by NSW, Queensland and Western Australia – even though this is what the federal government said needed to be done. In particular, while both governments have moved to develop a new body to address *police* corruption, neither government has moved to directly address risks of official corruption throughout the *remainder* of the public sector.

Does there remain a need for further institutional development in these jurisdictions? The answer is yes, but as seen through the remainder of the chapter, there is no simple answer as to how this should be done. In particular, as a starting point, there is a clear need for more objective methods for determining both the case and direction for reform, than have informed the *ad hoc* decisions to date.

Estimating the 'Net Value' of Integrity Agency Resourcing

In the hot debate over the wisdom of different institutional approaches, how might more objective methods be arrived at for estimating whether there is a case for reform, and if so, how much? Basic questions as to whether additional resources were needed, and if so in what configuration, were at the heart of recent reforms both in Victoria and at a federal level. In both cases, the response to a short-term integrity challenge involved the familiar assumption that a new government agency was automatically needed, as a means of demonstrating that more resources were to be thrown at the problem.

For example, by bypassing the establishment of a royal commission and a new agency, and simply expanding the Ombudsman's Office, the initial Victorian response was calculated to appear more measured and cost-effective than an institutional response on the Queensland or Western Australian model. State government figures were even happy to cite the (unfair) description of Queensland's Crime and Misconduct Commission, given by the Opposition in that state, as a 'multimillion-dollar joke … that couldn't track an elephant through snow' (see Victorian Parliament 2004, 12). Nevertheless the Victorian government quickly came under pressure to be seen to be throwing 'enough' resources at the problem. In April 2004, it announced that the Ombudsman's budget would be boosted by \$1 million per annum (from \$3.5 to \$4.5 million) to deal with police corruption. In June 2004, the size of the boost was increased tenfold to \$10 million per annum, with the addition of the new Office of Police Integrity (OPI) expected to increase the Ombudsman's Office from around 30 to around 100 staff (see Bracks 2004; Victorian Parliament 2004).

These announcements came as direct responses to escalating media commentary on the significant budgets of the anti-corruption bodies in NSW, Queensland and Western Australia, even though the Victorian government had determined it was not following any of these models. This comment was reinforced by the arguments of the Victorian Opposition parties and federal government, that a 'properly formulated' independent commission was the way to go (Rudduck and Ellison 2004). However, for its part, the media comment itself referred only to the raw staff numbers and budgets of the interstate bodies (e.g. Bottom and Medew 2004), without demonstrating why this data was necessarily comparable. Assuming they faced similar corruption risks, the scale of the agencies and programs of different Australian governments already varied greatly, in line with their quite different areas and populations.

This knee-jerk approach to institutional design has obvious limitations. Not least is the fact that, given the different elements of 'capacity' listed earlier, it is simply unsafe to assume that the creation of a new integrity body will necessarily guarantee that corruption is more effectively addressed, especially if the new agency is weak or easily sidelined. As discussed below, these are real questions in relation to the federal government's approach. However the debates confirm that even if there is real commitment to injecting sufficient capacity to make up a perceived shortfall, governments tend to go into such reforms flying blind, without any reliable basis for gauging the original shortfall let alone what might represent an appropriate 'target' level of resources – irrespective of precise institutional configuration.

A first step towards a more informed approach is to take advantage of the opportunity for comparative analysis provided by a federal system, but provide some more realistic basis for comparing the level of resources given to integrity bodies in different jurisdictions. In the national integrity system assessment this was done by examining the financial and human resources given by governments to their core integrity agencies – individually and in aggregate – relative to the overall size of government business (see Brown and Head 2004). In other words, rather than comparing raw figures that on any analysis would be expected to be different, it is possible to compare the ratios of staffing and financial resourcing of these agencies to the total public sector staffing and total public expenditure of each jurisdiction. These ratios remain comparable over time, without adjustment needed for inflation.

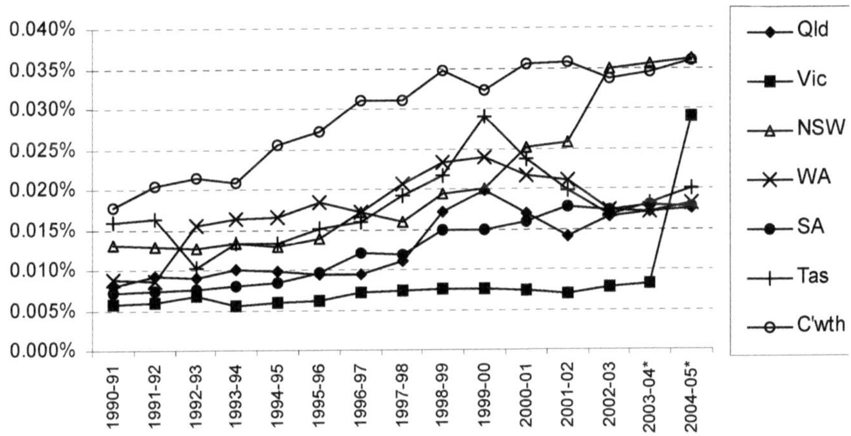

Figure 10.2 Ombudsman staffing ratios – 1990–2005

Figures 10.2 to 10.4 shows the resourcing trends for most of the agencies depicted in Figure 10.1, over a 14 year period.

Figure 10.2 demonstrates the method by showing the staff numbers for each of the federal and state Ombudsman's Offices, as a ratio of the total public sector staffing in that jurisdiction. The Commonwealth Ombudsman was the largest such office, in relative terms, until recent expansions in the NSW Ombudsman's Office brought these into alignment. It also confirms that the Victorian Ombudsman was the smallest (and potentially weakest) such office in Australia, relative to the size of the Victorian government's own operations, until the substantial expansion in 2004 with creation of the OPI.

As already shown, however, Ombudsman's Offices do not exist in isolation in Australia's integrity systems, but share their accountability roles with other core agencies. Figure 10.3 shows the staffing ratios for all these core agencies combined (not including crime commission functions, which are not necessarily focussed on public sector integrity). This analysis reveals a number of points. It suggests that Victoria's arrangements were indeed still the weakest in staffing terms. However it also shows the Ombudsman's expansion with the creation of OPI did little, overall, to make up the extent of the comparative shortfall. It also confirms that having more agencies does not necessarily translate into having a stronger staffing ratio – as shown by the fact that NSW drops from the equal strongest in terms of Ombudsman staffing, to only the middle of the group when all agencies are considered, despite having more agencies.

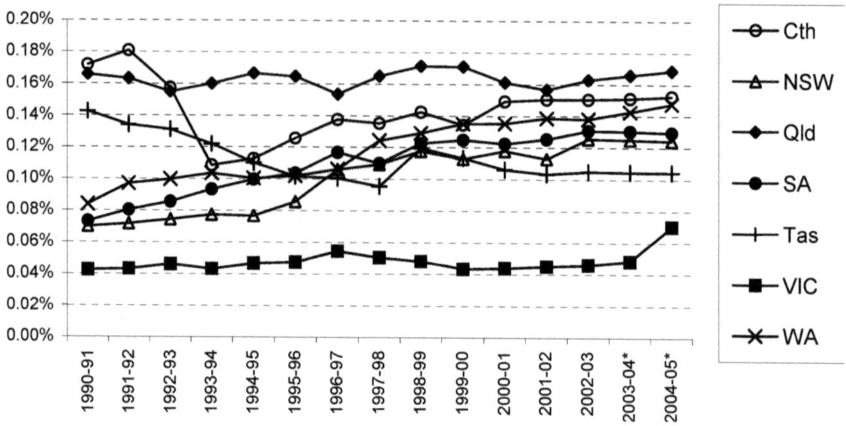

Figure 10.3 Core watchdog agencies – staffing ratios 1990–2005

Figure 10.4 compares the resources of the same core agencies on a different measure again – based not simply on core agency staffing, but a combined ratio reflecting *both* agency staffing relative to total public sector staffing *and* agency budget size relative to total public sector spending (with each factor given equal weight). The different results in this figure, from the previous, indicate that staff numbers are not the only measure of the resources used by integrity agencies. This points to differences in the types of activities and functions of different bodies. It is well established that normal Ombudsman-style complaint-handling is less expensive than the more resource-intensive activities regarded as effective responses to corruption, including more complex investigations, intelligence gathering and proactive corruption prevention activities (such as workplace education and training) (see ACLEI 2007, 18).

On this last measure, the combination of relatively strong staffing and budget ratios suggests that the three jurisdictions with the highest overall levels of resources are, indeed, those with general purpose anti-corruption agencies (Queensland, NSW and WA). Again, the result for NSW shows that this is irrespective of the number of individual agencies across which these resources are spread. By contrast, Victoria still retained the lowest overall resourcing at least until the addition of OPI, which still did not bring it up to par with any other state apart from Tasmania, but the gap was considerably less. These results suggest that irrespective of whether OPI is part of the Ombudsman's Office, or an independent agency as it has now become, Victoria still has some way to go in terms of additional injections of resources if it wishes its core integrity arrangements to be comparable with other states.

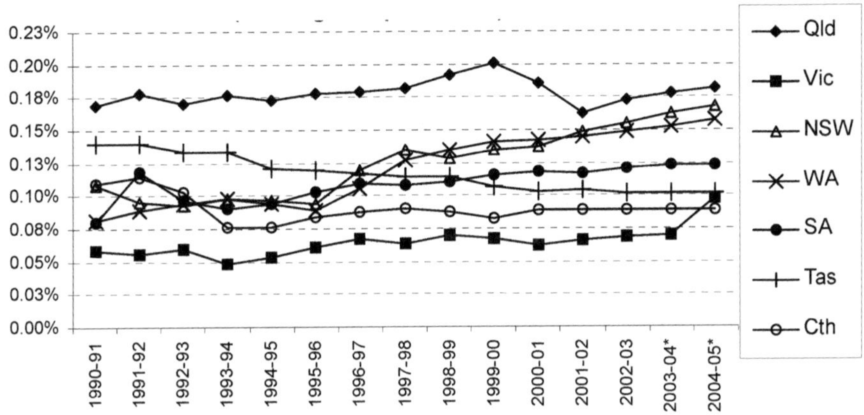

Figure 10.4 Core watchdogs – averaged resourcing ratios (staffing and expenditure) 1990–2005

A further significant result, is that the same conclusion flows in respect of the federal government. Whereas Victoria always rated low on all measures, on this last combined measure the federal government appears to have had the least well resourced integrity sector overall, at the point that it took the decision to create the new Australian Commission for Law Enforcement Integrity (ACLEI). However by contrast with Victoria's expansion of the Ombudsman's Office through OPI, the federal government position has not significantly changed since that time – notwithstanding that it elected to form a whole new agency, rather than expand an existing one. Since commencing operations on 30 December 2006, ACLEI has functioned with just 11 staff and an operating budget of $2.022 million per annum (ACLEI 2007, 22, 40). Given the small scale of this injection, the federal government is still essentially vying with Victoria and Tasmania for the honour of the least well-resourced integrity sector, irrespective of whatever appearances it might seek to claim from having created a new body.

This gap between appearance and reality should be accepted as a real problem by current and future federal governments. On one hand, the addition of any new agency to the federal integrity system represented, almost by definition, the most significant development in that system in 20 years (Brown 2005; see Senate 2006b, 20; ACLEI 2007, 1). Yet the net value of its creation remains open to question. By the end of ACLEI's establishment phase, the acting commissioner (Professor John McMillan) had concluded that while ACLEI had 'significant investigation powers' on paper, including the power to conduct telephone interception and covert surveillance, 'the reality' was that the agency did not have the budget to exercise those powers (Stewart 2007). Noting that only five staff members were involved in investigation work, Professor McMillan suggested that the agency probably needed a staff of 'around 50' in order to exercise all the functions it had been given, even if it did not uncover any major new patterns of systemic corruption.

This result falls into line with warnings that the creation of a new anti-corruption body could be of relatively little substantive value, beyond some simply superficial or symbolic strengthening, if sufficient capacity did not follow (Brown and Head 2004, 88).

What scale and type of further institutional development would be needed, for these less well-resourced jurisdictions to approach parity with their better resourced cousins? As discussed through the second half of the chapter, in addition to more resources to address law enforcement more effectively, a larger need remains both in Victoria and at a federal level to address corruption risks across the wider public sector, not simply those in the 'hot button' area of policing. Indeed this need is now demonstrably higher for the federal government than it is in Victoria. Before sketching how these needs might be addressed, however, it is necessary to address pervasive assertions that for some reason, Australia's federal government has less overall exposure to corruption risks than its state governments. Such assertions have long been made, in a manner that might justify a continuing low level of resources.

Is the Commonwealth Different?

The arguments of individual governments that they are less prone to corruption, and therefore do not need comparable integrity institutions, are not actually restricted to federal governments. In Victoria, as late as 2004, the choice of a different institutional path to NSW, Queensland and Western Australia was still defended on the basis that no evidence had emerged of the 'systemic' corruption present in other states. Subsequently, however, the anti-corruption investigations of Victoria Police and the OPI confirmed that the picture was, in reality, much the same (Rennie 2007). Is the same thing true of the Commonwealth?

The suggestion of a reduced level of federal need was explicit at the birth of ACLEI, when the relevant ministers stated that 'no evidence' existed of systemic corruption within the Australian Crime Commission (ACC), Australian Federal Police (AFP) or other federal law enforcement agencies, with the government determining simply that 'an independent body' should be available to address corruption at the federal level 'should it arise' (Ruddock and Ellison 2004). In March 2006, the Attorney-General repeated this position in the second reading speech for the Bill establishing the Commission. This had been a familiar refrain for many years – even on the part of the Harrison inquiry into federal police misconduct in 1997, which led to the dismissal of eight AFP officers (ACLEI 2007, 11, 13).

The presence of this presumption of relatively low corruption risk does much to explain the weak state of integrity resourcing, including the 'shell-like' quality of ACLEI noted above. Effectively without apology, the new body was set up not to fail, but simply to do very little, on the assumption that very little needed to be done. Even within the policing field, however, its establishment commissioner described the assumption that federal officers were less corruption prone than state officers as inherently 'risky' (Stewart 2007). Coming as the apparent fruition of a long history of proposals to enhance the effective capacity of any external oversight body to deal effectively with police corruption risks (ACLEI 2007, 7–13), the result has potentially done little more than shift an existing problem from one body (the office of the Commonwealth Ombudsman) to another.

While there is a self-evident need for the federal government to at least resource any body in ACLEI's position to a level that allows it to fulfil its minimum statutory functions, there is also now wider evidence to challenge claims that the federal jurisdiction is generally different to state jurisdictions, in a manner that significantly reduces the need for standing integrity agencies. This includes empirical evidence of integrity risks as perceived by public servants themselves, and evidence of actions taken by government itself in response to various integrity challenges.

The empirical evidence takes the form of the responses of public employees to a 2006 survey about wrongdoing of which they had direct knowledge within their organization, for the purposes of a large-scale study of whistleblowing (see Brown et al. 2007). Table 10.1 sets out the proportion of a random sample of over 7600 public officials, drawn from 118 different federal and state agencies, who had seen direct evidence of each of the nominated types of wrongdoing within their organization, sometime in the previous two years. This sample extended beyond simply law enforcement agencies.

While jurisdictions do vary in terms of the relative incidence of some observed behaviours, the broad pattern is similar. This result is consistent with the fact that all public agencies, having been established for important public purposes, involve their own risks of official positions or powers being abused – often irrespective of the precise nature of those positions or powers. Moreover, many of the integrity risks managed by public agencies are actually risks common to any type of organization. Many of the types of wrongdoing identified in Table 10.1 relate as much to breaches of *organizational* integrity as they do to *public* integrity, often with few bright lines to distinguish between the two. Poorly run agencies with low organizational integrity are also frequently identified as those in which breaches of public integrity are less likely to be readily detected and more likely to become systemic – again, irrespective of precise function.

Clearly, this result also suggests that if there is a legitimate need for institutional capacity to address a range of integrity risks across the larger public sector at a state level, then a similar need exists across the larger federal public sector.

Does this evidence of a general need to address comparable integrity risks translate into a need for a strengthened framework of 'core' integrity agencies, to a level comparable with some state jurisdictions in the manner suggested by the earlier figures? After all, other forms of institutional strengthening might potentially be used to address similar challenges. However, a more conclusive answer is suggested by the recent actions of the federal government itself in response to various integrity challenges.

These actions take the form of federal decisions to establish at least three major *ad hoc* inquiries into alleged abuses of federal official power – the Palmer/Comrie, Cole and Clark inquiries – independently of the agencies concerned, but outside the existing framework of standing integrity bodies. Each of these inquiries has also coincided with the period of the creation of ACLEI, even as

Table 10.1 Proportion of public employees surveyed with direct evidence of various wrongdoing types

Wrongdoing type	Cth (n=2307) %	NSW (n=2561) %	Qld (n=1729) %	WA (n=1007) %	Total[a] (n=7663) %
Covering up poor performance	30.9	30.0	30.7	24.2	29.6
Incompetent or negligent decision-making	27.7	26.4	25.6	21.4	26.0
Improper private use of agency facilities/resources	27.0	22.5	24.3	23.2	24.3
Rorting overtime or leave provisions	22.2	20.7	20.3	19.2	20.9
Theft of property	13.7	14.1	15.5	15.5	14.5
Use official position for personal services/favours	10.1	13.4	12.4	11.1	11.9
Failure to correct serious mistakes	12.3	11.3	11.7	8.9	11.4
Misuse of confidential information	10.1	10.9	13.4	9.1	11.0
Giving unfair advantage to contractor etc.	6.8	8.7	10.5	10.3	8.8
Theft of money	9.8	7.7	8.4	7.0	8.4
Intervening on behalf of friend or relative	6.1	7.7	8.2	5.7	7.1
Downloading pornography on a work computer	9.1	5.9	5.5	7.7	7.0
Racial discrimination against staff member	6.7	7.5	5.9	6.2	6.8
Making false or inflated claims for reimbursement	5.3	5.9	4.5	6.0	5.4
Racial discrimination against member of public	4.2	5.6	4.2	4.0	4.6
Misleading or false reporting of agency activity	3.7	3.6	3.5	2.9	3.5
Bribes or kickbacks	2.4	2.9	3.7	3.4	3.0
Unlawfully altering or destroying official records	2.7	2.7	3.1	1.6	2.7
Covering up corruption	1.6	3.2	2.1	1.2	2.2
Improper involvement of a family business	2.1	2.1	2.0	1.0	1.9
Hindering an official investigation	1.5	2.0	2.2	0.7	1.7
Failing to declare financial interest	1.0	1.6	1.3	1.6	1.4

a Includes 59 respondents for whom jurisdiction and agency unknown.

Source: Brown et al. 2007: 17.

the federal government has continued to maintain that the nature of its business involves significantly reduced risk of such abuses.

The Palmer and Comrie inquiries were administrative inquiries instituted by the federal minister for immigration in 2005, into growing evidence that federal immigration compliance and detention policies had resulted in the unlawful detention and deportation of a number of Australian citizens. In a bid to ensure public confidence, the commissioned inquiry heads were former commissioners of the Australian Federal Police and Victoria Police, who not only confirmed the key incidents alleged, but uncovered a far-reaching pattern of systemic organizational failures and confirmed that a defective management culture was largely responsible for the incapacity of the department to prevent such failures or detect and remedy them when they had occurred (see Palmer 2005).

Importantly, the decision to constitute these inquiries as *ad hoc* administrative inquiries was publicly contested, given that it meant the inquiries lacked a clear legal basis, including either authority to compel witnesses or an ability to allow them to speak freely, without risk of defamation action or other repercussions. This was only rectified by recommissioning the unresolved inquiries as cases under the investigation of the Commonwealth Ombudsman, followed by legislative and resource enhancements to allow that office to take on a more active, ongoing oversight role in relation to immigration compliance and detention activities.

The Cole Inquiry was established in early 2006 in response to a damning United Nations investigation indicating that the Australian Wheat Board (AWB) Limited had engaged in bribes of over $200 million to the government of Iraq, in breach of the UN sanctions regime, to secure and maintain lucrative wheat contracts (see Bartos, this volume). This time the inquiry was given the formal investigative powers of a royal commission, but as an *ad hoc* inquiry it remained formally limited by terms of reference set for the occasion by the government itself, restricting its ability to investigate full responsibility for the poor standards of accountability within AWB (a government agency until shortly prior to the events), the failure of the government's system of regulation and oversight of AWB, or the failure of the federal department of foreign affairs and trade – and relevant ministers – to heed warning signs regarding the company's illegal and unethical actions.

It was also publicly visible by the time that the Cole Inquiry reported in November 2006, that despite having originally promised to establish 'an independent national anti-corruption body' along the lines of NSW, Queensland and Western Australia (Ruddock and Ellis 2004), this had not actually occurred. Instead the body eventually established by the government – ACLEI – only had limited jurisdiction over two federal agencies, and was incapable of satisfying corruption investigation needs of the type fulfilled, somewhat incompletely, by the Cole Inquiry.

The third inquiry headed by former NSW Supreme Court justice John Clarke, was commenced in April 2008. It concerns police and immigration department actions in July 2007 against Dr Mohamed Haneef, the second cousin of the brother of a British terrorist. Despite terrorism laws being used to hold Dr Haneef for 12 days without charge, charges then laid by the Australian Federal Police were cancelled by the Director of Public Prosecutions, and deportation action by the minister for immigration was declared unlawful by the Federal Court, raising concerns that federal officials – including the minister – had abused or overstepped their powers.

While ongoing at the time of writing, this further, *ad hoc* administrative inquiry suffered the same criticisms of legal inefficacy as the Palmer and Comrie inquiries (see Maley 2008; see also *The Australian* 2008). It also highlighted the continuing fragmentation of the federal integrity system, even after the creation of ACLEI. No consideration had apparently been given to commissioning the inquiry under the *Ombudsman Act 1976*, perhaps because under that Act, the investigation could not have extended to actions of the minister. Neither was consideration apparently given to commissioning the inquiry under the ACLEI legislation, notwithstanding the central role of the Australian Federal Police. Perhaps this was because neither the minister, the immigration department or the security agencies fell within ACLEI's jurisdiction; or perhaps because ACLEI is expressly restricted to the investigation of 'corruption issues' (though this in fact has a wide statutory definition, including any serious abuse of office by an AFP staff-member).

Together, these recent inquiries show that in practice, the federal government is anything but immune from the need for standing institutional capacity to address a wide range of integrity issues. They also reinforce that the most significant recent enhancement of core integrity agency capacity, through the creation of ACLEI, has done little if anything to address many of these wider needs. Instead, the federal government's responses tend to reinforce the high degree of fragmentation and incoherence in its public integrity system, as suggested elsewhere in this volume (Roberts, this volume). Far from there being much plausibility to assertions that the federal government has lower need for enhanced integrity system capacity, the question becomes the reverse – what institutional design issues need to be confronted, if the federal government is to restore confidence that it has the capacity to keep serious risks of integrity breaches to a minimum?

Key Issues for Federal Institutional Design

As previously reviewed elsewhere, objective analysis of existing integrity institutions exposes a wide range of roles, structures and powers (Brown and Head 2004; 2005). These differences translate into a complex range of institutional choices. Assuming a new agency is needed, is it intended to act independently or work closely with the agencies it oversights? Is it to be reactive, for example by responding to complaints, or more proactive and intelligence-driven? Are its investigations to be conducted in public or private? Does it have positive standard-setting, education and corruption prevention responsibilities as well as the usual compliance roles? What should be the limits of its jurisdiction? How should it relate to other integrity bodies, and be held accountable?

The first part of the chapter demonstrated that while some of these questions have been approached in a rational manner in recent years, most responses have remained piecemeal. Five major issues stand out as needing to be addressed in the federal government's approach to integrity institutional design:

1 how to bring all federal officeholders within a realistic scheme of integrity scrutiny;
2 how to include senior officials such as ministers within the scheme;
3 how to ensure that information about integrity breaches is rapidly transmitted to the place where most effective action can be taken;
4 how proactive integrity-building and corruption resistance strategies, rather than reactive investigations into alleged integrity breaches, are best pursued and monitored across the public sector; and
5 how the different integrity institutions are best to be coordinated.

A Comprehensive Approach to Integrity Scrutiny

The first part of the chapter demonstrated the continuing need for an integrity agency of general jurisdiction for the federal public sector. As described elsewhere (Roberts, this volume), the Commonwealth Ombudsman has played some of this role over the last 30 years, and can be expected to continue to play a leadership role in the setting and maintenance of high standards of public administration. However, over the same period that ACLEI has been created, resource demands and investigative needs in the anti-corruption field have made it clearer that 'in broad terms', the Ombudsman 'should not be the chief agency responsible for investigating corruption allegations' (Commonwealth Ombudsman 2004, ch. 1).

Similarly, the Australian Public Service Commission (APSC) has its own important roles in the maintenance and monitoring of professional standards in the public sector. However these roles have not historically extended to more complex integrity investigations, of the kind dealt with by the core integrity agencies in other jurisdictions or the increasing number of *ad hoc* federal inquiries. Moreover the jurisdiction of the APSC is somewhat illogically limited to 'Australian Public Service' (APS) agencies, whose employees account for only around half of the Commonwealth public sector.

Given that the identified need is for standing capacity to oversight and undertake more complex corruption-style investigations, one persistent argument against a more comprehensive approach has been that this function can be handled by existing law enforcement agencies – notably, the Australian Federal Police. On this theory, the creation of the Australian Commission for Law Enforcement Integrity was all that was needed to bolster the integrity system, by bolstering the extent to which the AFP could continue to be trusted to handle such investigations in other areas of the public sector. This theory is perhaps the most rational explanation, if one is required, for the government's failure to adopt the type of 'properly-formulated independent Commission – similar to those in WA, New South Wales and Queensland' that it insisted should be the model for Victoria (Ruddock and Ellison 2004). In all three of those states, it will be remembered, the anti-corruption agencies cover the entire public sector and not just policing.

The idea that public sector corruption matters can be left to the AFP, however, is one that has now clearly been exploded. The role of the AFP is to investigate criminal offences, but as shown earlier, the nature of complex integrity investigations is such that often, the sources and reasons for integrity breaches are not likely to be criminal. As much is confirmed by the definition of 'corruption issue' under section 6 of the *Law Enforcement Integrity Commissioner Act 2006* (Cth), which as already noted, takes as its starting point whether there has been an 'abuse of office' rather than whether behaviour is necessarily criminal.

In practice, the AFP *may* become involved with major corruption investigations where criminal behaviour is clear – for example, in major fraud by a federal officer. However in general, unless the matter is exceptionally serious or sensitive, individual federal agencies are currently expected to investigate and prosecute such matters themselves. By contrast there is currently no expectation that the AFP would ever help deal with other types of alleged official misconduct, such as conflicts of interest, even in complex or serious cases. When reviewing the provisions of the *Law Enforcement Integrity Commissioner Bill*, the Senate Legal and Constitutional Committee concluded that, clearly, there were 'limits to the effective jurisdiction of the AFP in relation to broader corruption or integrity issues that fall short of criminal behaviour' (Senate 2006b, 26).

Consequently, the federal decision to limit ACLEI's jurisdiction has been extensively questioned – from a number of perspectives. First, even law enforcement agencies have questioned why the jurisdiction is limited to just two such agencies: the Australian Federal Police (AFP) and Australian Crime Commission (ACC). In evidence to the Senate Legal and Constitutional Committee in April 2006, the AFP commissioner (Mr Mick Keelty) confirmed that in his view, this left 'a gap' in the integrity system, given that many other federal agencies also operated in the law enforcement field, with comparable powers and risk of abuse, who would not be subjected to oversight by the new body (Senate 2006a):

> If we are serious about this, and if it is not just a quick fix, then the AFP could benefit in its investigations if the ACLEI had a wider remit than what is proposed in the Bill.

In response to this, the Senate Committee concluded that there was 'a strong rationale for ensuring that a wider group of law enforcement agencies' were brought within the new agency's jurisdiction, including Customs, the Australian Taxation Office and the Department of Immigration (Senate 2006b, 27). Indeed had this occurred, then in 2008, there may well been no need for the separately established Clarke Inquiry.

For its part, in June 2006 the federal Opposition moved an amendment to the Bill, seeking to add Customs, Immigration and the Australian Transaction Reporting and Analysis Centre (AUSTRAC) to ACLEI's jurisdiction. However this extension was rejected by the government and defeated (Senate 2006c, 269). Instead the relevant minister (Senator Ellison) responded that he envisaged that 'in the future' the jurisdiction 'will be expanded to encompass other Commonwealth agencies which have a law enforcement function', adding that there was 'no doubt' this would be the case (Senate 2006c, 272). One year later, however, a new minister

(Senator Johnston) indicated there was as yet no plan to extend the jurisdiction (Stewart 2007).

A second objection to this limited jurisdiction was that its extension, if it ever occurred, was legislated so as to take place via regulation. This facility for allowing the government to add or remove further individual agencies from ACLEI's jurisdiction by regulation, was itself criticized by the Opposition's Senator Ludwig as 'completely unacceptable':

> The Minister proposes to add [additional agencies] at his whim and convenience … There is no guarantee that any of these agencies are or will be able to be investigated… Why should a Minister have a roving discretion to decide when an agency should or should not be investigated for corruption? (Senate 2006c, 270)

A third and final objection to the jurisdiction similarly highlights its fragmentary, piecemeal nature. Under the current legislation, even if the jurisdiction were extended to further law enforcement agencies, then sub-section 6(2) of the *Law Enforcement Integrity Commissioner Act* restricts ACLEI to dealing only with conduct relating to 'the performance of a law enforcement function of the agency'. Consequently even if a department such as Immigration were added to the jurisdiction, it would remain unclear – and likely be contested legally – whether corruption or misconduct involving functions such as the issuing or cancellation of visas, or the administrative detention of individuals, could be captured. Even in respect of the AFP and ACC, this attempt to focus the jurisdiction on 'law enforcement' means that there are some types of corruption allegations that ACLEI may not be able to investigate – for example, it is not clear that an AFP officer who accepted a kickback for an information technology contract would be performing a 'law enforcement' function (see also Senate Committee 2006b, 27).

Anticipating these issues, the Senate Legal and Constitutional Committee concluded that the creation of the ACLEI should not be the end of the story:

> The committee also considers that a Commonwealth integrity commission of general jurisdiction is needed, and there is an accountability gap that would be closed by such a body. … [C]onsideration should also be given to developing such a commission in the longer term (Senate 2006b, 28).

Consistently with the first recommendation of the national integrity system assessment (Brown et al. 2005a, 65–6, 92–3), the time has clearly arrived for the creation of such an agency. The only real question is whether the federal government – having made its institutional choices in an *ad hoc* manner to date, somewhat akin to NSW – will continue that trend and create an entirely new body; or face the reality that these issues should have been dealt in conjunction with the creation of ACLEI in the first instance.

The history of these matters, the weak resourcing of ACLEI, and the more general need for the federal government to comprehensively revisit the fragmented state of its integrity system, all point to one conclusion. The federal government's clear need is for a standing agency with the capacity to undertake complex investigations on integrity matters, including but not restricted to those that might fit narrow definitions of 'corruption', wherever this might arise within federal government administration. Properly constituted, this body would be well able to service government demands for particular inquiries, such as the Palmer/ Comrie, Cole and Clarke inquiries, in addition to conducting more routine reviews and investigations into less high profile matters, as well as other integrity functions. The important lesson from history to date, is the need for such a body to have a comprehensive, general jurisdiction. This means both an inclusive organizational catchment covering all federal employees and officeholders, and a wide conception of the breadth of issues into which the agency may need to enquire when investigating any particular kind of integrity breach, as opposed to a jurisdiction constructed in narrow or technical terms.

If the workload and/or existing resources of ACLEI meant that it was already a large body, then reason might exist for considering the creation of an additional body. However the reality is that no existing federal core agency is actually very large. As seen, ACLEI in particular is quite diminutive, to an extent that makes it questionable whether, as it stands, it is capable of building and retaining a critical mass of the necessary expertise even for its current basic functions. Consequently, the logical options for the future involve either expanding the jurisdiction of ACLEI, or rolling that agency into an existing or new body with appropriate investigative capacity.

As shown earlier, similar considerations also still apply in Victoria. The question there is similarly, how to expand the general anti-corruption jurisdiction for the remainder of the public sector – whether to create a new agency, expand the Office of Police Integrity (OPI), or entrust this function to the Ombudsman (see Hughes 2007). However in that jurisdiction, there are some differences. Unlike ACLEI, OPI was established with significant resources and a mission to find work. There may well remain a case for police corruption issues to be handled by a larger anti-corruption agency, much as there remains a case for the NSW Police Integrity Commission to be made a division of the ICAC rather then left as a stand-alone body. However, the size and roles of OPI mean that the decision to separate it from Ombudsman Victoria at least appears sustainable.

The situation in Victoria is further different to the federal government because Ombudsman Victoria has already commenced to handle some corruption issues, outside its traditional administrative complaint-handling roles. This is due to a separate jurisdiction over corruption complaints and disclosures granted by the *Whistleblowers Protection Act 2001* (Vic). The fact that the Ombudsman is already dealing with such matters – unlike, or at least to a much greater extent than the Commonwealth Ombudsman – makes it more logical to evaluate that experience before assuming that a new or different body should be handling them. This is especially the case given that even if a new or different body was needed, a decision would also be needed regarding its own roles, vis-à-vis the Ombudsman, under the *Whistleblowers Protection Act*.

The Necessity of Including Senior Officeholders

When the federal government moves to establish a general anti-corruption agency, an issue demonstrated by recent experience is the importance of ensuring its jurisdiction does not stop at the door of politicians. When the federal government originally pointed to Queensland, NSW and Western Australia has possessing 'properly formulated' corruption bodies, it was also pointing to three jurisdictions where parliamentarians are not exempted from the integrity regime. Instead, albeit in sometimes differing ways, parliamentarians are recognized as being public officials to which any comprehensive public integrity framework should also apply.

This is not the situation at the federal level, where actions of ministers and other members of parliament are excluded from investigation by the Commonwealth Ombudsman. Indeed the lack of any standing arrangements for ensuring a high level of integrity on the part of federal parliamentarians has been described as a system of 'puzzling self-regulation' (Uhr 2005,147). The need for this to be rectified is well demonstrated by recent history, where even in the absence of evidence of any systemic corruption on the part of federal politicians, several of the most serious inquiries have included questions about the actions or inactions of ministers. Similar questions have been asked in Victoria, about why, when governments are upgrading the integrity regimes that apply to public servants, there is no clear commitment to ensuring the same or equivalent regimes also apply to political representatives (Hughes 2007).

There are different options for how different political representatives might best be brought within the integrity system. They include equipping the parliament itself with a stand-alone integrity mechanism, such as an ethics or integrity commissioner, answerable to a multi-party parliamentary ethics committee, and capable of receiving and resolving information about any impropriety by individual politicians in a more transparent way. It is important, however, that such a commissioner also be able to draw on the resources of a more general integrity agency when more complex investigations arise, and that the general integrity agency not be restricted from investigating ministerial actions or failures in political accountability for events within government, wherever the public interest demands.

Sourcing and Referring the Crucial Information

The developments reviewed in the first part of the chapter also highlight an important shift in the way in which information about integrity breaches can, and should, come to core integrity agencies. Historically, integrity agencies have often been expected to be reactive – only undertaking an investigation in response to a specific allegation or complaint. While this may remain appropriate for some integrity functions, such as the public complaint-handling functions fulfilled by ombudsmen, it is now widely appreciated as insufficient in respect of corruption issues and other forms of official misconduct:

> Ombudsmen's offices are complaint bureaux for dissatisfied citizens. They are incapable of dealing with organised corruption. Corruption is a consensual crime. Both parties to the arrangement are unlikely to complain – illegal gain flows to the police officer while criminals are unhindered in their pursuits. By the time, if ever, the matter is manifest as a complaint, the problem has usually assumed serious proportions. (Le Grand 2004)

A more comprehensive approach to integrity recognizes that information regarding integrity breaches and risks is best sourced in a number of ways: including public complaints; other public information, such as media reporting of problems; risk assessment methods; intelligence-gathering; management observation; and employee disclosures ('whistleblowing'). In many of these areas, core integrity agencies cannot act in a totally independent manner from the government agencies they are intended to oversight, because it is clear that much of the crucial information already exists within those agencies. Moreover as indicated by Le Grand, in many instances it will only be very late in the piece that problems already visible within organizations manifest themselves to an external agency as an independent complaint.

Institutional arrangements to ensure that the right information flows to an integrity agency in a timely way, rely both on having the right processes, and sufficient resources. An important breakthrough in the processes of Australian integrity systems was been the development of clearer relationships for the reporting of such matters between core integrity agencies and the government bodies they service. Part of the efficacy of integrity systems modelled on Queensland experience, lies in their adoption of the principle of 'mandatory reporting', whereby the heads of all government agencies are obliged to notify the core agency (in that case the Crime and Misconduct Commission) of all cases of suspected official misconduct. This in itself ensures that agencies have systems in place to deal with such matters, do not try to 'sweep them under the carpet', and that they are addressed to a consistent standard across different agencies. Mandatory reporting arrangements also enable the core agency to form an overall picture of integrity risks and trends, and ensure its own resources are devoted to assisting in those matters where its involvement is most needed.

The establishment of ACLEI saw the federal government directly confront this issue. Initially, a more reactive, complaint-handling model of oversight appeared to be proposed for this agency, which was to be titled the 'Inspector-General of Law Enforcement' comparable to the existing Inspector-General of Intelligence and Security (see Brown 2005). However in a positive development the *Law Enforcement Integrity Commissioner Act 2006* ultimately introduced a mandatory reporting arrangement for the first time in the federal jurisdiction, under which an agreed framework must be reached by which the agencies involved (AFP and ACC) report all matters in their own knowledge to the oversight agency. This provides a valuable precedent for the establishment of a more general anti-corruption jurisdiction at the federal level.

In Victoria, a measure of mandatory reporting was introduced for the first time in serious integrity matters, through a requirement for the Ombudsman to be notified of public interest disclosures under the *Whistleblowers Protection*

Act 2001. This development provides a separate reminder of the special circumstances in which such an arrangement may be necessary – for example, where an employee's internal disclosure about defective administration might place them at risk of reprisal without external oversight, even though it might not otherwise justify referral to an independent agency in the same manner as a 'corruption' matter.

The management of complex disclosures of this kind, including a measure of independent oversight of the welfare of public officials involved, further dictates that the resourcing of core integrity agencies must be realistic. An effective integrity agency must have the capacity to service this ongoing interchange of information with the bodies in its jurisdiction, but also to conduct its own research and build its own intelligence, initiate investigations of its 'own motion', and use complaint trends and information from the public domain to identify systemic issues that call for larger investigations. Attracting the necessary information about serious corruption from whistleblowers, informants and those not benefiting from favourable treatment, requires having a reasonable public profile. No matter how strong its legal powers, an agency without the financial and staff resources to satisfy these operational needs is hampered in its ability to make a credible contribution to public integrity.

'Positive' Integrity-building and Corruption Resistance

Since at least 1996, when the establishment of a new federal police oversight body was first recommended (ALRC 1996), it has been assumed that such an agency should follow the model of the Queensland and NSW anti-corruption agencies and undertake more than simply compliance and investigation functions. In 2004, arguments for a new integrity agency in Victoria similarly pointed out that additional resources were needed for more positive capacity-building, research and prevention functions, including workplace education on integrity issues, corruption risk assessments, and proactive reviews of the adequacy of agencies' systems and procedures for preventing and minimising integrity lapses.

Consistently with these broader, more positive functions, the federal government established the ACLEI with statutory objectives to not simply investigate corruption in the relevant agencies, but also 'to prevent corrupt conduct' and 'maintain and improve the integrity' of their staff members (section 3 of the *Law Enforcement Integrity Commissioner Act* 2006).

Two obvious problems stand out in relation to these heavy responsibilities. First, the corresponding section 15 of the same Act gives the Commission no specific functions aligned with achieving these objectives. Secondly, as discussed earlier, the Commission has not been given the resources to undertake such functions in any event. While ACLEI has indicated it will 'review the anti-corruption plans of law enforcement agencies, conduct assessments of high-risk corruption areas of operations, and appraise the adequacy of agency safeguards to detect corrupt activity' (ACLEI 2007, 30), it remains unclear whether its need to respond to specific cases will ever allow it the time and resources to undertake these activities. It is well known that 'one of the risks inherent in any complaints system is that the processing of large volumes of complaints becomes the sole function', detracting from prevention by preventing 'a larger research-based risk management approach to integrity' (Prenzler 2004, 109).

For these reasons it remains an important design issue, not simply whether ACLEI or a larger commission will be given appropriate resources to pursue these functions, but whether they will be properly recognized in the enabling legislation. One of the few ways for legislative action to help ensure that resources are devoted to these objects, in the face of inevitable internal pressure to service investigations, is to require the agency to also fulfil specific statutory functions – for example to:

- conduct the types of reviews cited above by ACLEI itself;
- independently assess levels of corruption resistance in the agencies within its jurisdiction, e.g. through annual surveys and reports;
- ensure that staff and clients of relevant agencies are aware of the Commission's existence and their responsibilities to report corrupt conduct, including empirical research to monitor that awareness;
- formulate and deliver training and education programs to agency staff on integrity and corruption issues; and
- undertake, coordinate and/or supervise integrity testing programs relating to agency staff.

It is also possible for these roles to be institutionalized in the structure of the organization, for example by creating the person responsible for them as a statutory officer – such as an Assistant Commissioner (Intelligence, Research and Corruption Resistance), alongside an Assistant Commissioner (Investigations).

At the same time, many of the research, evaluation and outreach functions that need to be performed by an effective corruption agency are also not actually unique to that agency. Just as public integrity relies on more than simply an absence of corruption, so too other agencies, such as the Ombudsman, audit office and public service commission have similar responsibilities to help public sector bodies embed effective approaches to high quality government administration and public sector standards. For these reasons, it is particularly important that the positive, integrity-building programs of any new anti-corruption agency are well integrated with the roles of other agencies. This issue raises its own important institutional design principles.

A Coordinated and Coherent System

As discussed throughout this volume, and throughout the Australian national integrity system assessment, ensuring that institutional reform contributes to a coherent integrity system is vital. Given that the maintenance of public integrity relies on the harmonious operation of so many different institutions and institutional forces, it is no surprise that such systems can become characterized by gaps, fragmentation and unintended *ad hocery* in the manner laid out in the first part of this chapter.

In the face of this risk, there are nevertheless positive trends at a federal level. The introduction of systems of mandatory reporting to core agencies on integrity issues, discussed earlier, itself is an important measure to close communication gaps and ensure greater coherence.

A second positive trend is the abandonment of the assumption that because each agency within the integrity system exists to serve a different primary function, it must therefore also have a legally exclusive jurisdiction. For example, unlike proposals as recent as those of the Australian Law Reform Commission (ALRC 1996), the establishment of ACLEI recognized that the creation of new anti-corruption oversight over federal agencies, did not mean that they should *not* also continue to be covered by the Commonwealth Ombudsman in relation to complaints that might not amount to corruption. Instead, these agencies have concurrent jurisdiction over the AFP and ACC:

> The Ombudsman will have a continuing role in relation to the AFP and the ACC, except in dealing with corruption issues. This will enable two complementary approaches to investigation to be brought to bear on different types of issues. Together, the Integrity Commissioner and the Ombudsman will provide the Australian public with the guarantee that the conduct of the key Australian Government law enforcement agencies is subject to comprehensive external review. (Senator Ian Campbell, Senate 2006c, 54)

The proven problem of multiple agencies with exclusive jurisdictions, is not only conflict between agencies over who has power, but the tendency for matters that are on the periphery of either jurisdiction to fall through a crack between both of them. For example, in this situation, a complaint involving a 'minor' corruption matter may not be sufficiently significant to demand attention from ACLEI, relative to other matters, but might nevertheless be positively excluded from investigation by the Ombudsman, even when it would be considered serious by complaint-handling standards.

While the benefits of concurrent jurisdictions has been realized for some time in several Australian states, it has come late to the federal government. One example of where it persists is in a statutory bar under section 5(2)(d) of the *Ombudsman Act 1976* preventing the Commonwealth Ombudsman from investigating any action relating to the employment of a public servant. While intended to prevent complaints to the Ombudsman from being used as an alternative mechanism for raising employment-related grievances, the fact that the Ombudsman cannot investigate an employment-related matter even on their own initiative, also prevents that office from making employment-related inquiries or taking any action to protect a federal officer who discloses defective administration, or otherwise assists an Ombudsman investigation. An effective solution would be a concurrent jurisdiction in which the Ombudsman could investigate such matters where he determined there was a public interest in doing so, but was not otherwise obliged to investigate any employment-related grievances.

The price of the greater coherence made possible by concurrent or overlapping roles, is the need for cooperation and coordination between agencies. In practice this already often occurs, and where it does not, structural incentives for doing so are in any event clearly desirable. In particular, as already noted, systems are particularly needed which require coordination between agencies in respect of their dealings with the government bodies they service, in the areas of outreach, education, monitoring and evaluation.

For example, the Australian Public Service Commission is currently the main collector of information relevant to awareness and adherence to public sector standards, through the annual State of the Service surveys and reports, at least in respect of APS agencies. The public sector would be better served by seeing this role enhanced to serve as many as possible of the information needs of all integrity agencies, rather than seeing all agencies develop their own surveys. Even more importantly, coordinated workplace education and executive training packages that incorporate the many different elements of public integrity are more likely to contribute to the maintenance of integrity, than confusing, fragmented packages.

One mechanism for supporting a coordinated approach is the institution of a coordinating committee or council of integrity agencies. This has been taken up in a number of jurisdictions (see Brown et al. 2005a, 86–9). At a federal level, a valuable precedent exists in the form of the Administrative Review Council.

A coherent integrity system is also one in which the accountability of core integrity agencies is clear. Following the principles of mutual accountability discussed in many parts of this volume, the presence of multiple core agencies can help entrench public integrity because each is also held accountable by each other. For example, even though these agencies must also work as partners in the integrity system, the accountability of the new ACLEI is enhanced by the fact that it is subject to scrutiny by the Commonwealth Ombudsman (ACLEI 2007, 36). This principle of mutual accountability is an important one to be maintained in further reform.

The final mechanism for accountability is a sensible arrangement for oversight by the people through the parliament. Here there also remain signs of fragmentation at the federal level, which stand to be rectified in the event of more coherent reform. A number of important parliamentary committees exist which play vital roles in relation to public integrity, such as the Parliamentary Joint Committee on Public Accounts and Audit, but their roles are themselves largely uncoordinated. The Commonwealth Ombudsman receives occasional special attention from the Senate Standing Committee on Finance and Public Administration, but otherwise its pivotal role in the federal public integrity system goes largely unsupported at a parliamentary level.

This contrasts with the approach taken under the *Law Enforcement Integrity Commissioner Act 2006*, which created a special Parliamentary Joint Committee to oversight that agency alone, notwithstanding is comparatively small size and narrow role. Indeed a more logical arrangement would have been for a new Parliamentary Joint Committee on Law Enforcement, replacing the existing parliamentary committee on the Australian Crime Commission, to also oversight the AFP, ACLEI, and any other significant law enforcement issues (see Senate 2006b, 41–4). However in the absence of this, another more logical arrangement would be the establishment of a joint committee on public integrity, to help oversight and coordinate a number of the institutions that make up the federal integrity system. Whenever a general integrity commission is created to replace or expand the Australian Commission for Law Enforcement Integrity, this would provide a logical opportunity for this further reform.

Conclusion: Towards a New Federal Integrity System

This chapter has reviewed some of the complex issues that confront any government when considering how to respond to pressures for institutional reform to the integrity system. Frequently those pressures will be 'scandal-driven' and, as seen in the first part of the chapter, the decisions made will often have a tendency to be *ad hoc* or 'knee-jerk'. There is a clear need for a considered approach, in which a more comprehensive process of institutional design is used to determine how public integrity systems are to be strengthened. This chapter has suggested, using recent Australian experience, some key questions that can help inform that process.

The first part of the chapter exposed these deficiencies in respect of the approaches both of the Victorian state government and, especially, Australia's federal government. Rather than flying blind in respect of assumptions about the levels of resources needed to make up shortfalls in the integrity system, it was shown that objective analysis is needed before assessments can be seen as reasonable. The data suggest that assumptions in 2004, that Victoria had allowed the capacity of its core integrity frameworks to stagnate compared to other jurisdictions, were broadly correct. However the data also showed that this was also true of the federal government, and most importantly, that in both cases, the further injection of resources that came with new police anti-corruption strategies did comparatively little to change the overall picture. This analysis helps demonstrate that while nations and governments can sometimes *appear* to have all the necessary institutions and processes in place, their actual capacity to pursue integrity may be very different. It also demonstrates that by attempting a more objective view of the way in which institutions have evolved, integrity system assessment can help gauge the extent of the 'hollowness' in particular integrity pillars.

This second finding also exposed the most significant flaws in the federal approach. Having criticized the Victorian government for failing (at least initially) to create a new independent agency, the federal government's own position was not substantially improved even once it did so. Indeed its creation of a new anti-corruption body restricted only to law enforcement, and resourced only weakly, was more typical of an attempt to create an appearance of action, than a coherent contribution to strengthening of the federal integrity system. The 'silver bullet' solution of creating a new agency did little to meet the demonstrated need for reform across the larger system.

These events provide a salient reminder that the creation of 'core' integrity agencies of this kind should not be pursued as if representing a total solution to corruption risks, either as an act of political symbolism or as a surrogate for the other, more systemic reforms that might be needed. The unresolved debate over the creation of an effective anti-corruption commission at Australia's federal level highlights that even industrialized countries with well-entrenched democratic institutions can battle to find the right mix of integrity institutions.

The second part of the chapter suggested five major issues of institutional design that need to be satisfied in the development of the federal integrity system, arising from this situation. In line with the views of the Senate Legal and Constitutional Legislation Committee, the first major issue is the now almost inevitable need for the expansion or replacement of the most recently created federal agency into a general integrity or anti-corruption commission capable of operating across the entire public sector. However, it is important that this occur in a way which takes account of the lessons learned, and strengthens the integrity system as whole. The remaining four key issues provide guidance to that end.

As a concession to the criticisms of the Senate Legal and Constitutional Committee in 2006, the Australian government allowed at least one useful amendment to the *Law Enforcement Integrity Commissioner Act 2006* – under section 223A, that legislation must be reviewed either by a parliamentary committee or independently, after three years of operation. The test will be whether this review is taken as an opportunity to address the original concerns of the committee, and of the many observers of the federal government's reforms, that a more comprehensive and visionary approach was not only possible, but necessary.

Corruption issues, by their nature, attract political attention and excite public passion. The issues of institutional reform on which public integrity really depends are, by comparison, extremely dry, complex, and burdensome. Once created, the important roles played by integrity institutions are easily forgotten until the next scandal, when pressure for a new or different institution arises again. It requires a long view of history to see how integrity systems are built, maintained and renewed – or alternatively, built and quietly eroded. Australia's federal integrity system continues to experience a period when the trend could go in either direction.

References

ACLEI (2007), *Annual Report of the Integrity Commissioner 2006–2007* (Canberra: Australian Commission for Law Enforcement Integrity).

ALRC (1996), 'Integrity: But not by Trust Alone – Australian Federal Police and National Crime Authority Complaints and Disciplinary Systems', *Australian Law Reform Commission Report No. 82* (Sydney: Commonwealth of Australia).

The Australian (2008), editorial, 'Wider Powers Needed', 1 May, 15.

Bottom, B. and Medew, J. (2004), 'The Unfair Fight: Why Corruption's Unchecked', *The Age*, 23 May.

Bracks, S. (2004), 'Ombudsman to Receive Additional Funds and Resources', *Media Release: Office of the Premier of Victoria*, 3 June.

Brown, A.J. (2005), 'Federal Anti-corruption Policy Takes a New Turn … But Which Way? Issues and Options for a Commonwealth Integrity Agency', *Public Law Review* 16:2, 93–8.

Brown, A.J. (2006), 'What are we Trying to Measure? Reviewing the Basics of Corruption Definition', in C. Sampford, A. Shacklock, F. Galtung, and C. Connors (eds) *Measuring Corruption* (Aldershot: Ashgate Publishing).

Brown, A.J. and Head, B. (2004), 'Ombudsman, Anti-Corruption Commission or Police Integrity Authority? Choices for Institutional Capacity in Australia's Integrity Systems', refereed paper to *Annual Conference of the Australasian Political Studies Association*, Adelaide, September.

Brown, A.J. and Head, B. (2005), 'Institutional Capacity and Choice in Australia's Integrity Systems'. *Australian Journal of Public Administration*, 64:2, 84–95.

Brown, A.J. et al. (2005a), *Chaos or Coherence? Strengths, Challenges and Opportunities for Australia's Integrity Systems*, National Integrity Systems Assessment (NISA) Final Report, Transparency International Australia and Griffith University.

Brown, A.J., Uhr, J., Shacklock, A. and Connors, C. (2005b), 'Developing Policy Assessment Measures for Integrity and Corruption Prevention Activities: The Australian Experience', *Public Sector Integrity: A Framework for Assessment* (Paris: Organisation for Economic Cooperation and Development), 225–96.

Brown, A.J., Mazurski, E. and Olsen, J. (2007), 'The Incidence and Significance of Whistleblowing', in A.J. Brown (ed.) *Whistleblowing in the Australian Public Sector*, Draft Report, Griffith University; paper to the First Australian Public Sector Anti-Corruption Conference, Hilton Hotel, Sydney, 24 October.

Commonwealth Ombudsman (2004), *Annual Report 2003–2004* (Canberra: Commonwealth Ombudsman).

Gilchrist, M. and Bachelard, M. (2004), 'Stopping The Rot', *The Australian*, 26 May.

Hughes, G. (2007), 'Calls for a Watchdog with Teeth', *The Australian*, 13 June.

Le Grand, M. (2004), 'Bracks Team Keeps Fiddling while Garden State Burns', *The Australian*, 18 June.

Maley, P. (2008), 'Haneef Witnesses Risk Civil Lawsuits', *The Australian*, 1 May, 3.

Mulgan, R. and Uhr, J. (2001), 'Accountability and Governance', in G. Davis and P. Weller (eds) *Are You Being Served? State, Citizens and Governance* (Sydney: Allen and Unwin).

Palmer, M. (2005), *Inquiry into the Circumstances of the Immigration Detention of Cornelia Rau*, Commonwealth of Australia, Canberra, July.

Prenzler, T. (2004), 'Stakeholder Perspectives on Police Complaints and Discipline: Towards a Civilian Control Model', *Australian and New Zealand Journal of Criminology* 37:1, 85–113.

Rennie, R. (2007), 'Corruption does Happen: Overland [Victoria Police]', *The Age*, Melbourne, 14 September, available at <http://www.theage.com.au>.

Ruddock, P. and Ellison, C. (2004), 'Commonwealth to Set up Independent National Anti-corruption Body', *Joint Media Release, Offices of the Commonwealth Attorney-General and Minister for Justice*, Canberra, 16 June.

Senate (2006a), Transcript of Hearing, Senate Legal and Constitutional Legislation Committee, NSW Parliament House, Sydney, 27 April.

Senate (2006b), *Provisions of Law Enforcement Integrity Commissioner Bill 2006* [and related measures], Report of the Senate Legal and Constitutional Legislation Committee, Parliament House, Canberra, May.

Senate (2006c), *Parliamentary Debates* (Hansard), Australian Senate, Parliament House, Canberra, 21 June.

Stewart, C. (2007), 'Police Watchdog Toothless', *The Australian*, Sydney, 12 July, available at <http://www.theaustralian.news.com.au/story/0,20867,22059735-601,00.html>.

Victorian Parliament (2004), 'Police: Corruption and Organised Crime', *Legislative Council of Victoria – Parliamentary Debates (Hansard)*, 9 June, 5ff.

PART 3
A Best Way to Assess Integrity Systems?

Chapter 11

Police Oversight Agencies: Measuring Effectiveness

Colleen Lewis and Tim Prenzler

Introduction

This chapter focuses on an often neglected aspect of police oversight: what performance indicators should be used to best measure the effectiveness of independent, civilian agencies established, among other things, to monitor, review and/or investigate complaints against police and enhance police integrity. In attempting to address this question the authors wrote to the heads of agencies which oversight complaints against police in all Australian states and at the federal level. They also analysed the annual reports of the oversight agencies to identify which performance indicators they use when measuring their effectiveness. The findings show that the majority adopt a fairly basic and largely quantitative approach that focuses primarily on matters processed. This method is supplemented by self-selected, qualitative case studies that highlight the positive impact of the civilian oversight process. A very limited number of agencies also use stakeholder surveys and independent audits. The chapter concludes by recommending that police oversight agencies adopt a broader, multi-faceted approach when measuring their effectiveness. The authors suggest a four-part model that draws together notions of 'procedural integrity', 'procedural rigour', 'timeliness' and 'contribution to police integrity'.

Background

Repeated police corruption and abuse of power scandals and evidence of police bias when responding to citizens' complaints against police meant that by 1986 all Australian states and the Commonwealth had created an independent, civilian agency to oversight the complaints against police process (Lewis and Prenzler 1999). Table 11.1 shows the institutions responsible for police oversight in Australia from 1973 to 2004. The South Australian (SA) Police Complaints Authority, the New South Wales (NSW) Police Integrity Commission and the newly formed Office of Police Integrity in Victoria are the only agencies that currently deal exclusively with police related matters. Table 11.1 also shows that NSW has, and Western Australia (WA) had, a tiered system of oversight, split between an

Ombudsman dealing with the majority of complaints and a Commission dealing with the most serious types of misconduct. Other states have adopted what is commonly referred to as a 'one stop shop' approach.

Table 11.1 Police oversight agencies

Jurisdiction	Name	Responsibility for police
Commonwealth	Ombudsman	Since 1976
New South Wales	Ombudsman	Since 1979
	Independent Commission Against Corruption	1988–1996
	Police Integrity Commission	Since 1996
Northern Territory	Ombudsman	Since 1978
Queensland	Police Complaints Authority	1982–1989
	Criminal Justice Commission	1989–2001
	Crime and Misconduct Commission	Since 2002
South Australia	Police Complaints Authority	Since 1985
Tasmania	Ombudsman	Since 1978
Victoria	Ombudsman	1973–1986
	Police Complaints Authority	1986–1988
	Deputy Ombudsman (Police Complaints)	1988–2004
	Police Ombudsman	2004
Victoria	Office of Police Integrity	Since November 2004
Western Australia	Ombudsman	1985–2003
	Anti-corruption Commission	1996–2003
Western Australia	Crime and Corruption Commission	Since 2003

Traditionally, there has been a distinction between the role and functions of an Ombudsman's Office and Commissions.[1] When the Ombudsman's office first became involved in the police complaints process its role was largely confined to a paper review of police investigations. Commissions were seen as more powerful bodies that had greater coercive powers and the capacity to engage in independent investigations. But over time these differences have blurred with some Ombudsmen gaining greater coercive powers and investigative capacities and Commissions

1 The term Commissions in this chapter does not refer to *ad hoc* royal commissions or commissions of inquiry established for a limited period of time to address a specific problem. It is used to denote standing independent, external, civilian bodies that have an on-going oversight function.

increasingly undertaking review functions (Lewis and Prenzler 1999). But despite the blurring of the roles between Ombudsmen and Commissions and the creation of some form of civilian oversight in all Australian jurisdictions, the bulk of complaints investigation and adjudication is still performed by police internal investigation units. Independent oversight agencies audit, monitor and/or review the police investigations and only conduct their own independent investigation in the most serious of cases, following a public scandal, or at the request of a complainant.

Performance Indicators

Police oversight agencies are in effect citizens' watchdog bodies. Their role is to ensure that police complaints are properly investigated and that police departments operate with integrity. However, there is also a need to 'ensure' that oversight agencies are 'performing competently themselves' (Alexander and Burgess 1999, 54). Evaluating their impact is difficult because of the number of variables involved, conflicting ways of interpreting data (Lewis 1999) and the problem of hidden misconduct (Walker and Bumphus 1992). For example, an increase in complaints appears to be an obvious way to measure effectiveness, and it can reflect citizen and police confidence in the independent complaints process (Brereton 1999). But an increase in complaints received could also be the result of a legislative amendment that compels an oversight agency to be involved in all complaints against police, even those of a minor nature.

Resources and powers, which vary enormously between agencies (Lewis 2004a), are also an important factor when evaluating performance. Even if an oversight agency has the power to conduct its own investigation it may not have the resources to do so (Lewis 1999). Lack of resources also impacts on the time it takes agencies to process complaints, which in turn can negatively affect police and citizens' satisfaction with the complaints process. Some complainants and the public may be dissatisfied with sanctions imposed on police, but may not be aware that it is the police and not the oversight agency that determines disciplinary decisions (Kappeler et al. 1994). Also, just because there is a large increase in the number of complaints against police it does not automatically follow that an even larger problem of undetected corruption does not exist.

Despite these and other problems, there is an emerging set of indicators that are potentially useful in measuring effectiveness. Many are drawn from the growing interest in measuring police integrity, and from the wider field of police and regulatory agency performance evaluation. The number of complaints received and the nature of those complaints are inevitably linked to issues of agency performance, in the same way that reported crime is viewed as a measure of police performance (Grabosky 1989). The number of complaints monitored, reviewed and investigated and the subsequent disciplinary sanctions imposed can act as a guide for determining the ethical culture of a police organization and for devising strategies to improve police behaviours by deterring or re-educating erring officers or by punishing or dismissing recalcitrant officers (Brereton 2002). Outcome data, which includes complaints that are both substantiated and resolved informally, provide a complete picture of the extent to which an oversight agency has been able to 'solve' complaints and is similar to the way police crime clearance figures are used to determine how effectively police are dealing with the crime problem (Grabosky 1989). But complaints data and any reduction in complaints received should also be used more creatively to judge broader compliance strategies. In the same way that police need to be involved in problem-oriented, proactive strategies when trying to reduce crime, oversight agencies need to engage in research and preventive strategies to minimize the causes of citizen complaints. In other words they need to also concentrate on changing police behaviour and procedures where possible. (Brereton 2000). Disaggregated complaints data is important for this type of focused evaluation – particularly in relation to high risk areas such as police use of force, strip searches, interview methods, harassment or inaction (CJC 2000b; 2000c; 2000e; Herzog 2002).

A number of other performance measures show potential. Surveys designed to gauge police perceptions about the fairness, rigour and deterrent effect of the oversight processes can offer valuable insights into effectiveness (CJC 1997). Where agencies undertake their own investigations, substantiation rates can be supplemented by case file audits, where a group of experts – including judicial officers and experienced investigators – examine randomly chosen case files to see if appropriate methods have been pursued, if findings are appropriate and if recommended sanctions have been imposed by the police (Committee on the ICAC 2000; CJC 1996). This applies to the oversight agency an audit review similar to what the oversight agencies apply to police. Monitoring the outcomes of actions taken by oversight agencies in complaints tribunals, appeal tribunals or courts can also be a measure of agency effectiveness. Because not all people with a legitimate grievance against police will make complaints, anonymous surveys of detainees, crime victims and the general public can be used to assess the nature of people's interactions with police. Longitudinal studies also allow any change to be measured over time (Brereton 2002). 'Ethical climate surveys', in which police respond anonymously to scenario-based ethical dilemmas, can also be valuable when trying to gain insight into whether the culture, which can support or inhibit misconduct, has changed (CJC 1997).

Stakeholder confidence and satisfaction with the complaints process provides another dimension to performance evaluation. Complainant satisfaction surveys focus on the way complaints are handled and their outcomes and are similar to the satisfaction surveys of crime victims used by police. Here though, stakeholders should include police who are the subjects of complaints. This is necessary as police work in an environment that sometimes gives rise to vexatious complaints. As a result, police need to feel confident that they will be given a fair and timely hearing by the oversight agency should citizens or colleagues report against them. Opinion surveys can also provide information about the public's knowledge of, and confidence in, the work of the oversight agency, as well as levels of general confidence in police integrity. This is analogous to the way in which safety surveys are used to measure police effectiveness (ICAC 2000; Grabosky 1989).

Part of the problem with using substantiation rates as a performance measure is that the bulk of complaints against police typically lack sufficient evidence to convict or exonerate officers, even when the 'balance of probabilities' standard is applied. An important mission, therefore, is to reduce grievances through a variety of resolution strategies other than prosecution (Barnes and Ede 2002). This task addresses what many argue should be the primary goal of oversight agencies: 'to invoke public confidence in the police and thereby ensure good police-community relations' (Landau 1996, 294). It also addresses the concern of most complainants who frequently express the view that what they most want is an opportunity to be heard, an apology, or a behavioural or procedural change that will prevent the alleged misconduct being repeated. They do not complain just so that the officer(s) involved will be punished (Maguire and Corbett 1991).

The complexity of the environment in which performance is measured means that no one measurement or cluster of measures provides an objective demonstration of the effectiveness of an oversight agency in terms of changing behaviours, preventing corruption or effectively adjudicating allegations of misconduct. A diverse set of indicators needs to be used to gather different perspectives. As Sparrow (2000) points out, the more 'real' the measure, the less it will count activity and the more it will reflect achievement.

Research Methodology

The aim of this study was to identify and discuss the measures and categories of performance indicators used by police oversight agencies in Australia and to identify their perceptions of factors that do and could impede effectiveness. The study began in December 2000, when police oversight agencies across Australia were invited, by letter, to participate in a survey. They were asked to describe two aspects of their work:

1 what performance indicators they used to evaluate the effectiveness of their organization when overseeing complaints against police; and
2 the identification of factors that currently impede effectiveness and those (if any) that could impact negatively on effectiveness in the future.

By 2002 all agencies had responded. Sections on performance indicators taken from the agencies annual reports 1999–2000 and 2002–2003 were also examined. As the Crime and Corruption Commission was not established until 2003 it first annual report (2003–2004) was examined. At the time of writing, the Office of Police Integrity, established in late 2004, had not tabled an annual report. It will do so for the first time in 2005.

The responses in relation to performance are reported below by agency. This is followed by an analysis of annual reports and responses from agencies in relation to obstacles affecting performance.

Commonwealth

The Commonwealth Ombudsman has responsibility for overseeing complaints against police and police integrity in the Australian Federal Police (AFP). The main 'performance target' cited in the annual reports is the Ombudsman's ability to finalize the review of 75 percent of complaints processed by the AFP's Internal Investigations unit within a three month period. In the annual report for 1999–2000 a figure of 70 per cent of matters concluded within four weeks is cited. The performance indicators section also focuses on 'remedies' negotiated with government departments. These are reported by percentages in terms of actions such as 'explanation given', 'apology/error admitted' or 'financial remedy'. (Commonwealth Ombudsman 2000, 16–17). Another key measure, which addresses the degree to which government departments acted on the Ombudsman's advice, is reported primarily through case studies. In the 2002–2003 report, remedies are broken down with separate figures noted for complaints against the AFP and a slightly modified version of the timeliness standards being retained along with advice reports. There is also a section on internal reviews of complaints against the Ombudsman's processes and decisions; including numbers and type of complaints received and their outcomes. (Commonwealth Ombudsman 2003, 16–18).

In response to the question about matters that impede effectiveness, the obligation to review 'minor complaints' was cited as a drain on resources and a misuse of expertise. The requirement that the Ombudsman 'obtain the agreement of the AFP Commissioner before commencing investigation of most types of complaints', is seen to create problems in relation to 'controversial matters' and one that also has the potential to raise 'conflicts of interest' issues. The matter of police informing or complaining about other police is also identified as a particular problem as it remains outside the Ombudsman's jurisdiction.

A 2004 television documentary, which exposed corruption problems in the recently formed Australian Crime Commission (ACC), led to the Federal Government announcing the establishment of a new oversight body to take over the Ombudsman's role in relation to the oversight of the ACC, AFP and Customs (*Four Corners* 2004; McIlveen 2004). The *Law Enforcement Integrity Commissioner Act* 2006 commenced operation on 30 December 2006 and established ACLEI's jurisdiction over the AFP and ACC.

NSW – Ombudsman

The Ombudsman's response to the authors' survey begins by identifying 'improvements to complaint investigation outcomes' as a measure of effectiveness:

> For example, last year adverse findings were made in relation to 42 percent of matters investigated. A total of 2,567 investigations were carried out. Last year investigations led to 79 police officers being charged with criminal offences. This number is about the same as last year. We believe that this indicates that the complaints system is working effectively to identify those police officers who engage in misconduct.

In similar terms, the NSW Ombudsman refers to the identification of deficiencies and delays in police investigations of complaints and notes outcomes from monitoring the extent to which police implement Ombudsman's recommendations. The response also includes a suggestion that quantitative data can be 'restrictive' in showing incremental changes to police practices and on its own does not provide a macro perspective on reform.

The *Annual Report 1999–2000* includes a statistical summary of complaints against police and outcomes which resulted in a police response. Reportage that focuses on the Ombudsman's own performance is noted. This includes percentages of cases assessed within a given time frame; cases conciliated and recommendations implemented by the Police; as well as the number of monitored and direct investigations undertaken (NSW Ombudsman 2000, 10). Diverse case studies outlining the work of the Ombudsman in successfully resolving complaints, and in correcting inadequate police investigations and sanctions are also reported. In addition, the Annual Report notes the number of recommendations for changes to laws, policies or procedures. The 2002–2003 Report maintains this approach but enlarges on explanations about how the monitoring process is carried out (NSW Ombudsman 2003).

On the question of impediments to effectiveness, the Ombudsman notes the importance of police cooperation and the gradual improvement in police implementation of recommendations.

NSW – Police Integrity Commission (PIC)

In responding to the survey, the then Commissioner enclosed the Corporate Plan and Annual Report, both of which contain key information on performance indicators. The Commissioner notes that a major source for evaluating the PIC's work is its own review of the way the NSW Police manage complaints – titled *Project Dresden*. This report represents the first detailed review by the PIC of the operations of the NSW Police Internal Affairs. It is highly critical of police investigations and notes a lack of will by police in terms of implementing reform. It also provides a detailed account of weaknesses in police processes (PIC 2000b).

At the time of the survey the PIC was developing a new performance measurement framework for its Investigations Unit. This was later enlarged into an agency-wide framework as the *Corporate Plan and Performance Measurement Framework 2003–2006* (PIC 2003b). The document sets out three key objectives:

1. Effective Deterrence – Contribute to the effective deterrence of serious police misconduct.
2. Ongoing Reform – Ensure the development and provision of high quality advice on police reform.
3. Improved Assurance – Improve the level of assurance in the NSW community that there is vigilant oversight of police. (PIC 2003b: 2–3)

The rest of the document is set out in tables with language that is somewhat complex. Table 11.2 below presents a sample of categories. The 1999–2000 *Annual Report* uses performance indicators in a fairly rudimentary form largely in terms of goals. The 2002–2003 Report reflects the developments described above in roughly the same format as Table 11.2 (PIC 2000a; 2003a).

Table 11.2 Sample 'outcomes' and 'measures' from the PIC

	Performance framework
Outcome	**Measures**
Identification of aspects of the nature and extent of, opportunities for, factors contributing to, and evidence of, serious police misconduct.	Proportion of convictions in prosecutions that arise from investigations in which the Commission is involved. (Target: baseline of 80% set for first year). Proportion of Commission reports that identify aspects of the nature and extent of, opportunities for, or factors contributing to, serious police misconduct. (Target: baseline of 80% set for first year).
Identified serious police misconduct is addressed.	The proportion of recommendations relating to disciplinary action that are accepted by the NSW Police. (Target: baseline of 80% set for first year). Proportion of convictions that arise from investigations in which the Commission is involved. (Target: baseline of 80% set for first year).
Increased community and other stakeholder awareness of the nature and extent of aspects of, opportunities for, and factors contributing to, serious police misconduct.	Number of references in media to Commission investigations/projects. (Target: baseline of 80% set for first year). Proportion of Category 1 [most serious] complaints which are made directly to the Commission. (Target: baseline of 80% set for first year). Number of public hearing days. (Target: baseline of 40% set for first year).

Source: PIC 2003b: 4–6.

At the time of responding, the Commissioner reports that there are no significant factors impeding the PIC's effectiveness. He notes, however, that reductions in funding or the curtailing of investigative powers would impede future effectiveness, as could an adverse change in relations with the Police Service. For example, there had been problems with police implementation of the reform process as detailed in *Project Dresden,* which have since been overcome.

Northern Territory (NT)

The NT Ombudsman cites turnaround times as an important performance indicator. He also refers the researchers to measures in the *Annual Report*. Under the heading 'Performance Indicators and Targets', targets are listed with 'actual performance' in a parallel column, including figures for the preceding year which allow for comparisons. These are set out in a summary form in Table 11.3 as an example of this type of reportage.

Table 11.3 Summary of performance indicators and targets, NT Ombudsman 1999–2000

Performance Indicator	1999/2000 target	1999/2000 performance	1998/99 performance
Acknowledgement of written complaints within 48 hours	95%	95%	–
A decision will be made on how a complaint will be treated within 7 days	98%	98%	98%
Time taken to finalize complaint and advise complainant			
(a) General	75%	62%	72%
Within 3 months	85%	76%	81%
Within 6 months	95%	91%	90%
Within 12 months			
(b) Police	30%	26%	20%
Within 3 months	60%	49%	46%
Within 6 months	85%	96%	87%
Within 12 months			
Reduce the number of current complaints outstanding at year end			
General	120	80	115
Police	50	62	63
Conduct visits to Centres outside of Darwin and Alice Springs	8	8	6

Source: NT Ombudsman 2000: 53.

The *Annual Report 2002–2003* uses a different format with more detailed information about categories, targets, demographics and outcomes of complaints (NT Ombudsman 2003). A new umbrella term 'approaches' is utilized to separate enquiries from complaints proper. Case studies are used in both reports to illustrate successful interventions by the Ombudsman. The following is an abbreviated example of the case study approach to reporting performance:

> A woman bystander reported observing a police office assault and racially abuse an Aboriginal man being apprehended in Alice Springs. When she attempted to speak to the officer about the incident he became threatening and offensive. The matter was thoroughly investigated by a senior police officer under the supervision of the Joint Review Committee ... The JRC considered that the evidence of the complainant and her partner, as disinterested bystanders, was sufficient to warrant the commencement of disciplinary proceedings against the officer of excessive force and offensive language. (Northern Territory Ombudsman 2000, 176)

When responding to the question about impediments, the Ombudsman argues that a legislated six months completion time for disciplinary matters is too restrictive, especially when the legislation states that a matter lapses after that date. Investigations are conducted by police (with the most serious complaints being supervized by a joint Ombudsman/Police Committee) but treated as a performance standard for the Ombudsman. The Ombudsman also notes that a recent court case determined that his Office did not have own motion powers in relation to police conduct issues other than for 'administrative' matters. The implications of this are spelt out by the Ombudsman as follows:

> If serious allegations are made against the NT Police and are the subject of media speculation, unless there is a complaint made directly to the Commissioner or the Ombudsman about the matter, it cannot be the subject of an own motion investigation.

Furthermore, there is some ambiguity about whether police can approach the Ombudsman directly with an allegation. Resources are also identified as a major factor impeding effectiveness. The Ombudsman notes that police matters amount to approximately one third of complaints dealt with by his office but can account for up to 50 per cent of its workload:

> With limited resources and the staff available to me, I am not able to initiate many investigations in my own right. This is an important area as it would enable me to respond to the criticism of police investigating in their own right most complaints and thus the outcomes being viewed suspiciously.

Political factors also impact to constrain the Ombudsman's work. For example, the sixth month limit on disciplinary matters is thought to be the result of negotiations between the Government and the Police Association.

Queensland Crime and Misconduct Commission (CMC)

The then Commissioner notes that the requirement to report to Treasury means a concentration on 'throughput of work, timeliness, etc.' Beyond this, he argues that, 'it is extremely difficult to develop simple and reliable quantitative measures of effectiveness'. Nonetheless, he asserts that:

> The Commission is acutely aware that we must be able to persuade government and the general public that we are effective in our police oversight role, if we are to continue to maintain budgetary and political support. To this end, a priority within our research area has been to develop a 'basket' of different indicators, including qualitative data, with which to monitor whether progress is being made in raising standards of behaviour within the Queensland Police Service.

As an example, the major report *Integrity in the Queensland Police Service* (CJC 1997) uses a range of innovative measures in relation to police conduct and the Commission's impact on police behaviour. These include interviews with police, surveys of police, an analysis of police implementation of the Commission's recommendations, analyses of complaint outcomes, public opinion surveys, a study of police reporting against other police, and a study attempting to assess any inhibiting effect the Commission's presence might have on police arrest activity (see also *Reform Update*, CJC 2001).

CMC annual reports include performance indicators across a variety of activities, including an analysis of special risk areas for police misconduct such as drug-related corruption and excessive force. There is extensive use of the types of surveys described above. Under 'investigations' there is a mix of activity and achievement reports, with data on things such as:

- number of standard complaints assessed and finalised;
- number of investigations conducted or reviewed;
- percentage and number of complainants and subject officers satisfied with the process …;
- substantiation rate …;
- percentage and number of standard complaints finalised within 12 weeks…; and
- cost per complaint assessed. (CJC 2000a: 23)

There are also several case studies outlining investigations and their outcomes that are used to illustrate the achievement of the Commission. An example of this type is provided below:

> Operation Craven
> This covert investigation began in late 1998 after we received allegations that police officers in a regional Queensland town were involved in the protection of drug offenders.
> The investigation, which closed in February 2000, resulted in the arrest of three police officers on drug and corruption charges. Three civilians were also charged with serious drug offences. One of these men pleaded guilty to trafficking dangerous drugs and was sentenced to a term of imprisonment; the remainder await trial. (CJC 2000a, 28)

Performance indicators for 'research, prevention and reform' include a similar mix of activity and achievement measures, including:

- number of reports;
- number of presentations …;
- number and significance of instances in which agencies adopt changes; and
- qualitative evaluation using peer review. (CJC 2000a, 35)

Of particular note in the 2002–2003 Report is the inclusion of the following targets:

- Percentage of audited misconduct investigations that meet quality standards …; and
- Stakeholder satisfaction with prevention and intelligence reports. (CMC 2003, 68)

Results are reported separately in a *Ministerial Portfolio Statement*, but in a somewhat cryptic form (90 per cent and 95 per cent respectively) without explanation of the method (Queensland Government 2004, 8, 4).

The Commissioner did not identify any major impediments to the Commission's work, but did note the following as having the potential to cause difficulties in the future:

- a reduction in resources. This would be particularly detrimental given the broad jurisdiction of the CJC;
- effectiveness in reducing misconduct being seen as a reason for reducing the CJC's responsibility to oversee all levels of police misconduct. Such action could cause conduct problems to reappear;
- a change in police leaderships that might be less cooperative.

SA Police Complaints Authority

The Authority identifies two performance indicators:

- time taken to finalize a file after completion of investigation; and
- a calculated file completion rate.

He does, however, argue that 'performance indicators are at best crude indicators of poor performance and at worst are mistakenly read as indicators of worth and value'. The Authority referred the researchers to a conference paper he delivered at the 1999 conference of the International Association of Civilian Oversight of Law Enforcement, in which he proposed a number of targets, including the need to:

> Ensure public confidence in the police force and the complaints system;
> Be fair to complainants, police and staff;
> Be accessible to the community;
> Promote appropriate standards of conduct [by police]; and
> Provide the appropriate response to the full range of complainants. (Wainwright 1999, 3–8)

In the conference paper the Authority also indirectly questions the value of complainant surveys:

> In a complaint driven system, one might be tempted to think of complainants as clients and to operate in such a way as to obtain a benefit for them in every case. This is to be resisted. Some complainants will indeed have well founded grievances. In other cases it will appear, once the matter has been investigated, that the police have acted well and that the complainant's perceptions or expectations have been unrealistic (1999, 4).

The Authority's 1998–2000 *Annual Report* focuses on completion times for investigations as a measurable performance indicator. This is not included in the 2002–2003 Report, but percentage of cases informally resolved is included; along with a focus on how citizens can access the Authority (PCA 2000; 2003).

The Authority argues that the time taken to process complaints is the biggest obstacle to effectiveness: 'In the vast majority of cases, the sooner a complaint is answered the better the chance of achieving a satisfactory outcome and maintaining or restoring confidence in the police force'. Related to this was 'thoroughness', which he argues can be lacking in initial investigations by police which in turn leads to complainant dissatisfaction.

Tasmania

The Ombudsman's Office reports use of the following performance indicators:

- number of complaints against police, (compared with the number of complaints received by the Police Internal Investigations Unit);
- outcome of complaints (whether they are substantiated); and
- timeliness of complaint handling (average age of a complaint) – although this is often affected by the period of time taken by the Internal Investigations Unit to respond to the matter.

The 1999–2000 *Annual Report* records changes in the number of complaints against police, the outcomes of police internal processing, and the number of appeals dealt with by the Ombudsman. The 2002–2003 Report also covers this ground. In addition there is data on the time taken to finalize complaints (but without targets) (Tasmania Ombudsman 2000, 40; 2003, 41).

The Ombudsman reports three factors that impede his effectiveness:

- power being limited to recommendations not determinations;
- delays affected by the requirement to deal with most matters in writing; and
- budget constraints that 'affect officer workload and the ability to engage consultants or technical experts in investigations'.

More generally, though, the Ombudsman notes that his office 'is not strictly a 'police oversight body' as it does not oversight all complaints against police. Rather, it only handles those complaints 'that come to the Ombudsman's Office in its normal functioning of investigating complaints about government departments'.

Victoria

The former Victorian Ombudsman, in his role as Deputy Ombudsman (Police Complaints), reports that over time his office has experimented with numerous performance indicators and supplied an extensive list of abbreviated indicators:

'Efficiency' indicators include:

- timeliness;
- output:
  - cases on hand at end of reporting period;

  - number of old cases on hand;
  - total number of cases completed;
  - number of telephone enquiries;
- efficient use of resources:
  - use of informal handling;
  - number of own investigations;
- accessibility to Office by complainants.

A large number of indicators are listed under 'effectiveness', and include such things as:

- identification of ethical misconduct;
- complainant satisfaction – process and outcome;
- public confidence in/community approval rating of police force;
- outcome of cases investigated (1) by Ombudsman, (2) by police.

The latter is divided into three areas: 'Facts ascertained', 'Punishment' and 'Remedial'. The acceptance of recommendations by the Chief Commissioner of Police and changes in police attitudes is also listed.

The 1999–2000 *Annual Report* describes and justifies the Ombudsman's review processes; and includes quantitative data on complaints processes, their outcomes, the percentage informally resolved, and cases where the Ombudsman instigated further action by police investigators. It also provides summaries of special investigations into major areas of alleged misconduct, such as police raids on allegedly mistaken targets. The Report sets out achievements from these processes in a qualitative form, mainly in terms of changes to police management practices. The 2002–2003 Report follows the same model, but with the inclusion of data from previous years to show trends (Victorian Ombudsman 2000, 18–19; 2003, 76).

There has recently been a major overhaul of the complaints against police process in Victoria. In response to a staggering number of gangland killings and allegations of organized crime, police corruption and links between the two, the Deputy Ombudsman Police Complaints was replaced by a Police Ombudsman in 2004. In a classic example of policy on the run (Lewis 2004b) the Police Ombudsman was then replaced by the Director Police Integrity in an Office of Police Integrity in the same year. However, the Ombudsman fulfils both roles: he is simultaneously the Ombudsman and the Director Police Integrity, a situation, which in Australia at least, is peculiar to Victoria.

The Office of Police Integrity has not been in operation long enough to have tabled an Annual Report to the Parliament. Consequently, which performance indicators it will use to measure effectiveness and what methods it will use in the measurement process are unknown. However, given the extensive powers bestowed on the Director, Police Integrity, and the controversy surrounding the establishment of the office, the performance indicators selected will be of great interest to all who have an interest in the effectiveness of the civilian oversight process.

WA – Ombudsman

The Ombudsman referred the researchers to the 1999–2000 *Annual Report*, where performance indicators focus on 'efficiency', in terms of 'how quickly' the Office processes complaints, and 'effectiveness', in terms of 'the extent to which the Office has been able to provide assistance to complainants and have agencies improve their practices and procedures' (WA Ombudsman 2000, 13). For police, 'key effectiveness indicators' are reported as percentages of 'allegations finalized where complainants received assistance', the number of 'improvements to practices and procedures' and the number of allegations where Police 'took further investigative action at the instigation of my Office' (2000, 15). 'Performance measures' that set 'target' against 'actual' are the number of allegations finalized, average finalization times, and costs (2000, 18). These are maintained in the 2002–2003 report (WA Ombudsman 2003).

A number of impediments to effectiveness are identified:

- a lack of defined powers in legislation;
- the probable absence of own motion powers;
- a requirement that police be allowed 42 days to investigate a complaint before the Ombudsman could conduct his own investigation;
- inadequate resources for carrying out independent investigations;
- reliance on review that meant matters often devolved into disagreements with police about how complaints had been investigated rather than focusing on the complaint itself;
- the enormous geographic size of WA further limited the capacity for independent ('primary') investigations;
- a possible duplication of work under the 'three-tier system' involving police, the Ombudsman and the Anti-Corruption Commission.

These concerns fed into a review of external oversight of police by the WA Royal Commission in 2002. It resulted in the Ombudsman's role in police oversight being taken over by a Crime and Corruption Commission (CCC), which was created in late 2003 (Kennedy 2004).

WA – Anti-Corruption Commission (A-CC)

The A-CC respondent referred the researchers to the section on performance indicators in its annual reports. The core indicator being the extent to which Commission members (the top management group) accepted Commission recommendations. This target is broken down across 'assessment and investigation reports', 'review reports' and 'audit reports', with a standard of 'accepted first time: 90%'. Results for the current and previous year are reported and include costs per hour (A-CC 2000, 34–5; 2003, 44–5).

In terms of impediments, the A-CC referred to its inability to hold public hearings. It referred the researchers to the Royal Commission for further information.

The Royal Commission review in 2002 concluded that the A-CC lacked sufficient powers and accountability (Kennedy 2002; 2004). In late 2003 the A-CC was replaced by the Crime and Corruption Commission which, as mentioned above, also took over the Ombudsman's police-related tasks.

Crime and Corruption Commission

The new agency, the CCC, is similar to Queensland's CMC. It has own motion powers; the authority to conduct public hearings, covert investigations and integrity tests; coercive powers to obtain information; and a proactive role in research, education and the reporting of findings.

In its first Annual Report (2003–2004) the CCC identifies the performance indicators it will use in 2004–2005. It also notes that they were developed before the recruitment of Directors was complete and consequently may have to be modified to 'better reflect the Commission's strategic plan' (CCC 2004, 54).

The performance indicators are located in the following 'outcome statements'.

1 Improved integrity and reduced incidence of misconduct in the public sector.
2 Appropriate use of powers to address organised crime. (CCC 2004, 53)

The CCC's achievements in meeting these outcomes will be measured through the following three output based performance indicators:

1 Investigations into misconduct in the public sector
2 Corruption prevention reviews and education
3 Investigations facilitated into organised crime. (CCC 2004, 53)

What is not clear at this early stage is how the measurement will take place.

Towards Optimum Performance Indicators

The results of this research show that performance indicators are of concern to police oversight agencies. The format of annual reports and special reports demonstrate a definite attempt to evaluate performance. Nonetheless, respondents see the development of reliable indicators as problematic, with some more sceptical than others. Despite this, there is an understanding that a range of indicators is required to obtain the best possible assessment of an oversight body's performance in monitoring, reviewing and investigating complaints, and reducing and preventing police misconduct. It is also clearly understood that performance indicators are an inescapable part of accountability.

As a baseline, oversight agencies typically collect the following statistics, either in term of reviewing complaints processed by police or in direct processing of complaints:

- the number of complaints received and finalized per annum;
- time taken to finalize complaints; and
- outcome in terms of decisions such as substantiation, referral to mediation and penalties.

In some cases it is conceded that these are measures of activity, rather than achievement. Despite this, they do provide an important picture of agency work. Complaint finalization times are popular indications of effectiveness, but they are not always set against a target. In addition, it is clear that, in part, oversight agencies judge their performance based on the extent to which police achieve satisfactory performance targets in processing complaints and preventing misconduct. There are efforts to assess this by scoring the number of recommendations judged to have been implemented, and by providing narrative accounts of investigative processes leading to changes in police procedures or improved outcomes for complainants.

The Queensland CMC stood out for its more comprehensive, social science based reports – including extensive stakeholder surveys, and some limited application of case file audits. This can be attributed in large part to the fact that it was established with a well-resourced research division with research-qualified staff (Lewis 1999).

The most commonly identified issue impeding effectiveness is budgets and their impact on resources. Ombudsmen are most likely to complain that insufficient funding constrains their capacity to properly oversee police. Other impediments to effectiveness, identified by some agencies, relate to legislative capacity and include lack of own motion powers, the inability to compel testimony and determine sanctions. Some respondents also emphasize how reliant they are on police co-operation, which could change when police leadership changes.

Taking these diverse practices and opinions into account, the following section provides a set of performance targets and indicators, using four larger categories that cut across issues of inputs and outcomes, and efficiency and effectiveness. The model is not put forward as the optimum in performance measurement; rather it is designed to stimulate discussion and advance the development of fair and meaningful performance indicators.

Procedural Integrity

Procedural integrity is concerned about compliance with procedural standards in the areas of complaints investigation techniques, the development of appropriate intelligence and the application of sanctions. It is designed, among other things, to prevent interviewees feeling intimidated, to ensure the appropriate communication of rights, and to prevent discrimination toward or against accused persons and complainants. This is where surveys of complainants, witnesses, subject police officers and others involved in the process can be useful. Through their feedback, perceptions of impartiality and professionalism are able to be measured. The process can be triangulated by analysis of sample case files by an expert audit panel. Performance can also be judged in terms of outcomes, or 'forensic integrity', through the success of a brief and any positive or adverse comments from judicial officers.

Procedural Rigour

'Rigour' refers to the thoroughness of investigations in terms of properly following leads and asking the appropriate questions, while quality can be examined through the stakeholder surveys mentioned above. The independent case audit process is a vital component of this performance indicator. Performance can also be judged here in terms of successful prosecutions, judicial comments on briefs, and reviews of failed prosecutions.

Timeliness

Heads of oversight agencies identify the quick resolution of matters as an indicator of agency effectiveness. It is a very important issue for all stakeholders including police and complainants. However, timeliness needs to be balanced against procedural thoroughness. How quickly complaints or referrals are processed and resolved is easily measured by tracking a complaint. Fair turn-around times can be established by benchmarking with similar agencies and through surveys, which include questions about expectations of what is a reasonable time for the resolution of matters. Resources are an important factor as inadequate resources will result in an overburdened oversight agency. Regardless of how efficient the oversight agency is in processing complaints, without appropriate resources it will not have the capacity to keep pace with complaints received.

Contribution to Police Integrity

This can be understood in terms of both deterring police corruption and the agency's contribution to wider integrity maintenance. Deterrence can be measured, in part, by surveys of police, with direct questions covering perceptions about the probability of officers being 'caught' and sanctioned for misbehaviour. Other sources will include surveys of the public and police regarding perceptions of corruption levels. Changes in the volume, seriousness and types of complaints, and intelligence about misconduct, which draw in some of the findings from 'procedural integrity indicators', would assist in measuring the agency's contribution to police integrity. Ethical climate surveys will also have relevance; as will surveys of the public regarding their confidence in, and knowledge of, the oversight agency and its processes. Complainant satisfaction surveys can also be useful here. The appropriateness of outcomes (including sanctions) is important for ensuring a productive balance between punishment, remedial interventions and reconciliation of complainants. Complaints data will need to be disaggregated in order to monitor specific areas of risk – such as incivility, false arrest and excessive force – and outcomes. Separate studies will need to be done on potential problem areas where complaints may not be a good indicator of the magnitude of a problem. Special surveys or incident data collection will be required here.

The above constitutes a list of tasks that is potentially very expensive. However, many of the more ambitious surveys only need to be conducted every few years to provide useful time-series measures. In some instances it may be more economical to subcontract surveys to commercial firms who specialize in such matters. But the need for an investment of resources away from core business to evaluation of business cannot be denied. Commenting on the general neglect of performance measures for oversight agencies world-wide, David Brereton, a long-term Director of the Queensland CMC's Research and Prevention Division, emphasized that:

> The grounds for retaining these bodies are philosophical as well as utilitarian – concepts such as accountability and transparency are important, even if they are not readily susceptible to measurement. ... However ... in a world in which governments are placing ever greater emphasis on the need to show 'value for money', appeals to abstract principles may not be enough to win funding arguments – evidence that external oversight has value in a concrete sense is also required. (1999, 4)

Conclusion

Measuring the performance of police oversight agencies is not an easy matter. Basic statistics about numbers of complaints processed, times and costs of processing, and outcomes give a picture of the demand pressures on agencies and how they prioritize and spend the resources allocated to them. However, more sophisticated measures are needed to assess the extent to which agencies are succeeding in their common mission as citizens' watchdog bodies. Regular surveys of stakeholders will help to establish performance benchmarks and a series of vital indicators about deterrence, rigour, impact, fairness, timeliness, appropriateness of outcomes, and stakeholder confidence. Regular case auditing will add another dimension to independent expert review. Without such measures there is no reliable evidence that the core business of independent, civilian oversight agencies is being done as efficiently and effectively as possible.

References

Anti-Corruption Commission (ACC) (2000), *Annual Report 1999–2000*, Perth.

Anti-Corruption Commission (ACC) (2003), *Annual Report 2002–2003*, Perth.

Alexander, P. and Burgess, M. (1999), 'The Effectiveness of Standing Commissions', *NSW Police News* 79:2, 53–9.

Brereton, D. (1999), 'Evaluating External Oversight Bodies', *1999 IACOLE World Conference*, Sydney, 5–9 September.

Brereton, D. (2000), 'Policing and Crime Prevention', in D. Chappell and P. Wilson (eds) *Crime and the Criminal Justice System in Australia* (Sydney: Butterworths).

Brereton, D. (2002), 'Monitoring Integrity', in T. Prenzler and J. Ransley (eds.) *Police Reform: Building Integrity* (Sydney: Federation Press).

Crime and Corruption Commission (CCC) (2004), *Annual Report 2003–2004*, Perth.

Criminal Justice Commission (CJC) (1994), *Informal Complaint Resolution in the Queensland Police Service*, Brisbane.

Criminal Justice Commission (CJC) (1996), *Submission to the Queensland Police Service Review Committee*, Brisbane.

Criminal Justice Commission (CJC) (1997), *Integrity in the Queensland Police Service: Implementation and Impact of the Fitzgerald Inquiry Reforms*, Brisbane.

Criminal Justice Commission (CJC) (2000a), *Annual Report 1999–2000*, Brisbane.

Criminal Justice Commission (CJC) (2000b), *Complaints Fact Sheet*, Brisbane.

Criminal Justice Commission (CJC) (2000c), *Defendants' Perceptions of Police Treatment*, Brisbane.

Criminal Justice Commission (CJC) (2000d), *Police Strip Searches in Queensland*, Brisbane.

Criminal Justice Commission (CJC) (2000e), *Protecting Confidential Information*, Brisbane.

Criminal Justice Commission (CJC) (2000f), *Public Attitudes Toward the CJC*, Brisbane.

Criminal Justice Commission (CJC) (2000g), *Reported Use of Force by Queensland Police*, Brisbane.

Crime and Misconduct Commission (CMC) (2002), *Monitoring the Ethical Climate of Organisations*, Brisbane.

Crime and Misconduct Commission (CMC) 2003. *Annual Report 2002–3*, Brisbane.

Committee on the ICAC (2000), *The ICAC: Accounting for Extraordinary Powers*, Parliament of NSW, Sydney.

Commonwealth Ombudsman (2000), *Annual Report 1999–2000*, Canberra.

Commonwealth Ombudsman (2003), *Annual Report 2002–3*, Canberra.

Ede, A. and Barnes, M. (1991), 'Alternative Strategies for Resolving Complaints', in T. Prenzler and J. Ransley (eds) *Police Reform: Building Integrity* (Sydney: Federation Press).

Four Corners (2004), 'Corruption Inc.', 14 June, ABC TV, Sydney.

Grabosky, P. (1989), 'Efficiency and Effectiveness in Australian Policing', in D. Chappell and P. Wilson (eds) *Australian Policing: Contemporary Issues* (Sydney: Butterworths).

Herzog, S. (2002), 'Police Violence in Israel: Has the Establishment of a Civilian Complaints Board Made a Difference?', *Police Practice and Research: An International Journal* 3: 119–33.

Independent Commission Against Corruption (ICAC) 2000, *Annual Report*, Hong Kong.

Kappeler, V., Sluder, R. and Alpert, G. (1994), *Forces of Deviance: Understanding the Dark Side of Policing* (Prospect Heights, IL: Waveland Press).

Kennedy, G. (2002), *Royal Commission Interim Report* (Perth: Government of Western Australia).

Kennedy, G. (2004), *Royal Commission into Whether There Has Been Any Corrupt or Criminal Conduct by Western Australian Police Officers: Final Report, Volume I* (Perth: Government of Western Australia).

Landau, T (1996), 'When Police Investigate Police: A View from Complainants', *Canadian Journal of Criminology*, July, 291–315.

Lewis, C. (1999), *Complaints against Police: The Politics of Reform* (Sydney: Hawkins Press).

Lewis, C. (2004a), 'Why Our Police Must Face a Probe', *Age*, 6 April: Opinion Page.

Lewis, C. (2004b), 'How Best to Use Fitzgerald', *Age*, 4 June: Opinion Page; 'The Wrong Way to Fight Corruption', *Age*, 28 August: Opinion Page.

Lewis, C. and Prenzler, T. (1999), 'Civilian Oversight of Police in Australia', *Trends and Issues in Crime and Criminal Justice* 141, 1–6.
Maguire, M. and Corbett, C. (1991), *A Study of the Police Complaints System* (London: Stationery Office).
McIlveen, L. (2004), 'Corruption Force to Check Top Officers', *The Courier Mail*, 17 June, 16.
NSW Ombudsman (2000), *Annual Report 1999–2000*, Sydney.
NSW Ombudsman (2003), *Annual Report 2002–3,* Sydney.
NT Ombudsman (2000), *Annual Report 1999–2000*, Darwin.
NT Ombudsman 2003. *Annual Report 2002–3*, Darwin.
Police Complaints Authority (PCA) (2000), *Annual Report 1998–2000*, Adelaide.
Police Complaints Authority (PCA) (2003), *Annual Report 2002–3*, Adelaide.
Police Integrity Commission (PIC) (2000a), *Annual Report 1999–2000*, Sydney.
Police Integrity Commission (PIC) (2003a), *Annual Report 2002–3*, Sydney.
Police Integrity Commission (PIC) (2003b), *Corporate Plan and Performance Measurement Framework 2003–2006*, Sydney.
Police Integrity Commission (PIC) (2000b), *Special Report to Parliament: Project Dresden, An Audit of the Quality of NSW Police Service Internal Investigations*, Sydney.
Prenzler, T. (2004), 'Stakeholder Perspectives on Police Complaints and Discipline', *Australian and New Zealand Journal of Criminology* 37:1, 85–113.
Queensland Government (2004), *Ministerial Portfolio Statement, 2004–5 State Budget, Honourable the Premier and Minister for Trade, Crime and Misconduct Commission*, Brisbane.
Sparrow, M. (2000), *The Regulatory Craft* (Washington, DC: Brookings Institute).
Tasmania Ombudsman (2000), *Annual Report 1999–2000*, Hobart.
Tasmania Ombudsman (2003), *Annual Report 2002–3*, Hobart.
Western Australian (WA) Ombudsman (2000), *Annual Report 1999–2000*, Perth.
Western Australian (WA) Ombudsman (2003), *Annual Report 2002–3*, Perth.
Wainwright, T. (1999), 'Evaluating the Effectiveness of Civilian Oversight', *1999 IACOLE World Conference*, Sydney, 5–9 September.
Walker, S. and Bumphus, V. (1992), 'The Effectiveness of Civilian Review', *American Journal of Police* 11: 1–26.

Chapter 12

Integrity Assessment Tools: A Preliminary Comparison

Arthur Shacklock, Carmel Connors and Angela Gorta

Introduction

The world of business and public sector management has changed dramatically in Australia over the past 20 years, as regards attitudes towards poor governance and corrupt behaviour in both the public and private sectors. The major excesses of the 1980s and 1990s gave birth to a movement in public sector ethics, leading to the establishment of anti-corruption agencies, major inquiries into ethical misconduct and a myriad of integrity building strategies. Internationally, major corporate excesses and collapses, such as Enron, Worldcom and others, have jolted citizens out of their lethargy. In Australia, the collapse of companies such as HIH and OneTel, and the recent Australian Wheat Board (AWB) involvement in the 'oil for foods scandal' have heightened public awareness of the need to address ethics and corporate governance at the highest levels in both the private and public sectors (Cole 2006; Prasser 2004, 94; Bower and Gilson 2003, 20; Houghton and Jubb 2003, 67; Leibler 2003, 61; Leung and Cooper 2003, 505; Mellema 2003, 125; Riley 2003, 31; Veasey 2003, 839; Clarke, Dean, and Houghton 2002, 58–72; Dabscheck 1998, 155–87; Glasbeek 1998, 188–221).

Royal Commissions, Senate Inquiries and other forms of public sector investigations and reviews have yielded alarming incidents of corruption with high-ranking officials charged and gaoled. Such events have pressured both the public and private sectors to focus attention on ethics, integrity and good governance. The approach by both government and private sectors has involved passing legislation, developing codes of ethics/conduct, delivering training in ethics and governance issues, instituting rewards and sanctions, and establishing compliance systems and 'watchdog' agencies.

Following on from these activities, there has been an interest in assessing the degree to which such approaches have been successful in enhancing ethical behaviour and integrity. There is now a range of Integrity Assessment Tools (IATs) in use in both the public and private sectors. However, the literature is undeveloped in analysing the usefulness, comparability or compatibility of these various tools, except, perhaps for research which highlights the difficulties and complexities of measuring specific areas of integrity and good governance, such as the quality of corporate directors or corporate reputation (Cravens et al. 2003, 200; Epstein and Roy 2004, 1; Scissons 2002, 20–26).

These tools differ in many respects, and it is not possible in this chapter to identify all that may be in use and their special characteristics.[1] Our primary purpose is to begin a more focused examination by selecting a sample applied in both sectors. Our comparisons will highlight various approaches adopted for assessing integrity-building strategies by both the public and private sectors, and, hopefully encourage further research, analysis, enhancement and development of assessment tools.

Before commencing our discussion, it is useful to acknowledge some definitional issues. The literature abounds with numerous definitional approaches to what is meant by the terms 'integrity' and 'corruption'. This confounding factor in the interpretation of data means that the use of such terminology can differ significantly between authors, organizations, sectors, cultures and countries. Precision about what is being described is difficult to establish across the various assessments or studies (Langseth 2006; Philp 2006; Brown 2006; Duncan 2006, Gorta and Forell 1994, 4–22; Independent Commission Against Corruption 1997, 22–32). Major international measurement tools, such as those used by Transparency International and the World Bank have attracted ongoing debate over what their respective indexes actually measure and the methodology they employ (Lambsdorff 2006; Galtung 2006). It is not the place of this chapter to re-enter this debate, but merely to identify definitional problems. The purpose of this chapter is to examine some of the IATs now in use for assessing the impacts of integrity building strategies.

Assessing Integrity in Australia

For more than 20 years, significant governance reforms have been implemented in Australia. Yet, new cases of high-level unethical conduct are regularly reported. This raises an important question: to what extent have the numerous anti-corruption and ethics building activities and strategies been effective in curbing corruption and unethical practices and in building integrity?

Only limited research has been undertaken on the impact and effectiveness of the any intervention undertaken to reduce corruption since one consequence of the hidden nature of some forms of corruption is that it is not possible to ascertain a simple measure of the level of corruption before the intervention; how much corruption there would have been if the intervention had not occurred; or, how much corruption is currently occurring (Gorta 2006, 204, 205, 207).

On the other hand, measurement techniques can be used to assess an organization's ability to identify and consider high-risk functions, to examine corruption prevention strategies in place, and to gauge the awareness of employees of the relevant organizational issues, policies and strategies. Such data can

1 Information about a more comprehensive analysis undertaken by the authors can be obtained from a.shacklock@griffith.edu.au.

form the basis upon which to obtain a clear profile of the organization, similar organizations or the entire sector (Gorta 2006). It has also been argued that qualitative rather than quantitative measures are the most effective in yielding usable information (Gorta 2003).

We are not concerned with the detail of strategies themselves or with the global assessments made by such organizations as Transparency International) or the World Bank, except as might be useful in contextualizing examples. Rather, we are interested in the specific features of Australian tools. For this task, we have selected several key strategies employed within the public and private sectors. The tools selected cover both theoretical frameworks and applied examples for monitoring and assessing integrity practices within and across public and private organizations.

In the public sector, the results of this assessment activity eventually become public, appearing in special reports to parliament, review documents from watchdog agencies, departmental annual reports and other forms of public communication such as agency web sites. In the private sector, it is often more difficult to elicit information that reviews the effectiveness of integrity building strategies. This factor does not suggest that such activities are not occurring in the private sector or that the public sector is more ethical than the private sector, or *vice versa*, but it merely recognizes the reality that private companies and corporations operate in a competitive marketplace and are more likely to protect such information 'in-house'.

Public and Private Sectors – An Era of Change

In recent decades, changes brought about by deregulation, commercialization, corporatization and privatization have fundamentally altered public sector management across the world. A shift to a more entrepreneurial management style, increasing managerialism, compulsory competitive tendering and outsourcing of the delivery of many government services, the set-up of discrete purchaser/provider units within departments, successive restructurings and retrenchments, has left a residual public sector to operate in an environment where the skills, culture and value systems differ significantly from that of a traditional bureaucracy. The operational environment of the private and public sectors have become much more enmeshed.

The public sector shift towards private sector style self-governing agencies tests the customary mode of accountability with tension emerging between managerial independence and managerial accountability. The intermingling of public and private sector values within organizations involved in these new governance arrangements and bodies where both public and private values co-exist (spanning the public/private divide) are under the most stress to develop a new culture to update their working practices (Mulgan 2000, 93).

Many doubt whether business administration theories and techniques – and hence governance and integrity measures – can be easily transposed, let alone imitated in the public sector (Argyriades 2003; Clatworthy et al. 2000; Grimshaw et al. 2002; Kickert 1997; Klijn and Teisman 2003). Generally, the literature argues that the main impediment is the fundamental differences in role, environment, culture and organizational characteristics of public and private sector agencies. Theobold (1997, 490), for example, argues that the importance of a market driven philosophy and the need for openness and accountability (which is an indispensable feature of all public sector organizations) are incompatible. Management in the public sector has to deal with more values above and beyond effectiveness and efficiency criteria, such as legitimacy and social justice. Additionally, it may be more constructive to recreate public institutions 'built on a fuller understanding of the essential distinction between public and corporate management' (Gregory 1999, 68).

Nevertheless, the reforms to the public sector, which have come to be known as 'New Public Management' (NPM), amount to an administrative philosophy that has become widely accepted (Clark 2002; Haque 2001; Pollitt and Bouckaert 2000; Terry 1998). However, there is increased concern about the impact of NPM reforms on public service ethics (for example, OECD 1996; 2000) suggesting a decline in public service ethical standards and an increase in unethical behaviour (Maesschalck 2004, 468).

The private sector in Australia has fared no better and has been under similar but different pressures to undertake reforms to improve ethical standards and corporate governance. Executive remunerations have increased exponentially at the same time as organizations have been downsized and workers' salaries held in check (Wishart 2006).[2] Australian shareholders, even those with small holdings, are taking a greater interest in the management and accountability of corporations in which their retirement savings are invested (Bartholomeuz 2006).

Likewise, business ethics has become more important (Kusku and Zarkada-Fraser 2004; Milton Smith 1997; McMahon 1995). Since the late 1980s in Australia as elsewhere, evidence of entrenched corruption in many areas of public and business life has surfaced with ethical standards and guidelines becoming key issues for management, boards and governments to address. Therefore, it is important that both private and public sector organizations address ethics as a corporate culture issue to be strategically managed and monitored by top management. To do this, the capacity of public and private sector managers to enhance integrity and control corruption must be reinforced. Will is not enough.

2 A recent example is the retiring CEO of Macquarie Bank, Alan Moss, who is reported having retired on 24 May 2008 with a $50m retirement package comprising 'amounts quarantined from previous pay packets, profit sharing and share options'. The same report quotes the ACTU President, Sharan Burrow stating that: 'Qantas … management gets between $3–7m as a base salary … yet they're trying to tell workers to take a real pay cut, to take 3 percent …. Surely we haven't lost our moral compass to the point where people can take away tens of millions of dollars in salary every year and yet the very workers who have made their companies profitable won't get a fair share of those profits' (AAP General News, 21 May 2008), available at <http://global.factiva. com>, accessed 21 May 2008).

Skills and tools are needed for engaging with workplace realities by measuring the success or otherwise of integrity reforms in delivering positive outcomes.

The signposting of ethics has been assisted, to a large extent, by legislation and other regulatory changes. In recent times, the Australian government and regulators have strengthened governance arrangements (CLERP 9,[3] the ASX Guidelines, extension of privacy legislation etc.). The implications of these changes are that private bodies have become subject to stronger integrity regimes. The increasing convergence of the public and private sectors has been largely driven by the increased contestability of the provision of public services (Barrett 2004). Outsourcing of government services and the adoption by the public sector of many private sector management techniques means that while public bodies have been trying to go private and take on aspects of the private sector model, the private bodies have also been tending to go more public in their approaches to accountability.

Because of these factors, a number of Australian companies are building their own internal integrity systems through measures such as instituting codes of ethics, setting clear values and compliance standards, ethics training, and in some cases, visibly punishing breaches and rewarding ethical behaviour. These changes vary from highly aspirational activity through to risk avoidance and punitive processes. Whatever the reason, it is apparent that the Australian private sector, like its counterpart in the public arena, is moving forward in developing and employing strategies for integrity.

Choice of Integrity Assessment Tools (IATs)

An IAT can be considered as operating, broadly, at three levels. First, what we might call 'global integrity measures' which focus on whole countries, such as the various indexes, indicators and measures used by Transparency International, the World Bank, or the OECD (Carayannis and Laget 2004; Davis 2004; TI 2004). A second level is 'sectoral or industry measures' which examine smaller geographic entities such as state public sectors or an industry group. A third level applies to individual organizations such as single public sector agencies or companies.

Our focus in this chapter is on the latter two types of measures currently in use in the Australian public and private sectors. The public sector tools chosen include those used by the Independent Commission Against Corruption in New South Wales, the Crime and Misconduct Commission in Queensland, and the Australian Public Service Commission. In the private sector, our chosen instruments were selected from those developed by the major ('Big Four') consultancy companies – Deloitte Touche Thomatsu, KPMG, PricewaterhouseCoopers and Ernst and

3 The Corporate Law Economic Reform Program (Audit Reform and Corporate Disclosure) Act 2004 (also known as CLERP 9) became law on 1 July 2004. Under these reforms, organizations must have adequate measures, processes and procedures to meet the obligations of the Act, especially if they are involved in auditing and company financial reporting. See <http:/www.asic/gov.au>.

Young. These companies engage in consultancies across a wide range of industries and organizations. While some of these private sector tools are used more widely than the Australian context, we are interested in their local application.

Towards a Cross-sectoral Comparison of Assessment Tools

The belief that there is a link between ethical and effective organizational performance has broad based relevance both in the public sector and within corporations, but the means of embedding ethics is open for debate (APSC 2003; Ashkanasy et al. 2000; Christie et al. 2003; Haynes and Jones 1999; Jose and Thibodeaux 1999). Hence, a variety of surveys and measures have evolved which attempt to assess the effectiveness of various types of strategies for institutionalizing ethics within different types of organizations.

How real is the 'divide' between the public and private sectors? There are similar efforts being made in both sectors to address related problems of ethics, governance and integrity. At the present time, the methodologies and outputs are often different and range from examining and verifying specific troublesome issues, through to less focused searches to identify potential risks. The availability of output data also varies widely sometimes due to 'commercial-in-confidence' restrictions or copyright protection of a commercial product.

Usually when we speak of a 'typology', we mean the establishment of a means of classification, based upon various agreed characteristics that are deemed to be of importance and then representing these in a way that presents clear boundaries between them, but which is conducive to comparative analysis. Such a categorization allows others, whether theoreticians or practitioners, to understand the properties of any given phenomenon – in this case, the tools that seek to measure integrity and corruption. Moreover, a 'typology' is usually developed progressively as a result of grounded research, which slowly yields the data needed for classification. We have departed from that process in that we have examined a sample of the available evidence of existing measurement tools currently used in Australia and have attempted to identify their characteristics according to a predetermined estimate of what might be expected to be found.

In attempting to compare and contrast any phenomenon with the ultimate aim of devising a 'typology', we must be mindful that such typologies are difficult to establish, given the wide array of potential variables that can be considered. To accommodate these difficulties, there can often be forced categorizations based on debatable criteria. This difficulty has been alluded to by several authors, most recently (Pursey et al. 2004) who remind us that there will always be a need to deal with classificatory anomalies and issues related to boundaries, but that it is essential to recognize that there are barely any comprehensive and mutually exclusive typologies in the social sciences.

In comparing our selection of IATs, we have attempted to examine and describe a small number in terms of characteristics which we felt would be important in assessing their applicability and expected effectiveness. Of course, not all measures yield all of the information suggested. The characteristics generally chosen for our examination were:

- **Objectivity**: who conducts the assessment: whether an objective observer organization or one which may have a vested interest in the outcomes.
- **Scope**: whether international *via* multi-country surveys etc., national (unique to Australia) or local (regional, intra-company/intra-agency).
- **Coverage**: whether the tool measures only one factor (e.g.: corruption or fraud) or whether it reports on multiple factors.
- **Respondents**: whether respondents are from the public sector, private sector, civil society (i.e. the general population) or a combination of these.
- **Sample**: size, method of selection, whether random, convenience etc.
- **Methodology**: how data is collected (mail, email, phone, paper, interviews).
- **Analysis**: analytical methods used, whether quantitative or qualitative, or both.
- **Occurrence**: how often data is surveyed and publication of data produced.
- **Output**: whether a written report, publicly/readily available data files, graphs/diagrams/tables etc.
- **Cross-referencing**: whether there are any obvious links with similar survey work, within or across sectors.
- **Users/use**: the main users of the information to date and for what purposes they may use it.
- **Accessibility**: the ways in which these outputs can best be accessed (reports, contacts, website etc.).

Australian Public Sector Integrity Assessment Tools

Most of the ethics components in current public sector training and practice still seek to instil ethical practices primarily through rule-based compliance measures. This approach adopts the development of codes of conduct, induction programmes, collection of data on misconduct, and regular training programmes to explain new or changed regulatory regimes (Bishop and Connors 2003; Doig and Wilson 1999). Such programmes can be incongruent with a shift from *government* to *governance* and the kind of managerial and organizational latitude that the reformed environment is meant to promote (Bishop and Connors 2003). Nevertheless, the 'public expectation of due process and fairness in the use of public resources has not significantly reduced for the public sector' (Mulgan 2003, 253). Hence, both public and private organizations (which are increasingly involved in delivering taxpayer funded services to the community) can and should be subjected to similarly searching regimes of accountability.

Australian Public Service

Ethics are important in any organization, but there are particular reasons why they are especially important in the public service. Trust, protected by ethical behaviours, supports the public confidence in the government and in the democratic process (MAB/MIAC 1996). The involvement of numerous Australian watchdog bodies and central agencies, at both the federal and state level, in the monitoring, maintenance, and ongoing development of ethical and probity standards demonstrates its importance to government.

Australian Public Service Commission State of the Service Report The Australian Public Service Commission (APSC), through 'ORIMA Research' a research consultancy company, conducts the State of the Service Employee Survey. The survey examines the embedding of core Australian Public Service (APS) values and the APS Code of Conduct. The survey results are used to prepare the State of the Service Report for presentation to Parliament. The report draws on a range of information sources. However, the main sources are the staff survey across agencies with more than 100 staff and an agency survey of APS agencies with more than 20 staff employed under the Public Service Act. The surveys are part of a quality assurance mechanism which examines how well the APS adheres to its values framework in delivering its services to the public and the Parliament.

NSW Independent Commission Against Corruption (ICAC)

The Independent Commission Against Corruption (ICAC) was established in March 1989 to expose and prevent corruption in the New South Wales public sector. The ICAC has three main functions: investigations of allegations of corruption, corruption prevention and education. The following section contains a synopsis of selected ICAC research and tools.

Community Attitude Surveys[4] Since its inception, the ICAC has conducted periodic community attitude surveys – Community Attitudes to Corruption and the ICAC (ICAC 1993; 1994; 1995; 1996; 2003; 2006) and Community and Journalists' Attitudes to Corruption and the ICAC (ICAC 1999) – to explore community perceptions about a range of issues, including attitudes to corruption and support for and awareness of the role of ICAC. The results of the surveys are used to inform the ICAC's corruption prevention and education programmes which are part of the statutory functions of the ICAC. These surveys provide information as part of a longitudinal study on the effectiveness of the ICAC's policies and programmes in combating corruption and give an indication of the organization's profile within the community.

What is ethical culture? Key issues to consider in building an ethical organization This report contains a summary of the results of the Ethical Culture Survey which was designed and conducted by the ICAC. An aim of the research was to explore in an Australian context the findings of past research (primarily in the USA) about the relationship between different aspects of an organization and how they impact on its ethical tone (ICAC 2000). The findings indicated that the features most strongly

---

4 All available Surveys are accessible at: <http://www.icac.nsw.gov.auto be>.

associated with perceptions of workplace integrity were behaviours of leaders, punishment of wrongdoing, and existence and enforcing of organizational, values, rules and rewards (ICAC 2000). As a result of the findings, an Ethical Culture Survey Kit was produced for use by New South Wales public servants.

Ethical Culture Survey Kit Ethical tone or culture has traditionally been considered a difficult aspect of an organization to understand or measure. To assist organizations in measuring those aspects of their organization, which impact upon its ethical practices, the ICAC has developed a survey kit. Organizations can use this kit to conduct their own assessment of the issues that impact on their ethical practices.

Do It Yourself Corruption Resistance Guide The purpose of the guide is to assist organizations to assess how well they are building corruption resistance across their functions and locations; to identify any gaps and the steps that are needed to remedy them; as a benchmarking tool to measure progress over time (ICAC 2002). This guide, together with *The First Four Steps* (ICAC 2001)[5] and *Corruption Troubleshooting* (ICAC 2001),[6] is designed to allow agencies to develop appropriate corruption strategies to fit within their usual corporate planning processes and integrate corruption prevention within their overall business planning (ICAC 2002).

Profiling the NSW Public Sector This comprehensive report summarizes a sector-wide survey across the NSW public sector and provides a 'snapshot' of the range of functions, corruption risks and the corruption prevention strategies in place. The survey asks a variety of questions about corruption prevention strategies already in place, perception of corruption risk within the organization, and the types of activities undertaken by the organization. The report allows individual organizations within the NSW public sector to benchmark their efforts against the rest of the NSW public sector and to identify areas where they may be able to improve resistance. The ICAC re-ran this survey in 2007.[7]

---

5 This quick guide outlines what *organizational integrity* is, how it can benefit an organization, and four steps to achieve integrity. This booklet is available online from <http://www.icac.nsw.gov.au/>.

6 This publication is intended for managers, Chief Executive Officers and General Managers in the public service and local government. Based on ICAC research into common corruption risk areas, the publication outlines key corruption trouble spots, then suggests actions that management can take to overcome these risk areas and lists resources from The Audit Office of NSW, Ombudsman and the ICAC, that managers can use. It is therefore intended as a guide to identifying and addressing the areas and issues that most frequently cause problems for agencies. The booklet is available on line from <http://www.icac.nsw.gov.au/>.

7 The Crime and Misconduct Commission in Queensland undertook a similar *Profiling the Queensland Public Sector* released in 2004. In 2007, the scope was expanded and the research replicated to further identify risks and examine changes in the risk profiles over time.

Local government risk profile The ICAC recognizes that the corruption risks and probity issues that affect local government are often quite different from those that arise in the wider public sector. This tool was used to identify major corruption risks specific to local government. The ICAC subsequently produced and then evaluated tools to assist councils to manage each of these risks (procurement, planning, and misuse of resources).

Queensland's Crime and Misconduct Commission (CMC)

The CMC was created on 1 January 2002 when the Criminal Justice Commission (CJC) and the Queensland Crime Commission (QCC) merged to form the new organization. The CJC was established by the *Criminal Justice Act 1989* to help restore confidence in Queensland public institutions following the revelations of the 1987–1989 Fitzgerald Inquiry into police corruption (Fitzgerald 1989). In addition to investigating police and public sector misconduct, for several years the CJC assisted police in investigating organized and major crime. In 1997, this crime function was taken over by the newly formed QCC, under the *Crime Commission Act 1997* (Qld). The QCC was also specially tasked with investigating paedophilia. In 2001, the state government decided to amalgamate these two Commissions to form a single body to fight crime and public sector misconduct: the CMC (http://www.cmc.qld.gov.au). The following section contains a synopsis of some selected CMC/CJC research and tools.

Public attitudes surveys Since 1991, CJC/CMC has conducted periodic public attitude surveys. The latest report being *Public Perception of the Queensland Police Service* published in June 2006. The primary focus of the surveys was to measure public attitudes towards the Queensland Police Service, as well as public knowledge, confidence and experiences regarding the complaint process. Changes in attitudes can be determined over time by the repeated use of the survey. The survey has undergone some modifications over the years, including the recent addition of questions relating to public service and local government employees and various questions relating to the CMC. The surveys provide information as part of a longitudinal study on the effectiveness of policies and programmes in combating corruption and give an indication of the CMC's profile within the community.

Monitoring the ethical climate of the Queensland Police Service This survey was developed by the CMC to monitor 'ethical climate' of the Queensland Police Service and to track changes in that climate over time. The surveys conducted between 1995 and 2002 were based on scenarios that described various forms of improper conduct. The surveys indicated that there had been a measurable increase in awareness of ethical issues and a stated willingness to report misconduct.[8]

8 The CMC has continued to collect this information from recruits and first year constables and are currently analysing the information that had not yet been reported with a view to releasing a further report.

The authors consider the method to be applicable to the monitoring of 'ethical climates' in other organizations, including non-policing bodies (CMC 2002).

Some Private Sector Assessment Tools

To gain an insight into the tools that are used within the private sector, we began by contacting the 'Big Four' consulting firms, Deloitte Touche Tohmatsu, KPMG, PricewaterhouseCoopers and Ernst and Young. Two of these, KPMG and Deloitte Touche Tohmatsu, have a specifically designed tool of their own used for forensic governance work.[9] We also comment briefly on two other organizations who have researched integrity issues in the private sector: RepuTex, and the Sydney Chamber of Commerce (NSW).

Deloitte Touche Tohmatsu

Deloitte Australia conducts surveys for both public and private sector clients. It has developed a tool known as 'Dtermine' (a trade marked and copyright name). This tool was developed and pilot tested over a number of years by consultants from Deloitte and academics in the USA and Australia (Deloitte 2004). It is a web-based tool that can also be administered through paper-based distribution. Its purpose is to determine the culture in an organization based on a range of determinants, including the openness of communication, willingness to deliver bad news, the tone at the top and employee awareness of issues affecting the organization. Deloitte has found this tool to be useful cross-sectorally (Deloitte 2004).

KPMG

Through its forensic group, KPMG provides 'integrity risk services' to measure integrity and corruption within individual company contexts, as well as consultancy services to assist organizations to identity and deal effectively with specific corruption risks that are identified (KPMG, 2004). KPMG uses its own tool known as the 'Integrity Thermometer' which evaluates the ethical climate of an organization against eight dimensions: *Discussion, Awareness, Code of Conduct, Feasibility, Support, Clarity, Accountability and Example Setting*. This instrument is normally completed online and consists of two parts, the first being a generic tool which is similar globally, the second tailored to the specific needs of clients undergoing this assessment.

---

9 It must be acknowledged that these consulting organizations conduct integrity assessments for both public and private sector clients. The instruments are not used exclusively for the private sector.

PricewaterhouseCoopers (PWC)

PricewaterhouseCoopers has developed an online report known as their 'Management Barometer'. This tool takes a wide sweep and assesses a range of different management issues, not focusing on Integrity *per se*. PWC conducts an Annual Global CEO Survey which now covers over 1400 CEOs across 45 countries and which contains questions relating to integrity issues such as corporate social responsibility.[10] PWC emphasizes its 'Power of the People' focus which, rather than relying on survey data, adopts a targeted approach to individual organizations seeking analysis. This approach examines how business strategies align with management and people strategies to ensure a positive organizational culture (PWC 2004).

Ernst and Young

Ernst and Young do not use a specific tool of their own, but undertake this type of assessment through their national Global Investigations and Disputes Advisory Services. Instead, their assessments are tailored to specific company needs and often adopt as a base the standards emanating from the Australian Standard, AS 8001 – Fraud and Corruption Control mechanisms (the AS 8001–2003) and/or by reference to the principles adopted by the New South Wales Auditor's office (Ernst and Young 2004).

Sydney Chamber of Commerce

A survey carried out by the Sydney Chamber of Commerce in 2001, to gain a measure of Corporate Social Responsibility, found that a major disincentive for Australian businesses in engaging in corporate social responsibility (CSR) is the complexity surrounding the measurement of returns from investment in CSR activities (SCC/NSW 2001). In order to further this work, Ernst and Young, while not having a specific standard tool did participate in the development of a 'Corporate Responsibility Index' in collaboration with the St James Ethics Centre, *The Sydney Morning Herald* and *The Age* newspapers. This work has a long history based upon previous work in the UK. The redeveloped survey has one hundred and eleven in-depth questions covering areas that identify strengths and weaknesses in a company's CSR practices. It is possible to benchmark Australian companies against data from other sources, for example the UK. In this way, the Corporate Responsibility Indicators (CRI) can provide a focus on corporate responsibility and guide the achievement of best practice. While this is only one aspect of private sector organizational integrity, it is, nevertheless, a very important one.

---

10 For example, see report No. 9 of 2006 available at <http://www.pwc.com/extweb/aboutus.nsf/docid/11BEE3BA4F529D2DCA2570490017D844/$file/9th_Annual_Global_CEO_Survey.pdf>.

RepuTex Measurement Pty Ltd

RepuTex has, in the past, carried out surveys to determine the reputation of companies via their Reputation Index Category Survey, but now prefers to carry out data collection against very specific criteria, which it considers more reliable than traditional survey methods. RepuTex considers that traditional surveys can be misleading in that survey respondents often provide a theoretical answer rather than disclose actual practice. RepuTex argues that the standard survey approach can skew answers to the centre and does not allow sufficient scope for more comprehensive qualitative information, which can sometimes help to qualify and clarify what may appear to be an overly negative or positive statistic. The firm now undertakes more specific work by means of public domain searches and actual site visits (RepuTex 2004).

Discussion

Table 12.1 provides a prototype for categorization of some of the main IATs discussed in this chapter, using the characteristics previously outlined. This has been possible because of the availability of these particular IATs to examine and information in the public domain. For some others, detailed analysis is more problematic. Broadly, the majority of public sector IATs are readily available in the public domain with the exception of some agency-specific internal data outputs. In the private sector, access to particular instruments for analysis is more restricted. Private sector IATs are usually commercial property, often developed, trialled and administered in the international domain. Their outputs, for the most part, remain the property of the private sector client.

While the nature of these instruments may differ markedly in terms of selected criteria adopted for analysis, there is considerable common ground cross-sectorally. For example, many instruments examine organizational strategies employed to combat corruption and the extent of the adoption of appropriate underpinning values supporting the ethical culture of the organization. This consideration is an important adjunct to client service or business success. An observation is that, where an IAT is used over time to produce longitudinal data, it is likely to be far more effective in providing reliable and useful information for benchmarking (e.g., the ongoing studies of the Queensland Police Service). One-off surveys, while providing a useful snapshot of an organization, do not yield the important organizational information that is needed to monitor organizational culture and embed strong and appropriate values. Similarly, those IATs which are readily able to be benchmarked – either with other external studies or with other internal reports (as is the case with ICAC's work) – are more likely to yield useful comparative information.

Ideally, key objectives worth pursuing with IATs include:

- sharing instruments across sectors;

Table 12.1 Comparison of selected Australian integrity assessment tools

ICACs IATs	*Ethical Culture Survey* **Kit (ICAC)**	***Do It Yourself Corruption Resistance Guide* (ICAC)**	***Profiling the NSW Public Sector* (ICAC)**	***Local Government Risk Profile* (ICAC)**
Objectivity	Internally administered (ICAC instrument)	Internally administered from ICAC instrument	Externally administered by ICAC	Externally administered by ICAC
Scope	Agency level	Agency level	Within and across public sector agencies	Local government sector
Coverage	Ethical culture/climate	Corruption prevention strategies	Measures corruption risks and corruption prevention strategies in place	Corruption risk areas
Respondents	Agency staff	Agency	Agencies + sample of staff	NSW Councils and staff
Sample	Determined by individual agency	Agency elects to use instrument	Public sector agencies + random sample of staff	All council + random sample of staff
Methodology	Anonymous questionnaire	Self assessment against benchmarks	Mailed survey + pre-promotion + reminders	Mail Questionnaire
Analysis	Quantitative	Quantitative	Qualitative and quantitative	Qualitative and qualitative
Occurrence	Ad hoc	Ad hoc	Conducted in late 2001 and in 2007 in NSW + similar survey conducted by the CMC in Queensland in 2003 and 2007.	One-off
Output	Benchmarking data	Agency level data	Presentations + tailored reports	Summary reports and tools
Cross-referencing	Various ICAC publications/ instruments		Links to local government risk profile	Public sector risk profile
Users/use	NSW public sector agencies	NSW public sector agencies	ICAC, NSW government agencies	ICAC and NSW councils
Accessibility	Freely available to NSW public sector agencies	Public domain (web)	Additional information – ICAC website	Additional information – ICAC website

Other organizations IATs	Monitoring the Ethical Climate of Organisations (CMC)	Public Perception of the Queensland Police Service (CMC)	State of the Service Report (Australian Public Service Commission)	KPMG 'Integrity Thermometer	Deloitte Touche Thomatsu 'DTermine'
Objectivity	Internally administered from CMC instrument	Internally administered from CMC instrument	Externally administered (private consultancy)	Externally administered by KPMG	Externally administered by Deloitte
Scope	Agency level (Queensland Police Service)	Agency level	APS wide	Organization based	Organization based
Coverage	Culture and attitudes to misconduct	Public attitude to the QPS, public servants and local council employees, as well as public knowledge and confidence in the complaints process.	Values	Ethical climate	Organizational culture
Respondents	Agency staff	Queensland residents	APS employees and agencies	Public and private sector employees	Public and private sector employees
Sample	Target groups based on location, task etc.	Random sample	Stratified Random Sample	Dependent on organization	Usually employees at all levels
Methodology	Scenario based	Telephone surveys	On line survey	Online survey	Online survey
Analysis	Quantitative and qualitative	Quantitative and qualitative	Quantitative and qualitative	Quantitative and qualitative	Quantitative and qualitative
Occurrence	Ongoing	Six survey conducted since 1991*	Annually	Ad hoc	1–2 years or organization change
Output	Report	Report	Formal Report	Report	Report
Cross-referencing	Ethics Survey of First Year Constables: Summary of Findings 1995–1998	Public Perception series	Previous surveys/reports	Benchmarking data held by KPMG	Benchmarking data held by Deloitte
Users/use	Queensland Police Service	Qld Public Sector Agencies and law enforcement bodies Document available publicly	Parliament and PS agencies	International clients (large public and private sector organizations)	Corporate HR and risk management
Accessibility	Additional information – CMC website	Public Domain (and printed report)	Public domain (web and printed report)	Reports issued to management	Reports issued to management and usually made available to staff.

Note: In a July 2006 media release for its 2006 report on the CMC website http://www.cmc.qld.gov.au/asp/index.asp?pgid=10814&cid=5201&id=945 – media release states that CMC has carried out six surveys since 1991.

- sharing outputs to maximize benchmarking opportunities across agencies/sectors;
- commitment to longitudinal studies (particularly by central agencies); and
- replications of IATs in other settings (either within the same sector in different states, or cross-sectorally.

Conclusion

While the convergences of the public and private sectors will continue to introduce new levels of complexity and risk to the public sector, when it comes to operational circumstances, the needs of managers to understand, influence and, where necessary, rectify the standards of accountability in their workplace are remarkably similar. It is important, therefore, that both private and public sector organizations address ethics as a corporate culture issue to be strategically managed and monitored by top management. The capacity of public and private sector managers to enhance integrity and control corruption must be reinforced. Will is not enough. Skills and tools are needed for engaging with workplace realities.

Can the public and private sectors learn from each other? It is argued that businesses can learn a great deal 'about service to the public, public accountability and general financial probity from the values of the public sector' while the public sector can learn from business 'the importance of operationalizing their values and in linking them directly to the delivery of their product or service' (Vallance 1999, 202).

There is no one, ideal design for IATs that can satisfy all purposes. Doubtless, when such assessments are made, there are overlapping areas some of which we have discussed. But there are also likely gaps with an inherent danger that some key elements of knowledge may fall between the tools. Nevertheless, we consider that there is value in utilizing IATs in a cross-sectoral approach so as to present a more complete picture of the Australian integrity system. Additionally, there is potential for greater cross-fertilization and integration between the various measures across the public-private divide. Any integrated IAT should also attempt to gather data on the impact of reward and punishment systems on ethical behaviour as well as attempting to gain accurate measures of the impact of enforcement and the role of regulators in producing an enhanced integrity environment. Ideally, it would be valuable to develop IATs that could simultaneously evaluate information across all three sectors: public, private and civil society.

In this chapter, we have provided an insight into the ways in which integrity assessments are being carried out in the public and private sectors in Australia and attempted to describe tools in a form that may assist further investigation and comparison. Individually, the tools can provide helpful information for policy makers and practitioners about the current status of integrity strategies operating in particular domains. We stress that there is no intention or attempt by us to make value judgements about the relative merits of the different tools and approaches which we have highlighted. Our primary aim has been to describe briefly and objectively how each tool operates. Future empirical research is needed to extend this limited analysis, with the objective of establishing a 'typology' of IATs useful in the Australian setting. Such a 'typology' may provide practitioners and theoreticians with a wider view of the Australian integrity system and enable the design of more specific research. In short, the aim is to enable practitioners to selectively choose the best practices, decide on suitable elements and combine resources in order to design new and better IATs.

References

APSC (2003), *State of the Service Report 2002–2003* (Canberra: Australian Public Service Commission).

Argyriades, D. (2003), 'Values for Public Service: Lessons Learned from Recent Trends and the Millennium Summit', *International Review of Administrative Sciences* 69:4, 521–33.

Ashkanasy, N., Falkus, S. and Callan, V.J. (2000), 'Predictors of Ethical Code Use and Ethical Tolerance in the Public Sector', *Journal of Business Ethics* 25, 237–53.

Barrett, P. (2004), *Corporate Governance – A More Private Public Sector* (Canberra: ANAO).

Bartholoileuz, S. (2006), 'Not Happy Chaps: Investors Revolt Over Executive Pay', *The Sydney Morning Herald*, 2 December.

Bishop, P. and Connors, C. (2003), 'The New Public Sector: Changing Management Organisation and Ethics', in P. Bishop, C. Connors and C. Sampford (eds) *Management, Organisation, and Ethics in the Public Sector* (Aldershot: Ashgate).

Bower, J. and Gilson, S. (2003), 'The Social Cost of Fraud and Bankruptcy', *Harvard Business Review* 81:12, 20.

Brown, A.J. (2006), 'What are We Trying to Measure? Reviewing the Basics of Corruption Definition', in A. Shacklock, C. Sampford, C. Connors and F. Galtung (eds) *Measuring Corruption* (Aldershot: Ashgate).

Carayannis, E.G. and Laget, P. (2004), 'Transatlantic Innovation Infrastructure Networks: Public-Private, EU-US R and D Partnerships', *R and D Management* 34:1, 17–31.

Christie, P.M.J., Kwon, I.W.G., Stoeberl, P.A. and Baumhart, R. (2003), 'A Cross-cultural Comparison of Ethical Attitudes of Business Managers: India, Korea and the United States', *Journal of Business Ethics* 46:3, 263–87.

Clark, D. (2002), 'Neoliberalism and Public Service Reform: Canada in Comparative Perspective', *Canadian Journal of Political Science-Revue Canadienne De Science Politique* 35:4, 771–93.

Clarke, F., Dean, G. and Houghton, E. (2002), 'Revitalising Group Accounting: Improving Accountability', *Australian Accounting Review* 12:3, 58–72.

Clatworthy, M.A., Mellett, H.J. and Peel, M.J. (2000), 'Corporate Governance under New Public Management: An Exemplification', *Corporate Governance-an International Review* 8:2, 166–76.

CMC (2002), *Monitoring the Ethical Climate of Organisations* (Brisbane: Crime and Misconduct Commission).

CMC (2004), *Councillor Information Kit* (Brisbane: Crime and Misconduct Commission).

CMC (2004), *Profiling the Queensland Public Sector* (Brisbane: Crime and Misconduct Commission).

CMC (2006), *Public Perception of the Queensland Police Service* (Brisbane: Crime and Misconduct Commission).

Cole, T. (2006), *Report of the Inquiry into Certain Australian Companies in Relation to the UN Oil-for-Food Programme*, vol. 1 (Canberra: Australian Government).

Cravens, K., Oliver, E.G. and Ramamoorti, S. (2003), 'The Reputation Index: Measuring and Managing Corporate Reputation', *European Management Journal* 21:2, 200.

Dabscheck, B. (1998), 'The Waterfront Dispute: Of Vendetta and the Australian Way', *Economic and Labour Relations Review* 9:2, 155–87.

Davis, J. (2004), 'Corruption in Public Service Delivery: Experience from South Asia's Water and Sanitation Sector', *World Development* 32:1, 53–71.

Deloittes (2004), *Dtermine: Assessing, Understanding and Strengthening Organisational Culture*, available at <http://www.deloitte.com/dtt/article/0,1002,sid%253D8564%2526cid%253D24904,00.html>, accessed 16 May 2007.

Doig, A. and Wilson, J. (1999), 'Ethics, Integrity, Compliance and Accountability in Contemporary UK Government-business Relations – Till Death do us Part', *Australian Journal of Public Administration* 58:4, 26–31.

Duncan, N. (2006), 'The Non-perception Based Measurement of Corruption: A Review of Issues and Methods from a Policy Perspective', in A. Shacklock, C. Sampford, C. Connors and F. Galtung (eds) *Measuring Corruption* (Aldershot: Ashgate).

Epstein, M.J. and Roy, M. (2004), 'Improving the Performance of Corporate Boards: Identifying and Measuring the Key Drivers of Success', *Journal of General Management* 29:3, 1.

Ernst and Young (2004), *Ernst and Young Global Investigations and Dispute Advisory (GIDA)*, retrieved 14 June 2004 from <http://www.ey.com/global/content.nsf/Australia/Global_Investigation_and_Dispute_Advisory>.

Fitzgerald, G.E. (1989), *Report of the Commission of Inquiry into Possible Illegal Activities and Associated Police Misconduct* (Brisbane: QPrint).

Fitzgerald. G. (1992), *Electoral and Administrative Review Commission, Queensland: Report on the Review of Codes of Conduct for Public Officials* (Brisbane: Queensland Parliament).

Galtung, F. (2006), 'Measuring the Immeasurable: Boundaries and Functions of (Macro) Corruption Indices', in A. Shacklock, C. Sampford, C. Connors and F. Galtung (eds) *Measuring Corruption* (Aldershot: Ashgate).

Glasbeek, H.J. (1998), 'The MUA (Maritime Union of Australia) Affair: The Role of Law vs the Rule of Law', *Economic and Labour Relations Review* 9:2, 188–221.

Gorta, A. (2003), *Identifying Corruption Risk Areas to Measure Corruption Resistance* (Brisbane: unpublished).

Gorta, A. (2006), 'Corruption Risk Areas and Corruption Resistance', in A. Shacklock, C. Sampford, C. Connors and F. Galtung (eds) *Measuring Corruption* (Aldershot: Ashgate).

Gorta, A. and Forell, S. (1994), 'Unravelling Corruption: A Public Sector Perspective – Survey of NSW Public Sector Employee's Understanding of Corruption and Their Willingness to Take Action. Independent Commission Against Corruption', *Research Report No. 1*, April.

Gregory, R.J. (1999), 'Social Capital Theory and Administrative Reform: Maintaining Ethical Probity in Public Service', *Public Administration Review* 59:1, 63–75.

Grimshaw, D., Vincent, S. and Willmott, H. (2002), 'Going privately: Partnership and Outsourcing in UK public services', *Public Administration* 80:3, 475–502.

Haque, M.S. (2001), 'The Diminishing Publicness of Public Service under the Current Mode of Governance', *Public Administration Review* 61:1, 65–82.

Haynes, B., and Jones, H.M. (1999), 'Ethics and Public Sector Management: The Western Australian Experience', *Australian Journal of Public Administration* 58:2, 70–82.

Houghton, K.A. and Jubb, C.A. (2003), 'Auditor Selection: What Influences Decisions by Listed Companies?', *Australian Accounting Review* 13:3, 67.

ICAC (NSW) (1993), *Community Attitudes to Corruption and the ICAC 1993* (Sydney: Independent Commission Against Corruption).

ICAC (NSW) (1994), *Community Attitudes to Corruption and the ICAC 1994* (Sydney: Independent Commission Against Corruption).

ICAC (NSW) (1995), *Community Attitudes to Corruption and the ICAC 1995* (Sydney: Independent Commission Against Corruption).

ICAC (NSW) (1996), *Community Attitudes to Corruption and the ICAC 1996* (Sydney: Independent Commission Against Corruption).

ICAC (NSW) (1997), *Corruption and Related Issues: An annotated Bibliography* (Sydney: Independent Commission Against Corruption).

ICAC (NSW) (1999), *NSW Journalists: What Do They Know About Corruption and the ICAC?* (Sydney: Independent Commission Against Corruption).

ICAC (NSW) (2000), *What is an Ethical Culture? Key Issues to Consider in Building an Ethical Organisation* (Sydney: Independent Commission Against Corruption).

ICAC (NSW) (2001a), *The First Four Steps* (Sydney: Independent Commission Against Corruption, April 2001).

ICAC (NSW) (2001b), *Corruption Troubleshooting: Lessons Learnt from ICAC Research about Identifying and Dealing with Corruption Hotspots* (Sydney: Independent Commission Against Corruption, November).

ICAC (NSW) (2002), *The Do It Yourself Corruption Resistance Guide* (Sydney: Independent Commission Against Corruption).

ICAC (NSW) (2003a), *Community Attitudes to Corruption and the ICAC* (Sydney: Independent Commission Against Corruption).

ICAC (NSW) (2003b), *Profiling the NSW Public Sector: Functions, Risks and Corruption Resistance Strategies* (Sydney: Independent Commission Against Corruption).

Jose, A. and Thibodeaux, M. (1999), 'Institutionalization of Ethics: The Perspective of Managers', *Journal of Business Ethics* 22, 133–43.

Kickert, W. (1997), 'Public Governance in the Netherlands: An Alternative to Anglo-American Managerialism', *Public Administration* 75, 731–52.

Klijn, E.H. and Teisman, G.R. (2003), 'Institutional and Strategic Barriers to Public-Private Partnership: An Analysis of Dutch Cases', *Public Money and Management* 23:3, 137–46.

KPMG (2004), *Integrity Thermometer*, available at <http://www.us.kpmg.com/ethics/>, accessed 16 June 2004.

Kusku, F. and Zarkada-Fraser, A. (2004), 'An Empirical Investigation of Corporate Citizenship in Australia and Turkey', *British Journal of Management* 15:1, 57–72.

Langseth, P. (2006), 'Measuring Corruption', in A. Shacklock, C. Sampford, C. Connors and F. Galtung (eds) *Measuring Corruption* (Aldershot: Ashgate).

Lambsdorff, J. (2006), 'Measuring Corruption – The Validity and Precision of Subjective Indicators (CPI)', in A. Shacklock, C. Sampford, C. Connors and F. Galtung (eds) *Measuring Corruption* (Aldershot: Ashgate).

Leibler, M. (2003), 'True and Fair – An Imaginary View', *Australian Accounting Review* 13:3, 61.

Leung, P. and Cooper, B.J. (2003), 'The Mad Hatter's Corporate Tea Party', *Managerial Auditing Journal* 18:6/7, 505.

MAB/MIAC (1996), *Ethics Standards and Values in the APS*, MAB/MIAC Report 19 (Canberra: Australian Public Service Commission).

Maesschalck, J. (2004), 'The Impact of New Public Management Reforms on the Public Servants' Ethics: Towards a Theory', *Public Administration* 82:2, 465–89.

McMahon, L. (1995), 'Corporate Accountability in Australia – Managing the Information Environment for Corporate Accountability', *Journal of Business Ethics* 14:8, 673–81.

Mellema, G. (2003), 'Responsibility, Taint, and Ethical Distance in Business Ethics', *Journal of Business Ethics* 47:2, 125.

Miller, W. (2006), 'Perception, Experience and Lies: What Measures Corruption and What do Corruption Measures Measure?', in A. Shacklock, C. Sampford, C. Connors and F. Galtung (eds) *Measuring Corruption* (Aldershot: Ashgate).

Milton Smith, J. (1997), 'Business Ethics in Australia and New Zealand', *Journal of Business Ethics* 16:14, 1485–97.

Mulgan, R. (2000), 'Comparing Accountability in the Public and Private Sectors', *Australian Journal of Public Administration* 59:1, 87–97.

Mulgan, R. (2003), *Holding Power to Account: Accountability in Modern Democracies* (Hampshire: Palgrave Macmillan).

OECD (1996), *Ethics in the Public Service: Current Issues and Practices* (Paris: OECD).

OECD (2000), *Trust in Government: Ethic Measures in OECD Countries* (Paris: OECD).

Philp, M. (2006), 'Corruption Definition and Measurement', in A. Shacklock, C. Sampford, C. Connors and F. Galtung (eds) *Measuring Corruption* (Aldershot: Ashgate).

Pollitt, C. and Bouckaert, G. (2000), *Public Management Reform: A Conceptual Analysis* (Oxford: Oxford University Press).

Prasser, S. (2004), 'Poor Decisions, Compliant Management and Reactive Change: The Public Sector in 2003', *Australian Journal of Public Administration* 63:1, 94.

PriceWaterhouseCoopers (2004), *Management Barometer* and *The Power of the People*, available at <http://www.pwcglobal.com/>, accessed 15 June 2004.

Pursey, P.M., Heugens, A.R., Kaptein, M. and Oosterhout, J.H. van (2004), 'Ties That Grind? Corroborating a Typology of Social Contracting Problems', *Journal of Business Ethics* 49:3, 235–52.

RepuTex (2004), *Reputation Index Category Survey*, available at <http://www.reputationmeasurement.com.au>, accessed 16 June 2004.

Riley, J. (2003), 'Protection for Employment Entitlements: A Legal Perspective', *Australian Bulletin of Labour* 29:1, 31.

SCC (NSW) (2001), *Taking the First Steps: An Overview of Corporate Responsibility in Australia* (Sydney: State Chamber of Commerce (NSW)).

Scissons, E.H. (2002), 'All Numbers are not Created Equal: Measurement Issues in Assessing Board Governance', *Corporate Governance* 2:2, 20–26.

Terry, L.D. (1998), 'Administrative Leadership, Neo-managerialism, and the Public Management Movement', *Public Administration Review* 58:3, 194–200.

Theobald, R. (1997), 'Enhancing Public Service Ethics – More Culture, Less Bureaucracy?', *Administration and Society* 29:4, 490–504.

Transparency International (TI) (2004), *Transparency International Surveys*, accessible at <http://www.transparency.org/ >, accessed 30 May 2004.

Vallance, E. (1999), 'Sleeping with the Enemy or Learning from Each Other?' Sharing Ethical Experiences between the Public and Private Sectors', *Long Range Planning* 32:2, 199–206.

Veasey, E.N. (2003), 'Corporate Governance and Ethics in the Post-Enron WorldCom Environment', *Wake Forest Law Review* 38:3, 839.

Wishart, D. (2006), 'Executive Pay a Fraud on Society', *The Age*, 1 December.

Chapter 13

Assessment Strategies and Practices for Integrity and Anti-corruption Measures: A Comparative Overview[1]

Stuart C. Gilman and Jeffrey Stout

Introduction

Corruption prevention systems are some of the least understood and least frequently evaluated programmes in contemporary government. As effective assessment is critical to the future of integrity programmes, this comparative chapter provides an overview of methods and solutions used in countries to assess the effectiveness of their pro-integrity and anti-corruption programmes. It is not meant to be an exhaustive analysis, but rather to review strengths and weaknesses of assessment methods and conditions for their success. This chapter also lists measures that work well, and vulnerabilities of existing prevention programmes resulting from assessment.

Integrity is essential to modern government. It not only provides a foundation for effective governance, but also assures citizens that their government is working on their behalf. Corruption of political processes and institutions both undermines the capacity of government to carry out its critical missions and distorts economic, social and political relationships that democratic government erect. Eventually, unfettered corruption gives rise to demagogues and authoritarians who then blame democracy for corruption. In truth, democracy provides the vehicle to make corruption public, whereas in most authoritarian regimes it remains hidden through intimidation and secrecy. For this reason, stable democracies require robust pro-integrity systems and anti-corruption regimes.

---

1 'Assessment Strategies and Practices for Integrity and Anti-Corruption Measures: A Comparative Overview, Measures for Promoting Integrity and Preventing Corruption: How to Assess?', 30th Session of the Public Governance Committee 28–29 October 2004, Public Governance and Territorial Development Directorate, GOV/PGC(2004)24, © OECD 2004. This chapter is published with the kind permission of the OECD. The findings, interpretations, and conclusions expressed in this chapter are those of the authors and do not necessarily reflect the official views of the OECD or of the governments of its member countries. Stuart C. Gilman, PhD is currently Head, The Global Programme against Corruption, and the Anti-Corruption Unit, United Nations Office on Drugs and Crime, Vienna, Austria.

Modern anti-corruption regimes tend to limit their focus to investigation and punishment. Although such reactive measures are important components of the integrity framework, punishment as deterrence has limited impact. Even if individuals are punished for corruption, the resultant headlines lead many citizens to believe that the case is indicative of massive undetected corruption. Public officials must be aware of the penalties for doing the wrong thing, but it is more effective and less expensive to motivate officials to do the right thing in the first place. Therefore, a critical element of any effective integrity system is corruption prevention and effective evaluative measures for such systems. Preventative elements typically exist as ethics or compliance programmes, taking on various forms as detailed below.

The organization of this study is fairly straightforward. After describing the nature of ethics or integrity systems, there will be a brief discussion about the concept of assessment. Organizing the rest of the study around each potential element of an integrity system, the chapter will address the type of assessment, with recent examples where available, the strengths and weaknesses of the approach, and the criteria for success.

What is an Integrity System?

Integrity systems[2] are designed to prevent corruption before it occurs. With this as a strategic mission, there are a variety of laws, institutions and systems that are used to anticipate potential corruption. It is not suggested that determined, corrupt officials will be absolutely deterred from committing crimes or violating the public's confidence, but that a number of acts that either appear to be, or are actually corrupt, often begin as relatively benign actions by individuals who are blindly focused on policy ends. This is critical because in government, the means are as important as the ends. Well-constructed prevention systems can both help individuals and protect the integrity of government. Furthermore, some 'bad actors' will be deterred if they believe that everyone in their agency will recognize unethical behaviour and have an ability to report it.

Integrity systems use a variety of institutions to accomplish their goals. They may be part of a larger agency (for example, in ministries of justice, comptrollers), a separate agency, or in some rare cases they are truly independent. Their authorities also vary widely. Some prevention systems are only responsible for civil servants. Other agencies have responsibility for political officials (both appointed and elected), and still others have oversight of legislative and judicial officials. There is no one dominant pattern. In some cases agencies exist with an appointed head and civil servants to carry out its functions. In some such cases, heads are appointed to serve at the request of the appointing authority, while others have lengthy fixed term appointments to assure independence. Other forms of prevention systems include commissions. Some commissions are comprised

2 For purposes of this chapter the terms integrity system, prevention system or ethics system are used synonymously.

solely of individuals who are part of the government, some are comprised of external stakeholders (citizens, NGOs, economic interests) and still others have a mixed makeup.

Integrity systems also vary in terms of level of government. Some regimes cover all government employees within a nation state. Other programmes focus only on the national level, with the national government requiring each constitutional sub-national level (province, state) to have an integrity system. Other countries, such as the United States, have different integrity systems for each branch of the federal government, but do not mandate programmes at the state or local level. Nonetheless, the prolific growth of state and local ethics systems in the United States over the past 20 years suggests that national government mandates are not necessarily required.

Assessment: The Focus of This Study

The purpose of this study is to understand the assessment strategies currently employed by government integrity programmes. Within the term 'assessment' is included any effort, quantitative or qualitative, to evaluate programme effectiveness. This study does not examine the actual methodology used nor the validity or reliability of the measures utilized. Instead it provides an overview of approaches governments or and public organization have taken to evaluate ethics programmes. Interestingly, despite all of the emphasis on performance measures over the past decade, no prevention programme has attempted to evaluate overall performance. Rather, most programmes look only at pieces of the programme, and often use indirect measures to evaluate those elements.

While the findings of this analysis could also serve as lessons for enforcement activities, this study focuses only on prevention. Thus, the purposeful omission of assessment tools for prosecution, investigation, audit, adjudication, penal institutions, or legislative oversight.

In the past, many programmes claimed that, because their focus was on the prevention of unethical or corrupt actions, they could not measure something that *did not happen*. Unfortunately, this perspective takes a very narrow view of evaluation. The effectiveness of most government programmes cannot be directly measured. Nonetheless, a number of indirect measures of programme and programme effect can provide reasonable understanding of programmatic outcomes. Importantly, if assessment is done regularly there can be both a contemporary assessment as well as comparative assessments over time.

The study, rather than using a random sample, contacted a number of individuals and agencies that specialize in preventative programmes. These contacts were used to not only provide assessment examples, but also to recommend other programmes with which they were familiar. In addition researchers utilized the internet and printed materials to gain a better understanding of assessment approaches. Despite the limitations, it cannot be considered as either exhaustive or wholly representative, this study does present a reasonable picture of the assessment landscape, pointing to some potentially exciting approaches and critical vulnerabilities.

Types of Assessment

Typically, there have been three types of assessments used to evaluate integrity programmes:

1 The first type is a *baseline perception survey*. Perception surveys focus on how a system is viewed by stakeholders – citizens, business leaders, or foreigners doing business within the country. The best known in the anti-corruption area is Transparency International's annual Corruption Perception Index. This index ranks countries throughout the world in terms of the perceptions about corruption within the country. While this type of measure is an indirect way of evaluating integrity programmes, it could be argued that perception surveys and the effectiveness of ethics programmes are independent of each other.[3]
2 A second approach to assessment looks at the *general state of affairs*. For example the state of Queensland in Australia has sponsored this kind of assessment focused on singular measures, such as prosecutions for corruption, estimated economic loses due to corruption and some perception measures. Although there is no attempt to correlate these elements, or identify how they explain the success or failure of prevention systems, this type of assessment does provide potential comparative data that could be used to view changes across time.
3 Finally, there are *agency evaluations*. These are usually comportment evaluations rather than performance evaluations. They focus on whether ministries or agencies are comporting with legal or structural requirements. For example, they do not try to assess the effectiveness of ethics training programmes, but rather focus on the number of training classes, the percentage of employees took training, and what was the focus. One can be critical of the lack of impact assessment, but comportment is a critical element in understanding the efficacy of ethics programmes.

Integrity Framework

Overview

In designing integrity systems government officials must take into account a variety of concerns. Culture and type of government both have an impact,

3 A hypothetical case might explain how this could occur. The TI Corruption Perception Index is completed annually. Country X was ranked at number 55 because of the perception that it has a poor record of prosecuting corruption. For the next two years, it completely redesigns its prosecution system, firing and bringing to court corrupt prosecutors, and finds that after two years it is ranked at number 68 in the TI rankings. Why? Because broad media coverage leads to the perception that corruption is actually more rampant rather than less. Secondly, other countries might also be getting 'better'. Despite Country X's improvements, its progress is overshadowed.

not only in terms of what are to be considered legitimate areas of privacy and personal issues, but also the influence of the media and NGOs. And, obviously the commitment of leadership will have a profound impact.

While acknowledging the differences between programmes, it is important to recognize that there are identifiable, general elements that can be found within integrity programmes. The following is a model framework that will be used to understand what is meant by a prevention system, as well as help for organizing the analysis presented in this chapter:

a) codes of conduct;
b) transparency systems;
   simplification of administrative procedures;
   elimination of secrecy;
   financial or interest disclosure/asset declaration;
c) training systems;
d) communication strategies;
e) counselling;
f) whistleblower hotlines and help lines;
g) control and enforcement;
   criminal code;
   conflict-of-interest code;
   post-employment code;
   ombudsmen;
   audit agencies;
   NGOs;
   media;
h) independence.

Each of these is a discrete element that can be found in an integrity system. However, it would be overstating to conclude that ethics programmes that do not include all of the elements are insufficient. Many governments put elements of these programmes in other agencies, and in some societies, issues such as post-employment, are not terribly relevant. The obvious problem with such a framework is that as it organizes it can also limit it. The intention here is not to exclude other elements, but to organize the most common programmatic themes. The overall purpose of this chapter is to raise issues and is not exhaustive in order to provide a starting point to understand the dynamics of evaluating an ethics programme. Future work building on the framework will rethink, modify and go beyond the framework presented here.

The Content of the Framework

Code of conduct Integrity systems often begin with a code of conduct, code of behaviour or code of ethics. No matter which term is used, they usually begin with either a series of principles or a delineation of behaviours that public servants are expected to avoid or observe. These codes are generally in addition to anticorruption laws, and they attempt to refine behaviours in a broader and encompassing fashion. They are often helpful because they provide the basis for other ethics elements. For example, a counselling system needs to have guidelines – usually law or code – upon which to base advice.

Some governments supplement the code with a series of interpretations to ensure uniform application of the code. For example, the US Office of Government Ethics (OGE) has supplemented the code of conduct with Informal Advisory Opinions that are used to give guidance to both ethics counsellors and employees on the application of the code.[4] Other programmes stand on the simplicity of principles (for example, fairness, objectivity) and rely on employees to behave in a way that reflects those principles and use them to both advise and, if necessary, punish civil servants. Some criticize the lack of specificity of such programmes as entrapping government employees by the whims of superiors. Others defend it on the grounds that simplicity offers far more clarity of expectations for the individual civil servant.

Transparency systems Perhaps the most misunderstood elements in integrity programmes are transparency systems. Often, transparency systems are considered only in terms of financial disclosure. Well-designed disclosure systems can work to maintain the confidence of citizens in governmental institutions. Having effective review of disclosures, and elimination of subsequent potential conflicts of interest or other ethics problems, can have a positive impact both within government as well as on public perception. Some programmes use disclosures for prosecution rather than counselling. This focuses on the issue of 'illicit enrichment', which in most cases can be better detected in other ways. While disclosure is the most common transparency programme, the openness of procurement and contracting procedures should also be included. Even simplifying and clarifying administrative processes can be excellent ways of increasing transparency.

Training Training is also a common element included in most integrity systems. Training on ethical principles and their application is diverse. Some governments require only new employees to undergo training, while others require regular training. Additionally, some ethics regimes focus on certain levels of employees – senior political officials – or positions that are considered particularly vulnerable, such as tax collectors or contracting officials. Types of training also vary. For some programmes all training is in person, while others use computer training. Some training is focuses solely on the 'rules', while other types of training use vignettes or actually have employees play ethics games.

Communication strategy Most effective ethics programmes have communication strategies. Often, the communication strategy is not planned, which leads to the accusation that it is 'the best kept secret in government'. A dynamic

4 See the Informal Advisory Opinions of the United States Office of Government Ethics, available on the USOGE website, <http:// www.usoge.gov/pages/advisory_opinions/advisory_opins.html>. These documents were originally published in three volumes by the US Government Printing Office covering the period 1979–1998.

communication strategy can range from broad media coverage to posters and/or speeches encouraging citizens to provide input on new regulations. Admittedly, many ethics programme officials are reticent to engage in broad communication for fear that it will unfairly draw the attention of the media to their limitations, rather than their successes.

Counselling Most ethics programmes have counselling mechanisms through which they give employees advice in response to ethics questions. Such systems vary considerably from centralized to highly decentralized. The advice can be agency specific or government-wide. The counselling can be done verbally, or in writing. And finally, investigative authorities may question the advice, or it can bind employees to respect the advice given. The logic behind the latter reasons that if an employee has gone to an objective third-party for advice (appointed by the government for that purpose), it is unfair to punish said employee for following that advice.

Whistleblower hotlines and help lines Whistleblower programmes, or hotlines, are probably the most well-known prevention systems. In some cases, hotlines to report misconduct are supplemented with 'help lines' that allow employees to ask ethics questions. Both require effective staffing and follow up. Often hotlines become vehicles for disgruntled employees, so hotline staff must be trained to separate the 'wheat from the chaff'. Assessing the feedback provided through hotlines and 'help lines' has become an essential tool in anticipating corruption and dealing with it before it becomes debilitating.

Control/enforcement It is important to recognize that an effective enforcement programme is an essential compliment to any prevention system. Effective enforcement deters those who would be corrupt and assures honest employees that they will not have to work in a corrupt environment. 'Effective' should not be confused with 'severe' enforcement. One can threaten someone with lengthy prison terms, but if no one ever goes to jail the penalty soon becomes ridiculed. Sureness of punishment for violators is a far greater deterrent than severity. As one official suggested, 'rather than a ten year jail sentence that has never been imposed, I would get greater impact with a $100 fine'.[5]

Independence Finally, effective ethics programmes require independence. Independence can mean many different things. The key to understanding independence is not necessarily in terms of a separate agency or ministry, separate budget or limited reporting responsibilities. Rather, the foundation of independence is whether the prevention system can act as an objective third party in judging a particular question, and whether those seeking the advice can ignore, or worse, change the advice to suit their own interests. Independence is probably one of the most critical features in assuring the effectiveness of integrity programmes. Although legitimate evaluation of independence is difficult, it is essential that it be addressed.

5 Interview with an ethics official in one of the US states, February 2002.

At this point we turn to assessment and evaluation instruments used by ethics programmes, focusing on the most effective techniques and interesting approaches. There is no single right way to design an integrity system. Many of the variations are designed to make programmes more effective. However, one would be naïve to think that some integrity programmes are not created to camouflage corruption, rather than prevent it. Some governments have created an ethics office, but then denied it the basic resources to make it successful (Hermann 1997). Ultimately, integrity systems are one of the most innovative anti-corruption programmes developed by governments in the last 100 years.

Measuring the Impact of Preventative Systems

This section describes methods of assessment for each component of an integrity system listed above, detailing strengths and weaknesses and listing criteria for success. The following overview in no way intends to be comprehensive. The examples presented below originate from many sources and include the efforts of international organizations such as Transparency International, the World Bank, Organisation of American States, the UN and the OECD.[6] Other examples include programmes of a national or provincial coordinating ethics body, and still others are the work of an individual department within the national or provincial government. Examples are cited that refer to individual questions within a management assessment survey designed not to measure ethics specifically, but rather to assess the performance of department management practices. An attempt is made to select examples of assessment methods from a diverse range of sources and to focus on those that enable future assessment efforts.

The efforts of international organizations on this front are to be complimented. While most, to date, have concentrated specifically on baseline assessments and on anti-corruption systems, as opposed to ethics systems, the efforts that lead the way in demonstrating the importance of evaluation and assessment of anti-corruption systems are also to be commended.

Assessments by International Organizations

Transparency International,[7] for example, is engaged in a range of important efforts aimed at gauging the state of corruption in countries. Transparency International's Corruption Perception Index measures the extent to which corruption is perceived to exist in government. It is a composite index derived from seven separate surveys. This index measures perceived corruption rather than actual corruption. It aims to minimize possible biases, including differences in

6 For a more complete explanation of multilateral involvement see Cooper and Yoder (2002).

7 TI emerged as the leading international NGO over the past decade. They have developed general tools for assessing perceptions related to corruption and bribery, such as the Corruption Perception Index (CPI).

the notions of corruption and culture specific ethical standards across countries by pooling surveys from various sources. For example, the Bribe Payer's Index ranks countries based on the degree to which international companies pay bribes to foreign officials. TI's index provides an external assessment based primarily on perception and a useful check for official government analysis on the health of their integrity systems. The National Integrity Systems Country Studies outline the state of integrity systems and the political context for 18 countries. These reports focus on the presence and effectiveness of the institutions and laws that comprise an integrity system. They are unique in their comprehensive approach and provide a useful baseline description of how the government's integrity system is organized. They describe efforts to identify potential weaknesses in the system, as opposed to specifically assessing integrity system components.

A more recent, and sophisticated approach, has been *the Public Integrity* Index[8] issued by the Center for Public Integrity in Washington, DC. Utilizing both perception data and aggregate data the index assesses 21 different dimensions of integrity in 25 different countries. The analysis utilized both in country experts as well as panels of experts to evaluate the meaning of the data and assure its objectivity. Certainly, the index and ranking of countries will catch the eye of the media and politicians, but arguably the most valuable contribution of the index are the qualitative evaluations of each country. These provide a model for qualitative assessment that can be used in many other contexts.

The World Bank has developed an Anti-Corruption Toolkit, including a series of questionnaires designed for institutional assessment of policy-making institutions and the civil service, as well as surveys focused on corruption in civil service delivery and a country's commitment to reform.[9] The Organisation of American States has also engaged in efforts to help members assess the existence and adequacy of the legal framework and enforcement mechanisms related to corruption. It has developed a questionnaire as a follow-up instrument to determine the extent to which its member nations are working to improve their anti-corruption systems.[10]

The United Nations Global Programme Against Corruption, introduced in 1999, provides a framework for standardized assessment to document corruption in public administration and business. The four-part framework includes surveys of business, public administration, and media; focus groups including labour, parliament, media and prosecutors; an analysis of the legal and institutional framework; and finally an analysis of the societal context. A good example of such a study is the Country Corruption Assessment of South Africa.

The Organisation for Economic Cooperation and Development (OECD) has developed monitoring process to ensure the effective implementation of the

---

8 See The Center for Public Integrity *Public Integrity Index* website, <http://www.publicintegrity.org/ga/ii.aspx>.

9 See World Bank *Anti Corruption Toolkit* website, <http://www.worldbank.org/publicsector>.

10 See Organisation of American States website, <http://borwww.oas.org/juridico/english>/. Results listed by country.

Convention on Combating Bribery of Foreign Public Officials in International Business Transactions. The monitoring process, based on the OECD peer-review principles, is divided in two main phases, namely:

- Phase 1 evaluates whether relevant legal texts meet the standard set by the Convention;
- Phase 2 reviews, started in 2000, studies the structures put in place to enforce the laws and rules implementing the Convention and to assess their application in practice. This includes reviewing national investigations and prosecutions and conducting 'on site' interviews with government and regulatory authorities and other persons concerned with application of the Convention.

In the public governance area, a series of ground-breaking studies (see OECD (2003; 2002; 2000; 1999; 1996)) from general approaches to ethics to a detailed analysis of conflicts of interest have been published in the last decade. Although these studies did not explicitly assess ethics programmes in OECD countries, rather that provide a detailed description of the ethics regimes within a country. For example, the OECD[11] reviewed the application of the 1998 Recommendation on Improving Ethics in the Public Service. The resulting report 'Trust in Government' provides standards against which ethics programmes can be evaluated.

The intention is to supplement the reports listed above by focusing on assessment of ethics systems, as opposed to corruption or enforcement systems. More specifically, focus is on methods used to assess the effectiveness of integrity system components on a more granular level than institutional analysis. While it is important for a country to take honest stock of its institutions, how they interact and where potential exists for inappropriate actions, it is essential to be armed with tools to assess specific integrity system measures.

Instead of describing criteria for success of a system component focus is on how one can assess the success of that component. Methods that a governing entity can use to discover whether or not a policy is accomplishing the desired results are addressed, rather than what specific considerations make a successful policy. It is also worth noting that a finite number of programme assessment methods exist. The discussion of the strengths and weaknesses of surveys to measure a code of conduct may well overlap with the strengths and weaknesses of surveying training systems. In the case of overlap those advantages or disadvantages unique to the relevant assessment method will be highlighted.

Performance Assessment

Before discussing measures that assess specific integrity system components, using the framework articulated earlier, it is important to note that no country was found to have all of these measures fully implemented and that the integrity

11 Through its Public Management Service (PUMA) which was transferred to Public Governance and Territorial Directorate in 2002.

systems of many countries are in the very early stages of programme development. As governments work to implement integrity systems, a parallel effort to improve performance and managerial assessment, in general, will help create work environments that encourage ethical behaviour. The management sciences literature and innovative efforts by organizations to improve their workplace environment on many levels is very much related to our discussion, as ethics exists within the context of a living workplace with human beings who happen to be managers and workers.

An exceptional model for widening the framework of performance assessments beyond managerial results to include leadership, people management and organizational environment is provided by the Treasury Board of Canada Secretariat (TBS) Management Accountability Framework (MAF).[12] It is an encouraging trend that management can now address broader goals including ethics, but it is also important to note that in practice, the disruption caused by the ebb and flow of management approaches in the public sector has often adversely affected existing ethics programmes (Gilman 1999).

Codes of Conduct

Measuring the success of a code of conduct is inherently difficult. However, a wide variety of assessment tools can shed light on the efficacy of this important integrity tool. By far the most common is the survey, which has the advantage of being relatively inexpensive and replicable. Of course, it matters who is surveyed and how, and it is helpful to compare survey results between organizational levels (that is, management and employee level responses).

Code Assessment Method 1: Surveys

Surveys come in several forms including:

- ones that measure the 'ethical climate' of the organization;
- direct questions about the presence of misconduct, pressure to commit, reporting of and pressure not to report; and
- performance reviews with some ethics relevant questions.

Additionally, there is a range of variations and combinations of each form, as detailed below, can be helpful.

Management surveys Some management level surveys have been designed specifically to assess ethics programmes, but far more common are performance review surveys that happen to include a question or questions regarding ethics, and codes of conduct in particular.

---

12 See Treasury Board of Canada Secretariat Management Accountability Framework website, <http://www.tbs-sct.gc.ca/maf-crg/maf-crg_e.asp#Introduction>.

Example: The US Office of Government Ethics reports (1990–1998). The United States Congress required the US Office of Government Ethics to issue biennial reports between 1990 and 1998. Many of the biennial reports used survey data to support conclusions about the success of various programme elements, and several of the reports provide summary data. These reports used aggregate data reported by ethics officials in more than one hundred ethics offices. The types of data included items such as the number of full and part-time officials working on ethics, the number of advisory opinions issued, the number of financial disclosure form filed (and their timeliness), the number of administrative and criminal actions taken against employees.

Aggregate data is often not seen as relevant to assessment, yet it can be reasonably claimed that this kind of data – collected over time – can provide some strong indirect indicators of effectiveness.

Example: Survey of top management in Finland. This survey of management and personnel from 170 agencies focuses on changes in values of governance, principles of civil service ethics, unethical practices and factors affecting civil service ethics. The objective of the survey is to paint a general picture of ethics in civil service, specifically in public administration. Transparency of political decision-making and the operations of government enterprises are not included. Finland serves as an example for surveying both the employee and management level, allowing for a useful comparison of factors affecting civil service ethics. The Finnish survey also stands out in that the impetus for its undertaking was not the perception of high levels of unethical behaviour in government but rather the perception of risk for increasing levels of unethical behaviour.

Example: State of the Service Report in Australia. The Australian Public Service Commissioner draws on a range of information sources for the annual State of the Service Report. One of the main sources is an agency questionnaire which is aimed at, among other things, assessing agency approaches to upholding and embedding the APS Values and Code of Conduct. The structure of the State of the Service Report in recent years has been based around the four groups of the APS Values reflecting the key relationships and behaviours they reflect:

- the relationship between the APS and government and the parliament;
- the relationship between the APS and the public; and
- relationships in the workplace and personal behaviours.

There are questions in the agency survey on all these matters as well as questions focussing specifically on the Code of Conduct, including the reporting and investigation of suspected breaches of the Code.

Example: Learning advisory panel survey of middle managers in Canada. While not designed specifically for integrity system assessment, this survey targeted middle managers and its ethics related results could be compared to a survey of public servants undertaken by Canada's Treasury Board. For example, while managers recognized a need for accountability measures and assessment of those measures, they raised concerns that their departments do not have the 'capacity to lead and sustain the dialogue'. In such an environment, the results of the public servant survey which indicated perceptions of unfairness in promotions are not surprising.[13]

Employee surveys Employee surveys are an effective way to determine if management has effectively implemented a code of conduct. Below, several examples are presented.

Example: public servant survey in Puerto Rico. In 2003 the Ethics Resource Center worked with the Office of Government Ethics of Puerto Rico (OGE-PR) to survey all public sector employees (Government of Puerto Rico 2003). Teams were created by both organizations to assure that the data would reflect the culture and institutions of Puerto Rico, while assuring the validity and reliability of the survey questions. The focus of the survey was on how employees 'viewed' ethics in their own organizations, capturing ethics values as well as pressure to commit misconduct. The OGE-PR also recognized the necessity of a broad communications strategy to encourage a large response to the survey and as a result, 65,000 employees responded to the questionnaire.

Example: KPMG 'Integrity Thermometer' in South Africa. Agencies in South Africa have used a survey, initially developed by KPMG for use in businesses, to gauge the existing ethical climate within an organization. The goal is to identify gaps between official policy and company culture in a way that facilitates comparison between offices. The initial attempt to survey employees failed because of reliance on the Internet and employees simply did not have enough access to computers. Further, the question of whether business ethics surveys are directly translatable to the public sector is debatable.

Strengths of employee surveys The importance of employee surveys in assessing the effectiveness of a code of conduct cannot be overestimated. Whether a code of conduct is just a document in the employee handbook or whether it has become part of the agency culture can be determined by understanding the 'view from the trenches'. Employee surveys are an important strategy. The Ethics Resource Center's (ERC) 2003 National Business Ethics Survey (NBES) is a good example of a study designed to understand how employees viewed ethics in their own organizations.

Example: ERC's 2003 National Business Ethics Survey. Although entitled a 'business' survey, the data represents public and non-profit employees as well. Additionally, the data set was able to take advantage of the validity and reliability of other ERC surveys of specific organizations, as well as the two previous NBES surveys in 1993 and 2000. The NBES provides measures to understand the impact of codes of conduct, as well as their relationship to organizational culture, leadership and ethics systems, thus identifying strong relationships among these variables. For example, a robust ethics programme (defined by specific elements) is linked to both a reduction in perceived misconduct and an increase in the willingness to report that misconduct. In the review of assessment of employees

13 See Office of the Auditor General of Canada website, <http://www.oag-bvg.gc.ca/domino/reports>.

there have been very few surveys that look for explanatory relationships between variables. Many organizations resist such studies for fear that some might view these as causal relationships. Although often lost on layman, this distinction is critical. It also demonstrated the greater vulnerability of young managers in organizations as well as a strong correlation between robust ethics systems and a decline in ethical misconduct.

Client Surveys

An alternate angle, most appropriate for agencies that directly serve the public and/or another agency in the government, can be provided through client surveys. While primarily designed to measure performance, surveys of the clientele of civil service agencies can shed light on integrity issues as well. The potential for politicization of the process is very high, but inter-agency scorecards can be a useful check on activity that takes place at the depths of bureaucracy with little public exposure. No examples were found of interagency scorecards, although the Queensland NISA included an inter-agency questionnaire aimed at determining the level of coordination between ethics related bodies (KCELJAG/TI 2001, 146). More common are report cards or scorecards for agencies that directly serve the public.

Example: civil service report cards in Bangalore, India. The 1999 Civil Service Report Card survey in Bangalore, India is an example of a client survey aimed at assessing integrity. An important result of this survey was an indication of an increase in perceived corruption, as evidenced by the growth in both the numbers of respondents who paid bribes and the amounts they paid (World Bank 1999).

Example: South Africa country assessment. The Public Service Commission of South Africa commissioned three surveys:

1 one measuring public perceptions of government corruption;
2 one of businesses; and
3 one regarding public administration.

A selection of four agencies participated in the Public Administration Survey that collected data from service users, managers and public officials. Where most surveys focus on public perception or of government corruption, this survey offered interesting insight into public corruption. It was shown that public officials perceive that clients often sought 'back door' solutions to their issues (PSC News, 2003/3004), suggesting that it is important also to measure public expectations and tolerance for corruption in addition to their perception of its existence.

Strengths and weaknesses of client surveys The public sector can learn from extensive work in private sector customer surveying. The strengths of client surveys in assessing the effectiveness of a code of conduct include:

1 avoiding the conflation of output and outcome that often takes place in internal reviews;
2 capturing public perception regardless of actual practice; and
3 creating a benchmark against which change can be measured. The primary weakness of client surveys is that their relevance is limited to service agencies. This limitation can be relaxed slightly by expanding the use of this tool to inter-agency assessment, but even then they are only relevant to agencies serving others. After that, a careful distinction must be made between the perception of code of conduct violations and actual violations. While an understanding of public perceptions of misconduct is fundamental to programme design considerations, the end goal is to eliminate actual violations of the code of conduct.

Media Surveys

Media plays an important role as agencies assess the effectiveness of a code of conduct. Negative attention can provide a powerful disincentive for transparency and cooperation with the media. At the same time, media provides an outlet for whistleblowers and momentum for investigations, reprimand and stronger ethics practices. The mantra 'do nothing that you wouldn't want on the front page of the Post' for some agency offices in Washington, DC, can be viewed as a positive.

Example: 2002 country assessment of South Africa. An example of the use of media coverage to characterize the success of a code of conduct are two complementary studies that formed part of the 2002 Country Assessment of South Africa. The studies measure the types of corruption reported by the media, who is responsible for bringing the corruption to light and which agencies are responsible for responding to the charges and following up.

Strengths and weaknesses of media surveys The weakness of using media surveys to measure the effectiveness of a code of conduct is that most violations of a code of conduct do not find their way to the media. Nevertheless, such studies provide a useful third party verification of the effectiveness of certain ethics programme instruments. Media participation may be more useful on expert panels and focus groups than surveys as discussed in a later section of this chapter.

Institutional Framework Studies

Further discussion of what are referred to as 'institutional framework studies', such as the National Integrity System Assessment, is warranted as these comprehensive studies form the groundwork for ethics programme assessment. Collaboration between the Key Centre for Ethics, Law, Justice, and Governance at Griffith University in Australia and Transparency International Australia is an important example of such a study. The two groups undertook an ambitious investigation of integrity system components in Queensland, Australia.

Their objective was to provide an in-depth understanding of the laws and institutions comprising the state's integrity systems, to point out the strengths and weaknesses of these components and to identify gaps and areas of overlap (KCELJAG/TI 2001).

The undertaking included documenting the political context and history of the state as related to ethics, as well as a description of the specific laws and institutions. The main study was comprised of three bodies of information:

1. interviews with senior executives of agencies;
2. focus groups to discuss best practices; and
3. a survey aimed at establishing the effectiveness of interaction between agencies within the integrity system.

A parallel study of the private sector, assessments of other states and jurisdictions, attitude surveys among the public and business community and an international comparison of integrity systems were added to the initial study.

Mapping the integrity system landscape by using a framework study such as the NISA Queensland is a vital first step in establishing an effective integrity system. Framework assessments strive to 'identify, analyse, and record institutions, laws, procedures, practices and attitudes' (KCELJAG/TI 2001, Section 2). They primarily focus on questions such as, 'Does a code of conduct exist?' But due to their comprehensive nature, such an assessment can only go so far in answering, 'Has the code of conduct been effective?' The Queensland NISA questionnaire does distinguish between the two, asking respondents to document formal provisions related to each integrity system component and also 'what actually happens?' (KCELJAG/TI 2001, 139). The intention of this chapter is to focus on the latter question by comparing assessment measures used internationally.

Strengths and Weaknesses in Using Surveys in Assessing the Effectiveness of a Code of Conduct

Surveys are a familiar tool that managers and personnel already use in many cases. Retooling human resource/performance related surveys to include ethical considerations is a feasible way to gather data. The strengths of surveys, in general, are that they can be replicated – baseline can be established and comparisons can be made over time.

The principal challenge facing surveys is self-reporting. Collaboration is often required in cases of misconduct, thus almost guaranteeing under-reporting. This limitation was noted in the documentation of South Africa's National Victims of Crime Survey conducted by the Department of Safety and Security and it is applicable to surveys. Employees and managers may also be unlikely to indicate violations exist for fear of reprisal. Effective survey design can avoid the obstacle of self-reporting.

Other challenges surveys face are that they often reflect perception of misconduct as opposed to actual misconduct and cultural differences among organizations or jurisdictions may make comparisons difficult. The code of conduct is intended to standardize notions of acceptable and unacceptable behaviour, but answers to survey questions regarding the effectiveness of a code of conduct, just as actual compliance, may vary from place to place and agency to agency.

Finally, a weakness of surveys in general is a lack of an effort to correlate the perceptions described in surveys with empirical data such 'complaints filed', or the lack of aggregate data for overall reference. Presumably, progress made integrating a code of conduct should be reflected in frequency or output data.

Criteria for success Designing a survey that can adequately measure the effect of a code of conduct is extremely difficult, but some criteria will improve its validity:

- ease of use;
- anonymity;
- a mechanism in place to analyse results and feedback;
- comparison – comparing management vs. employee or provider vs. client;
- a benchmark is set and surveys are replicated. An example of a survey created with this in mind is the Canadian Department of Defense survey of military and civilian employees that provide a baseline assessment of values, used by employees, values respondents supported, respondent expectations of the ethics programme and an assessment of ethical concerns (Department of National Defense 2004);
- good technique. for example, ensuring the validity and reliability of the survey and that it is distributed in a way that encourages a high response rate;
- revealing questions, ensuring that they provide insights into the effectiveness of the programme, rather than programme outputs (for example, how many financial disclosures were filed?).

Code Assessment Method 2: Focus Groups, Expert Panels and Interviews

Focus groups, expert panels and interviews provide an alternative to surveys and have the advantages of fomenting discussion and a more nuanced insight. For the purpose of this chapter, all three situations are referred to as focus groups. Whereas surveys are extremely focused and limited to the research question and the imagination of the surveyor, focus groups leverage group dynamics to widen the discussion to include any consideration deemed relevant by participants. However, focus group conclusions are purely qualitative and, therefore, difficult to compare over groups or over time. Additionally, the selection of participants and moderator play an important role. Both a potential advantage and limitation is the group dynamic. Hearing other participants voice similar concerns could encourage others to voice their own or make others wary of openly discussing certain issues.

Employee focus groups The Australian Public Service Commission's report 'Embedding APS Values' documents the strategies of six case study agencies' efforts to embed the Australian Public Service Values and Code of Conduct and then correlates them to views of employees that were collected in focus groups. As an example of findings from such a focus group, the following shows its importance and utility. Employee focus groups yielded the following conclusions, among others (APSC 2004):

- leadership is crucial to ensuring that the Values and Code of Conduct are taken seriously;
- unethical behaviour by leaders and managers would cause employees to consider the Values and Code of Conduct as rhetoric and to lose confidence in them;
- leaders perceived to be modelling the Values are strongly supported;
- the Values and Code of Conduct as presented in some corporate documents are not made meaningful by corporate practice;
- the relevance of the Values and Code of Conduct to everyday duties is not widely understood;
- some managers and leaders do not seem to be upholding the Values;
- the 15 Values are quite long. some embody more than one concept, are difficult to remember and to put into context;
- grouping the Values is a useful tool in helping to gain an understanding of the Values and making them relevant – makes the Values come alive.

Strengths and weaknesses of employee focus groups Focus groups have many benefits, however organizations must be cautioned not to over analyse the results. Focus group research is best used as groundwork for a scientific survey. It is very seldom the case that a focus group represents a scientific sample, and therefore it is wrong to conclude that the summary of the focus groups is representative of a population. Further, focus groups responses – no matter how well organized – have a subjective element within them. There are judgments and interpretations of not only responses, but also body language, and the dynamics of interchange. This is not to suggest that these are necessarily bad, but rather that one must take into consideration the subjective nature of focus groups when reviewing summaries.

Management focus groups and interviews Management interviews represent one subset of focus group methodology. Usually, the management group in any organization is relatively small and, as a result, the interview process is relatively uncomplicated. The key to doing this successfully is a fairly detailed research framework that clearly articulates issues, question sets, and links between questions. When these interviews are done well it allows the organization to get a picture of how the managerial level views each other's ethical perspective as well as the ethical culture of the organization.

Example: Ethics Resource Center – Corporate Leadership Review. In order to identify integrity issues among top management, the Ethics Resource Center conducted a series of interviews with over 80 executives at a multinational corporation as a part of a 360° executive leadership review. Corporate officers and their direct reports were asked to describe their perceptions of the ethical leadership and overall ethical climate of the organization. The exercise provides the information necessary to assess the integrity programme as viewed 'at the top' and assisted in the development of reports for each member of the leadership team, as well as an overall organizational report. The information also provides foundation and direction for future surveys and assessments. This example from the private sector can serve as a model for government agencies, particularly at the executive level.

Example: Badaracco and Webb. Another example from the private sector, involving focus groups rather than interviews, is 'A View from the Trenches' by Joseph Badaracco and Allen Webb. The work is based on in-depth interviews with Harvard MBAs in their first position out of business school. Emerging from the interviews is that intense focus on job and career goals allows pressure to exist. Getting ahead requires making your numbers no matter what; being a team player, and having a name clean of whistleblowing.

The interviewees also stress that examples are more important than words when it comes to an ethics programme.

Strengths and weaknesses of management focus groups and interviews Management focus group methodology can help to gauge the impact of ethics programmes. However, conclusions from focus groups and interviews must be viewed in light of the limits of the methodology. In the review of public service ethics programmes no system was found that took advantage of this relatively inexpensive approach to understanding the ethical dynamics of organizations. There are several likely reasons why public agencies avoid their use:

1 they appear 'too subjective'. However, all methodologies – including scientific surveys – have an element of subjectivity.
2 public agencies are sensitive to the politics of the results. Surveys can generally couch conclusions more generally; focus groups are far more personal.
3 most ethics programmes are too new to deal with new methodologies.

Client Focus Groups

Client focus groups are a common method used to collect public opinion, especially with regard to the provision of public services and ethics is only one among many considerations, including quality of service and efficiency. Northern Ireland's Review of Public Administration (UK Government 2005) uses focus groups to collect feedback on public service provision. As with surveys, public focus groups are limited in their reach to integrity issues involving service provision to the public.

Strengths and Weaknesses in Using Focus Groups and Interviews in Assessing Codes of Conduct

Focus groups provide a quick way to generate a qualitative comparison of stakeholder viewpoints. For example, in South Africa, under the UN GPAC framework, focus groups were conducted as part of its Country Assessment

Report. Five focus groups were convened consisting of parliamentarians, prosecutors, magistrates the media and trade unions.[14] A discussion guide was used to focus the conversation on certain issues and elicit responses from the various representatives. While this particular set of focus groups was focused on corruption, it serves as an example for future investigations into a wider array of ethics related issues. Particularly useful were the immediate comparisons of the priorities of various stakeholders. Generating candid feedback from all relevant stakeholders helps minimize the chance that important issues are swept under the rug. Focus groups are a way to elicit candid responses from experienced professionals and the interplay between colleagues may spur ideas that would not surface in a paper survey.

On the other hand, focus groups are not meant to be a wholly representative sample and therefore, one must use caution in drawing valid generalizations from their results. The data gathered is qualitative and depends very much on who is involved in the focus group, who is conducting the focus group and what the goals of the discussion guide are. Focus groups rely heavily on the opinions of a few people and to that extent they work best as a means to point out problems or potential risks rather than to scientifically measure the effectiveness of integrity system components.

Criteria for Success

In order to be successful, focus groups should be as representative as feasibly possible and steps should be taken to use an independent group leader. To assure independence, one can use an outside evaluator, as shown through the ERC Corporate Leadership review example presented above. As in all measurements discussed, the proper resources must be allocated to collect, interpret, and publish the results. Follow up focus groups are encouraged, to get a sense for what changes have taken place.

Code Assessment Method 3: Audits and Performance Reviews

Performance audits and reviews are another way to assess the level of compliance with codes of conduct. Two types of audits are distinguished:

1 an audit focused specifically on ethics related requirements; and
2 a more general performance audit that may indicate ethics related performance issues.

Output methods, in this case, provide the source for assessment. For example, the Disclosure of Wrongdoing and the Harassment Policy (including the numbers of complaints, types of cases, etc.) used in Canada creates a baseline for understanding the state of affairs in this area. There are inherent problems

---

14 See UN Global Program website, <http://www.unodc.org/southafrica>.

with relying on output statistics as they do not illuminate the actual outcome of policies and therefore may be more misleading than helpful.[15]

Another example of an ethics related audit is the Operations Review Committee of the Independent Commission Against Corruption in New South Wales, Australia which performs both internal and external management audits focusing on key elements of the ethics regime.[16]

Additionally, the United States Office of Government Ethics Management Audits primarily focuses on the regulatory compliance of federal agencies under its responsibility. Within the regulatory regime every department or agency is required to have a Designated Agency Ethics Official (DAEO) who is responsible for the management of the agency's ethics programme. As examples, these audits review whether the DAEO complied with financial disclosure requirements (number, review and timeliness), training requirements, and even the accuracy of advice given to employees.

The State Services Commission (SSC) in New Zealand has one of the most advanced integrated performance system in use at this time. Originating through the *Integrity Project* the SSC has carefully created a risk matrix for both 'people integrity' and 'organizational integrity'. This risk matrix was initially used in the New Zealand Customs Service and produced a series of critical indicators for integrity. These indicators were then used to evaluate managerial and organizational practices leading to informed policy adjustments (SSC 2005).[17]

Strengths and Weaknesses of Using Audit and Performance Reviews in Assessing Codes of Conduct

The weakness of relying on output statistics to measure compliance with the code of conduct is that extreme detail allows one to 'lose the forest for the trees'. The importance of context makes the analysis of output statistics extremely tenuous. On the other hand, audits designed specifically to account for the integrity system components and procedures can be useful in measuring the success of a code of conduct. Perhaps more importantly, such audits can encourage compliance. Because regular audits of compliance will only promote the generation of audited paperwork and not actual ethical conduct, it is important that audits are not the only assessment of integrity system components. Another shortcoming of this method is the high cost associated with a detailed audit.

The risk analysis employed by New Zealand appears to avoid many of the pitfalls of audits, but its potential 'Achilles heel' is that it must rely on the integrity of managers and leadership to effectively carry out this sophisticated evaluation.

---

15 See Treasury Board of Canada Secretariat website, <http://www.tbs-sct.gc.ca>.

16 See NSW Independent Commission Against Corruption website, <http://www.icac.nsw.gov.au/>.

17 See State Standards Commissioner (NZ) (2002) *Integrity Conduct – Setting Standards for Crown Entities* website, <http://www.ssc.govt.nz/display>.

Criteria for Success

Ultimately, good management audits in the ethics area must focus on both compliance, and impact. The latter is harder to measure, but not as difficult as many assume. Effective management audits can take the form of perception measures, or correlate actually criminal or administrative violations with programme elements. Public agencies are reticent to undertake such evaluations because it makes them vulnerable to criticism. There is a certain amount of ethical courage necessary to say we are not perfect, we risk discovering weaknesses in a programme, but it is the only way to make them better. From outside government such a sentiment seems both rational and compelling. However, given the fury of political winds within some agencies, and certain governments, it might be perceived as a reasonable survival strategy.

Code Assessment Method 4: Public Hearings

Public hearings are a common top down approach to measuring agency heads accountability for compliance to the code of conduct and other ethics programme components. In the United Kingdom, The Committee on Standards in Public Life publishes annual reports on the conduct of public officials. Its methodology includes publishing a 'consultation paper' establishing the issues of principal concern, inviting submissions on the relevant issues, conducting informal interviews/meetings with stakeholders and finally public, formal hearings. The committee has published ten such reports focusing on a range of issues from conduct in the House of Lords to defining the boundaries of acceptable behaviour at the executive level.

Other examples include legislative hearings that focus on ethical accountability of individual agencies or ethics offices themselves. Such hearings are noteworthy because the legislative oversight is often an effective counterbalance to the tendency of some bureaucracies to interpret their responsibilities minimally. Using oversight or budget authority, legislative committees can wield effective power in ensuring that executive agencies take their ethical responsibilities seriously.

Strengths and Weaknesses of Using Public Hearings in Assessing Codes of Conduct

The formal and legal nature of hearings brings this method of assessment a high degree of legitimacy. It should be noted that depending on the composition of the body conducting the hearing, political rivalry might encourage extremely rigorous examination. It is also significant that busy legislative calendars ensure that such hearings are limited in time and scope and that testimony is limited to the agency heads.

Criteria for Success

In order to be effective, hearings must recur at a regular frequency, attendance and candid answers must be required by law and enforceable, committee members must be representative of the government in place and not exclusively from one political group or another. Hearings should also be public because they serve both as an effective transparency mechanism and an essential element in a communications strategy. They add to transparency because the public has the ability to see into and understand the governmental process. They are an essential component of a communications strategy because hearings make the average citizen cognisant that ethics is important and that there are systems in place to ensure the ethical behaviour of public employees.

Transparency Systems

Laws and processes that guarantee access to information about government decision making are integral to an effective integrity system. Assessment of transparency measures can occur at the agency or programme level, or alternatively it can focus on individual transparency provisions such as interest and financial disclosure. Agency level assessments include framework analysis to determine the existence of and adherence to a range of international standards, the agency performance review or audit, and independent community oversight. Provision level assessments include process audits and surveys of officials that administer interest and financial disclosure regulations.

Transparency Systems Assessment Method 1: Standards and Administrative Simplification

The development of standards for transparency in day-to-day public operations and output measures provide a baseline against which agencies can assess their activities.

Example: IMF ROSC reports. The IMF publishes *Reports on the Observance of Standards and Codes (ROSC)*, which detail the level of compliance with internationally recognized standards including 'accounting; auditing; anti-money laundering and countering the financing of terrorism (AML/CFT); banking supervision; corporate governance; data dissemination; fiscal transparency; insolvency and creditor rights; insurance supervision; monetary and financial policy transparency; payments systems; and securities regulation'.[18] As such, the ROSC reports provide a broad-based assessment of the transparency systems in place in various countries from a third party perspective. Measuring the absence of misconduct, while difficult, makes standards especially important. A related

18 See World Bank Group *Report of the Observance of Standards and Codes* website, <http:// www.imf.org/external/np/rosc/rosc.asp>.

area where standards play an important role is in administrative simplification as shown in the example below.

Example: trade and transport facilitation in Southeast Europe. Administrative simplification is an important element of a transparency system and one that lends itself to analysis through output statistics. An example is the Trade and Transport Facilitation in Southeast Europe Programme, a coalition of area governments, the World Bank, US Government and the American College at Thessaloniki.[19] This organization developed an administrative simplification manual for participating agencies. Specific measures include import and border entry clearance times, reported cases of corruption, and revenue and salary analysis. Setting a standard for administrative efficiency is an important step towards insuring that the public can fairly participate in the government decision-making process.

Example: Chilean procurement process. Chile has created a state of the art procurement process by making it absolutely transparent to anyone who is interested. All procurements are announced, processed and awarded over a secure Internet site. Objections and questions about the process or awards are also coordinated through the web. This system not only provides integrity to the public tender process, but it also reassures the public of its fairness. 'Public-ness' is an intriguing way of doing evaluation as it allows the public to provide the evaluation elements by way of their feedback throughout the process. This not only provides a unique evaluation perspective, but it is also relatively inexpensive.

Strengths and Weaknesses of Using Standards to Assess Transparency Systems

Administrative reform can be an important integrity tool if it is effectively implemented. Simplifying systems, writing regulations and policies in common, straightforward language, reducing the number of approvals for any process can have a positive impact on the integrity of government. This is appealing because it makes government both 'citizen friendly' as well as gives the citizen more confidence in the integrity of government institutions.

Unfortunately, in many countries there is little effort made beyond modification of laws or policy. Administrative simplification can be viewed as an end in itself, and simplification does not necessarily lead to integrity. It can lead to a consolidation of power in a few hands, and if those few are corrupt the 'cure can be worse than the disease'.

Criteria for Success

Standards and simplification can be effective tools if there is a commensurate set of checks and balances. The tendency is to view all checks and balances as potentially redundant, and therefore unnecessary. In fact a few elements,

19 See Trade and Transport Facilitation in Southeast Europe Programme website, <http://www.surecom.org/ttfse>/.

that are independent from one another and where there are reward systems for ensuring that the system both works and maintains integrity, can be successful. Ultimately, the tests for simplification are citizens who feel that there is both greater responsiveness to their requests and a sureness that the public servant is working on their behalf.

Transparency Systems Assessment Method Two: Agency Audits and Performance Reviews

Transparency issues will arise in both financial and performance audits. The Government Accountability Office (GAO) in the US conducts such audits. Hong Kong, along with many other countries has an Independent Commission Against Corruption to review procurement procedures of various departments. Transparency systems can also be effectively combined with codes to provide an effective integrity strategy.

Example: Finland's 'Values as Part of the Daily Job' and management barometers. Based on a 1998 employee survey, the State Employer's Office created avenues for value-based daily activity and management into the everyday work-life of Finnish civil servants. The idea was to create a system where fundamental public service values could be used as a basic management tool. Managers and executives in Finland are evaluated annually using integrity indicators for themselves and their organizations. Up to one quarter of a manager's performance will be based on their ability to implement values in practice. These are measured through integrity barometers as well as self-assessment tools.

Strengths and Weaknesses of Agency Audits and Performance Reviews in Assessing Transparency Systems and Criteria for Success

Many factors determine the efficiency and effectiveness of agency operations, but in some cases such measurements indicate institutionalized misconduct. Of course, the usefulness of output measurements is limited to the evaluation of those agencies with measurable outputs and even then must be considered relevant only in so far as output is a reliable proxy of outcome. Careful interpretation of the outputs of procurement divisions, customs agencies and law enforcement agencies can shed light on the extent to which transparency requirements are effective.

The more abstract perception indicators used by Finland can answer some of these concerns. First, it ties real time performance to integrity indicators. Second, it utilizes employee and stakeholder perceptions to evaluate the 'atmosphere' in a department or agency. Third, it ties a large segment of managerial success to their ability to influence that environment by focusing on the highest values of public service.

Transparency System Assessment Method 3: Community Visitors or Advisory Committees

Directly involving the public in the role of an advisory committee improves the dissemination of information to the public, which is particularly useful in the case of technically complex regulation that affects large numbers of people, such as public health and communications policy. In Canada, the Public Advisory Committee of the Health Products and Food Branch reports directly to the Assistant Deputy Minister and the Branch Executive Committee. The Public Advisory Committee was established to improve the flow of information to citizens about health protection issues and facilitate public involvement in the policy making process.[20] Especially in the developing world, NGOs often act independently to monitor large government contracts.[21]

Strengths and Weaknesses for Community Visitors or Advisory Committees in Assessing Transparency System and Criteria for Success

Community visitors or advisory committees can be very effective in lending voice to the average citizens concerns. Their success really depends on how they are selected, their independence, effective resources, and clear authorities. Unfortunately, it is seldom the case that governments will cede these necessary ingredients to committees or commissions.

Transparency System Assessment Method 4: Surveys

In the case of assessing the effectiveness of specific transparency related measures, such as financial and interest disclosure requirements, surveys provide a useful tool. For example, the US Office of Government Ethics surveyed ethics officials about the workflow and effectiveness of the financial disclosure process.[22] One issue to consider while implementing effective transparency measures is that regulations must be understandable. This is significant because surveys can also help determine the extent to which participants understand and interpret reporting requirements and gauge the need for training.

Strengths and Weaknesses of Surveys in Assessing Transparency Systems and Criteria for Success

These surveys can contribute in an important way to understand the administrative processes and problems in asset declaration systems. The weakness of such surveys

20 See Health Products and Food branch Public Advisory Committee website,<http://*www.hc-sc.gc.ca/hpfb-dgpsa/pac*>.

21 See Green Salvation website, <http://www.greensalvation.org/English/Partners/transparency.htm>.

22 See US Office of Government Ethics website, <http://www.usoge.gov/pages/forms_pubs_otherdocs/fpo_files/surveys_ques/ srvy450questions_03.pdf>.

is that they generally ask output questions, for example how many disclosures were collected, how questions were asked or answered based on the disclosures. In the limited sample, no government had ventured to ask questions about the outcome of disclosures. Examples of such measures would include a correlation between the number of negative administrative actions taken because of ethics problems and the number of cleared financial disclosures.

The criteria for success should be both administrative and policy based. Surveys can ensure that ethics asset declarations are being collected and reviewed. As importantly, there should be an assessment that the declarations are revealing and addressing ethics questions that are raised by them. As an example, too often such surveys ask how many declarations were collected, but do not ask how quickly they were reviewed, and how many problems were identified and resolved.

Transparency System Assessment Method 5: Process Audits

In addition to soliciting feedback from Designated Agency Ethics Official (DAEO) about the efficacy of the financial disclosure process, the US Office of Government Ethics (OGE) audits ethics programmes in all agencies. To ensure the effectiveness of audits, OGE has legislative authority to issue orders of corrective action to agencies. In case of non-compliance with orders of corrective action, OGE must notify the President and Congress in writing.

Strengths and Weaknesses in Using Standards and Outputs in Assessing Transparency Measures and Criteria for Success

Standards and output statistics, as measurement tools, are less relevant for transparency systems, such as financial disclosure and freedom of information statutes. Submission rates for financial and interest disclosure, the number of requests and the turnaround time for requests under the freedom of information guidelines, for example, may be relevant performance assessments, but understanding the effect of such statutes on the behaviour of government employees is much more difficult. Output statistics fail on several accounts. The context of the output is extremely important because if procedures or regulations change, comparisons are not possible. More importantly, what is captured is output and not outcome. Other methods of assessment are more relevant for financial disclosure.

Perhaps the most important assessment measure is the institutional framework study, which identifies the existence and enforceability of disclosure statutes. The existence of such regulations, the existence of a review and audit body, frequency of filing, counselling on problems, the existence of real deterrence in the form of jail terms or extensive fines etc. are all involved in the development of an international standard for disclosure regulations.

The primary obstacle to effectiveness access to information is the oversupply of information. Often, agencies will collect large amounts of irrelevant information that will overwhelm any attempt to do a manageable analysis. It is simply not feasible for any public body to adequately analyse all of the information available.

In this sense, public scrutiny is an effective method of assessment. The media and interest groups play an important role here by analysing voting records, campaign contributions and financial statements.

Training Systems

Training provides employees with the decision-making tools to deal with situations that fall outside of the most common case studies. Again, the concern here is not specifically what makes up an effective training programme, but rather how an institution knows if its training programme is effective. Assessing the effectiveness of training programmes can be done on several levels:

1 testing the trainee's understanding of the programme objectives;
2 trainee's evaluations of trainers;
3 trainer's evaluations of trainees;
4 surveys of ethics officials.

Training Assessment Method 1: The Trainers and/or Exit Quizzes

To the extent that ethics training is done in person and on an ongoing basis, trainers provide an important source for the evaluation of training programmes. Trainers have the ability to perform qualitative assessments of the participation they receive in classes. Do the participants take the issue seriously? Do participants believe managers take the issue seriously? Are participants simply developing the skills to choose the right answer on an ethics test, or are they gaining a better understanding of the values underlying ethical decisions? Post session feedback from trainers provides an important source of training programme evaluation criteria.

Because of its ease of use and cost effectiveness, online ethics training has become popular. Providing exit quizzes and maintaining minimum requirements is an effective way to ensure that a participant has not just clicked 'next' a dozen times until the training session is complete. In researching this chapter, it was possible to do just that and 'complete' a training session without reading a word of it. A review of unobtrusive measures, such as time per question, could provide an indication of whether participants are taking the training seriously. Alternatively an exit quiz could signal a passing or failing grade. Some online training programmes include an exit feedback questionnaire.[23]

---

23 See Texas Department of Criminal Justice website website, <http://www.tdcj.state.tx.us/ace/ethics/ethics-feedback-form.htm>.

Strengths and Weaknesses in Using Trainers and/or Exit Quizzes in Assessing Training Systems and Criteria for Success

It has been suggested that ethics training should be done early in an employee's tenure and is integrated with other socialization and training activities. It also stands to reason that one-time training is probably insufficient when it comes to instilling core values. Measuring compliance with timing and frequency standards is a good place to start, however these measure should not take the place of qualitative assessment of the training programme.

The Office of Government Ethics in the US conducted a survey of 175 ethics officials in various departments regarding ethics training including:

1 programme successes, problems and solutions;
2 satisfaction with guidance and assistance provided by the Office of Government Ethics;
3 satisfaction with executive branch agency senior management support;
4 employee satisfaction with ethics training; training objectives; measures of compliance;
5 effectiveness of training methods;
6 effects of budget cuts.[24]

Not surprisingly, most ethics officials reported that their programmes were successful. More interestingly, officials rated the effectiveness of certain training methods and reported that videos and case study discussions were the most effective, whereas distribution of regulations was the least effective measure. They also noted that they had more success when training methods were interactive, fun and convenient.

Communication Strategies

The role of communications strategy of an integrity system is to provide ethics 'marketing' on an ongoing basis to all stakeholders. Training programmes can be thought of as a subset of communications efforts and as formal educational opportunities targeting specific employee groups at specific times with specific objectives. In comparison, communications strategies may entail:

1 the issuing of ethics related documents;
2 posting related documents in the workplace;
3 reference to the code of conduct in speeches and day-to-day operations;
4 press conferences and any other ongoing effort to elevate and maintain awareness of the organization's values.

---

24 See US Office of Government Ethics website, <http://www.usoge.gov/pages/daeograms/dgr_files/1997/etsurvey.pdf>.

Assessing the effectiveness of a communications strategy is similar to assessing training effectiveness in that compliance with frequency and timing standards can be measured, but surveying to determine the extent that understanding and internalization of core values is more important.

For example, South Africa instituted the National Anti-Corruption Initiative in 1999 resulting from the National Anti-corruption Summit and the Public Sector Anti-Corruption Conference (Selby and Baqwa 2001, 21–4). This led to a series of legislative and administrative initiatives but lacked the effort to assess the effectiveness of communicating these issues to the public or public servants. However, it did lead to the creation of a number of innovative offices, including the Public Protector and the Registrar of Assets.

In 2002, the Office of Government Ethics of Puerto Rico (OGEPR) surveyed all of the public employees in the Commonwealth. As part of their strategy to increase the response rate to the survey the OGE PR engaged in a broad media campaign. Using radio, television and newspapers the office did interviews and placed ads to emphasize the importance of getting accurate survey data.

In so doing, they also raised significant awareness among non-government employees about their concerns towards the integrity of public servants and a significant increase in telephone calls to their hotlines. The questions were both about reporting suspicious actions and general questions about ethics in government. This was an unanticipated, but potentially effective way of measuring the impact of a communications strategy.

Communication Strategy Assessment Method 1: Surveys

Communications strategies generally focus on communicating core values To begin with, an organization must determine if a coherent communications strategy exists at all. Once in place, surveys are a commonly used method of assessment, as seen in Finland, South Africa and Canada. Each of these includes questions aimed at whether employees understand departmental values and reporting procedures on general management performance questionnaires. Some of the relevant survey questions follow:

1 rate the clarity of the principles of ethics (Finland 1998);
2 who would you report problems to? (South Africa);
3 I can clearly explain the values of my department (Canada).

Other questions regarding the modelling of ethical behaviour by management, frequency of impact with tenets set forth in the code of conduct, and the extent to which day to day practices embody company values may also indicate the extent to which a communications strategy has worked. One of the newest and most ambitious evaluation and communication strategies has been employed by the Korean Independent Commission Against Corruption (KICAC). Although a recently established agency it has created and used more than ten distinct evaluation systems since 2002. These include client surveys on transparency, quality of service, awareness of municipal integrity systems, fairness of government systems and the role of leadership in the integrity of public servants. These ultimately were used in an assessment model by agency, evaluating each agency's integrity with integrity scores. KICAC adopted a 'naming and blaming' communications strategy releasing performance results to the media using this as a catalyst to encourage voluntary efforts to meet this integrity challenge. The public nature of the strategy also resulted in legislative hearings for any recalcitrant departments.[25]

Strengths and Weaknesses of Using Surveys in Assessing a Communications Strategy

Surveying to determine the effectiveness of a communications strategy has the same strengths and weaknesses as surveying to assess the effectiveness of a code of conduct as described previously. In this particular case, it can be especially difficult to disentangle the effect of a communications strategy from the effect of a training programme on public servants. However, surveys can provide a distinct perspective from citizens or key NGO and private sector groups.

Criteria for Success

As mentioned above, the criteria for success for communications is often tangled in the training strategy. However, if there is an expansion of the survey group to include both stakeholders as well as civil servants, the comparative date will allow a meaningful differentiation between the training and communications strategy.

Counselling

Ethics counselling services include counselling on conflicts of interest and opinions clarifying statutes. The extent to which ethics counselling services are successful can be assessed several ways including independent review of output and client satisfaction surveys.

Counselling Assessment Method 1: Independent Review

When an independent ethics body offers opinions on conflicts of interest or interpretation of a statute for a concrete case, a sample of the advice should be tracked and audited. The US Office of Government Ethics does do a sample audit of the advice given, but this is done only in terms of legal accuracy. There is no attempt to find out if the advice was followed. This study did not find a formal process for the review of ethics body counselling, although this is most certainly performed by personal attorneys and the press.

---

25 See Korean Independent Commission Against Corruption website, <http://www.kicac.go.kr/?ACTION=english_home>.

Counselling Assessment Method 2: Surveys

The feedback of those who solicit the advice of counselling agencies is important to assessing their effectiveness, although no survey examples of this type are available to share. For example, was the request turned around in a timely manner? Was the advice given relevant, helpful and objective?

Strengths and Weaknesses of Assessing Counselling Programmes and Criteria for Success

Counselling should be the critical element for any integrity programme. These programmes are designed to prevent corruption, or the perception of corruption, before it occurs. If effective personal counselling is not available the overall effectiveness of the programme is in question. The strength of such programmes is their ability to provide timely and consistent advice for government officials.

The criterion for success is whether public employees believe that they can rely on the advice that is given them. Further, a good counselling system should create an environment of ethics, where employees both know that it is legitimate to ask ethics questions and see it as a regular part of the management system.

Whistleblower Hotlines and Help Lines

Whistleblower hotlines and help lines are meant to provide a safe, independent outlet for reporting misconduct and receiving ethics advice. The existence of a hotline alone is presumably preventative, but as in other cases discussed above, measuring the overall efficacy of whistleblower hotlines as a preventative measure is extremely difficult. It is possible, however, to determine if:

1 there is willingness to use the hotlines or if they exist in name only;
2 the cases reported are fairly and efficiently dealt with.

Hotline and Help Line Assessment Method 1: Surveys

Generally, surveys play an important role as an indirect measure of the effectiveness of ethics programmes. Ethics surveys can take two different approaches. The first is the general societal perception survey. This type of survey emphasizes the perception of citizens, groups, or key stakeholders about ethical values and corruption in a country (or state). The more widely used survey targets the ethical culture of the organization in which people work, exploring the ethical culture and pressures to commit misconduct. These types of surveys can be very useful in targeting the effectiveness of key components of the ethics programme such as hotlines and help lines.

Example: South Africa's country assessment 2002. One of the component surveys of South Africa's Country Assessment of 2002 asked employees and managers about their understanding of whistleblowing procedures and their own willingness to report. Willingness to report is an indicator of the perceived level of protection afforded whistleblowers. Training and communication strategies can directly address any gap between perception and actual procedure.

Example: ERC's National Business Ethics Survey 2003. As previously mentioned, the Ethics Resource Center's general US perception survey, despite the title, does include private and public sector, as well as the non-profit community. The survey looks at the role of leaders, supervisors and peers, as well as focusing on how often employees see misconduct, feel pressure to commit misconduct and their willingness (or ability) to report misconduct, thus provides crucial feedback on programme elements such as help lines or hotlines. Variations of this survey have been used by ethics centres in South Africa and Turkey.

In addition, this perception survey can be used as a benchmark for government or agency specific surveys. Although this is common in the private sector, it is seldom used in the public sector. The one major exception was the Puerto Rico's Office of Government Ethics 2003 survey. The agency wanted to consciously benchmark in order to better understand the dynamics of ethics on the island.

Hotline and Help Line Assessment Method 2: Stakeholder Analysis

Stakeholder analysis is used to identify and assess the importance of key actors that may affect the programme in question. More specifically, the expectations, perceptions and constraints of each stakeholder are documented and analysed. Such analysis is often done informally as a starting point for any evaluation. A formal and detailed stakeholder analysis can be extremely useful, especially in cases where confidentiality is of the essence. For example, tracking the complaints that enter a hotline system may illuminate how many complaints are being elevated and to whom, on a post hoc basis. A more proactive review of the system would identify the actors in the process and assess their expectations, perceptions and constraints.

A detailed analysis of callers, operators and any actors involved in the various levels of review of complaints can illuminate the observed outputs of the system. For example, a low rate of complaints elevated for review could be due to caller misunderstanding of the purpose of the hotline, limitations on elevation options available to operators, or simply a lack of cases requiring elevation. Stakeholder analysis, not output statistics, will illuminate the answer.

Example: Public Service Human Resource Management Agency of Canada. Stakeholder analysis is particularly useful where surveys and other quantitative analysis are not possible. Canada's Public Service Human Resource Management Agency conducted stakeholder analysis of issues surrounding the disclosure of wrongdoing (PSHRMAC 2004). Their discussions with complaint processors indicated the need for independent and confidential investigations, as well as improved protection for whistleblowers and measures to protect the accused.

Stakeholder analysis is an important first step to an in depth process review. By analysing the perceptions, expectations and constraints on the relevant actors, it is possible to understand how the participants in a process are shaping the outcome of it. Furthermore, by identifying gaps between perceptions and expectations and by documenting the constraints on actors this tool provides the foundation for a plan of action for managers wishing to improve the process in question.

Strengths and Weaknesses of Assessing Help Lines and Hotlines and Criteria for Success

Assessing the effectiveness of the hotlines in terms of either providing counselling to whistleblowers or efficiently and responsibly investigating the issue reported can be done in a number of ways. First, client feedback, while complicated by the anonymous nature of some reports, can be collected. Next, many unions encourage members to file a simultaneous report with them in order to maintain an independent record for comparison with official action. Other, perhaps even more independent, tracking procedures could be devised. In fact, for high profile cases, the press often plays this role.

Coordinating Ethics Bodies

The existence of a coordinating ethics body in itself can be an assessment of the effectiveness of a country's integrity system. However, even when such a body exists, determining a reliable method to assess the assessors is critical. Coordinating bodies often fill a number of roles, including acting as a watchdog agency, counsellor and promoter or marketer of ethics standards (PSHRMAC 2004). Having already discussed counselling and communications strategies, focus is on assessment of the coordinating body's role as a watchdog agency and their overall assessment.

Coordinating Ethics Bodies Assessment Method 1: Legislative Oversight

Ethics bodies must be accountable to a legislative body with respect to operational and financial performance. Legislative hearings, where the ethics body reports on its progress toward its performance goals and its budget performance, should be held regularly and publicly. Most coordinating bodies are obligated to publish annual performance reports and/or testify before a legislative body regarding their performance. For example, the US Office of Government Ethics issued biennial reports to Congress from 1990 to 1998 until Congress repealed the requirement. From 1999 OGE has provided a publicly available Annual Performance Report to Congress in conjunction with its annual budget request and justification. Canada's Ethics Counsellor regularly reported to Parliament, as does the Committee on Standards in Public Life in the United Kingdom.

Coordinating Ethics Bodies Assessment Method 2: Self-assessment

The US Office of Government Ethics publishes a self-assessment of their progress toward reaching their annual performance goals in the aforementioned Annual

Performance Report. In the United Kingdom the Committee on Standards in Public Life has its own code of conduct, publishes performance goals and progress, and publishes its financial performance in an annual report.

Coordinating Ethics Bodies Assessment Method 3: Independent Audits

New South Wales' Independent Commission Against Corruption appoints independent auditors every three years to assess processing of complaints, financial performance and the control of formal investigations.[26] In many countries around the world, inspectors general (or those who are responsible for such a function) do management audits of ethics programmes. In Turkey and the United States this is done through the individual agency responsibility of each Inspector General, while in Chile government-wide inspectors general do this. Sometimes supplementing this oversight is the supreme auditor in a country who takes legislative responsibility for auditing ethics agencies.

The Supreme Chamber of Control, Poland's supreme audit institution, also undertakes some risk assessment of integrity systems. However, it is not clear as to the extent of the current approach. Risk assessment methodologies can be one of the more effective approaches in reviewing output measures. However, good risk management assessment requires a fairly sophisticated quantitative background requiring vector analysis and often factor analysis of distinct interval level variables.

Coordinating Ethics Bodies Assessment Method 4: Public Scrutiny

Common to most coordinating bodies is a commitment to detailed reporting of activities online. This enables media and public scrutiny of the agency's activities. Most government ethics offices have a presence on the worldwide web. However, there has been no attempt to evaluate these, or create a portal to take advantage of cross-government institutional knowledge.

Coordinating Ethics Bodies Assessment Method 5: Surveys

One goal of a coordinating body is to facilitate the process of harmonization among agencies regarding ethics related procedures. The only method uncovered that is used to systematically assess progress on this front is the interagency questionnaire discussed previously, the Queensland National Integrity Systems Assessment (NISA) report. Intended to assess the effectiveness of Australia's National Integrity Systems at Commonwealth, state and territory level and also in the business sector, NISA was launched first in Queensland and findings have been published on the Internet as the Queensland NISA Handbook (KCELJAG/TI 2001).

---

26 See NSW Independent Commission Against Corruption website, <http://www.icac.nsw.gov.au/>.

Strengths and Weaknesses in Assessing Coordinating Ethics Bodies and Criteria for Success

There is very little attempt to assess the various coordination roles among the integrity functions and other anti-corruption agencies despite what seems to be an obvious area for evaluation. There are obvious issues of competition for scarce resources, but it would seem that everyone benefits from a clearer picture. In more complex systems there are competing integrity systems, and there appears to be little interest in evaluating how they impact one another. For example, in one agency in a large government there is a government ethics office, a research ethics office, business compliance and integrity office, and a clinical ethics office.

Control and Enforcement

While this chapter focuses on preventative measures, the effectiveness of any integrity system component is dependent on the likelihood of punishment for misconduct and the enforceability of statutes once a violation is known. The Ethics Resource Center's National Business Ethics Survey (NBES) 2003 found that employees were more likely to report ethical misconduct if they thought something was going to be done about it. Thus, if employees feel that those who violate the code will be punished, compliance with an organization's code of conduct will increase. Often this discussion of punishment is mistaken for severity. Actually, it is the sureness that a penalty will occur and how quickly it occurs that affects behaviour. The Philippines has capital punishment for 'public plundering' but as it is never enforced it provides little deterrence. On the other hand, governments that punish misconduct immediately with penalties such as reduction in pay or a day off without pay, appear to have more success with compliance.

A discussion of the methods to measure the effectiveness of control and enforcement mechanisms deserves its own work. Comments are limited to the obvious; for each case or type of violation, it should be clear who will conduct investigations, how they will go about it, how administrative violations will be distinguished from criminal violations, and in what way violations will be punished. The goal of an integrity system is to instil shared values that will prevent misconduct, but to achieve this goal control and enforcement mechanisms must be present and effective. Unfortunately, much of this falls outside the scope of the discussion.

Report Cards

External reviews and report cards provide an important check on the potential bias of internal assessments. The Maxwell School Government Performance Review provides a good example of a review that rates the management capacity of city, county and state governments in the US.[27] However; none of these report cards include ethics or integrity. In a recent article published in the Public Performance and Management Review titled *A Report on Report Cards*, over forty different report cards, assessing various government programmes and policies, were critiqued with equally disappointing results (Coe 2003). Report cards could serve as ideal vehicles for external assessment if governments could get researchers interested in issues of integrity.

Conclusion

There are many obstacles to the successful assessment of integrity system components. The nature of these obstacles is such that there is an important role for multilateral organizations. However, there first must be recognition of the importance of assessments to integrity programmes, and how to communicate this need to governments. Consensus, rather than mandate, is critical to the success of such an endeavour. Experience has shown that mandates produce iconic measures designed to please the external evaluators rather than measure the actual effectiveness of the programme. If ethics programmes are to be of value, internal evaluation measures should be part of on going operational processes and seen as a natural part of programme management.

In outlining some of the assessment methods that are currently being used around the globe, several challenges to effective evaluation have become apparent.

First, the ethics practice is young. For most countries in the world it is little more than a decade old. For that reason there is no general agreement on a common language (OECD 2003; 2005) or a broad concurrence on set of standard system components. Within this discussion there must be a recognition that a broad based integrity system – with prevention as its focus – is a recently arrived at paradigm. For that reason, the concept of evaluating the components is even newer. So it is not surprising that evaluation instruments, as well as what is to be evaluated, vary widely in the international community. Where one country emphasizes evaluating the effectiveness of training, another will focus on how effectively public servants understand the code of conduct. Even within each of these evaluation issues there is wide variance as to *how* a component should be measured. For example, training is measured through questions that emphasize technical understanding, application, and even whether the individual enjoyed the course. Therefore, it is also clear that there is not one, uniform system of evaluation even within governments, and sometimes ministries. The variance is in some large part due to a lack of consensus as to what government agencies are trying to measure. Because of this there is an emphasis on distinct elements of the programme, rather than having an evaluation that takes into account how all of the pieces of an integrity programme fit together.

---

27 See Maxwell School Government Performance Review website, <http://www.maxwell.syr.edu/gpp/about/goals.asp>.

Secondly, as is the case in most countries, responsibility for evaluation is decentralized. In all of the research no one single entity responsible for the evaluation of all elements of an integrity system was found. Even the 'governing' agencies such as ICAC in Hong Kong and Australia, the US Office of Government Ethics or the Registrar of Assets in South Africa are only responsible for a part of the overall evaluation. And often, even in the most sophisticated systems, there is very little actual evaluation.

Third, the incentive structure for integrity systems is often upside down. That is, in many ways it is in an agency's best interest not to know whether they are effective or not. Any critical report can bring unwanted legislative or executive oversight, and in the worse case a reduction of funding. For this reason, care must be taken to ensure that the incentives for valid evaluation outweigh the incentives for the appearance of success to any overseeing body.

Fourth, there is a persistent belief that given the nature of ethics programmes, effective evaluation is not possible. The argument generally made is that since ethics programmes are designed to prevent something before it occurs, one cannot measure something that does not happen. This is a variation on the proverbial 'if a tree falls in the forest and no one is around, does it make a sound?' So the conclusion drawn from this belief system is that gross measures of corruption (arrest rates, monies recovered, etc.) are not meaningful measures of the effectiveness of ethics programmes. This myth usually persists because of a lack of evaluation skills and the false assumption that if something cannot be directly measured, it cannot be measured at all. In fact there appear to be a number of robust indirect measures that, collectively, give a clear picture as to the success of ethics programmes, including surveys, stakeholder analyses and public hearings.

Finally, organizations continue to focus on observable outputs as opposed to outcomes in their evaluation of programme effectiveness. It is much easier to count how many people received training, how many asset declarations were filed and how many hotline calls were received. This echoes of the analogy of a man who lost his car keys in a dark alley but insists on only searching for them directly under the street lamp. Outcome measures would redirect attention to more appropriate concerns, such as whether public officials could apply ethical principles they learned to specific circumstances. What is needed is a much more nuanced approach that addresses the relationship between outputs *and* outcomes in order to get an effective understanding of the successes and vulnerabilities of ethics programmes.

Of the challenges mentioned above, lack of a standard, the disincentive to succeed (that is, an incentive not to uncover and/or publish ethical issues, particularly if solutions are not readily available), and over reliance on observable outputs all point to an important role for multilateral organizations. This chapter has identified only some of the key assessment strategies in use, but there remains an important gap between what is described here and a reliable plan of action for assessment. With the wide variance within integrity programmes it would be impossible to develop a set of standard measures. However, this problem does not preclude developing a framework that identifies the critical institutional elements of an ethics programme and examples of efficacious measures.

Recommendations

Ethics programmes seem to be struggling around the issue of effective evaluation. If they are to survive as deterrence systems, they must be able to demonstrate their efficacy. Multilaterals can provide a lifeline so that the organizational leaders, as well as the political leadership, can better understand how to measure impact, to distinguish success from failure. The potential role for multilaterals in this regard is multifold:

1 The first responsibility for a multilateral is to provide a primer for governments that describes legitimate methods for using secondary measures of performance of anti-corruption systems – their advantages and disadvantages. Until there is common acceptance of the advantages of such measures, they will never be put into place and, without them, there is little chance of evaluating the various elements of an integrity system.
2 Second, multilateral organizations can help to eliminate the dangerous misconception that integrity programmes cannot be accurately evaluated. In so doing they can help identify valid and reliable indirect measures thereby promoting the secondary measures as legitimate techniques for evaluating integrity systems.
3 Third, they can use this report as a starting point for developing a catalogue of effective evaluation techniques. Such a catalogue would emphasize that no 'one size fits all', yet programmes can learn from how other programmes have approached evaluation problems.
4 Next, there would be considerable value in creating evaluation instruments that can be modified for use in a variety of settings. Such instruments should contain concrete examples of evaluation frameworks for each of the elements of an integrity programme and explain interrelations between elements (for example, the importance of a code of conduct to inform effective reviews of asset declarations) as well as providing examples of surveys and aggregates analysis.
5 To accompany the above resources, it would be useful to provide an in-depth analysis of effective evaluation strategies along with case studies would allow others to learn the details programme evaluation elsewhere. For example, a systematic analysis of survey methodology intended for the assessment of an organization's ethical climate could allow organizations to learn from past successes and failures. Such an endeavour should highlight failed and ineffective methods of assessment by way of providing bureaucracies with a list of methods to avoid.

The goal would be to prepare a toolkit of evaluation instruments that could be modified for use in a variety of settings. This toolkit would include a discussion of how to determine which method is appropriate for each setting. For example, the Puerto Rico Public Servant Survey of 2003 is an excellent model for the evaluation of ethics in public service provision but may not be appropriate for a particular agency. Evaluation techniques will differ from programme to programme and agency to agency. A multilateral could play an important role in helping organizations navigate this decision-making process and providing model programmes for consideration.

Improving the value of integrity systems requires evaluation of their effectiveness, which, in turn requires willingness to self-evaluate, and the implementation of secondary methods of assessment. The OECD and other multilateral organizations have a singular and critical role to play in facilitating the sharing of information about successes and failures in integrity system assessment and providing a framework for implementation.

The OECD, among other multilateral organizations, has a unique position and capability to accomplish this. Because it has a finite set of members, most of which have robust integrity systems, it can easily develop the critical components discussed above. In addition, because of the existence of the SIGMA[28] (Support for Improvement in Governance and Management a joint initiatives of the OECD and the European Union, principally financed by the EU) programme, it can simultaneously use these newly developed integrity systems as laboratories for testing effective evaluation.

For a number of reasons citizens, governments, NGOs, and multinational organizations have an investment in the success of integrity programmes. They are the natural compliment to anti-corruption enforcement, and arguably effective enforcement cannot occur without an effective ethics programme. Knowing what is effective is the key here. And evaluation is the only way to open that door into insight.

For that reason, assessment should be a natural part of any integrity programme, but currently it is seldom the case. Multilaterals can provide the tools and the discipline to achieve this, and avoid the degeneration of these corruption prevention programmes. As attributed to Victor Hugo:

> He who every morning plans the transaction of the day and follows out that plan, carries a thread that will guide him through the maze of the most busy life. But where no plan is laid, where the disposal of time is surrendered merely to the chance of incidence, chaos will soon reign.

References

Coe, C.K. (2003), 'A Report Card on Report Cards', *Public Performance and Management Review* 27:2, 53–76.

---

28 See OECD/EU Support for Improvements in Governance and Management website, <http://www.sigmaweb.org>.

Commonwealth of Puerto Rico (2003), *Report to the Office of Government Ethics: 2003 Employee Ethics Survey* (Puerto Rico: Government of Puerto Rico).

Cooper, T.L. and Yoder, D.E. (2002), 'Public Management Ethics Standards in a Transnational World', *Public Integrity* 4:4, 333–52.

Gilman, S.C. (1999), 'Effective Management of Ethics Systems: Some New Frontiers', in V. Mavuso and D. Balia (eds) *Fighting Corruption: Invitation to Ethics Management* (Pretoria: Unisa Press).

Hermann, F. (1997), 'Bricks without Straw: The Plight of Government Agencies in the United States', *Public Integrity Annual*, 13–21.

KCELJAG/TI (2001), *Queensland National Integrity System Assessment Report* (Brisbane: KCELJAG/TI).

OECD (1996), 'Ethics in the Public Service: Current Issues and Practice. OECD', *Public Management Occasional Paper* 14.

OECD (1999), *Public Sector Corruption: An International Survey of Prevention Measures* (Paris: OECD).

OECD (2000), *Trust in Government: Ethics Measures in OECD Countries* (Paris: OECD).

OECD (2002a), *Public Sector Transparency and Accountability: Making it Happen* (Paris: OECD).

OECD (2002b; 2005), *Conflict of Interest in the Public Service* (Paris: OECD).

OECD (2003), *Managing Conflict of Interest in the Public Service: OECD Guidelines and Country Experiences* (Paris: OECD).

PSC News (2003/2004), 'Turning the Tide on Corruption', December/January.

Selby, A.M. and Baqwa, S.C. (2001), 'Anticorruption Efforts in South Africa', *The Journal of Public Inquiry* Fall/Winter, 21–24.

Chapter 14

Consequences, Capacity and Coherence: An Overall Approach to Integrity System Assessment

A.J. Brown and Brian W. Head

The assessment of an integrity system may draw upon a wide range of information relevant to whether the institutions and governance strategies that make up the integrity system are achieving their desired results and impacts. Unfortunately this information is often patchy and partial, and is not integrated in ways that support conclusive judgements about the performance of single institutions, let alone the system as a whole. This is an international problem, as shown by the OECD, whose surveys of member-countries' public sector ethics programmes provided extremely scant evidence when it came to hard performance assessment information (OECD 2000, 69–72). In this chapter we provide a summative approach to integrity system assessment by focusing on three key dimensions – consequences, capacity and coherence.

Consequences of an Integrity System

The 'consequences' or direct impacts of integrity systems are difficult to quantify. As in many areas of governance or public policy, it is not feasible to integrate all available information on the direct consequential impacts (or outputs) of integrity systems into one single 'model' for monitoring their behaviour – not in the same way, for example, that diverse economic indicators are often combined to evaluate the changing health of the economy.

The analysis of Australia's National Integrity System revealed that existing performance measurement regimes were fragmented and uncoordinated to an unnecessary and undesirable degree by comparison with other very complex and contestable areas of public policy. While the resulting analysis was necessarily limited, it supports no overall single assessment of the direct consequences of an integrity system, but instead points to strengths, opportunities and challenges in the methods by which consequences can be better measured and monitored on an ongoing basis. In all sectors, however, the development of more regular, agreed methods of monitoring the performance of integrity systems is clearly crucial to achieving smoother processes of institutional adaptation and adjustment, as well as counteracting the influence of *ad hoc* policy crises, scandals, and officeholders' shorter-term perceptions of their own self-interest in major decisions of integrity system design.

Evidence-based Tools to Monitor Effectiveness

One area of current strength of the Australian Integrity System is the extensive and regular use by some core public integrity agencies of evidence-based techniques for gaining thorough pictures of how particular ethics measures are being taken up in organizations, principally through employee surveys drawn from random representative samples. The NSW Independent Commission Against Corruption pioneered much of this work in the 1990s, and (along with the Queensland Crime and Misconduct Commission and WA Corruption and Crime Commission) has continued this research in the form of Public Sector Profiling and corruption risk assessment surveys. However, the most prominent recent example is the Australian Public Service Commission's Employee Surveys, complementing self-reporting by agencies with perceptions data from employee surveys, as part of its annual State of the Service Report (Uhr 2005b).

The particular importance of this work lies in the fact that social-science analysis of employee perceptions and experiences can provide a much more holistic and useful barometer of how integrity systems are working than, for example, tables of statistics on numbers of investigations launched, criminal or administrative charges laid, or successful criminal or disciplinary action. The latter data can be ambiguous – high numbers could indicate either a successful integrity system, in terms of investigative capacity and strength of the rule of law, or an unsuccessful system in terms of high incidence of offences, low ethical standards, and poor prevention. In Australia, numbers of criminal prosecutions for corruption are generally regarded as low, often provoking questions as to whether the cost of investigative bodies is justified, but paradoxically, this statistic is also a likely sign of overall success.

An important opportunity exists for supplementing empirical quantitative research into employee attitudes and experiences with greater qualitative ethnographic work involving the same individuals over time, rather than different random samples. Despite the difficulty of finding reliable measures, some of the most persuasive indications of progress in the NISA research came from asking agency representatives whether the handling of integrity issues was better or worse over time. In the New South Wales (NSW) study, 16 out of 18 agency respondents were satisfied that the NSW public sector had improved its handling of integrity issues over the past ten years, and this was true even of respondents who judged integrity issues to be badly handled (see Smith in this volume). Similarly, when the project asked a group of 28 senior integrity practitioners from across public and private fields to identify how well they thought integrity issues were handled, a substantial number thought things had improved (though much less for the private sector). Finally, the Australian study showed that all jurisdictions face the challenge of better coordinating and integrating such data with other measures, to provide a more holistic overview.

Public Feedback, Satisfaction and Trust Measures

A special strength in performance measurement for the overall integrity system lies in monitoring public awareness and satisfaction with key integrity services. Such research is used by a variety of core agencies including the Commonwealth Ombudsman, NSW ICAC, and Queensland CMC. Some agencies (such as the ICAC) also have advisory committees with public participation, a related feedback mechanism.

Whereas the proportion of substantiated complaints or investigations can have ambiguous implications, public attitudinal research can provide more objective, longitudinal benchmarks. For example, in the Commonwealth Ombudsman's third survey of past complainants in 1997, 50 per cent of respondent clients whose complaint had not been taken further by the office, indicated they found the office's decision unreasonable; up from the previous year, when 38 per cent had so indicated. This increase was seen as cause for 'significant concern' given the importance of the Ombudsman's reputation as an independent decision-maker (Commonwealth Ombudsman 1997, 95–9). By contrast in the year 2000, 78 per cent of those whose complaints the office had declined to investigate, still indicated that they would consider using the office in the future – a significant indication of confidence in the competence and impartiality of the office (Commonwealth Ombudsman 2000, 4).

Important opportunities exist for extending the use of such approaches across more agencies; developing more consistent methodologies for their conduct; and exploring more independent means of conducting such research. University-based research of direct relevance is provided by the Australian Survey of Social Attitudes (ASSA 2003), which could be extended to canvass public attitudes to all core integrity institutions, for example. What is most revealing is whether confidence increases or falls, and how this might be linked to possible causes. The opportunity exists to develop a much more comprehensive evaluation programme, including making better use of independent research of this kind.

Parliamentary Oversight Committees

Australia's public sector integrity systems include a major role for parliamentary committees whose main task is to oversight core integrity institutions, such as ombudsman's offices and anti-corruption commissions. Relatively recent examples include the NSW Parliamentary Committee on the Independent Commission Against Corruption; NSW Parliamentary Committee on the Office of the Ombudsman and the Police Integrity Commission; the Queensland Parliamentary Crime and Misconduct Committee (formerly Parliamentary Criminal Justice Committee); and the WA Joint Standing Committee on the Corruption and Crime Commission. In addition, all jurisdictions have a Public Accounts Committee that typically oversights Auditors-General, and these all have a long history. Such committees are also increasingly linked nationally through conferences (for example, WA Parliament 2003; Smith 2005). Parliamentary committees review integrity agencies' annual reports, and conduct hearings on their performance using reported outcomes, public or 'in camera' evidence given by the agencies, public submissions or complaints against the agencies, and research by parliamentary staff. These committees, therefore, function not only as a mutual accountability mechanism, but as a primary means by which society conducts a holistic and regular evaluation of the performance of key integrity bodies.

Activity and Efficiency Performance Measures

Integrity institutions and programmes have a variety of published activity and efficiency measures. However, at present, there is little consistency in the compilation of this data, sufficient to support meaningful comparative analysis. Variations in definitions, methods and data-collection limit their usefulness as measures of good or bad practice. Australian governments require the collection and publication of such information, but do not appear to use it to assess anything other than efficiency of past performance, which is itself subject to many variables.

A major opportunity exists to turn such data to more useful effect, albeit with substantial research and policy development needed to rationalize, standardize and expand the basic activity and efficiency measures applying to integrity bodies. Standardization is crucial before effective comparative analysis (one of the simplest evaluative tools) can be used to judge the relative performance of like bodies, and promote the identification and transfer of best practice. Expansion is needed to identify meaningful qualitative performance indicators, where this is possible. Such a revamped approach to performance evaluation may appear expensive and time-consuming to agencies with limited budgets, but compared to most areas of public policy in which comprehensive benchmarking is now regarded as unavoidable – for example, health and other social services – such an overhaul is, in reality, the minimum that should reasonably be required.

While some like agencies have engaged in discussions regarding common benchmarking, this reform is likely to require external triggers and independent research, as well as resource injections from outside. Accordingly, the need for strategic investment in the redevelopment of core agency activity and efficiency measures is an important issue.

Trust in Leadership

According to Dobel (1999, xii) the ultimate measure of the design and leadership of institutions is 'the quality of integrity and judgment that they produce', highlighting that the consequences of a well-functioning integrity system should include quality decisions and services. On one hand, integrity cannot be measured simply in terms of whether governments achieve their goals. Public integrity is a subject that will never lend itself to definitive performance measurement of the kind used in most areas of service delivery or reporting.

Overall, the most important consequences of effective integrity systems may relate to evolving features of civic participation, institutional cohesion and community well-being that are not easily measurable other than in highly qualitative or subjective ways over a long period of time. The best immediate surrogate for these may be a hybrid of public confidence and public trust. Although public confidence and trust are not 'catch-all' indicators of good governance (Bouckaert and Van de Walle 2003), they are, in some respects, the essential focus of integrity systems, given that citizens are forced 'as far as they can, to economize on trust in persons and confide instead in well-designed political, social, and economic institutions' (Dunn 1988/2000, 85–6).

The challenge is to develop ways to measure public confidence in the leadership of institutions that more accurately reflect both the value placed on integrity in our society and realistic expectations that it can be achieved. This challenge requires a new methodology for developing better overall indicators of these ultimate outcomes. This would be assisted if governments provided additional funding to allow their core public integrity agencies to collaborate in a joint long-term research programme into the optimum use of social science and other evidence-based research for evaluation of integrity system performance.

Fragmented Data Gathering

As the previous sections make clear, the information that is already available relating to integrity system performance is fragmented, not least because there have been few attempts to design and apply systematic and objective assessment methodologies. Most prominent evaluation efforts are still *ad hoc*, and sometimes driven by responses to scandals. Integrity institutions and practices are not sheltered from institutional politics, but are linked to the real-world policy and political environment. Reporting and evaluation by agencies are often flavoured by the perennial need to justify existing or requested resources. Anti-corruption bodies tend to survey public employees on issues of corruption perception and risk, whereas public service commissions tend to survey on awareness of positive codes of conduct and adherence thereto, without clear links between these two sides of the same coin. The task of developing a more systematic framework for regular, credible and publicly intelligible evaluation of the consequences of integrity systems is a larger challenge. Until major sources of information about the impacts of the integrity system are better integrated and larger gaps are filled, there can be no truly comprehensive assessment in any single jurisdiction or across jurisdictions. There is certainly scope for better research to monitor the effectiveness of a wider range of integrity system elements, both positive and enforcement-related.

In Australia as elsewhere, it is difficult to identify effective institutional champions to promote such an approach, which would entail a coherent, evidence-based evaluation framework. This gap could be filled by establishing governance review councils with wide ranging mandates and with a permanent secretariat to steer public reviews and compile reports. Membership could include core integrity institutions (Ombudsman, Auditor-General, anti-corruption commissioner, public service head, parliamentary standards commissioner, etc.), expert and community representation, and an independent chair.

The Capacity of Integrity Systems

The second theme of the assessment framework moves beyond the evidence of how integrity systems are performing, to examine evidence of gaps or deficiencies in the basic resources – 'capacities' – which the system needs to function. One of the most common conclusions of governance assessment approaches is that the jurisdiction or sector *appears* to possess the necessary institutional ingredients of a 'model' integrity system, but that these institutions are actually incapable of functioning effectively.

Even with the best intentions, governments may pass laws or establish institutions related to integrity, but not know how to guarantee them the necessary skills, financial resources or legal powers to have an impact. Even well-resourced institutions may fail if their strategies are not well-grounded in key elements of existing bureaucratic, business or public culture, or because their staff do not possess the necessary skills. All these problems raise issues of 'capacity' – ranging from institutional capacity in both 'core' and 'distributed' institutions, to broader social or community capacity in understanding and support for integrity processes. The key capacities in integrity systems include:

- Legal capacity. Are integrity institutions properly constituted, and do integrity institutions and practitioners have the formal powers or jurisdiction they need to fulfil their tasks?
- Financial capacity. Are the budgets of integrity institutions right for their tasks, and is the right share of financial resources across society and within organizations being devoted to integrity functions?
- Human resource capacity. Are sufficient numbers of employees dedicated to integrity functions either in core institutions or distributed among organizations?
- Skills, education and training. Do integrity practitioners or staff in general have the right professional training and background to discharge their important roles?
- Political/community will. Do senior political and business officeholders possess, or are they sufficiently empowered by the community to find, the will to provide genuine leadership in integrity matters?
- Community capacity. Is there sufficient broader social or community understanding and support for integrity processes?
- Balance. Are financial, human, legal and management resources being directed adequately to both 'positive' strategies, such as effective leadership training, and 'negative' enforcement strategies such as criminal investigations?

A number of significant strengths, opportunities and challenges in key areas of financial, legal and human resource capacity may be readily identified.

Financial Accountability

For integrity systems in all jurisdictions, strong financial accountability processes play a cornerstone role. This is not least because they permeate the entire sector, with no institution or officeholder beyond their reach – even when other integrity strategies remain patchy, fragmented, or limited in their application to groups of officials or elected leaders. Financial accountability processes thus also provide some of the major 'glue' holding basic elements of the integrity system together. Financial accountability includes robust systems for fraud control, auditing of expenditures, probity in procurement systems, investigation and prosecutorial capacity and high quality reporting.

Ethics and Enforcement Frameworks

The second area of strong capacity lies in the introduction by most governments of comprehensive legislated ethics regimes, including both ethical standard-setting and enforcement dimensions. Current ethics regimes in Australia, developed in the 1990s period of 'new public management', emphasize devolution of responsibility for values-based governance to individual agencies and their management. The assessment has confirmed the pivotal importance of the overarching legislative framework within which this occurs, providing requirements and incentives for ethical standard-setting processes to be embedded, including minimum standards and frameworks of enforceability through codes of conduct adapted to agencies' individual missions and circumstances. One of the clearest strengths of such frameworks is their comprehensiveness, providing a better overall articulation of the values and principles that should guide *all* public officers, irrespective of their specific roles – for example the Queensland *Public Sector Ethics Act 1994*.

Paralleling the extension of these 'positive' ethics frameworks, a matching strength is the extension of more comprehensive compliance (or investigation and enforcement) frameworks. In some Australian jurisdictions, *all* public officials are now covered by statutory definitions of corruption or official misconduct, irrespective of their particular role, as well as subject to relevant investigative agencies (New South Wales ICAC and Queensland Crime and Corruption Commission). Applicable definitions of wrongdoing are not restricted to criminal behaviour but take public service values, duty and trust (or breach thereof) as more comprehensive points of reference for independent review and action. This approach contrasts with 'traditional' but fragmented models in which ombudsman's offices can investigate administrative wrongdoing by appointed officials, but not elected ones; any other forms of ethical breach and any breach by elected officials must effectively transgress criminal thresholds to be independently investigated or actioned.

Resources for Core Investigation Agencies

The effective working of public integrity systems relies not only on having a comprehensive legislative approach to ethics and enforcement, but also on ensuring core investigation agencies have the basic financial and human resources to perform their tasks (Brown and Head 2005). Benchmarks for adequately resourcing these core integrity functions remain undeveloped. Suitable benchmarks could be found if further policy and financial analysis was undertaken through an appropriate public review process and linked with a standardized approach to understanding agency caseloads.

The Australian study showed the value of a more coordinated strategy of skills and career development for current and prospective staff in the integrity system. Not only are administrative and anti-corruption investigations complex and delicate by nature, but increasingly the positive problem-solving and management roles of integrity practitioners are being recognized. Interdisciplinary postgraduate or vocational training in key areas of integrity practice is currently limited. There is a clear opportunity for a strategy to grow and consolidate advanced skills.

Corporatization and Contracting Out

All jurisdictions face difficulties ensuring integrity and accountability in the delivery of public services in areas restructured through corporatization and contracting-out, with some attendant risks for agency oversight. Contracting-out also poses identifiable integrity risks within the private sector, due to agency incapacity and lengthened supply chains. Despite increased efficiency and responsiveness, corporatized and out-sourced services since the late 1980s have been characterized by significant accountability 'gaps'. However, the only real reason why public integrity oversight often still stops at the point of contracting-out is an outdated formulation of integrity agency jurisdiction based on the legal character of the organization as a commercial entity, rather than the public nature of its services. In relation to government-owned corporations (GOCs), there should be no doubt that when it comes to the 'fundamental choice' needed on questions of governance, accountability and ethical behaviour, 'we must treat GOCs as if they were public entities' (Bottomley 2003). Increasingly, there is little reason to differentiate between the basic integrity standards and strategies needing to be employed by public and private service providers (see Demack 2003, 12).

The solution adopted by some jurisdictions is to extend core public integrity institutions' jurisdictions to include discretion to investigate complaints into publicly-funded services regardless of provider. While other responses exist, including industry-specific integrity mechanisms (for example, industry ombudsman's offices), these responses do not provide universal coverage of contracted services and particularly where industry-controlled such responses can appear compromized. Such mechanisms also do not typically extend to programmes funded by government grants, rather than contract.

Devolved Governance

Beyond the 'core' audit and investigation capacities, ethical leadership and problem-solving capacities need to be embedded in the everyday management systems of all organizations. These 'distributed' and devolved capacities are obviously vital in all organizations, across the government, business and civil society sectors. Although integrity-focused legislative frameworks are a strength of many present Australian systems, many issues surround how effectively these frameworks currently play out at organizational levels. More research is needed into the level of financial and human resources devoted to ethical standard-setting, education, prevention and the institutionalization of integrity, as against the more expensive response processes involved in the investigation and remediation of integrity breaches. There is also need for more effective coordination between 'core' and 'distributed' institutions. A major opportunity exists to better institutionalize ethical leadership capacities in the everyday management of organizations, by formally embedding these capacities in the career structure of managers through recruitment and appointment processes. Basic management processes often do little to help organizations 'walk the talk'. If governments, regulators and organizational leaders are serious about ensuring that integrity is core business in organizations, it is time for public agencies and larger businesses and civil society organizations to require staff to complete accredited training in integrity, accountability and ethics as a prerequisite for appointment to middle and senior management levels. Formalising integrity education and training standards is one of the few effective ways for organizations to ensure a heightened integrity capacity and clarity about management standards.

A particular structural deficiency in distributed integrity capacity across the public sector is in the area of local and regional governance. In Australia, local government has traditionally been under-resourced, constraining the extent to which local democratic systems have been able to realize high standards of integrity. Commonwealth and state governments should fund a comprehensive review by Australian local government of the most effective framework for building integrity system capacity at the local and regional levels of government, recognising the historic under-resourcing of local government, the growing responsibilities of local government in the Australian federal system, and the increasing complexity of regional-level public institutions.

Parliamentary Leadership and Integrity

Several areas of challenge arose from our assessment of integrity system capacity. In the public sector, the first and most striking challenge is the lack of effective ethical standard-setting and enforcement regimes governing elected parliamentarians and ministers. Whereas oversight and enforcement capacities are typically strong in relation to appointed officials, they are weaker in relation to elected ones. Most public jurisdictions and much of the corporate sector in Australia now function under statutory schemes requiring development of enforceable codes of conduct or statements of official responsibilities, but the development of legislative and ministerial ethics regimes has been 'a saga of avoidance, delay, resistance and doubt' (Preston 2001). The Commonwealth parliament's system, in which 'neither house has a code of ethics or conduct, and there is no move towards an ethics or integrity commissioner' is one of 'puzzling self-regulation' (Uhr 2005a, 147). This lack of enforceable parliamentary and ministerial standards contrasts strongly with the systems in place for other public officials and most private sector officeholders.

At the state level, New South Wales, Victoria, Western Australia, Queensland and the Australian Capital Territory had a code of conduct for members and ministers (Parliamentary Research Service 2006). While all had interest disclosure regimes, these contained deficiencies. The most significant problem is the lack of any real enforcement capacity in relation to any of these regimes. Better practice is found in Queensland and NSW, which have both ethics advisors (but with no enforcement role), and integrity agencies whose coverage may include a 'substantial breach of an applicable code of conduct' by parliamentarians (NSW ICAC) or official misconduct by parliamentarians (Queensland CMC).

While traditionally legislators have argued that their accountability to the ballot-box and ongoing scrutiny from electors and the media are sufficient, attempts to rely on such mechanisms for continual assurance in integrity matters is now widely recognized as inadequate. While it can be argued that positive advisory implementation capacities remain important (Sampford 2001), it is clear that leaving enforcement to the legislature itself without avenues for public complaint has become a 'deficiency that needs to be remedied if there is to be any improvement in the level of public confidence in the integrity of the parliamentary system' (Carney 2000, 396). A comprehensive overhaul of these regimes is crucial to addressing lack of public confidence in parliamentary and ministerial self-regulation. Such reform would also function to restore the degree of effective accountability of the executive government to the parliament. This is achievable through boosting the independence and authority of parliaments' presiding officers, as well as parliamentary rather than executive control over the gazettal of codes and appointment of a commissioner to investigate possible breaches, including secondary employment and other non-official interests; post-separation or post-retirement employment of ministers (Holland 2002); abuse of parliamentary privilege; abuse of cabinet privilege in respect of documents requested under FOI; and honesty in public statements.

Whistleblower Protection

A further challenge lies in the restricted capacity of Australian integrity systems to make full use of one of their most important assets – the ethical standards and professionalism of those employees prepared to speak up about integrity breaches that would otherwise go uncorrected ('whistleblowers'). Whistleblowing is a fundamental resource for the integrity system; organizations' capacity to manage whistleblowers positively and encourage further reporting of wrongdoing by others is vital (McMillan 1994; Brown 2001; Brown et al. 2004). The implementation of even a simple public sector whistleblower protection regime is sometimes questioned, and the Commonwealth's scheme has been identified as completely inadequate (Dempster 1997; Martin 1997; De Maria 1999). Within the Australian public sector, there are substantial differences across state and territory regimes; and no single government has currently achieved what would constitute 'best practice'. In 2005, a consortium of 13 public integrity agencies and Transparency International Australia commenced a major research project into the development of more effective approaches to whistleblower protection within organizations, legislative frameworks, and coordination between core and distributed integrity institutions (see www.griffith.edu.au/whistleblowing).

Civic Education, Awareness and Rights

A vital component of integrity systems is the level of citizens' awareness, vigilance and legal capacity to seek the rectification of wrongs – whether against themselves personally or in relation to the broader public interest. Australian citizens feel a strong sense of duty to participate directly in the governance of their institutions, as reflected in arrangements for compulsory electoral enrolment and voting; with the positive effect that even when critical of official conduct, citizens nevertheless remain engaged in the governance process (Goot 2002).

Four signs of weakness in these vital areas of capacity have been identified. The first of these is the low level of civic and community education about the importance of integrity in the institutions that govern society. The lack of effective civic education in primary and secondary schooling became widely acknowledged in the 1990s (Krinks 1999), and much more needs to be done besides a few recent curriculum reform initiatives. There is also a need for the engagement of public interest groups and independent experts in the design of community awareness programmes about citizens' rights. The second major problem relates to gradual curtailment of the effective legal capacity of citizens to challenge government actions that affect them personally or conflict with the public interest. Significant liberalization of the ability of citizens to challenge government actions occurred in the 1970s–1980s, with the introduction of the 'new administrative law', but despite empirical evidence that judicial review of administrative action is effective, commitment to the philosophy of such review has somewhat lost its original impetus (Creyke and McMillan 1998). For example, the Australian government ministers have attacked such systems as harbouring a 'grievance industry' rather than supporting an integrity regime (Mulgan and Uhr 2001, 162). Over several years, the rights of non-citizens to equitable levels of administrative justice have been curtailed. More incrementally, issues of cost, access to justice, and limited availability of formal 'merits review' systems already mean that, for most Australians, even in less contentious areas, administrative justice is more difficult to attain. Citizens' civil and political rights are not buttressed by constitutional or legislative protection through a Bill of Rights. There is a need for substantial renewal of Australian systems for citizen-initiated review of government action.

The third area of concern relates to citizens' rights to know about interests that could reasonably be expected to influence the conduct of officials. The classic example of this problem lies in disclosure of electoral contributions, which typically does not occur until *after* the election concerned, by which time electors have already cast their vote based on incomplete knowledge. It is time to systematically overhaul disclosure regimes to satisfy the goal of up-to-date knowledge of disclosed interests on the part of those who need to know. The final challenge relating to citizen awareness concerns freedom of information (FOI). A recent Australian Public Service Commissioner has strongly questioned whether Commonwealth practices and attitudes are consistent with the express principle that FOI legislation should be interpreted to extend, 'as far as possible, the right of the Australian community to access information held by the Government' (Podger 2005). Achieving this principle necessitates higher standards of recordkeeping; curtailing the practice of formal FOI applications when it is readily within the discretion of administrators to simply release documents; abandoning exemptions based on 'classes' of records rather than actual contents; and reversing the present onus on applicants to challenge non-release (of records they cannot see) to ensure instead that non-release is justifiable in the eyes of an umpire who can see them.

Electoral Integrity and Political Parties

A major challenge lies in the capacity of Australia's integrity systems to ensure honesty and accountability within civil society organizations which play important roles in the good governance of society – the key example of organizations that are not well regulated is political parties. They have largely retained their historical status as private organizations, but their interrelationship with – and often control over – the workings of government give them a different and sensitive status in political practice. Political parties now draw on substantial public funding; a feature that arose as an integrity mechanism to curtail the need for parties to raise ever-larger amounts of private money. However, parties in receipt of public funds are not limited in the amounts or sources of private money that they can solicit; nor are they obliged to account in detail for how this money is expended. Candidate pre-selection and other party processes are also subject to limited scrutiny. There is a case for 'more interventionist and vigilant' regulatory approaches, and removal of responsibility for some key 'public interest' processes from their control (Orr 1999; Tully 2003).

Private Sector Regulatory Capacity

Analysis of 'public' integrity systems should extend beyond its traditional focus on government institutions, to all organizations with publicly-significant duties including those of business boards to shareholders, investors, consumers and fellow citizens. Previously, some governance reformers have assumed that the main relevance of the business sector to integrity systems was as one 'pillar' of public sector integrity in its own right (Langseth et al. 1999, 145; Pope 2000, 137–51), rather than as a group of institutions whose own integrity is often at issue (Brown and Uhr 2004, 7).). If there was any doubt regarding Australians' attitudes to this, it is dispelled by public opinion surveys which show relatively low levels of confidence in business integrity and indeed in the public regulation of business (for example, Bean 2005). Similar critical issues arise in relation to the mass media, which can play vital roles in ensuring integrity on the part of other institutions in society, but which themselves face ethical challenges and need to be governed by integrity regimes of their own (Johnson 2000; Gordon-Smith 2002; Sampford and Lui 2004). As mentioned in Chapter 6, business integrity systems also include a diversity of core integrity institutions whose roles and capacities could not be evaluated in this assessment. It is, nevertheless, important that the kinds of analysis conducted above in relation to public institutions are extended in further analysis of the business sector, and in the integrity regimes governing particular areas of business.

The Coherence of Australia's Integrity Systems

The third and final theme of the assessment is that of 'coherence'. It is now widely established that integrity systems rely not on single key institutions or laws, but on a diversity of agencies, strategies and measures, working in a mutually supportive fashion. The OECD's proposed assessment framework has also adopted the NISA approach and poses the final question: 'do the various elements of integrity policy coherently interact and enforce each other, and collectively support the overall aims of integrity policy?' (OECD 2004, 10).

Until recently, however, little attention has been given to how different elements of integrity systems *should* interact, given there are also occasions on which we expect them to conflict or work independently. When should integrity institutions stand apart, holding each other mutually accountable? When can their operations be more collaborative? How are 'core' and 'distributed' functions coordinated, and integration achieved between ethical leadership, enforcement and practical day-to-day management?

The first lesson of the analysis is that integrity systems involve quite different types of interrelationships between institutions, all working at the same time in an intricate network, 'lattice' or 'bird's nest'. A strong degree of coherence is fundamental to integrity systems' endurance and relative success. In most integrity systems there are significant gaps in the way in which these systems operate. Such gaps present a range of choices for the future. Even in areas of strong coherence, unless the opportunities to renew and build on these strengths are taken, there are reasons to be concerned for the long-term vitality of the systems. There are also a number of key challenges confronting the coherence of integrity systems, some revealing potentially deep fractures in the nation's ethical and accountability frameworks. While there is a natural element of 'messiness' in the operation of any integrity system, our overall conclusion is that integrity systems are often more chaotic and less coherent than is desirable, and that significant improvements could be achieved through relatively straightforward reforms.

Reinforcing Mutual Accountability

The first matter for commentary involves the extent to which the principle of mutual accountability at the heart of the integrity system has become more accepted. Much of the public debate concerning effective oversight has been expressed in terms of 'who guards the guards'. In several instances, this question has been answered through reliance on the judiciary's conventional powers of judicial review of the legality of actions taken by other government bodies. Key agencies are 'independent' in their exercise of statutory powers, but not 'unaccountable' in that the legality of their action remains reviewable by another independent institution (the courts). The breadth of such powers is ultimately a matter for parliament which may alter the framework but only through a public process for which legislators can be held accountable by the electorate.

In addition to the core investigation and review agencies, a wider range of key custodians of different integrity processes are now recognized as 'independent' (but still 'accountable') actors in the integrity system. Not all can be mapped here, but a key example is that of statutory electoral commissions. As recently as 20 years ago, some governments in Australia still determined parliamentary electoral boundaries and regulated the administration of elections through temporary commissions and other administrative processes under a high degree of political influence. Today, the independence of permanent electoral commissions is increasingly well-institutionalized, even if, at a federal level, there is potential for 'nibbling at the edge' (Hughes 2003).

The federal political system divides and constrains power in various ways, leading to circumstances where both federal and state governments may hold each other to public account. In terms of integrity systems, the fact that each federal and state jurisdiction has room to develop its own approach contributes indirectly to the integrity systems of others through demonstration of new approaches or competition in standards. Similar analysis of 36 different State Ethics Commissions in the United States has shown that the diffusion and adaptation of ideas is probably unavoidable (Smith 2003). In Australia, however, the advantages of this diversity have not precluded the benefits of significant national coherence, for example in the recent but increasing coordination of research and policy activity between state integrity agencies (for example, NSW ICAC, Queensland CMC, and WA Corruption and Crime Commission).

The practices of mutual accountability continue to evolve as much through conflict as through harmony; and while some key institutions may gain new independence, others may gradually lose it. For example, the traditionally independent judiciary has come under increased criticism from both legislators in general and the political executive in particular – even at the level of Australia's highest court (Patapan 2000). The revival of tensions has called into question a range of old relationships such as the traditional role of Attorneys-General (Justice Ministers) acting both as first law officers, and therefore as constitutional servants of the court, as well as government ministers. Related debates have emerged about the need for transparency in areas such as the use of judges in administrative roles and the mechanisms by which the executive make judicial appointments.

Questions remain about how mutual accountability is best institutionalized. The 'constitutionalisation' of a broader range of agencies is probably justified (as implied by Spigelman 2004), but this is not appropriate for all such agencies, and their needs may change over time. Australian practice confirms the understanding of contemporary mutual accountability to be a dynamic and unfolding story.

Parliamentary Oversight Committees

A second, more specific strength in the system of mutual accountability can be more readily identified. Special-purpose parliamentary committees have taken on an increasingly important role as both a performance assessment mechanism, and as an accountability mechanism standing at the interface between the newer 'core' integrity agencies, the parliament, the executive, and the public (see Smith 2005). While the roles of these committees may be defined as much by conflict as harmony, their place in the institutional framework ensures their deliberations are public, guaranteeing some transparency in the resolution of these conflicts.

Moreover, in receiving the reports and reviewing the performance of integrity agencies, parliamentary committees play a fundamental role in helping ensure the policy and operational coherence of the integrity system by also supporting these agencies' work. As well as providing critical review of integrity agencies, parliamentary committees often also identify or support their needs for additional resources or for legislative reform, and make it considerably more difficult for issues of operational importance to the integrity system to be ignored by executive government.

The role of parliamentary committees in strengthening integrity system coherence could be further improved. First, the review methodologies used by such committees could be made more coherent. Second, while oversight committees' deliberations are public, there is a role for the more structured use of *direct* public consultative mechanisms. These would assist in performance assessment and also enhance the transparency of the oversight process, for example, by creating another point of debate over how the performance of agencies should be judged. Third, there are significant gaps in the use of such committees for identifying where the integrity system lacks overall coherence. The most noticeable example is at a Commonwealth level where special-purpose joint parliamentary committees help in routine oversight of the Australian National Audit Office, Australian Electoral Commission, Australian Crime Commission, and Australia's security services; but it is left to general-purpose committees (usually the Senate Standing Committee on Finance and Public Administration) to occasionally review the role of the Commonwealth Ombudsman.

Relations Between Core and Distributed Integrity Institutions

The third area of clear strength in current integrity systems lies in the policy and operational coherence embedded in many jurisdictions' linkages between the roles of core integrity institutions and the distributed integrity functions lying with individual agencies. While the number and importance of core 'independent' regulatory and oversight agencies have increased, across both public and private sector integrity systems, it is well-established that bigger and better 'watchdog' agencies will never alone ensure high levels of integrity. The institutionalization of integrity is dependent on positive leadership across agencies and the ability of management to set and maintain appropriate ethical standards with the participation of staff, clients and the general public. While Australian integrity systems rely, in part, on core agencies with strong legal powers of investigation and oversight, in practice, the role of central agencies is at least as important as a supportive resource for those working in organizations to achieve coordinated outcomes 'on the ground' as agents of regulation and enforcement.

Best practice now involves principles of continuous disclosure, in which agency managers, notwithstanding their primary responsibility for the ethical culture of their own organization, should report all significant integrity issues or problems to 'core' agencies, to ensure effective decisions are made about solutions. Similarly, in some circumstances – such as whistleblower protection – the lack of clear statutory coordination in some jurisdictions has allowed doubts about the effective implementation of legislation to persist unaddressed for years. In some settings, the core-distributed relationship and its associated balance of approaches has worked in too cyclical a fashion, with strong regulation overshadowing managerial discretion in response to 'scandal' or 'crises', then largely withdrawn in order to 'let the managers manage'. An ongoing balance requires coordinated communication between integrity agencies and organizations in relation to individual integrity issues, systemic issues and the information needed by organizations and core agencies alike to monitor ethical climates over time. The opportunity for enabling legislation to better institutionalize constructive relationships between core institutions and organizational systems is required.

Parliamentary Leadership and Integrity

In principle, the integrity of ministerial (executive) action is ensured by the executive's accountability to parliament, and the integrity of ministers and parliamentarians alike is ensured by their accountability to 'the people'. In practice, the ability of 'the people' to hold their elected officials to account simply through an election every three or four years, means this constitutional relationship is attenuated. For this, arguably the most fundamental dimension of the integrity system to work, there must also be mechanisms to ensure that appropriate parliamentary and executive standards are set and maintained, and that alleged integrity breaches can be investigated and publicly reported upon, even when it might be in the perceived self-interest of all political parties to let the truth languish. The absence of comprehensive parliamentary integrity regimes can also have a debilitating effect on other parts of the integrity system if political leaders are not prepared to subject themselves to the same or equivalent integrity processes as other public officials.

Parliamentary Inquiries and Executive Accountability

The related challenge focuses more directly on executive accountability to parliament. The core principle of Westminster accountability is that the executive sits in parliament in order to remain accountable to it, not in order to control all parliamentary business (by virtue of its control of the lower house). However, the practical effects of executive control are widely recognized throughout Westminster systems. In Australia, there has been a series of deliberate strategies at Commonwealth level to strengthen the position of the executive *vis-à-vis* parliament and the public service (Weller 1989; Russell 2002).

There is also a countervailing trend, where politically feasible, for non-government-controlled upper houses and/or multi-party committees to initiate parliamentary inquiries even when this may be unpalatable to the government of the day. Principles of mutual accountability suggest that all parliamentarians should have some facility to use parliamentary powers to contribute directly to executive accountability, other than through the simple power to ask questions. Best practice would involve entrenching the availability of select parliamentary committees to play a stronger more independent role in the initiation of inquiries, thus encouraging bipartisanship in the conduct of parliamentary business and reducing the control of the Executive over such inquiries.

Ministers, Ministerial Advisors and the Public Service

A third challenge involves the current effectiveness of principles of mutual accountability to oversight ministers. This issue has been exacerbated by the increased numbers and roles of ministerial staff over the past 30 years, and increased powers of ministers (and staff) vis-à-vis the employment arrangements and relative independence of senior public servants. Ministerial staff are an important part of the accountability chain (Walter 1986; Maley 2000). However, at a federal level, the perceived integrity of this arrangement appears to have been substantially damaged, with the 'Children Overboard' affair in 2001 revealing that providing information to ministerial staff is no longer regarded as informing the minister, because ministers do not take responsibility for whether or not their staff passed on the information. The question has thus arisen whether these are now 'staff who can act on their own behalf, who can be disowned if necessary and who are not accountable to parliament ... the first steps down a path that leads to Haldeman and Ehrlichman, plausible deniability and the Nixon Whitehouse' (Russell 2002; Weller 2002; Tiernan and Weller 2003). Two Senate committees, the Australian Public Service Commission and others have suggested the need for a discrete code of conduct for ministerial staff, but this has been opposed by government Senators (Keating 2003, 94).

This failure is also linked with concerns that governments may not be keen to receive fully informed, frank or fearless advice from the public service (Uhr 2005a), and increasingly likely to use powers of direct appointment and dismissal over senior public servants. While there is no simple answer to questions as to whether public service 'responsiveness' has increased as a result of such powers, there is a problem 'not that the public service has been politicized in a partisan sense' but that public servants have been 'politically inept in an advisory sense... too keen to serve, and not sufficiently sceptical and alert to warn' (Weller 2002, 68–70). Some restoration of procedures to protect senior public servants from arbitrary dismissal has been suggested (Keating 2003, 95–7).

The roles of ministerial staff need to be tied back to their ministers and included in ministerial codes of conduct; and principles governing minimum due process should be followed by ministers in the event of disagreement leading to termination of senior officers. These matters could be appropriate subjects for the ministerial code – with the enforcement mechanism being the risk of public inquiry and exposure.

Coordination Between Core Integrity Agencies

With an increasing number of agencies playing 'core' roles in integrity, issues of coherence in policy and operational areas are important, and not only the issues of mutual accountability set out above. Within Australia, each jurisdiction has a different history and approach regarding policy and operational coordination.

For example, in Queensland the modern integrity system emerged from a comprehensive reform programme linked through the principles articulated by the Fitzgerald Inquiry and developed in more detail by the Electoral and Administrative Review Commission (EARC). However, there was fragmentation between some reforms from the outset, while others crept in at implementation. The winding-up of the EARC pursuant to its 'sunset' provisions left no clear institutional coordination mechanism. More recently, the challenge of better policy and operational coordination has been met by an 'Integrity Committee' comprising the Ombudsman, Auditor-General, Chair of the Crime and Misconduct Commission, Public Service Commissioner, and Parliamentary Integrity Commissioner. This committee has no formal basis, no fixed rules, and rarely comes to public notice (for example, Parnell 2004). Nevertheless, in the absence of any other significant mechanism, it is crucial to coordination of some of the activities of key bodies. In June 2005, in response to the draft NISA report, key Western Australian integrity agencies formed a similar 'Integrity Coordinating Group' (ICG). While also informal, this group adopted more explicit terms of reference. It is supported by an interagency working party, has publicized its own existence across the public sector, and has adopted a work programme based around key issues of operational coordination. In New South Wales, the development of core integrity institutions has been the most ad hoc, with successive criticisms of previous institutions leading to new ones. The result has been a proliferation of bodies with clear and distinct problems of coordination, including jurisdictional gaps, 'buck-passing' between organizations, increased 'gaming' or 'forum-shopping' by complainants, confusion in the eyes of citizens and end-users, and alienation of line agencies having to contend with multiple requirements and investigations. Thus a proliferation of integrity organizations does not necessarily guarantee higher 'capacity' overall. Nevertheless, the challenges of coherence demonstrated in NSW have also now provoked a very high level of informal cooperation and coordination between key agencies, if only from sheer necessity. While largely dependent on personal networks, a level of operational coherence has been achieved which appears to largely meet the needs of most agencies.

The Commonwealth public integrity system (Chapter 8), which governs Australia's fourth-largest public sector in employee terms, has had a different history again. Its core integrity investigation agencies have not multiplied in the same way as Queensland or NSW, at least until now. Commonwealth decisions regarding whether or how to expand the integrity system through creation of a new anti-corruption body have thrown up new challenges about policy and operational coherence, not necessarily all being comprehensively addressed. Issues such as the limited reach of the *Public Service Act*, APS Values, and Code of Conduct regimes, also suggest that a level of coherence which may have existed in previous eras of Commonwealth public management is often still assumed to exist, when in fact the nature of restructuring in the 1980s–1990s has made the integrity system quite fragmented. Financial accountability and fraud control regimes have played a stronger role in making the system operationally coherent than in other jurisdictions, but these are not necessarily integrated with other measures, and suffer some of their own coherence questions. While the effects of this fragmentation are difficult to directly gauge, and considerable institutional effort is still going into integrity-related strategies, the Commonwealth's integrity systems are, arguably, the least coherent in Australia in policy and operational terms.

At the same time, one of the stronger elements of the Commonwealth integrity system in recent history – the 'new administrative law' – also provides the nation's strongest institutional mechanism of policy and operational coherence. In the 1980s–1990s, many state integrity reforms drew on the 'new administrative law' reforms previously initiated by the Commonwealth in the 1970s–1980s, such as codifying and liberalising judicial review of administrative action, creating general-purpose merits review tribunals, and freedom of information (FoI). This alternative and earlier Commonwealth focus included a statutory policy coordination mechanism in the form of the Administrative Review Council. While the focus is on legal, quasi-legal and rights-based mechanisms of administrative review, in practice, it is the nearest thing to a Commonwealth integrity coordination mechanism, with a considerably stronger statutory basis and existence than any state mechanism.

Concluding Comments

We have seen that a variety of mechanisms have been developed for achieving policy and operational coherence across, or at least in major parts of, public integrity systems, confirming the significance of the coordination challenge. While informal committees and networks have natural advantages, the importance of integrity and of integrity system coherence are such that policy and operational coordination should not be left to chance, the changing enthusiasms of individual agencies, or the personal rapport that may or may not exist between individual agency heads. Among the most important policy issues requiring coordination in principle and practice are the research, performance measurement, capacity-building and capacity-sharing needs. Among the most important operational issues are the public's interest in more seamless and user-friendly complaint services, outreach and community education, shared information, research and intelligence, and better coordination of integrity policies at the 'coalface' of public sector management by better integrating and simplifying the diverse accountabilities imposed on individual public servants by the integrity regime.

Together, the experiences point to the need for governments to build and consolidate on the coherence of their integrity systems by establishing a statutory coordination body akin to the Commonwealth's Administrative Review Council, but with the broadened focus and membership of a 'governance' review council. By taking this opportunity, governments can bypass ongoing debate over whether there should be greater consolidation or pluralist dispersion of accountability mechanisms. The establishment of statutory 'governance review councils' would permit further expansion in specialist integrity agencies if required, even in jurisdictions which already possess multiple agencies, while still containing and compensating for the practical disadvantages of fragmentation. The largest apparent challenge is the lack of formal or 'whole of government' support for a coherent system.

References

ASSA (2003), *Australian Survey of Social Attitudes Dataset 2003* (Canberra: Australian Social Science Data Archive, Research School of Social Sciences, Australian National University), available at <http:\\assda.anu.edu.au>.

Bean, C. (2005), 'Is There a Crisis of Trust in Australia?', in S. Wilson, G. Meagher, R. Gibson and M. Western (eds) *Australian Social Attitudes: The First Report* (Sydney: UNSW Press).

Bottomley, S. (2003), 'Comments', in M.J. Whincop (ed.) *From Bureaucracy to Business Enterprise: Legal and Policy Issues in the Transformation of Government Services* (Aldershot: Ashgate).

Bouckaert, G. and Walle, S. van de (2003), 'Comparing Measures of Citizen Trust and User Satisfaction as Indicators of "Good Governance": Difficulties in Linking Trust and Satisfaction Indicators', *International Review of Administrative Sciences* 69:3, 329–43.

Brown, A.J. (2001), 'Internal Witness Management: An Art or a Science?', *Ethics and Justice* 3:2, 45–61.

Brown, A.J., Magendanz D. and Leary, C. (2004), *Speaking Up: Creating Positive Reporting Climates in the Queensland Public Sector* (Brisbane, Queensland: Crime and Misconduct Commission, Capacity Building No. 6).

Brown, A.J. and Head, B.W. (2005), 'Institutional Capacity and Choice in Australia's Integrity Systems', *Australian Journal of Public Administration*, 64:2, 84–95.

Carney, G. (2000), *Members of Parliament: Law and Ethics* (Sydney: Prospect).

Commonwealth Ombudsman (1997), *Annual Report 1996–1997* (Canberra: Office of the Commonwealth Ombudsman, Commonwealth of Australia).

Commonwealth Ombudsman (2000), *Annual Report 1999–2000* (Canberra: Office of the Commonwealth Ombudsman, Commonwealth of Australia).

Creyke, R. and McMillan, J. (eds) (1998), *The Kerr Visions of Australian Administrative Law – At the 25 Year Mark* (Canberra: Australian Institute of Administrative Law).

Demack, A. (2003), *Queensland Integrity Commissioner: Annual Report to the Premier* (Brisbane: Office of the Queensland Integrity Commissioner, Queensland Government).

De Maria, W. (1999), *Deadly Disclosures: Whistleblowing and the Ethical Meltdown of Australia* (Sydney: Wakefield Press).

Dempster, Q. (1997), *Whistleblowers* (Sydney: ABC Books).

Department of Parliament Library (Cth) (2006), *Codes of Conduct in Australian and Some Overseas Parliaments*, E-brief 19 July, available at <http:// www.aph.gov.au/library/ intguide/ POL/CodeConduct.htm>.

Dobel, J.P. (1999), *Public Integrity* (Baltimore, MD: Johns Hopkins University Press).

Dunn, J. (1988/2000), 'Trust and Political Agency', in D. Gambetta (ed.) *Trust: Making and Breaking Cooperative Relations* (Oxford: Basil Blackwell 1988); electronic edition 2000 Department of Sociology, University of Oxford, <http://www.sociology.ox.ac.uk/papers>, 73–93.

Goot, M. (2002), 'Distrustful, Disenchanted and Disengaged? Public Opinion on Politics, Politicians and the Parties: An Historical Perspective', in D. Burchell and A. Leigh (eds) *The Prince's New Clothes: Why Do Australians Dislike Their Politicians?* (Sydney: University of NSW Press).

Gordon-Smith, M. (2002), 'Media Ethics After "Cash for Comment"', in S. Cunningham and G. Turner (eds) *The Media and Communications in Australia* (Sydney: Allen and Unwin).

Holland, I. (2002), *Post-Separation Employment of Ministers* (Canberra: Research Note No. 40, Department of the Parliamentary Library, May 2002).

Hughes, C.A. (2003), 'The Independence of the Commissions: The Legislative Framework and the Bureaucratic Reality', in G. Orr, B. Mercurio and G. Williams (eds) *Realising Democracy: Electoral Law in Australia* (Sydney: Federation Press).

Johnson, R. (2000), *Cash for Comment: The Seduction of Journo Culture* (Annandale: Pluto Press).

Keating, M. (2003), 'In the Wake of "A Certain Maritime Incident": Ministerial Advisors, Departments and Accountability', *Australian Journal of Public Administration* 62:3, 92–7.

Krinks, K. (1999), 'Creating the Active Citizen? Recent Developments in Civics Education', Research Paper 15 1998–99 (Canberra: Politics and Public Administration Group, Commonwealth Department of the Parliamentary Library, Parliament House).

Langseth, P., Stapenhurst, R. and Pope, J. (1999), 'National Integrity Systems', in R. Stapenhurst and S.J. Kpundeh (eds) *Curbing Corruption: Toward a Model for Building National Integrity* (Washington DC: Economic Development Institute, World Bank), 127–48.

Martin, B. (1997), *Suppression Stories* (Wollongong: Fund for Intellectual Dissent).

McMillan, J. (1994), 'Whistleblowing', in N. Preston (ed.) *Ethics for the Public Sector: Education and Training* (Sydney: Federation Press).

Mulgan, R. and Uhr, J. (2001), 'Accountability and Governance', in G. Davis and P. Weller (eds) *Are You Being Served? State, Citizens and Governance* (Sydney: Allen and Unwin), 152–74.

OECD (2000), *Trust in Government: Ethics Measures in OECD Countries* (Paris: Organisation for Economic Cooperation and Development).

OECD (2004), *Measures for Promoting Integrity and Preventing Corruption: How to Assess?*, Report of OECD Public Governance Committee GOV/PGC(2004)24, October, available at <http://www.oecd.org/dataoecd/40/47/34406951.pdf>.

Orr, G. (2004), *Australian Electoral Systems – How Well Do They Serve Political Equality?*, Report No. 2, Democratic Audit of Australia, Research School of Social Sciences, ANU.

Parliamentary Research Service (2006), *A Survey of Codes of Conduct in Australian and Selected Overseas Parliaments* (Canberra: Commonwealth Parliament E-Brief).

Parnell, S. (2004), 'Integrity Essential as Justice Fighters Fly', *The Courier-Mail* 19 June.

Patapan, H. (2000), *Judging Democracy: The New Politics of the High Court of Australia* (Cambridge: Cambridge University Press).

Podger, A. (2005), 'Farewell Speech', *The Canberra Times*, 2 and 6 July.

Pope, J. (2000) (ed.), *Confronting Corruption: The Elements of a National Integrity System (The TI Source Book)*, 2nd edn (Berlin and London: Transparency International).

Preston, N. (2001), 'Integrity and Ministerial Ethics: The Qld Integrity Commissioner Case Study', in J. Fleming and I. Holland (eds) *Motivating Ministerial Ethics* (Aldershot: Ashgate).

Russell, D. (2002), 'The Role of Executive Government in Australia', Senate Occasional Lecture, Parliament House, Canberra, October 2002.

Sampford, C. (2001), 'Prior Advice is Better Than Subsequent Investigation', in J. Fleming and I. Holland (eds) *Motivating Ministers to Morality* (Aldershot: Ashgate).

Sampford, C. and Lui, R. (2004), 'Media Ethics Regimes and Ethical Risk Management in Australia', *Journal of Mass Media Ethics* 19:2, 86–108.

Smith, R.W. (2003), 'Enforcement or Ethical Capacity? Considering the Role of State Ethics Commissions at the Millennium', *Public Administration Review* 63:3, 283–95.

Smith, R. (2005), 'NSW Parliamentary Committees and Integrity Oversight: Comparing Public Sector Agency, News Media and NGO Perspectives', paper to Annual Conference of the Australasian Study of Parliament Group, 6–8 October, Parliament House, Sydney.

Spigelman, J.J. (2004), 'The Integrity Branch of Government', *Australian Law Journal* 78:11, 724–37.

Tiernan, A. and Weller, P. (2003), Submission to Senate Finance and Public Administration References Committee Inquiry, *Staff Employed under the Members of Parliament (Staff) Act 1984* (Canberra: Parliament House).

Tully, S. (2003), 'Party Registration and Preselection: A Minefield for Electoral Administrators', in G. Orr, B. Mercurio and G. Williams (eds) *Realising Democracy: Electoral Law in Australia* (Sydney: Federation Press).

Uhr, J. (2005a), *Terms of Trust: Arguments over Ethics in Australian Government* (Sydney: University of NSW Press).

Uhr, J. (2005b), 'How Do We Know If It's Working?', *Australian Journal of Public Administration* 64:2, 69–76.

Weller, P. (2002), *Don't Tell the Prime Minister* (Melbourne: Scribe Publications).

Western Australian Parliament (2003), *National Conference of Parliamentary Oversight Committees of Anti-Corruption/Crime Bodies* (Perth: Joint Standing Committee on the Anti-Corruption Commission, Report No. 7, Parliament of Western Australia).

Chapter 15

Promoting Integrity: Trends and Prospects

Brian W. Head

Promoting integrity, whether in public institutions or in the domain of private corporations, has had a variable history around the world. In the 'developing' countries, the scale and extent of corruption is generally perceived as much higher than in the 'advanced' democratic countries. In societies where there is little history of respect for institutions that reinforce fairness, equity, civility and tolerance, the effective promotion of institutional integrity is very difficult. For example, standards and codes of ethical conduct are difficult to establish and even more difficult to implement and enforce effectively, if the state itself is not a champion of civil rights and the rule of law. Conversely, it is difficult to expect state officials to form an oasis of integrity if the wider norms of business and civil society are characterized by opportunism and coercion.

Extent of Problems

Integrity matters not just for ethics but for economics. On a global scale, corruption is said to be significant, with corrupt transactions estimated to total around $1 trillion (Kaufmann 2005). Grand corruption, involving large-scale bribery and collusion between big business and public officials, is often seen as more typical of oligarchic regimes where nepotism is rife, equitable treatment before the law is rare, and the free flow of information is stifled. Yet even in societies with 'advanced' democratic systems, there are regular examples of bribery and corruption at the interface between politics and business. Moreover, petty corruption – involving 'side-payments' to facilitate favourable administrative decisions – may be seen as a constant risk in all countries, although more endemic (as a 'way of life') in some nations than others. Whether in rich or poor countries, the widespread flouting of standards for integrity and equity demonstrates some fundamental weaknesses in governance arrangements, including lack of clear standards and lack of effective resources committed to enforcement.

The proposition that bribery is less of a problem than poverty in developing countries is naïve. Even the proposition that bribery may assist in promoting economic efficiency (reducing transaction times, etc.) in some countries is short-sighted, since the long-term impacts of corruption create 'much larger negative effects', including regressive impacts on poorer households who are denied adequate health and education programmes and access to public services. According to a former Finance Minister for Nigeria:

> Systematic corruption has diverted resources, corrupted values, and led to rent-seeking activities in place of productive ones. While corruption damages a country's development, what is not at all sufficiently understood is that, in practice, it is highly regressive and inequitable. This is simply because corruption ultimately is most vicious on the poor. (Okonjo-Iweala 2007)

As Kaufmann (2005) has argued, a significant 'development dividend' can arise from good governance, thus enhancing a nation's capacity to provide economic and social benefits for citizens. On the other hand, the optimistic view that greater accountability and transparency tends to generate faster economic growth (and thus reduce poverty) is probably exaggerated, since the causal pathways are likely to be interactive (Goldsmith 2007).

From time to time, public officials may be prosecuted for misuse of their office. The capacity of a system to undertake such prosecutions is generally a mark of its sincerity. However, prosecution processes can also be abused. In one-party countries, the demonstration effect of trials for corruption is sometimes aimed more at intimidation of political opponents rather than at seeking to build cleaner systems of decision-making. A wider range of motivations for enforcing higher standards is beginning to emerge. In the People's Republic of China in May 2007, a senior official was convicted of recklessly and corruptly approving certification for food products which were later proved to have caused major health problems. His execution two months later illustrated the state's determination to show it was becoming more serious about the reputation of Chinese goods in global markets (*The Times*, 11 July 2007).

In the advanced democratic countries, public institutions and governance arrangements have generally been seen as reasonably 'clean' in recent decades, by comparison with the developing world – although an otherwise advanced country like Italy continues to have a chequered reputation in terms of high-level political corruption and collusion with business interests (Colombo 2004), and was ranked forty-fifth in the Corruption Perceptions Index 2006 published by Transparency International (TI 2007, 326). In the Scandinavian democracies, Canada, the United Kingdom, Australia and the United States, instances of serious misbehaviour by politicians and administrators stand out as exceptional events which have regularly attracted very close public scrutiny.

Public officials – whether elected politicians or appointed administrators – are increasingly aware that their behaviour is under constant surveillance and that standards for behaviour are becoming increasingly precise, with the overall effect that their actions are more likely to conform with established standards. Public culture reinforces the proposition that misbehaviour and abuse of public office warrant investigation and punishment. The standards by which such judgements are made have gradually become more systematic. In particular, codes of conduct for public employees have long existed, and oversight authorities play a role in ensuring these are taken seriously. However, codes for politicians have generally remained informal and self-regulatory in nature (or even non-existent in some jurisdictions), with the consequence that conflicts of interest are often not identified, for example, inappropriate mixing of business interests with public decision-making. Politicians have been especially slow to tighten the rules governing political donations, owing to the financial self-interest of incumbent or successful parties. The size of donations which will require public disclosure is a hotly debated issue, and mechanisms are constantly being invented for obfuscating the identity of donors.

Despite these countervailing examples of negative behaviour, there has been a discernible trend since the 1990s to place integrity issues in a more central position, as a foundation for good governance in both the public and private sectors. A concerted effort was being made on many fronts to identify and implement the most effective mechanisms for reducing fraud and corruption by public officials, and for improving the conduct of business leaders in the face of scandalous business failures. More positively, there has been a strong movement to promote better understanding of, and commitment to, integrity. A shared concern with identifying and measuring the dimensions of the problem has rapidly emerged. Governments, the media and researchers have joined in addressing these challenges. Scorecards and checklists have been developed to identify areas of risk and weakness. This has occurred within each country, but increasing attention has been directed towards comparative national performance and assessing the merits of adapting useful practices from neighbouring countries.

In the 'advanced' countries like Australia, which are rated as relatively 'clean' in terms of global league tables on corruption and integrity, there is some frustration that 'cleanliness' must be a matter of constant vigilance rather than a secure accomplishment that has been 'locked in'. Australia received a 'top 8' rating in Transparency International's 2004 Global Corruption Report (TI 2004, 155), and was ranked ninth in the 2006 Corruption Perceptions Index (TI 2007, 325). Nevertheless, even in such a relatively advanced country, there are regular outbreaks of dishonesty, leading to crises and scandals that demand political attention. As noted by the chair of the Australian chapter of Transparency International, Frank Costigan QC, a systemic pattern of greed, lies and secrecy tends to recur:

> For a country that is perceived not to be corrupt, a lot has happened in the last 20 years. Let me recall a few highlights, in no particular order:
>
> - The institutional corruption in Queensland under the Bjelke-Petersen government as shown by the Fitzgerald Inquiry
> - The institutional corruption in the New South Wales Police Force as shown by the Wood Royal Commission
> - Allegations of institutional corruption in the Western Australian Police Force resulting in the Kennedy Inquiry
> - Serious problems in the drug squad in Victoria (and that police force is widely regarded as the cleanest in the country with high standards and leadership of integrity)

> - Massive corporate scandals of which HIH and One-Tel are current and striking examples.
>
> All these incidents reveal a common thread of greed, whether for power or money or both, lies and secrecy. (Costigan 2004)

As then-commissioner Tony Fitzgerald had asserted with vigour some years earlier, a systemic response is necessary: 'there is no purpose in piecemeal solutions, which only serve to conceal rather than cure the defects in the existing system' (Fitzgerald 1989, 14). Public officials require both courage to act with integrity and good information on which to base their decisions. They also need frameworks for carefully assessing whether proposed solutions are merely piecemeal patchwork or are likely to strengthen the overall capacity of the public integrity system. In the long-term, more sophisticated policy analysis is needed than has been evident in recent debates, requiring reflection on basic questions of institutional choice and design. Once these questions are more carefully addressed, it may also be possible to develop improved methods for assessing integrity system capacity, sensitive to the need for ongoing innovation and reform to tackle modern accountability problems.

Measuring the Problem – Integrity Indicators

In recent years, and with great difficulty, several attempts have been made to assess and rank countries in a table of comparative performance. Much of the credit for this push for better performance in the integrity stakes is due to international institutions (such as the World Bank, the United Nations, and the Organisation for Economic Cooperation and Development) together with a number of non-government organizations (NGOs) with international reach (such as Transparency International in Berlin, the Centre for Public Integrity in Washington, and various major NGO bodies delivering foreign aid).

The Center for Public Integrity's study *Global Integrity* (Camerer 2004) studied corruption, accountability and openness in 25 countries including the USA (ranked first), Australia (ranked third) and four other OECD nations).[1] The Center compiled a list of indicators for a Public Integrity Index, across six main governance categories and 21 sub-categories. The Index is used to 'score' the institutional framework and safeguards at the national level to promote public integrity and accountability and prevent abuses of power (that is, corruption). The categories of information collected for the Public Integrity Index are summarized in Table 15.1.

---

1 The 25 countries surveyed for the 2004 report were Argentina, Australia, Brazil, Germany, Ghana, Guatemala, India, Indonesia, Italy, Japan, Kenya, Mexico, Namibia, Nicaragua, Nigeria, Panama, Portugal, Russia, South Africa, the Philippines, United States of America, Turkey, Ukraine, Venezuela and Zimbabwe.

Table 15.1 Fields of information for the Public Integrity Index

1 Civil society, public information and media: Civil society organizations Access to information law Freedom of the media	4 Administration and Civil Service: Civil Service regulations Whistleblowing measures Procurement Privatization
2 Electoral and political processes: National elections Election monitoring agency Political Party Finances	5 Oversight and regulatory mechanisms: National Ombudsman Supreme Audit Institution Taxes and customs Financial sector regulation
3 Branches of government: Executive Legislature Judiciary	6 Anti-corruption mechanisms and rule of law: Anti-corruption law Anti-Corruption Agency Rule of law and access to justice Law enforcement

For each of the 25 countries surveyed, the Public Integrity Index measured three dimensions of these governance categories:

> First, the *existence* of mechanisms – including laws and institutions – that promote public accountability and limit corruption; second, the *effectiveness* of these mechanisms; and third, the *access* that citizens have to public information to hold their government accountable. (Camerer 2004)

To summarize, this study found that all countries were:

> … susceptible to abuses of power, whether from a lack of transparency, a lack of accountability from an independent agency overseeing the electoral process, or having no disclosure requirements or limits on money from individuals and corporations flowing into the political system. (Camerer 2004)

Political party finances were secret in 10 of the 25 countries surveyed. Few of the 25 sampled countries were ranked 'strong' overall on this Public Integrity Index in 2004.

Australia ranked third out of 25 countries, falling into the strong tier. Australia's score was very strong (90–100) for Categories 1, 5 and 6, strong (80–90) for Category 2, moderate (70–80) for Category 3, and weak (60–70) for Category 4 mainly because of its lack of robust whistleblower protection. Even the United States, which finished highest of all these 25 countries, had low scores in some areas – owing primarily to lack of independent oversight mechanisms (national ombudsman role), and the perceived widespread buying of political favours. The USA was scored as very strong (90–100) for Categories 1 and 3, strong (80–90) for Categories 2, 4 and 6, and moderate (70–80) for Category 5. The performance of the USA and Australia is compared in Table 15.2.

Table 15.2 Public Integrity Index outcomes for USA and Australia

	Governance criteria	USA	AUSTRALIA
1	**Civil society, public information and media**	Very strong, ranking 1st	Very strong, ranking 4th
2	**Electoral and political processes**	Strong, ranking 5th	Strong, ranking 8th
3	**Branches of government**	Very strong, ranking 1st	Moderate, ranking 8th
4	**Administration and Civil Service**	Strong, ranking 2nd	Weak, ranking 8th
5	**Oversight and regulatory mechanisms**	Moderate, ranking 19th	Very strong, ranking 3rd
6	**Anti-corruption mechanisms and rule of law**	Strong, ranking 4th	Very strong, ranking 1st

Source: Adapted from Public Integrity Index: Camerer 2004.

In 2006 the Global Integrity study was expanded to focus on assessments of 43 countries,[2] mainly in the developing world, with a particular focus on countries which are 'large aid recipients and emerging markets'. None of the OECD countries were surveyed. The 2006 study noted a policy trend for wealthy donor countries to insist on greater action to curb corruption in exchange for increased investment and foreign aid. It noted that accountability of governments requires not just an electoral process, but also independent media, strong civil society organizations, institutional checks and balances, and internal anti-corruption mechanisms. The major gaps between theory and practice, regulation and enforcement, were also highlighted. Inadequate regulation of political financing was seen as the most significant issue for integrity and accountability, with a risk that the 'nexus' between money and power would be 'normalized' in many countries. Attention was drawn to the lack of will and capacity of legislatures to establish robust regulatory and accountability regimes, including freedom of information and protection of whistleblowers (Global Integrity 2006).

The World Bank Institute has recently argued that improvements in voice (participation) and in the flow of information required for accountability

2 The 43 countries surveyed for the 2006 report were Argentina, Armenia, Azerbaijan, Benin, Brazil, Bulgaria, Cambodia, Democratic Republic of Congo, Egypt, Ethiopia, Georgia, Ghana, Guatemala, India, Indonesia, Israel, Kenya, Kyrgyz Republic, Lebanon, Liberia, Mexico, Montenegro, Mozambique, Nepal, Nicaragua, Nigeria, Pakistan, Philippines, Romania, Russia, Senegal, Serbia, Sierra Leone, South Africa, Sudan, Tajikistan, Tanzania, Uganda, USA, Vietnam, the West Bank, Yemen and Zimbabwe.

(transparency) would go a long way towards improving the foundations for good governance and reduced corruption (WBI 2005). Information and transparency reforms could be assessed in relation to a check-list, which could include: disclosure of assets and incomes by officials and political candidates; disclosure of political campaign contributions; publication of draft legislation and details of legislative voting; strong regulation to prevent conflict of interest; black-banning further contracts with firms involved in bribery; freedom of media and freedom of official information legislation; high standards for public financial reporting; transparent procurement systems; and support for integrity surveys (WBI 2005, 92).

Transparency International drew attention many years ago to the range of activities, processes and institutions that are relevant to good governance and the need for legal, political and civil institutions to interact productively for good governance (see Pope, Chapter 2 in this volume, and Transparency International 2004). Information about a large number of these matters has been transformed into indicators of good governance, accountability and transparency. Correspondingly, as policy has turned towards identifying and implementing effective measures for good governance, checklists have been developed for implementation of reforms (see Gilman, Chapter 13 in this volume).

Different tools and approaches are necessary to address different issues. Experience in undertaking country assessments, and experience in using a wide range of tools and approaches, point to the need for flexibility and multiple levels of analysis. There is no single instrument suitable for every country, and no single recipe for institutional improvement. Hence, attention should be paid to 'the complementarities among the various tools and indicators – aggregate and disaggregate, subjective and objective' (Kaufmann and Kraay 2007). However, some donors and international organizations have yet to learn the lesson of how difficult it can be to impose specific solutions on the political, administrative and business leadership of developing countries. Existing cultural and behavioural patterns significantly constrain future pathways, and 'successful' institutionalization of new patterns always takes time to achieve (Larmour 2005).

Values Matter

Promoting integrity entails promoting ethical and competent conduct by public officials. Elected office-holders and professional public managers can best perform their public duties efficiently, effectively and honestly if they have a supportive institutional environment. It is unrealistic to expect the majority of managers and public officials to be successful in upholding ethical and honest conduct unless they are supported and assisted by several important features of public life:

- clarity and consistency of goals and values which support integrity;
- legislative authority to underpin equitable processes;
- operating systems designed to minimize fraud and dishonesty;

- effective training services backed up by reliable advisory services;
- efficient investigatory and enforcement services;
- monitoring, review and evaluation as a basis for improvement.

From another perspective, it can be seen there are two complementary sides to the promotion and achievement of integrity in the conduct of decision-makers. These may be termed the rule-based and the value-based aspects of appropriate conduct. It is clear that the successful introduction of formal rule-based initiatives (laws and regulations, enforceable codes, auditing, etc.) is essential. However, it is also increasingly clear that the efficacy of laws and codes is dependent on cultural and motivational aspects of integrity systems. The values espoused and modelled by leaders, the use of ethical reasoning based on values and principles, the qualities embodied in media discourses – these are just as important as the more formal arrangements defining the boundaries of acceptable behaviour.

John Uhr has provided a detailed account of the evolution of Australian public service documents concerning values and codes of conduct (Uhr 2005, ch. 6). He draws a useful distinction between approaches that emphasize taking personal responsibility (that is, internalizing the values and principles) and approaches that emphasize rules for conduct (that is, specifying those actions that are unacceptable). Uhr claims that a primary reliance on compliance with rules could threaten to hollow out the value base of institutional practices that are supposed to guarantee integrity and democratic governance. While agreeing with his proposition that values matter, it is argued here that the rule-based approach is also crucial, partly because different people need different kinds of guidance, but partly because situations of risk vary widely and some require precise guidance.

Values, processes and institutions need to be constantly adapted to meet the new pressures and problems. The major integrity challenges facing public officials are likely to change over time, even in a relatively stable country with solid achievements in governance arrangements. In the past, the central concerns underlying codes of conduct for officials were traditionally those related to professional competence, political neutrality, and avoidance of dishonest conduct in relation to all financial transactions including purchasing (procurement). However, in recent years the ground has shifted, at least in parliamentary countries such as Australia (Uhr 2005; Tiernan 2007) and the United Kingdom (O'Toole 2006; Doig 2006), towards a focus on two other kinds of integrity issues for senior officials. The first is the apparent 'politicization' of the senior executive service. There is a widely held perception that senior officials must increasingly protect the political interests of the government by publicising programmes, defending policy settings, and censoring critical advice. The second new issue is the growing cadre of ministerial advisors who are not subject to any meaningful accountability regime or ethical code. Although they work in the name of public office-holders, ministerial advisors currently escape responsibility and external accountability, and thereby weaken the overall regime of ministerial accountability. It is not just a handful of ministers and top officials who need to demonstrate integrity, but all who influence the tone of public life. In Australia, one third of public servants who had contact with ministerial staff indicated, in survey responses, that they had a 'challenge' in balancing the need for impartiality, responsiveness to government, and open accountability (APSC 2005, ch. 3).

Designing and Leading

Institutional design, we have argued in this book, is one important part of the story for assessing the capacity of integrity systems to flourish. Organizational structures, roles and functions are central. The creation of special-purpose bodies (anti-corruption commissions, auditors, etc.) designed to play a leading role in tackling corruption, setting standards and monitoring performance, has been a notable feature of recent decades. And yet, we have also shown that several important related factors must be examined for a full assessment of the integrity system and its effectiveness. Firstly, there are important issues concerning whether the specialist integrity bodies themselves have the required levels of staffing, financial resources and technical capacities to make a substantial difference. Secondly, the interactions and connections between these agencies are important: Are they mutually supportive? How coherent is their pattern of cooperative interaction? Thirdly, it is necessary to examine the extent of change in the operating climate and organizational culture of all the major agencies, where the bulk of everyday public administration and service delivery effort is located. Fourthly, the responsiveness of political leaders to tackling new challenges (for example, broadening the debate to include ministerial and political accountability) is crucial for the health of the system. Political leadership needs to complement the leadership derived from special-purpose independent bodies, if the integrity-system capacity is to be optimised. Political leaders need to champion the rule of law and public-interest legislation if special deals for 'mates' and lobbyists are to be eliminated.

This analysis has focused on public sector integrity institutions, while recognizing that many of the problems with corruption and lack of accountability have also featured highly in the commercial sector in recent years (see Kimber and Lucas, Chapter 6 and Bartos, Chapter 9 in this volume). The collapse of major corporations has provoked debates on raising the standards for financial reporting, public disclosure of full and accurate information, the ethical conduct of managers, and the duties of company directors in ensuring accountability. Public officials have a major role in drafting the regulatory changes needed to respond to these challenges for business corporations. Further comparative research is needed to analyse similar issues of institutional design, capacity and effectiveness in the business and civil society integrity systems.

Finally, many of the chapters in this book have emphasized the importance of transparency, open flows of information, and debate through the mass media. The quality of such communication depends largely on groups outside the state, those active in civil society, the professions and the business sector. It can be claimed that education is the foundation of such healthy debate. If so, the lack of support for education about rights and democratic values – both in the secondary school curriculum and in university professional education courses – is a major concern for the health of democracy.

Promoting integrity is partly about minimizing fraud and misconduct but ultimately it is about the quality of democratic accountability. Mark Warren has suggested that in a democracy, the real damage inflicted by corruption is its undermining of public trust in the norms of inclusive democratic decision-making which underpin the public sphere itself and make it different from the realm of private interests (Warren 2004). On this account, changes to electoral laws which make participation more difficult for some groups, or changes in disclosure rules for political donations which make donations less transparent, would be significant forms of corruption equal to fraudulent collusion with a private contractor to secure a government tender.

References

Australian Public Service Commission (2005), *State of the Service 2004–05* (Canberra: APSC, available at <http://www.apsc.gov.au>.

Camerer, M. (ed.) (2004), *Global Integrity: An Investigative Report Tracking Corruption, Accountability and Openness in 25 Countries* (Washington, DC: Centre for Public Integrity), available at <http://www.globalintegrity.org>.

Colombo, G. (2004), 'Integrity After "Clean Hands": Investigating Corruption in Milan', presentation to National Investigations Symposium, 4 November, Sydney.

Costigan, F. (2004), 'Is Corruption a Concern?', address to AGM of Transparency International Australia, November 2003, reprinted in *TI Australia News*, 37, January.

Doig, A. (2006), 'Half-full or Half-empty? The Past, Present and Future of British Public Sector Ethics', *Public Money and Management*, 26:1, 15–22.

Fitzgerald, G.E. (1989), *Report of a Commission of Inquiry into Possible Illegal Activities and Associated Misconduct* (Brisbane: Queensland Government).

Global Integrity (2006), *Global Integrity Report*, Washington, available at <http://www.globalintegrity.org>.

Goldsmith, A.A. (2007), 'Is Governance Reform a Catalyst for Development?', *Governance*, 20:2, 165–86.

Kaufmann, D. (2005), '10 Myths about Governance and Corruption', *Finance and Development*, 42:3, 41–3.

Kaufmann, D. and Kraay, A. (2007), 'On Measuring Governance: Framing Issues for Debate', *Issues Paper for Roundtable on Measuring Governance* (Washington, DC: World Bank Institute).

Larmour, P. (2005), *Foreign Flowers: Institutional Transfer and Good Governance in the Pacific Islands* (Honolulu: University of Hawai'i Press).

Okonjo-Iweala, N. (2007), 'Corruption in a Developing Country Context', Sabot Memorial Lecture, Center for Global Development, available at <http://www.globalpolicy.org/nations/launder/regions/2007/0725corruption.htm>.

O'Toole, B.J. (2006), 'The Emergence of a "New" Ethical Framework for Civil Servants', *Public Money and Management*, 26:1, 39–46.

Tiernan, A. (2007), *Power without Responsibility* (Sydney: University of NSW Press).

Transparency International (2004), *Global Corruption Report 2004* (Berlin: TI), available at <http://www.transparency.org>.
Transparency International (2007), *Global Corruption Report 2007* (Berlin: TI), available at <http://www.transparency.org>.
Uhr, J. (2005), *Terms of Trust: Arguments over Ethics in Australian Government* (Sydney: University of NSW Press).
Warren, M.E. (2004), 'What does Corruption Mean in a Democracy?', *American Journal of Political Science*, 48:2, 328–43.
World Bank Institute (2005), *Global Competitiveness Report 2005–2006* (Washington, DC: World Bank Institute).

Appendix

Recommendations of the National Integrity System Assessment of Australia

The 21 recommendations published in the NISA Report are intended for all Australian governments, the business community, the general public and civil society groups concerned to ensure continual improvement in Australia's integrity systems. The recommendations are not exhaustive. Rather than detailing every possible reform, they present a mixture of priorities and overarching principles for development of effective integrity systems as a whole. They reflect conclusions typically applicable throughout Australia, but in some cases relate more strongly to a particular identified jurisdiction.

The Table A1 summarizes the areas of the recommendations, their relationship with the assessment themes above, and the sectors/jurisdictions to which they most relate. The recommendations form three groups:

Recommendations 1–7 relate to core integrity institutions, i.e. bodies established wholly or largely to ensure proper discharge of power by organizations and their officeholders. As outlined in the preceding chapters, these relate primarily to the public sector.

Recommendations 8–15 relate to distributed integrity institutions, i.e. organizational strategies devoted to setting and maintaining integrity standards within the organizations through which most power is exercised. Recommendations 8–13 apply across all sectors, while recommendations 14 and 15 raise public sector issues.

Recommendations 16–21 relate to education, evaluation and research. Recommendations 16–19 reflect the need for further investment in community and official knowledge about integrity systems, and the last two emphasize the need for further research into capacity and coherence issues in the non-government society sectors.

Integrity from the Top: Core Institutions

Recommendation 1. Commonwealth integrity and anti-corruption commission

That the Commonwealth Government's proposed new independent statutory authority be tasked as a comprehensive lead agency for investigation and prevention of official corruption, criminal activity and serious misconduct involving Commonwealth officials, based on the following principles:

1 That the agency's jurisdiction not be limited to select agencies but include all Commonwealth officials from secretaries or equivalent down, including employees of Commonwealth-owned corporations, and any other persons involved or implicated in wrongdoing affecting the integrity of Commonwealth operations;
2 That the agency be made (i) an ex officio member of the Commonwealth Governance Review Council or other integrity coordination body created pursuant to recommendation 2, or failing that the existing Administrative Review Council, and (ii) subject to parliamentary oversight by a suitable parliamentary standing committee, preferably the same committee responsible for oversighting other core Commonwealth integrity agencies (see recommendation 3);
3 That the jurisdiction of the agency also include Commonwealth parliamentarians and ministers provided that, if recommendation 6 is taken up and an effective parliamentary and ministerial integrity system established, the agency's jurisdiction is only triggered by a request of the Parliamentary Integrity Commissioner, presiding officer of either House, or where in the opinion of the agency head an important matter of public interest would otherwise go uninvestigated;
4 That the agency be charged with a statutory responsibility to promote integrity and accountability as well as investigate wrongdoing, and be given a commensurate positive title rather than one defined by crime, misconduct or corruption;
5 That the agency be empowered and required to:
   (i) undertake inquiries of its own motion as well as receive and investigate complaints from whatever source;
   (ii) exercise concurrent jurisdiction and participate in a statutorily-based investigations clearing house with other federal investigative agencies including the Commonwealth Ombudsman and Australian Federal Police; and
   (iii) share all relevant information with other Commonwealth and state integrity institutions, and conduct cooperative investigations with them including delegating its own investigatory powers, when in either its or their opinion their own jurisdiction is also involved;
6 That the Commonwealth review its operational definitions of corruption to include internal fraud and any other offences or types of serious misconduct

with the potential to seriously affect public integrity, and revise its reporting, monitoring and prevention policies accordingly.

✓ **Capacity** ✓ **Coherence** ✓ **Consequences**

Recommendation 2. Governance review councils

That each Australian government establish, by constitution or statute, a governance review council or similarly titled body to:

(i) Promote policy coherence and operational coordination in the ongoing work of the jurisdiction's main core integrity institutions;
(ii) Coordinate research, evaluation and monitoring of the implementation of ethics, accountability and administrative review legislation, including the balance between different aspects of integrity systems (e.g. education, prevention and enforcement);
(iii) Report to the public on the 'state of integrity' in the jurisdiction;
(iv) Ensure operational cooperation and consistency in public awareness, outreach, complaint-handling, workplace education, prevention, advice and investigation activities, including greater sharing of information between integrity bodies;
(v) Foster cooperation between public sector integrity bodies, sector-specific or industry-specific integrity bodies and like integrity bodies in the private sector (e.g. industry ombudsman's offices);
(vi) Provide ongoing advice to government and the public on institutional and law reforms needed to maintain and develop the jurisdiction's integrity regime; and
(vii) Sponsor comparative research, evaluation and policy discussion regarding integrity mechanisms in other jurisdictions, nationally and internationally.

The council should have a permanent secretariat to hold occasional public reviews and compile complex reports, and have a membership including the heads of all the jurisdiction's core integrity institutions (Ombudsman, Auditor-General, anti-corruption commissioner, public service head, parliamentary standards commissioner, etc.), expert and community representation, and an independent chair.

✓ **Capacity** ✓ **Coherence** ✓ **Consequences**

Recommendation 3. Standing parliamentary and public oversight mechanisms

That all Australian parliaments establish (or where necessary, rationalize) a system of independent public oversight for all of their core integrity institutions, consisting of:

(i) a standing multi-party parliamentary committee, supported by staff; and
(ii) either a standing public advisory committee, or failing that, an extensive program of public participation when conducting annual or three-yearly parliamentary reviews.

✓	**Capacity**	✓	**Coherence**	✓	**Consequences**

Recommendation 4. Jurisdiction over corporatized, contracted and grant-funded services

That all governments review the traditional legislative methods for defining the jurisdictions of integrity institutions, away from characterizations of decision-makers or service-providers as 'public', 'private', 'commercial' or 'corporatized' and towards increased discretion for integrity bodies to investigate and/or hear any relevant matter involving any decisions or services flowing from an allocation of public funds.

✓	**Capacity**	✓	**Coherence**		**Consequences**

Recommendation 5. Access to administrative justice

That all governments join in a national review of the current availability of substantive administrative law remedies to citizens aggrieved by official decisions, recognizing:

(i) Partial, and often complete lack of protection for basic civil and political rights in Australia's Constitutions and other fundamental laws, and the extent to which this continues to constrain the operation of administrative law;
(ii) Continuing increases in the cost of legal services and continuing comparative lack of legal aid support for administrative as against criminal and family matters;
(iii) Continued lack of availability of hearing-based merits review systems in some jurisdictions, either with comprehensive jurisdiction or at all;
(iv) The continuing, but unmonitored conferral of administrative merits review functions on some lower state courts as a substitute to establishment of a merits review tribunal, with little evaluation of the value or equity of this approach;
(v) Current trends to a less equitable 'two-tiered' system of administrative review in which the only truly no-cost review mechanism (ombudsman) is only able to offer remedies based on negotiation and recommendation, and determinative remedies are available only to those in a position to pay; and
(vi) Widespread community concern regarding the need for effective legal protection of citizens against excessive use of official power by governments or individual officials in the name of border control and anti-terrorism.

That this review be overseen by the coordination body in recommendation 2, or otherwise by existing administrative review and/or law reform bodies or the national standing committee of Attorneys-General, with extensive public participation.

✓	**Capacity**	✓	**Coherence**		**Consequences**

Recommendation 6. Enforcement of parliamentary and ministerial standards

That all Australian parliaments establish, by constitution or statute, a comprehensive regime for the articulation and enforcement of parliamentary and ministerial standards including:

1 A statutory requirement for a code of conduct for each house of parliament, for presiding officers of each house, and for ministers (including ministerial staff), dealing with certain minimum subjects, prepared through a public process, and formally adopted and published;
2 A requirement for the appointment of the presiding officer by way of a two-thirds majority of the house, by secret ballot;
3 A multi-party ethics and privileges committee in each house responsible for:
   (i) preparing and updating the codes for that house and its presiding officers;
   (ii) preparing and updating the ministerial code, in the case of the lower house committee in consultation with the upper house committee and the government;
   (iii) making recommendations to parliament and government regarding appointment of the parliamentary integrity advisor and standards commissioner; and
   (iv) receiving and reviewing reports of the standards commissioner.
4 A parliamentary integrity advisor appointed by the government in consultation with the ethics and privileges committees of both houses, with the functions of (a) general guidance to members, ministers and their staff on integrity matters, (b) maintenance and publication of material interest registers of members, ministers and staff (see also recommendation 9), and (c) confidential written advice on conflicts of interests, probity of allowances and entitlements and like matters; and
5 A parliamentary standards commissioner, appointed:
   (i) by the government on the joint recommendation of the ethics and privileges committees and joint resolution of both houses;
   (ii) for a minimum term of 5 years, at a salary fixed by an independent remuneration tribunal, removable only by a two-thirds majority of a joint sitting of parliament on the basis of proven misbehaviour or incapacity;
   (iii) with power to: receive complaints from any person, or initiate any investigation of their own motion, regarding possible breach of a parliamentary or ministerial code of conduct or equivalent matter; make such inquiries as they see fit, including the power to enter premises and

compel evidence; refer matters to other relevant official bodies for joint or independent investigation; make reports of their investigations in the first instance to the ethics and privileges committee and/or the prime minister, and where in the public interest, to the parliament and the public; and, in their reports, reach such opinions as to facts and make such recommendations as they see fit.

✓	**Capacity**	✓	**Coherence**	✓	**Consequences**

Recommendation 7. Independent parliamentary select committees

That Australian parliaments adopt a new procedure for the initiation of inquiries by select parliamentary committee, and appointment of committee chairs, aimed at encouraging bipartisanship in the conduct of parliamentary business and reducing the control of the Executive over such inquiries. The new base procedures should be:

(i) for initiating an inquiry by way of select parliamentary committee, a system based on each member holding say five (5) votes that may be cast in favour of establishment of an inquiry in any one calendar year, with a fixed threshold of say twenty-five (25) such votes needing to be cast to establish an inquiry; and
(ii) for appointment of committee chairs, an election requiring a two-thirds majority of the committee (consistently with recommendation 5 above).

✓	**Capacity**	✓	**Coherence**		**Consequences**

Walking the Talk: Distributed Integrity Institutions

Recommendation 8. Statutory frameworks for organizational codes of conduct

That there be a legislated basis for all integrity systems for any sector in any jurisdiction, applying to all officials or officeholders irrespective of whether they are appointed or elected, including a statutory framework by which every organization is required to develop, monitor and implement an enforceable code of conduct relevant to its own mission and circumstances, based on consultation with staff and clients/community, reflecting statutorily-defined minimum contents, community-wide values, and mechanisms showing how rewards, incentives and sanctions are linked to standards of behaviour.

✓	**Capacity**	✓	**Coherence**	✓	**Consequences**

Recommendation 9. Relationships between organizations and core integrity agencies

That the statutory frameworks for each sector/jurisdiction's integrity system be reviewed to ensure more explicit key principles reflecting the mutually supporting functions of core and distributed integrity institutions, including requirements for:

1 Inclusion of organizational integrity capacity-building as a statutory object of core integrity institutions;
2 Core integrity institutions to consult with organizations and other integrity agencies in the preparation of policies, guidelines and capacity-building activities, with a particular focus on achieving coherence in their application in daily practice;
3 All managers to promptly inform senior management, and senior management to promptly inform relevant core integrity agencies, of all cases in which a reasonable suspicion is formed that corruption, official misconduct, organizational impropriety, serious maladministration or a similar integrity lapse has occurred; and
4 At least once every five years, all organizations to: evaluate the take-up of their code of conduct, including a formal survey of not less than 10 per cent of employees; in so doing, take account of guidelines for such evaluation published by core integrity agencies; make available the results of the evaluation (including anonymized raw data) to core agencies; and review and update their code of conduct in light of the evaluation.

✓ **Capacity** ✓ **Coherence** ✓ **Consequences**

Recommendation 10. Effective disclosure of interests & influences

That all regimes for the regulation and disclosure of material interests reasonably capable of being perceived as influencing the official or corporate duties of those in positions of trust, be reviewed to comply with new standards of minimum best practice, based on:

1 Continuous disclosure by officeholders of material interests (including political parties' gifts, contributions and electoral expenses) within statutory timeframes appropriate to the level of the interest, but in all cases within the shortest practical timeframe of the interest changing or arising;
2 Immediate publication and continual updating of interest disclosures by the registrars/regulators of such disclosure obligations, including the establishment of on-line disclosure registers and active advertisement of mechanisms for accessing such information to those entitled to know; and
3 Statutory prohibitions, supported by criminal sanctions, against officeholders acquiring any new personal or other material interest (including direct or

indirect acceptance of gifts, contributions or donations to political parties) other than in circumstances where those entitled to know have reasonable opportunity to become aware of the interest prior to relevant decisions (such as voting in an election).

✓	**Capacity**	✓	**Coherence**		**Consequences**

Recommendation 11. Whistleblower protection and management

That the legislated basis for all integrity systems for any sector in any jurisdiction, include a scheme to facilitate 'whistleblowing' by current and former employees about integrity concerns that is at least consistent with Australian Standard 8004-2003, plus the following principles:

(i) A statutory requirement, either directly or through organizational codes of conduct, for employees to report suspected corruption, fraud, defective administration or other integrity lapses to a person able to effect action;
(ii) The criminalization of reprisals against public interest whistleblowers or other internal integrity witnesses wherever this role is a factor of any significance in detrimental action taken against them (whether official or unauthorized);
(iii) Provision of statutory defences to any legal action for breach of confidence, official secrets or defamation where the whistle is blown to an authority empowered to take action; or to the media, in circumstances where this is objectively reasonable;
(iv) Training for managers in the avoidance, detection, investigation and prosecution of reprisal actions (whether giving rise to criminal, disciplinary or civil liability);
(v) Statutory requirements for all organizations to develop and promulgate internal disclosure procedures (IDPs) (including, in the private and civil society sectors, all organizations over an appropriate size); and
(vi) A statutory whistleblowing coordination role for a core integrity agency in each of sector, to which all significant employee disclosures must be notified, and whose duties include (a) guidance on effective investigation, resolution and management and (b) a discretion to directly and fully investigate alleged reprisals.

✓	**Capacity**	✓	**Coherence**		**Consequences**

Recommendation 12. Minimum integrity education and training standards

That the corporate governance regimes for public sector agencies, publicly-listed companies, and private companies and civil society organizations above a defined employee or financial threshold, be reviewed to require up-to-date training in integrity, accountability and ethics institutionalization systems through an accredited independent tertiary institution, as a prerequisite for the appointment of all senior managers (including directors, public officers and statutory officers).

☑ **Capacity** ☐ **Coherence** ☐ **Consequences**

Recommendation 13. Professional development for integrity practitioners

That Australian higher education institutions develop a nationally-relevant program of advanced professional training (including research-based training) in integrity systems, policy, inquiry and law reform, suitable for both government and business sectors and making up the core of a recognized postgraduate qualification in public administration, management, accounting and/or law.

☑ **Capacity** ☑ **Coherence** ☐ **Consequences**

Recommendation 14. Freedom of information

That all Australian governments revise their Freedom of Information laws to better respect the general principle of a public 'right to know', by establishing:

(i) A clear principle that citizens are entitled to free and immediate access to such government records as they may request, without the need for a formal application, other than in circumstances in which it can be demonstrated that release would specifically damage or compromise someone's rights or legitimate interests (other than public officials or agencies) or the public interest (other than as defined simply by the self-interest of public officials or agencies), or pose an unacceptable risk of such damage;
(ii) A reversed onus of proof so that where a public agency requires an applicant to submit a formal application for records due to its assessment of actual or unacceptable risk of damage, and then determines to reject that application for any reason other than privacy or personal (but not commercial) confidentiality, the agency must first make its own successful application for non-release of the records to the Information Commissioner, Ombudsman or other independent review agency – or release the records.

☑ **Capacity** ☑ **Coherence** ☐ **Consequences**

Recommendation 15. Regional integrity resource-sharing and capacity-building

That Commonwealth and state governments fund a comprehensive review by Australian local government of the most effective framework for building integrity system capacity at the local and regional levels of government, recognizing the historic under-resourcing of local government, the growing responsibilities of local government in the Australian federal system, and the increasing complexity of regional-level public institutions.

✓	Capacity	✓	Coherence		Consequences

Investing in Integrity: Education, Evaluation and Research

Recommendation 16. Civic education and community awareness

That Australian governments significantly expand programs for the development of civic education (both school-based and adult) to include a stronger direct focus on the theory and practice of the nation's integrity systems, with a focus on the nature of ethical decision-making, and awareness of public rights to complain, to access official information, and to independent review of official decisions; and that they directly involve public interest groups in the design of this expansion.

✓	Capacity	✓	Coherence		Consequences

Recommendation 17. Public review of integrity resourcing and performance measurement

That Australian governments collaborate in a national review of the optimum resourcing levels and arrangements for core and distributed integrity institutions, including:

1 Actual and preferred standards for resourcing of core public integrity institutions as a proportion of sector staffing and expenditure (taking into account levels of resources devoted to distributed integrity systems, and identifying where additional distributed capacity does or does not offset weakness in core capacity);
2 More consistent and transparent budget formulae for determining the appropriate levels for recurrent or new funds for core agencies;
3 More appropriate and consistent measures of the annual activities and efficiencies of core integrity agencies, along with methods for validating such measures;
4 More appropriate and consistent classifications of the government statistics needed to provide baseline information on integrity agency core business; and
5 Benchmarking of the resources spent on performance evaluation by or for integrity institutions, against performance evaluation in other public policy areas.

✓	Capacity	✓	Coherence	✓	Consequences

Recommendation 18. Parliamentary oversight review methodologies

That Australian parliaments commission a joint comparative study of the methods used by standing parliamentary and public advisory committees in the oversighting of core integrity institutions, with a view to identifying:

1 The range of information used by standing committees as indicators of the qualitative performance of integrity systems;
2 Current best practice in the methods used by parliamentary standing committees to monitor the effectiveness of integrity bodies;
3 The resource needs of effective parliamentary oversight of integrity bodies; and
4 Minimum and optimum best practice in the use of direct public consultation and participation in the evaluation and oversighting of integrity agency effectiveness.

✓ **Capacity** ✓ **Coherence** ✓ **Consequences**

Recommendation 19. Evidence-based measures of organizational culture and public trust

That Australian governments provide additional funding to their core public integrity agencies to collaborate in a joint long-term research program into the optimum use of social science and other evidence-based research for evaluation of integrity system performance, including:

1 Extension and consolidation of existing best practice in 'state of the service' and 'profiling the public sector' research by Commonwealth and state agencies;
2 Establishment of routine methodologies for workplace-based research by individual agencies, consistent with an ongoing evaluation plan coordinated by core agencies (see also recommendation 9);
3 More routine, consistent and independently validated research into public awareness and public experience of core integrity institutions in all jurisdictions; and
4 Longer-term research into measurement of public trust in institutions as a barometer on integrity system health and performance.

✓ **Capacity** ✓ **Coherence** ✓ **Consequences**

Recommendation 20. Core integrity institutions in the business sector

That a supplementary integrity system assessment be undertaken focusing on the consequences, capacity and coherence of core integrity institutions responsible for Australia's business sector – including their relationships with the distributed business integrity systems already studied – to more accurately gauge the health of Australia's business integrity systems including opportunities for enhanced best practice and their role in the nation's integrity systems as a whole.

✓	**Capacity**	✓	**Coherence**	✓	**Consequences**

Recommendation 21. Civil society integrity systems

That a supplementary integrity system assessment be undertaken focusing on the core and distributed integrity systems in Australia's civil society sector, recognizing overlaps with but also gaps between integrity regimes governing the government and business sectors, in order to more accurately gauge their overall health including opportunities for enhanced best practice and their role in the nation's integrity systems as a whole.

✓	**Capacity**	✓	**Coherence**	✓	**Consequences**

Table A1 Recommendations – National Integrity Systems Assessment (Australia) 2004

Recommendation	Relevant assessment themes			Sectors/jurisdictions to which this recommendation applies				
				Government			Business	Civil society
	Consequences	Capacity	Coherence	Common-wealth	State/ territory	Local		
Integrity from the top: core institutions								
1 Commonwealth integrity and anti-corruption commission		✓	✓	✓				
2 Governance review councils	✓	✓	✓	✓	✓	✓	✓	✓
3 Standing parliamentary and public oversight mechanisms	✓	✓	✓	✓	✓			
4 Jurisdiction over corporatized, contracted and grant-funded services		✓	✓	✓	✓	✓	✓	✓
5 Access to administrative justice		✓	✓	✓	✓	✓		
6 Enforcement of parliamentary and ministerial standards	✓	✓	✓	✓	✓			
7 Independent parliamentary select committees		✓	✓	✓	✓			
Walking the talk: distributed integrity institutions								
8 Statutory frameworks for organizational codes of conduct	✓	✓	✓		✓ (NSW)		✓	✓
9 Relations between organizations and core integrity agencies	✓	✓	✓	✓	✓	✓	✓	✓
10 Effective disclosure of interests and influences		✓	✓	✓	✓	✓	✓	✓
11 Whistleblower protection and management		✓	✓	✓	✓	✓	✓	✓

Table A1 cont'd

Recommendation	Relevant assessment themes			Sectors/jurisdictions to which this recommendation applies				
				Government			Business	Civil society
	Consequences	Capacity	Coherence	Common-wealth	State/territory	Local		
12 Minimum integrity education and training standards		✓		✓	✓	✓	✓	✓
13 Professional development for integrity practitioners		✓	✓	✓	✓	✓	✓	✓
14 Freedom of Information		✓	✓	✓	✓	✓		
15 Regional integrity resource-sharing and capacity-building		✓	✓	✓	✓	✓		✓
Investing in integrity: education, evaluation and research								
16 Civic awareness and community education		✓	✓	✓	✓	✓	✓	✓
17 Public review of integrity resourcing and performance measurement	✓	✓	✓	✓	✓	✓		
18 Parliamentary oversight review methodologies	✓	✓	✓	✓	✓			
19 Evidence-based measures of organizational culture and public trust	✓		✓	✓	✓	✓		
20 Core integrity institutions in the business sector	✓	✓	✓				✓	
21 Civil society integrity systems	✓	✓	✓					✓

Index

For Product Safety Concerns and Information please contact our EU representative GPSR@taylorandfrancis.com Taylor & Francis Verlag GmbH, Kaufingerstraße 24, 80331 München, Germany

Batch number: 10725973

Printed by Printforce, the Netherlands